Microsoft® Office 97 - Certified
with
Microsoft® Windows 95

A Susan Solomon Book

COURSE
TECHNOLOGY

ONE MAIN STREET, CAMBRIDGE, MA 02142

an International Thomson Publishing company I(T)P®

Cambridge • Albany • Bonn • Boston • Cincinnati • London • Madrid • Melbourne • Mexico City
New York • Paris • San Francisco • Singapore • Tokyo • Toronto • Washington

The *e-Course for Microsoft Office 97 – Certified with Microsoft Windows 95* is published by Course Technology.

Associate Publisher	Mac Mendelsohn
Series Manager	Susan Solomon
Product Developers	e-CourseWare, Corporation
Production Coordinator	Debbie Masi
Cover Designer	Doug Goodman

© 1998 by e-CourseWare, Corporation

For more information contact:

Course Technology
One Main Street
Cambridge, MA 02142

International Thomson Editores
Seneca, 53
Colonia Polanco
11560 Mexico D.F. Mexico

ITP Europe
Berkshire House 168-173
High Holborn
London WCIV 7AA
England

ITP GmbH
Königswinterer Strasse 418
53227 Bonn
Germany

Nelson ITP, Australia
102 Dodds Street
South Melbourne, 3205
Victoria, Australia

ITP Asia
60 Albert Street, #15-01
Albert Complex
Singapore 189969

ITP Nelson Canada
1120 Birchmount Road
Scarborough, Ontario
Canada, M1K 5G4

ITP Japan
Hirakawacho Kyowa Building, 3F
2-2-1 Hirakawacho
Chiyoda-ku, Tokyo 102
Japan

Trademarks
The e-Course logo is a registered trademark of e-CourseWare, Corporation.
Course Technology and the Open Book logo are registered trademarks and CourseKits is a trademark of Course Technology.
Custom Edition is a registered trademark of International Thomson Publishing.

I⊤P® The ITP logo is a registered trademark of International Thomson Publishing.

Some of the product names and company names used in this book have been used for identification purposes only and may be trademarks or registered trademarks of their respective manufacturers and sellers.

Disclaimer
Course Technology and e-CourseWare, Corporation reserve the right to revise this publication and make changes from time to time in its content without notice.

ISBN 0-7600-7224-8

Printed in the United States of America

1 2 3 4 5 6 7 8 9 MZ 02 01 00 99 98

To You from the e-Course Team

We're excited about e-Course Certified!

As experienced authors, educators, and publishing professionals, we are here to tell you that e-Course has provided us the opportunity to do what we've always wanted to do: cut through the red tape, go for quality, work as a team, be creative, be wildly entrepreneurial, and have fun.

We've also put in some long hours—writing, editing, testing, re-writing, re-testing, and testing again—and so we hope our work meets your expectations. Every e-Course product passes through various rounds of testing and checking by students, faculty, publishing professionals, and software specialists.

We believe e-Course—in combination with e-Test—is unmatched as a flexible, pedagogically sound, task-oriented way to learn microcomputer applications software. It's easy to use and will give you the results you want with a minimal investment of time. Each tutorial is designed to be worked through in about an hour. You can spend additional time working through the many Review Questions and Projects, over 60 per Tutorial.

And we're certified! On the cover you might have noticed the official seal of approval from Microsoft Corporation. If you take this entire e-Course, you will be prepared to take the exams for Word Proficient, Excel Proficient, Access Expert, and PowerPoint Expert, and become certified as a Microsoft Office User Specialist.

So let us know what you think about e-Course and e-Test at our Web site **www.e-course.com**.

Joe Adamski	John Nicholson
Judy Adamski	Fatima Nicholls
Bill Baker	Dan Oja
Stephanie Chenault	Sandi Poindexter
Cristal Ewald	June Parsons
Marilyn Freedman	Susan Solomon
Debbie Masi	Susanne Walker
Mac Mendelsohn	John Zeanchock

Thank You!

e- Course would never be all that it is without the hard work and sacrifices made by our authors, reviewers, testers, publishing professionals, and their families. This page is dedicated to the devoted, talented, and quality-minded people who helped us.

Thank you from the e-Course developers,
Dan Oja, June Parsons, and Susan Solomon

Hoober and Kirby Adamski

Joseph Adamski, Author

Judy Adamski, Author

Kevin Anderson, Beta Tester

Halvor Bailey, Student Tester

Jeannie Baker and the Baker Children

William Baker, Author

Wendy Benedetto, Proofreader

Greg Bigelow, Quality Assurance Manager

Mide Bradley, Web Page Consultant

Diane Breeman, Student Tester

Stephanie Chenault, Author

Lori Christner, Student Tester

Mark Ciampa, Beta Tester

The Entire Course Technology Sales and Customer Service Staff

Rachel Crapser, Associate Product Manager

Jodi Davis, Software Demonstrator

Cristal Ewald, Beta Tester and Project Assistant

Marilyn Freedman, Researcher and Project Assistant

Jeremy Gaboury, Student Tester

GEX, Inc.

Walid Ghanim, Project Assistant

Doug Goodman, Designer

Andrew Gorlick, Student Tester

Helen Heck, Web Page Consultant

Debbie Hughes, Beta Tester

Coco and Claire Jamrich

Matt Kenslea, Software Demonstrator

Everett Martin, Beta Tester

Peter, Alexa and Molly Masi

Debbie Masi, Production Coordinator

Mac Mendelsohn, Associate Publisher

John Nicholson, Author

Fatima Nicholls, Software Tester

Jane Pedicini, Copyeditor

Jane Phillips, Reviewer

Jared Phillips, Student Tester

Sandra Poindexter, Author

Thad Roelofs, Student Tester

Karl Smart, Faculty Tester

Paul, Max, Ginger and Cookie Solomon

Patty Stephan, Production Liasion

Paul Thacker, Beta Tester

Susanne Walker, Marketing Manager

Dave White, Beta Tester

Virginia Wiley, Beta Tester

Beth Zeanchock, Reviewer and Researcher

John Zeanchock, Author

Table of Contents

MICROSOFT WINDOWS 95

contents

MICROSOFT WORD – PROFICIENT

contents

contents

MICROSOFT EXCEL - PROFICIENT

contents

contents

MICROSOFT ACCESS - EXPERT

contents

MICROSOFT POWERPOINT - EXPERT

contents

TUTORIAL 2: POWERPOINT GRAPHICS, CHARTS, AND TABLES

Preface to the Student

e- **Course** is a new, fun way to learn how to use microcomputer applications, such as word processing and spreadsheets. Each e-Course product—let's take Excel, for example—is a CD and a WorkText that together teach you how to use computers in a way you have never been taught before.

HOW IS e-COURSE DIFFERENT?

With e-Course you have more control over how you learn, where and when you learn, and what you learn. Unlike a textbook or manual, the Steps you follow to learn the software are on the screen—so there's little chance you'll lose your place looking back and forth from the book to the screen to the book again.

Unlike most software tutorials, e-Course works "on top of" the live application software. In other words, you learn how to use the actual application, not merely interact with a series of simulated screens that only look like the application. You could compare this to learning how to ride a bicycle. Learning with simulated screens is like practicing on a stationary bicycle to learn how to ride a two-wheeler. Learning with e-Course is like practicing on a bike with training wheels.

HOW WILL e-COURSE HELP ME LEARN MORE EASILY?

e-Course has several features—on the screen and in the WorkText—that will help you master microcomputer tasks more easily. In general e-Course's philosophy is to provide context-sensitive help, that is, help where and when you need it.

Study Plans

This WorkText contains four modules—Word, Excel, Access, and PowerPoint. Each module is divided into Tutorials. We've included a Study Plan for each Tutorial. Use these Study Plans, and you will be glad you did. They help you plan what you'll tackle in each session and recommend which WorkText Projects you should complete if you've got limited time and can't do them all.

Introductory Tour

Before you begin the first Tutorial 1 that you decide to do, click the Introductory Tour button and take the tour. It provides helpful information about all the e-Course online learning features.

preface

Skill References

Forgot how to do a task that you already learned? Click any underlined text and you'll immediately see a Skill Reference—another context-sensitive feature that saves you time flipping back and forth through a textbook or manual for help.

Buttons in the e-Course Window

The buttons that appear along the right side of the e-Course window provide a variety of hints, tips, answers, animations, and other computer "movies" to help you master the material in e-Course. Included among these buttons is the Back on Track button—a quick way to update your progress in case you have made some mistakes along the way.

CAN I DO IT MYSELF?

With e-Course you have flexibility to learn at your own speed, at home, at the office, or in the lab. Anywhere you have a computer that meets the minimum specifications and the application software that e-Course teaches, you can use e-Course. It's well suited for traditional courses, as well as for self-study and distance learning courses. Using your Tracking Disk—a disk you will create at the beginning of e-Course—both you and your instructor can monitor your progress.

WHAT DOES THE WORD "CERTIFIED" MEAN IN THE TITLE OF THIS e-COURSE?

Microsoft has created a way to measure your mastery of Office applications. It's called the Microsoft Office User Specialist Program. By passing one or more Microsoft Office User Specialist Program certification exams, you can demonstrate to employers your proficiency in a particular Office application—at what they call the Proficient and Expert levels. Pass the test, and you become "certified." You'll get a real leg up in the job market, and it'll look great on your resume. And e-Course is the way to get certified. It's a Microsoft-approved product that covers all of the required objectives on the examinations for Word Proficient, Excel Proficient, Access Expert, and PowerPoint Expert. So take e-Course Certified, pass the exam, and get that job you want!

WHERE DO I GO FROM HERE?

When you're ready to begin, start by reading the e-SSentials chapter in the WorkText for the module you want to learn. Then on the computer, work through the Introductory Tour. Use the Study Plans and all the Help features. And have fun!

TechTalk

If you're planning to use your own computer at home or at work, you'll need to install the e-Course software. Here are the most frequently asked questions about e-Course software installation. You'll find additional technical tips on the e-Course Web site **www.e-course.com**.

WHAT DO I NEED TO USE e-COURSE?

- The e-Course WorkText
- The e-Course software CD-ROM
- A computer
- Microsoft Office 95 or Microsoft Office 97
- Floppy disks

WHAT ARE THE COMPUTER REQUIREMENTS FOR e-COURSE?

Before you install the e-Course software, make sure your computer has at least:

- A Pentium 75 MHz processor with 16 MB RAM—it is possible to run the e-Course software on systems with less memory and slower processors, but performance might not be acceptable.

- Windows 95 (or later version) or Windows NT 4.0—for information on Windows NT 3.51 see the Readme.txt file on the e-Course CD-ROM.

- A mouse or equivalent pointing device.

- 256 color or better display.

- A correctly installed Windows printer driver.

- A floppy disk drive configured as drive A.

- A CD-ROM drive is required for installation, but is not required on individual network workstations that run e-Course from a network file server. Additional network information is in the Readme.txt file on the e-Course CD-ROM.

A Windows-compatible sound card is optional.

techtalk

HOW DO I INSTALL THE e-COURSE SOFTWARE?

Make sure your computer is on and you're in Windows. To begin the installation, place the e-Course CD-ROM in your CD drive. The e-Course setup program should begin automatically. If it doesn't, click the **Start** button and then click **Run**. In the box, type **d:\setup.exe** (where d: is the letter of your CD drive), and then click the **OK** button.

Follow the instructions on the screen to compete the installation. If you're new to computers, use the **Next** button to accept the standard settings as you proceed through the installation.

HOW MUCH HARD DRIVE SPACE DOES e-COURSE USE?

The amount of hard drive space needed to run e-Course depends on whether you decide to run it from your hard drive or from your CD-ROM.

For example, the size of the Word e-Course Tutorial is approximately 20 MB. If you put the Word e-Course files on your hard disk, e-Course will respond faster to your commands; and you won't have to insert the CD-ROM each time you use e-Course. On the other hand, if you run the Word e-Course from your CD-ROM, response will be slower, but you won't need to use as much hard drive space.

Since you're using e-Course to learn all of Microsoft Office and Windows 95, you can choose to run some of these e-Course tutorials from CD-ROM and put the others on your hard drive. When you install e-Course, the on-screen instructions give you a choice of putting all files or only some files on your hard disk.

CAN I REMOVE THE e-COURSE TUTORIALS FROM MY HARD DRIVE WHEN I'M FINISHED USING THEM?

Yes. To uninstall the e-Course Tutorials, you should first run the Setnotro.exe program included on the CD-ROM. The program removes the write-only attribute from the e-Course files on your hard drive. Next, click the **Start** button, point to **Settings**, then click **Control Panel**. In the Control Panel window, click the **Add/Remove Programs** icon. Locate e-Course on the Install/Uninstall tab, and follow the instructions in the lower portion of the window.

HOW MANY FLOPPY DISKS DO I NEED?

When you use the Microsoft Office e-Course, you will store three types of files.

- files you use when following the Steps and completing Practices

- files you use for WorkText Projects

- files that track your progress on a Tracking Disk (optional)

In general, you'll have the option of storing your files on the hard disk or on a floppy disk for the Steps, Practices, and WorkText Projects. If you don't have much computer experience, it will be easier to use a floppy disk, so you should have at least five formatted floppy disks for these files.

Your Tracking Disk, however, *must* be a floppy disk. If you want to track your progress, have a formatted floppy disk handy when you first log into e-Course.

WHAT IF I LOSE MY DISKS?

Manage your disks carefully. Make sure they are labeled with your name and phone number. If you lose a Project Disk, you can recopy the Project files onto another disk. Of course, you might have to redo assignments that were on the disk you lost.

If you lose your Tracking Disk, just create a new Tracking Disk next time you log in. Your data from that date on will be stored. If you locate your original disk at a later date, your instructor can consolidate the information on both disks for grading.

Study Plans

Microsoft Windows 95

☐ **SESSION 1** Install your software, if necessary. Read the TechTalk section for installation instructions.

Read the overview chapter, *Operating System e-SSentials*.

☐ **SESSION 2** Read the Scenario for Tutorial 1.

Follow the instructions at the end of the Scenario to start e-Course, print your Task Reference, and start Tutorial 1.

Complete Tutorial 1 Topics 1 through 7 online, and print your CheckPoint Report.

☐ **SESSION 3** Answer the odd-numbered Review Questions, and then correct your answers by referring to the Answers section of your WorkText.

Complete the following Tutorial 1 WorkText Projects. Remember to refer to your Task Reference if you need help.

Project 2: Starting a Program and Manipulating a Program Window

Project 7: Improving Mouse Skills with a Game

Project 14: Running Multiple Programs, Moving Windows, and Passing Information from One Program to Another

☐ **SESSION 4** Complete the following Tutorial 1 WorkText Projects:

Project 3: Running Two Programs and Switching Between Them

Project 20: Using the Desktop Shortcut Menu and the Recycle Bin

☐ **SESSION 5 (OPTIONAL)**
Complete the following Tutorial 1 WorkText Projects:

Project 17: Exploring the Date/Time Control

Project 21: Smooth Operators

study plans

TUTORIAL 2

☐ SESSION 1   Read the Scenario for Tutorial 2.

Complete Tutorial 2 Topics 1 through 6 online, and print your CheckPoint Report.

☐ SESSION 2   Answer the odd-numbered Review Questions, and then correct your answers by referring to the Answers section of your WorkText.

Complete the following Tutorial 2 WorkText Projects.

Project 1:   Using Menus and Menu Conventions
Project 5:   Identifying and Using Print Dialog Box Controls
Project 12: Capturing a Screen Image and Pasting It into Paint

☐ SESSION 3   Complete the following Tutorial 2 WorkText Projects:

Project 8:   Comparing Menu Bars, Menus, and Toolbars
Project 16: Using a Program's Help Button
Project 18: Using the Answer Wizard

☐ SESSION 4   Complete the following Tutorial 2 WorkText Projects:

Project 11: Using Text Box Skills in WordPad
Project 17: Using the Help Button in a Dialog Box
Project 25: Menus by Design

TUTORIAL 3

☐ SESSION 1   Read the Scenario for Tutorial 3.

Complete Tutorial 3 Topics 1 through 6 online, and print out your CheckPoint Report.

☐ SESSION 2   Answer the odd-numbered Review Questions, and then correct your answers by referring to the Answers section of your WorkText.

Complete the following Tutorial 3 WorkText Projects.

Project 3:   Moving Files on Brenda's Disk
Project 6:   Copying a File Within a Folder
Project 17: Copy a Floppy

study plans

SESSION 3   Complete the following Tutorial 3 WorkText Projects:

Project 11: Organizing the Contents Pane

Project 14: Selecting Multiple Files

Project 24: Computers in Film: Two Thumbs Up?

SESSION 4   Complete the following Tutorial 3 WorkText Projects:

Project 15: Working with Found Files

Project 18: Using the Start Menu Documents Option

Project 20: Finding Files Containing Text

Microsoft Word - Proficient

TUTORIAL 1

SESSION 1   Install your software, if necessary. Read the TechTalk section for installation instructions.

Read the overview chapter, *Word Processing e-SSentials*.

SESSION 2   Read the Scenario for Tutorial 1.

Follow the instructions at the end of the Scenario to start e-Course, print your Task Reference, and start Tutorial 1.

Complete Tutorial 1 Topics 1 through 6 online, and print your CheckPoint Report.

SESSION 3   Answer the odd-numbered Review Questions, and then correct your answers by referring to the Answers section of your WorkText.

Complete the following Tutorial 1 WorkText Projects. Remember to refer to your Task Reference if you need help.

Project 1:   Congratulations

Project 5:   I'm the One

Project 18: Using the Memo Wizard and Create a Subdirectory

Project 22: Web Shopping

SESSION 4   Complete the following Tutorial 1 WorkText Projects:

Project 4:   Past Performances

Project 7:   The Lineup

Project 17: Additional Navigating Skills

study plans

☐ **SESSION 5**   Complete the following Tutorial 1 WorkText Projects:

  Project 13: Help: Wizards and Assistants
  Project 14: Help: Contents
  Project 15: ScreenTips

TUTORIAL 2

☐ **SESSION 1**   Read the Scenario for Tutorial 2.

  Complete Tutorial 2 Topics 1 through 6 online, and print your CheckPoint Report.

☐ **SESSION 2**   Answer the odd-numbered Review Questions, and then correct your answers by referring to the Answers section of your WorkText.

  Complete the following Tutorial 2 WorkText Projects.

  Project 2:   Ah, Poetry
  Project 7:   It's Too Delicious!
  Project 18: Readability Statistics
  Project 24: Readability

☐ **SESSION 3**   Complete the following Tutorial 2 WorkText Projects:

  Project 11: Additional Find Options
  Project 12: Advanced Find Features
  Project 16: Outlining
  Project 17: More Outlining

☐ **SESSION 4** Complete the following Tutorial 2 WorkText Projects:

  Project 9:   Let's Be Selective
  Project 13:   Replace Options
  Project 14:   More Replace Options

TUTORIAL 3

☐ **SESSION 1**   Read the Scenario for Tutorial 3.

  Complete Tutorial 3 Topics 1 through 6 online, and print your CheckPoint Report.

study plans

❒ SESSION 2 Answer the odd-numbered Review Questions, and then correct your answers by referring to the Answers section of your WorkText.

Complete the following Tutorial 3 WorkText Projects.

Project 1: Books and Bindings
Project 6: Ay, There's the Rub
Project 8: A Table for Pets
Project 23: What Typeface Should I Wear Today?

❒ SESSION 3 Complete the following Tutorial 3 WorkText Projects:

Project 11: Add Borders
Project 12: Insert Clip Art
Project 13: Formatting a Table and Using the Drawing Toolbar
Project 15: Take Care of Widows and Orphans

❒ SESSION 4 Complete the following Tutorial 3 WorkText Projects:

Project 16: Layer a Drawing Object
Project 17: Tables: Add Columns and Perform Calculations
Project 19: Use Overtype Mode, Sort a Table, and Rotate Table Text

TUTORIAL 4

❒ SESSION 1 Read the Scenario for Tutorial 4.

Complete Tutorial 4 Topics 1 through 5 online, and print your CheckPoint Report.

❒ SESSION 2 Answer the odd-numbered Review Questions, and then correct your answers by referring to the Answers section of your WorkText.

Complete the following Tutorial 4 WorkText Projects.

Project 4: Be-All and End-All
Project 12: Word's Envelope Option
Project 17: Creating Columns
Project 21: Create a Fax with Columns and a Watermark

study plans

☐ **SESSION 3**   Complete the following Tutorial 4 WorkText Projects:

Project 8:   Remember Drive-In Movies?

Project 11:   Shrink to Fit

Project 19:   Date Fields and Highlighting

☐ **SESSION 4**   Complete the following Tutorial 4 WorkText Projects:

Project 15:   Other Page Number Forms

Project 16:   Create Business Cards

Project 20:   Sorting Text

Microsoft Excel - Proficient

TUTORIAL 1

☐ **SESSION 1**   Install your software, if necessary. Read the TechTalk section for installation instructions.

Read the overview chapter, *Spreadsheet e-SSentials*.

☐ **SESSION 2**   Read the Scenario for Tutorial 1.

Follow the instructions at the end of the Scenario to start e-Course, print your Task Reference, and start Tutorial 1.

Complete Tutorial 1 Topics 1 through 6 online, and print your CheckPoint Report.

☐ **SESSION 3**   Answer the odd-numbered Review Questions, and then correct your answers by referring to the Answers section of your WorkText.

Complete the following Tutorial 1 WorkText Projects. Remember to refer to your Task Reference if you need help.

Project 1:   Advertising Megabucks

Project 3:   Get a Jolt

Project 16:   About Microsoft Excel

☐ **SESSION 4**   Complete the following Tutorial 1 WorkText Projects:

Project 6:   I'm Going to Disney World!

Project 9:   A What-if Analysis

study plans

☐ SESSION 5 (OPTIONAL)

Complete the following Tutorial 1 WorkText Projects:

Project 12: Pate Setup Options

Project 21: Spreadsheet Software History

TUTORIAL 2

☐ SESSION 1

Read the Scenario for Tutorial 2.

Complete Tutorial 2 Topics 1 through 5 online, and print your CheckPoint Report.

☐ SESSION 2

Answer the odd-numbered Review Questions, and then correct your answers by referring to the Answers section of your WorkText.

Complete the following Tutorial 2 WorkText Projects.

Project 1: RetroTV Guide

Project 5: The Midas Touch

Project 6: Eat at Joe's

☐ SESSION 3

Complete the following Tutorial 2 WorkText Projects:

Project 9: Bordertown Beatnik

Project 12: Honest Ernie's Order of Operations

Project 14: Motorcycle Mama's PMT Function

☐ SESSION 4

Complete the following Tutorial 2 WorkText Projects:

Project 15: The IF Function Settles a Challenge

Project 17: Help with the Auditing Toolbar

Project 20: Explore Date Functions

TUTORIAL 3

☐ SESSION 1

Read the Scenario for Tutorial 3.

Complete Tutorial 3 Topics 1 through 5 online, and print your CheckPoint Report.

☐ SESSION 2

Answer the odd-numbered Review Questions, and then correct your answers by referring to the Answers section of your WorkText.

Complete the following Tutorial 3 WorkText Projects.

Project 3: The Market Basket

Project 4: Deals on Wheels

Project 6: The Tao of the Dow

☐ **SESSION 3** Complete the following Tutorial 3 WorkText Projects:

Project 7: Rave Shades

Project 10: As Good as the Pros!

Project 11: More Alignment Options

Project 12: More Number Formats

☐ **SESSION 4** Complete the following Tutorial 3 WorkText Projects:

Project 13: Fill and Font Shortcuts

Project 15: Hide and Protect Cells

Project 19: Explore Styles

TUTORIAL 4

☐ **SESSION 1** Read the Scenario for Tutorial 4.

Complete Tutorial 4 Topics 1 through 5 online, and print your CheckPoint Report.

☐ **SESSION 2** Answer the odd-numbered Review Questions, and then correct your answers by referring to the Answers section of your WorkText.

Complete the following Tutorial 4 WorkText Projects.

Project 3: WigZine

Project 5: Why Not Spend It?

Project 7: Pink Floyd Fans

☐ **SESSION 3** Complete the following Tutorial 4 WorkText Projects:

Project 8: Chart Pro

Project 12: What Does This Chart Mean?

Project 15: Create a Picture Chart

study plans

☐ **SESSION 4**   Complete the following Tutorial 4 WorkText Projects:

Project 16: What's Wrong with These Charts?
Project 17: Trendlines to the Future
Project 18: Charts Illustrate What-if Models

Microsoft Access - Expert

TUTORIAL 1

☐ **SESSION 1**   Install your software, if necessary. Read the TechTalk section for installation instructions.

Read the overview chapter, *Database e-SSentials*.

☐ **SESSION 2**   Read the Scenario for Tutorial 1.

Follow the instructions at the end of the Scenario to start e-Course, print your Task Reference, and start Tutorial 1.

Complete Tutorial 1 Topics 1 through 7 online, and print your CheckPoint Report.

☐ **SESSION 3**   Answer the odd-numbered Review Questions, and then correct your answers by referring to the Answers section of your WorkText.

Complete the following Tutorial 1 WorkText Projects. Remember to refer to your Task Reference if you need help.

Project 1:   Inside Concerts
Project 6:   It's Your Witness
Project 12: More Ways to Fix Mistakes

☐ **SESSION 4**   Complete the following Tutorial 1 WorkText Projects:

Project 7:   Getting High
Project 11: Taped Reminders
Project 14: Orienting Your Printing
Project 20: Compact a Database

☐ **SESSION 5**   Complete the following Tutorial 1 WorkText Projects:

Project 10: Filling a Table
Project 13: Using a Form for Updating
Project 18: Help: Office Assistant

study plans

TUTORIAL 2

☐ **SESSION 1**   Read the Scenario for Tutorial 2.

Complete Tutorial 2 Topics 1 through 5 online, and print your CheckPoint Report.

☐ **SESSION 2**   Answer the odd-numbered Review Questions, and then correct your answers by referring to the Answers section of your WorkText.

Complete the following Tutorial 2 WorkText Projects.

Project 8:   Show Off
Project 11: Sorting Multiple Fields
Project 17: Update Data Using a Query

☐ **SESSION 3**   Complete the following Tutorial 2 WorkText Projects:

Project 13: Use Filters
Project 14: Find Specific Values for Specific Fields
Project 20: Perform Record Calculations and Create a Crosstab Query

☐ **SESSION 4**   Complete the following Tutorial 2 WorkText Projects:

Project 15: Sort Nonadjacent Fields
Project 16: Use Multiple Conditions
Project 18: Compare QBE and SQL

TUTORIAL 3

☐ **SESSION 1**   Read the Scenario for Tutorial 3.

Complete Tutorial 3 Topics 1 through 6 online, and print your CheckPoint Report.

☐ **SESSION 2**   Answer the odd-numbered Review Questions, and then correct your answers by referring to the Answers section of your WorkText.

Complete the following Tutorial 3 WorkText Projects.

Project 4:   The Name Game
Project 14: Grouping and Sorting In a Report Using Data From Two Tables
Project 16: Label Wizard

study plans

☐ **SESSION 3** Complete the following Tutorial 3 WorkText Projects:

Project 12: Change Chart Type

Project 13: Change an AutoFormat and Label a Report

Project 18: Add a Field to a Report

Project 23: Pie, Bar, Column, or What?

☐ **SESSION 4** Complete the following Tutorial 3 WorkText Projects:

Project 9: Who Knows What?

Project 19: Add Subtotals and Grand Totals to a Report

Project 20: Inserting an Access Query into Word

TUTORIAL 4

☐ **SESSION 1** Read the Scenario for Tutorial 4.

Complete Tutorial 4 Topics 1 through 5 online, and print your CheckPoint Report.

☐ **SESSION 2** Answer the odd-numbered Review Questions, and then correct your answers by referring to the Answers section of your WorkText.

Complete the following Tutorial 4 WorkText Projects.

Project 6: Old Family Photos

Project 13: Create a Form with Two Subforms and Change a Control Type

Project 17: Copy an Access Form

☐ **SESSION 3** Complete the following Tutorial 4 WorkText Projects:

Project 11: Create a Database and Use the Lookup Wizard

Project 12: Use the Database Wizard

Project 18: Import a Spreadsheet and Create an Append Query

☐ **SESSION 4** Complete the following Tutorial 4 WorkText Projects:

Project 9: Newspaper Work, Part 1

Project 14: Newspaper Work, Part 2 - Create a Table with a Lookup Field

Project 19: Newspaper Work, Part 3 - Define Relationships and Create a Four-Table Query

study plans

Microsoft PowerPoint - Expert

TUTORIAL 1

☐ **SESSION 1**   Install your software, if necessary. Read the TechTalk section for installation instructions.

Read the overview chapter, *Presentation e-SSentials*.

☐ **SESSION 2**   Read the Scenario for Tutorial 1.

Follow the instructions at the end of the Scenario to start e-Course, print your Task Reference, and start Tutorial 1.

Complete Tutorial 1 Topics 1 through 6 online, and print your CheckPoint Report.

☐ **SESSION 3**   Answer the odd-numbered Review Questions, and then correct your answers by referring to the Answers section of your WorkText.

Complete the following Tutorial 1 WorkText Projects. Remember to refer to your Task Reference if you need help.

Project 2:   Too Much of a Good Thing?
Project 7:   A Special Flyer
Project 11: Changing a Template

☐ **SESSION 4**   Complete the following Tutorial 1 WorkText Projects:

Project 6:   Playing it Safe
Project 12: 2-Column Text Layout
Project 15: Transitions and Effects with Multiple Slides

☐ **SESSION 5 (OPTIONAL)**

Complete the following Tutorial WorkText Projects:

Project 17: More on Transitions and Animations
Project 20: A Complete Presentation

study plans

□ **SESSION 1**   Read the Scenario for Tutorial 2.

Complete Tutorial 2 Topics 1 through 5 online, and print your CheckPoint Report.

□ **SESSION 2**   Answer the odd-numbered Review Questions, and then correct your answers by referring to the Answers section of your WorkText.

Complete the following Tutorial 2 WorkText Projects. Remember to refer to your Task Reference if you need help.

Project 2:   The Big Three in Conditioning
Project 3:   Bob and Sam
Project 4:   How Much Should You Eat?

□ **SESSION 3**   Complete the following Tutorial 2 WorkText Projects:

Project 5:   Let's Get Organized
Project 6:   Clip Art, Scanning, and AutoShape
Project 8:   Using Table AutoFormat

□ **SESSION 4**   Complete the following Tutorial 2 WorkText Projects:

Project 11:   Creating a Pie Graph
Project 12:   2-D Horizontal Bar Graph with Labels
Project 14:   Copying and Pasting an Image

□ **SESSION 5 (OPTIONAL)**

Complete the following Tutorial 2 WorkText Projects:
Project 15:   Using the Slide Master
Project 16:   Adding a Moving Figure and Speaker Notes
Project 18:   Cropping a Graphic and Using the Genigraphics and Internet Assistant Wizards
Project 20:   Using the Presentation Conference Wizard

Operating System e-SSentials

WHAT IS AN OPERATING SYSTEM?

An **operating system** is the software that works behind the scenes to help you run programs and use hardware resources such as memory and disk storage.

An operating system plays many roles, including acting as your personal executive assistant, clerk, telephone operator, mechanic, private tutor, and doctor. In each role, the operating system performs specific tasks, called **services**.

- The "executive assistant" starts the work you want to do by launching programs, then helps you switch from one task to another.

- The "clerk" files your documents and finds them when you want to use them.

- The "telephone operator" connects you to the Internet or to other computers.

- The "mechanic" installs and removes hardware and software.

- The "doctor" finds and fixes problems.

- The "tutor" explains things you don't understand.

Every personal computer is sold with an operating system. Two of the most popular operating systems for personal computers are **Microsoft Windows 95** and **Microsoft Windows NT**, or "**Windows**" for short.

Learning about your operating system is the first step to using your computer system effectively. Knowing what services it can provide and how to use these services will help you avoid frustration and let you focus on getting your work done.

overview

HOW DO I COMMUNICATE WITH THE OPERATING SYSTEM?

Wouldn't it be nice to have a personal staff that did what you wanted with hardly a word of direction? You point at a drawer in the filing cabinet and a clerk rushes over to open it. You want to work with a document? A gesture, and an assistant fetches the file and opens it on your desk. You hold up three fingers and another employee rushes off to print three copies of the document.

An operating system isn't quite as good as having a personal staff, but operating systems do include many features to help you manipulate files effectively. The **user interface** consists of the hardware and software that you use to communicate with a computer.

The Windows user interface was designed to be easy to use. It is intended to look like a desktop—in fact when you start your computer each day, the first screen you see is called the **Windows desktop**. The programs, data, and commands you'll work with are represented by pictures, lists, and buttons, called **objects**. Some of the most noticeable objects on the Windows desktop are small pictures called **icons**.

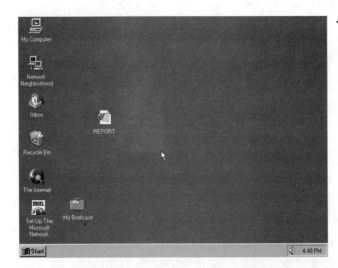

Figure 1 *Windows uses icons to represent programs or documents. The REPORT icon represents a document. If you don't want a document, you'll need to throw it in the Recycle Bin which is represented by the trash can icon.*

HOW DO I TELL THE OPERATING SYSTEM WHAT TO DO?

In addition to icons, the Windows user interface makes use of **menus** that provide you with lists of commands or tasks that the operating system can perform. When you select one of these commands, the operating system might display a **dialog box** like the one shown in Figure 2 so you can indicate how you want the task performed.

Figure 2 *If you want to turn off your computer, you'll select the Shut Down option from the Start menu. A dialog box appears so you can select one of the shut down options.*

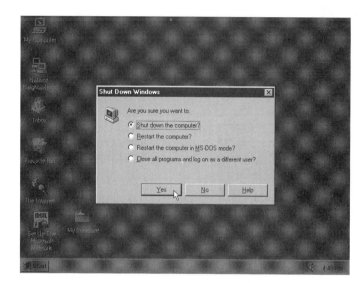

The Windows desktop would get pretty cluttered up if all of the menu options, files, and documents were visible at the same time. To simplify things, Windows uses rectangular viewing areas called **windows** (with a lowercase "w") to display logical groupings of files, icons, and menus as shown in Figure 3.

Figure 3 *The window for My Computer displays icons for various parts of the computer. Clicking the 3½ Floppy (A) icon displays another window showing the information stored there. You can open and close the windows as you need them, move them around, and change their size.*

HOW DO I USE A MOUSE?

A **mouse** is an **input device** that allows you to manipulate Windows objects and make menu selections. Most mice, like the one shown in Figure 4, have two buttons that you press or **click**.

Figure 4 *A two-button mouse*

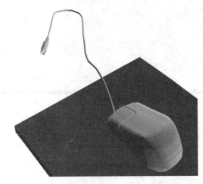

When you move the mouse on your desk, a **pointer**—usually shaped like an arrow—moves on the screen. When you move the mouse to the right, the pointer moves to the right, when you move the mouse away from you, the pointer moves up, and so on.

You select an object by positioning the pointer over the object and clicking the left mouse button. You can also use the mouse to point to an object, such as a graphic, then hold down the mouse button to drag the object to a new location.

You can click the mouse twice in rapid succession—called **double-clicking**—as a shortcut for some steps. You can also click the right mouse button—called **right-clicking**—to see an object's properties. Good mouse skills help you communicate effectively with the operating system.

HOW IS WINDOWS DIFFERENT FROM OTHER SOFTWARE?

An operating system like Windows provides general services. It doesn't directly enable you to apply your computer to tasks such as writing a letter, adding up your expenses, or storing information about the people you come in contact with. To do these tasks, you need **application software**. Word processing software, spreadsheet software, and database management software are examples of application software. Windows is an operating system that starts an application, then remains in the background to help that application store and retrieve your work.

THEN WHAT'S A WINDOWS WORD PROCESSOR?

A **Windows word processor** is one that works on a computer using the Windows operating system. Suppose you decide to purchase word processing software. You notice that there are several versions of the software listed in the software catalog—one for Windows, one for DOS, and one for the Apple Macintosh computer. Each version of the application is designed to work with a specific operating system. You need to buy the right one.

Windows applications, such as Windows word processors, all use the same system of controls, icons, and menus as the operating system. The advantage of this similarity? Learning new Windows applications is easy.

HOW DO I START WINDOWS?

When you switch on your computer, the operating system automatically starts and is ready for your commands in about one minute. You'll know it is ready when the Windows desktop appears and the pointer changes from an hourglass to an arrow shape. When Windows is ready, you can run programs and view documents using the Start button.

WHAT'S THE DIFFERENCE BETWEEN A PROGRAM AND A DOCUMENT?

A **program** is a set of detailed, step-by-step instructions that tell a computer how to solve a problem or carry out a task. The computer executes the program by carrying out the steps. Application software such as word processing software is essentially a program that tells the computer how to display what you type and follow your commands to insert and delete text.

A **document** is the data you work with and create when you use application software. Although the word "document" makes you think of reports and letters, the documents you create with Windows applications include databases and spreadsheets.

HOW DO I USE WINDOWS TO START A PROGRAM?

With the Start button of course. The **menu** which appears shows various things you can start to do. As shown in Figure 5, selecting the Programs option on the Start menu displays a **sub-menu** with a list of available programs.

Figure 5 *Pointing to the Programs menu option displays a sub-menu with a list of programs. You can click any program to start it.*

In Windows 95 and Windows NT you can create **shortcuts** to programs and documents that you use frequently. You can open the document or start the program just by double-clicking the shortcut icon. You can recognize shortcut icons, such as the Reports shortcut in Figure 5 by the little arrow at the bottom-left corner.

overview

HOW DO I ACCESS MY DOCUMENTS?

Typically you'll use one of two ways to access your documents. The traditional approach is to start an application such as your word processor, then use the application's File menu to locate and open the document you want to access.

Using the newer **document-centric** approach, you select the document you want to open and let Windows start the application needed to access the document. This association between a document and the software that created it is one of the distinguishing characteristics of the Windows operating system.

CAN I DO MORE THAN ONE THING AT A TIME?

When you're working on a project that involves several different tasks you might want to switch from a program that lets you edit a graphic to a program that lets you write a memo. An operating system such as Windows that allows you to do several tasks at the same time is called a **multitasking** system. The Windows taskbar at the bottom of the screen contains a button for every program that is currently running. You can easily switch to any one of these programs by clicking its button on the taskbar as shown in Figure 6.

Figure 6 Suppose you're working on a graphic and you want to switch to the WordPad program and write a brief memo. You can switch to WordPad by clicking its button on the taskbar along the bottom of the screen.

WHY ARE THERE DIFFERENT WAYS TO DO THE SAME THING?

An operating system provides several ways to do things because you might want the services it offers in several different contexts. For example, when you first start work it's convenient to have a menu of all the programs to choose from, whereas when you are already working it's convenient to use the taskbar to select among only the programs you are using.

Sometimes different ways are provided because some users prefer one approach over another. For example, pressing the Alt and Tab keys together is an alternative to the taskbar for switching between programs.

CAN I MAKE THE USER INTERFACE LOOK AND WORK THE WAY I WANT IT TO?

Yes, you can customize Windows. For example, you can change the desktop color scheme, add or eliminate sounds, and change the screen resolution using the **Windows Control Panel**. Customization isn't just a question of preferences and taste. Windows **accessibility options** provide customization options that make computer access possible for many handicapped users. The operating system should provide a pleasant, convenient and accessible interface through which any user can organize work and control application software.

HOW DO I ORGANIZE MY DOCUMENTS?

Every document you create is stored as a **file** on a storage device. When you store a file, the operating system looks for space on your disk. It puts the data in that spot, then makes a note of its location in case you want it to retrieve the file later. A basic key to organizing your files is the way they're labeled. A file must have a unique name, called a **filename**. All operating systems let you give your documents names, but in Windows 95 and NT the names you give your files can be long and descriptive.

It might not seem important to be able to use long names, but one of the biggest complaints about previous operating systems was that you could only use eight characters in a filename, which meant calling documents things like "prscrfrd" (which you immediately forget because it's unintelligible) instead of "personal correspondence with Fred".

The rules that specify what you can name your document are called **filenaming conventions**. Windows 95 and NT have few restrictions on filenames except for the 255-character maximum length and the prohibition that you cannot use the symbols \ / : * ? " < > |. Of course if you make your names too long they won't fit conveniently in lists and under icons so you do have to be reasonable. Generally speaking, you should avoid using filenames more than 25 or 30 characters in length. Filenaming conventions for Windows 3.1 and DOS limit you to 8 characters, so you might have to limit yourself to shorter filenames if you need to transfer files to computers that use Windows 3.1 or DOS.

ARE ALL FILES DOCUMENTS?

Both programs and documents are stored as files. There is a special part of the filename, called the **filename extension**, which you can use to distinguish between different kinds of files. An extension is a three letter code which goes at the end of the filename, separated from it by a period. For example, in the filename Goats.doc, .doc is the filename extension.

Application software automatically puts an extension on your filenames when you save your documents. Microsoft Word documents have a .doc extension, Excel uses an extension of .xls, and Access uses .mdb. You shouldn't add your own extensions to filenames because the application software may not be able to recognize the type of file you have created and you won't be able to work with the file.

Files that contain programs usually have an .exe extension, meaning they are files which can be run or executed.

HOW CAN I PUT MY DOCUMENTS IN LOGICAL GROUPINGS?

Any good clerk will establish a filing system which groups together related documents. The clerical services in Windows allow you to create **folders** and to give the folders names.

You can put documents or files into a folder. You can also put folders into other folders, creating as complex a filing system as you need. In Windows 95 the Windows Explorer performs many of the tasks of a file clerk. In Windows NT, these tasks are performed by the Windows NT Explorer. Menus at the top of the Explorer window allow you to select and execute common clerical functions such as filing and finding documents.

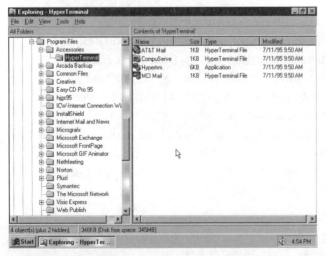

Figure 7 Windows Explorer shows the hierarchy of folders on the left. The folder called Program Files contains a folder called Accessories which contains a folder called Hyper Terminal which is depicted by an open folder icon. On the right are all the files stored in the Hyper Terminal folder.

overview

WHAT CAN I DO WITH MY FILES AND FOLDERS?

Just about anything you might need to do. You can **move files** if you want to put them in a different folder or storage device. For example, you might want to give a file to a friend, so you would move it to a floppy disk. You can also **copy files** to keep a duplicate in case your original is damaged. You can **create new folders and files** and **rename** existing folders and files. You can also **delete** un-needed files.

CAN A FILE BE MISPLACED?

You might have a problem finding files if you have many files and folders or if you haven't organized them well. If you forget where a file has been placed in the filing system you might have to look through many folders to locate it.

Windows has a special **Find** feature that helps you locate files. You provide Windows with the information you remember about the file: the date it was created or modified, its approximate size, its file type or extension, or even a word or phrase that is somewhere in the filename or the text of the file.

Suppose you used the Microsoft Word software to write a business letter about a refund. You saved the letter in a folder that seemed obvious at the time. Six months later you can't remember where you put it. You know it is somewhere in the "business" folder but that folder contains many subfolders and thousands of memos.

You can use Windows' Find feature to specify a range of dates which include the day you wrote the letter Since you know it was a Microsoft Word file, you can specify that you are looking for files of that type. You remember that the title had the word "refund" in it so you can specify that. The Find feature in Windows, Figure 8, will give you a list of all files that meet your specifications, and tell you where they can be found.

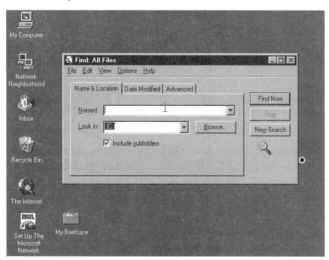

Figure 8 The Find feature is accessible from the Start menu as well as from Windows Explorer. Tabs at the top of this window select different ways of describing the file you are looking for.

overview

Windows Explorer and the Windows Find feature can help you find folders and files, but sometimes you need to tell application programs the path in which to locate a file.

HOW DO I SPECIFY A PATH?

A **path** describes the location of a file and typically consists of four components—a letter identifying the storage device, the name of the folder or folders in which the file is located, the filename, and the filename extension. The path C:\Letters\Linda.Doc indicates that this file is located on drive C, in the folder \Letters, has the filename Linda, and has a .Doc filename extension.

You can think of the Windows filing system as the branches and leaves of a tree. The trunk of the tree is the name of the physical device that stores files for your computer system. The trunk of the tree is called the **root directory** and all files and folders in it are said to be in the **root directory**. Folders, called **subdirectories**, branch off from the root directory. The files stored in these folders or subdirectories are like the leaves of the tree as shown in Figure 9.

Figure 9 *The figure on the left shows the files on a disk arranged as leaves on branches of a tree. The figure on the right shows the same files as seen in the Windows Explorer. Can you identify the path to the file A:\Business\Reports\Annual in both figures?*

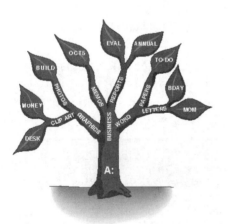
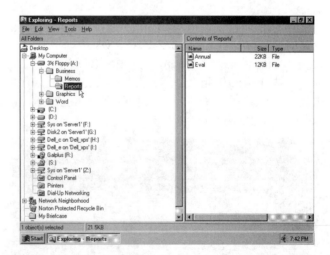

WHY INCLUDE THE STORAGE DEVICE LETTER IN THE PATH?

Your computer might have access to many storage devices. A complete path has to start by specifying which device holds the file. A personal computer typically has at least two disk drives. A **hard drive** with a large capacity hard disk, is usually hidden away inside the computer. A **floppy disk drive** appears as a slot in the computer case into which you can put a floppy disk. Many computers also have a **CD-ROM drive** that accepts CD-ROMs that look like audio CDs, but store data instead of music. The floppy disk drive is usually accessed as drive A. Storage device letter B is reserved for a second floppy disk drive. The hard disk drive is usually designated as drive C. The CD-ROM is usually accessed as drive D or E.

HOW DO I INSTALL NEW PROGRAMS?

There are thousands of Windows programs: drawing, graphing, money management, games, and so on. When you own a computer, you'll want to install new programs from time to time. The programs you purchase usually arrive on a floppy disk or CD-ROM. The **installation process** prepares the program for use on your computer. The operating system assists the installation process by finding space on your disk, transferring the program code from the distribution disk or CD-ROM to your hard disk, and making an entry in the Programs menu that you can use to start the program.

Usually software has installation instructions on the package. Often a special **setup program** that performs the installation is included on the floppy disk or CD-ROM that contains the software.

To install software from a floppy disk, you would put the disk in drive A. Then, you'd start the setup program by clicking the Run option on the Start menu and type a:\ setup.

Most programs that are distributed on CD-ROM are designed to self-install. You just place the CD-ROM disk into your CD-ROM drive—Windows examines the CD, finds the instructions for setting up the new software, asks if you want to install it, and proceeds with the installation!

HOW CAN THE OPERATING SYSTEM HELP ME COMMUNICATE WITH OTHER COMPUTERS AND USERS?

A **local area network** or **LAN** is a collection of computers that can exchange information. To connect your computer to a LAN you need a small circuit board called a **network interface card**, a cable, and **network client software** that handles the communication between your computer and the other computers on the network. The Windows operating system provides the network client software.

When your computer is connected to a LAN, you can use a Windows feature called **Network Neighborhood** to find out what computers, printers, and other devices you can access on the network.

overview

The **Internet** is a worldwide network of computers that stores, distributes, and communicates information of all sorts. To use the Internet, you must connect your computer to an **Internet service provider**. You can connect to a service provider over a local area network or over a dial-up connection. A **dial-up connection** is a communications link that uses a standard phone line instead of LAN cables. The Windows operating system provides the software you need to establish a dial-up connection.

Suppose you have a computer at home and you are using the local university as your Internet service provider. Your Windows dial-up connection software lets you dial into the university using your phone line to establish a connection to the Internet. But then what? You will need software to use Internet e-mail or search for information.

The software you use to send and receive e-mail is called **e-mail software** or an **e-mail client**. Microsoft has several e-mail software products, some included with Windows, and some that are "add-ons."

To search for information, you'll need **browser software** like the one shown in Figure 10. Some versions of the Windows operating system include Microsoft's browser software, called **Internet Explorer**. When not included, browser software can be installed just like any application software. Even a beginner will find it easy to use Internet Explorer to "surf" the Internet and find information from Internet sites around the world.

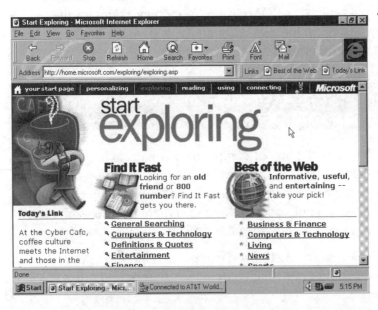

Figure 10 Microsoft's Internet Explorer is an example of browser software that you can use to search for information on the Internet.

WHAT KINDS OF PROBLEMS CAN THE OPERATING SYSTEM WARN ME ABOUT?

The Windows operating system spends some of its time being a doctor, checking to make sure that hardware is working properly, that the software you want to use is available, and that your data is accessible. Windows checks out your computer hardware every time you **boot up** (computer jargon for "switch on") your computer. If it spots problems with your hardware, the operating system often attempts to take care of them. For example, if the operating system spots some bad areas on the surface of your hard disk, it will cordon them off so data is not stored there.

During a computing session, the operating system keeps a watchful eye on your hardware and software, issuing **error messages** that warn you when problems occur. In some cases, Windows may detect problems and ask permission to try to fix them. It's usually a good idea to give Windows permission to fix problems so you don't lose data.

If you encounter serious problems with your computer hardware or software you might need help from a technical support person. Be prepared to describe your computer's symptoms as specifically and with as much detail as you can!

Finally, one principle is worth remembering: computers can fail and valuable information can be lost. Keep extra copies of documents that would be difficult to replace or do without!

WHAT'S A BACKUP?

A **backup** is a copy of one or more computer files. Because computers have been known to lose data, it is important to make a backup of the critical files you have stored on your computer. Usually, you will copy these critical files from your computer's hard disk to a floppy disk or to a computer tape device.

The Windows operating system provides several ways to copy information, including the Copy command, the Copy Disk command, and the Backup program. The Copy and Copy Disk commands are usually used when you back up to a floppy disk. The Backup program can be used when backing up to floppy disks or to tape.

HOW MUCH DO I NEED TO KNOW ABOUT WINDOWS?

Modern operating systems are powerful and complex. These e-SSentials present only an overview of concepts and basic services. The more you learn about your Windows operating system the more useful you will find it to be.

overview

Most users won't try to learn everything there is to know about Windows, at least not in the beginning. You need to know enough to be comfortable using Windows to run the applications you want to use without wasting too much time or getting too confused. If you go on to more advanced computing you might want to learn more, use a wider range of more powerful services, and become a Windows "power user!"

HOW CAN I FIND OUT WHAT I NEED TO KNOW?

There are books and tutorial systems, such as e-Course, that help you learn about Windows and other operating systems. There is also online **Help** available from Windows itself. Three ways to use online Help are available by selecting the tabs in the Help window shown in Figure 11.

Figure 11 *The Contents tab in Windows Help is structured into topics, represented by book icons. Sub-topics and more details are displayed as you selects areas of interest. The other two Help tabs, Index and Find, help you find information by entering a key word.*

WHAT ARE THE DIFFERENCES BETWEEN OPERATING SYSTEMS?

Because an operating system manages the hardware in a computer, operating systems are developed to run on a *specific* type of computer. One of the most important characteristics of an operating system is the type of computer it will run on. The Windows operating system is designed to run on computers whose main processor chip is manufactured by Intel Corporation. Intel chips or their equivalent are used in most of today's personal computers.

Windows was not designed to run on Macintosh computers because they use chips that are not compatible with those manufactured by Intel. Macintosh computers generally run an operating system called **MAC OS**. The MAC OS pioneered the use of graphical objects, such as icons, several years before they became a part of Windows.

Although most operating systems are designed for one type of computer, there are exceptions. **UNIX** is an operating system that was deliberately designed to be implemented on a variety of computers. It is a flexible and powerful operating system designed by and for sophisticated users, and requires some skill to use it effectively. The elegant approaches developed years ago for UNIX influenced the development of many operating systems and of the Internet. UNIX is available on so many different kinds of computers, because it is preferred by many computer professionals.

WHAT ARE THE DIFFERENCES BETWEEN THE DIFFERENT VERSIONS OF WINDOWS?

Windows 3.1, an early version of Windows, isn't generally considered a complete operating system because it requires DOS for many important computing tasks. Windows 3.1 provides the user with a graphical interface, while DOS and its not-so-friendly command-line interface hides in the background. Since it is the user interface that the user sees, the fact that Windows 3.1 calls on DOS for services may not seem important, but this dependence limited the growth and improvements possible to Windows in many serious ways. Microsoft eventually produced Windows 95 and Windows NT to take advantage of new hardware and new computing techniques.

The newer Windows operating systems such as Windows 95 and Windows NT have a user interface which is based on Windows 3.1, though new features have been added and improvements made. For example Windows 3.1 only allowed short, indecipherable DOS filenames, whereas Windows 95 allows long, descriptive filenames. It is expected that over the next several years most Windows 3.1 users will change to a more current version of Windows.

overview

CheckPoint

1 The Windows _____ includes hardware such as the mouse and the monitor, as well as software featuring graphical objects that you manipulate on the screen.

2 To tell Windows what you want it to do, you can select commands from _____ and indicate how you want a task performed by filling in _____ boxes.

3 True or False? Windows is considered application software because it enables you to apply your computer to specific tasks such as writing letters and adding up expenses.

4 Windows _____ use similar interface elements such as controls, icons, and menus.

5 A _____ is a set of detailed instructions that tell a computer how to solve a problem, whereas a _____ is the data you work with and create when you use application software.

6 An operating system that allows you to do several tasks at the same time is called a _____ system.

7 Every document you create is stored as a _____ on a storage device.

8 The _____ in Windows 95 and NT limit you to filenames of 255 characters and prohibit you from using the symbols / \ : * < > | in filenames.

9 Most executable programs have a(n) _____ filename extension.

10 The _____ C:\Letters\Linda.Doc describes the location of a file.

11 On most computer systems, the floppy disk drive is accessed as drive letter ____, the hard disk drive is drive letter _____, and the CD-ROM drive is accessed as _____.

12 The operating system provides _____ so you can connect your computer to a local area network.

13 List the ways that the Windows operating system helps you copy information as a backup in case of hard drive failure.

14 True or False? The Windows operating system was designed to run on the chips used in Macintosh computers as well as those used in computers with the Intel chip.

15 Place the following operating systems is chronological order: Windows 95, Windows 3.1, Windows NT, DOS.

Microsoft Windows

Tutorial 1: Windows Essentials

Tutorial 1

Windows
Essentials

Walking Through Windows

Windows are supposed to be clear, so you can see what's on the other side, right? Well, if Microsoft Windows isn't crystal clear to you, you're not alone—and this Windows tutorial is just what you need!

Doing the e-Thing

You'll find out how to get started with the e-Course software tutorials. This is a very easy way to learn how to use computer software.

Projects

Tutorial 1 Projects will help you practice and sharpen your newly learned Windows skills as you take a guided tour, play a game, view animations, and even design a computer game ad.

WHAT'S ONLINE

1 Meet the Windows Desktop
- The Windows Desktop
- Use a Mouse

2 Use the Start Menu

3 Start and Exit a Program
- Start a Program
- Exit a Program

4 Run Multiple Programs
- Start Multiple Programs
- Switch Between Programs
- Close Multiple Programs

5 Manipulate a Window
- Minimize
- Redisplay
- Maximize
- Restore
- Move
- Change Size

6 Use Desktop Icons

7 Use Help

Disks

If you'd like to keep track of your progress, you should have a blank formatted disk ready when you begin the online Steps for Tutorial 1. As you log in, the e-Course software will create a **Tracking Disk** for you. The Tracking Disk will keep a record of the length of time you spend on each e-Course session and your scores on the CheckPoint questions you answer online.

Walking Through Windows

o you shudder when you see yet another magazine or newspaper article about computers? Do you wish you could knowledgeably groan at the puns in article titles such as these actual examples:

MSN Around	*Backing Up Is Hard to Do*
Caught in the Web	*How Much Is the Degas in the "Windows"?*
Of Mice and Pens	*Dial M for Macintosh*
Scared Bitless	*Let the Chips Fall Where They May*
Send In The Clones	*The Wizards of OS*
Windows Without Walls	*Microsoft Office Binder: Docs in a Box*

Were you surprised when you heard or read about the PC wars, because you didn't even know there was a disagreement? Do you think that Windows is a home improvement option? Are you troubled when your child or a younger sibling uses terms such as "boot," "mouse," "virus," and "web crawler"? Do you think your favorite network news anchor is stuttering when he says, "Reach us at double-u double-u double-u… "? Would you like to take a ride on the information superhighway, but you can't find an entrance ramp?

The world of computers can be frightening to the uninitiated. So let's start your initiation right now. A computer is simply an electronic device that can store, retrieve, and process data. A personal computer, or PC for short, is a small computer used in homes and businesses. You issue commands to a computer via its operating system. For PCs, the most popular operating system is Microsoft's Windows.

Tutorial 1 presents Windows essentials—the basics you'll need to know how to use the Windows operating system. The ancient Chinese said it all with their proverb: A journey of a thousand miles must begin with a single step. You're ready now to take that first step, and then a second, and a third….

GET STARTED ONLINE WITH e-COURSE

The e-Course software is designed to teach you how to use the Microsoft Windows operating system. The first time you use the e-Course software, you'll probably want to set up a Tracking Disk, which keeps track of your progress and your CheckPoint scores. Now, it's time to use your computer.

To start the e-Course software and set up a Tracking Disk:

1: Label a formatted disk "Tracking Disk" and place it in the disk drive. (This step is optional, but if you do not insert a disk, you will not have an electronic record of your progress.)

2: Start your computer, then click the **Start** button.

3: Point to **Programs**.

4: Point to **e-Course**.

5: Click **e-course Windows**.

6: If you see the message "The tracking file was not found on drive A," click the button labeled "Copy the tracking database to a disk in drive A." This will copy some files onto your disk, and then display the Login window.

➔ If you're in a computer lab and e-Course is not on the Programs menu, ask your technical support person how to start the e-Course software. If you're using your own computer, you must install the e-Course software before you use it. Refer to the TechTalk section of this WorkText.

The first time you log in, e-Course asks you to enter your name and other information that automatically appears on your CheckPoint reports. This information is stored on your Tracking Disk, so you won't have to enter it the next time you log in.

To log in the first time:

1: On the Login screen, fill in the blanks with your **first name**, **last name**, **course section**, and **student number**. If you don't know your course section or student number, just type anything—you can change it later.

2: Click the **OK** button. In a few seconds, you should see the e-Course Welcome screen.

scenario

At the e-Course Welcome screen, you can print your Task Reference. The Task Reference will help refresh your memory about how to do the tasks you learn in the tutorials.

To print the Task Reference:

1: Click **Task Reference** on the Welcome screen menu bar.

2: Click **View/Print Task Reference**.

3: After the Task Reference appears, click **File** on the menu bar, then click **Print**.

4: When the printing is complete, click **File** again, then click **Exit**.

e-Course is easy to use. After the short e-Course Introductory Tour, you'll be ready to use all the e-Course features.

To start the e-Course Introductory Tour:

1: Click the **Introductory Tour** button on the Welcome screen.

2: Follow the instructions on the screen to navigate through the tour.

When you've finished the Introductory Tour, it's time to get started on Tutorial 1!

To start Tutorial 1:

1: Click **Tutorials** on the menu bar at the top of the Welcome screen.

2: Point to **Tutorial 1**.

3: Click a Topic—you should begin with Topic 1.

Review Questions

FILL-IN-THE-BLANKS

Fill in the blank with the correct word or phrase.

1 Microsoft _Windows_ is the most popular operating system in use today for personal computers.

2 In Windows terminology, a(n) _desk top_ is the workspace for projects and the tools needed to manipulate those projects.

3 A(n) _mouse_ is a pointing device that helps you interact with objects on the screen.

4 The _Pointer_ is a small object on the screen that moves as you move the mouse.

5 Positioning the mouse pointer on an object is called _Pointer_.

6 When you point to certain objects, a(n) _tool tips_ appears that tells you the purpose or function of the object.

7 A(n) _menue_ is a list of options.

8 The _start_ button provides access to programs, data, and configuration options.

9 When you point at a menu option that is followed by a ▶ (triangle), a(n) _Submenue_ appears.

10 The _tool bar_ is the area at the bottom of the screen that contains the Start button.

11 _multi task_ is that Windows feature that allows you to work on more than one program at a time.

12 When a program is running, a button for that program appears on the _task Bar_.

review questions

13   The three buttons in the right corner of a program's title bar are collectively called
     ___Sizing___ buttons.

14   When you ___minimize___ a program, the program window "shrinks" to a button on the
     taskbar.

15   You click the taskbar button for a minimized program to _____ that program's
     window.

16   When you ___maximize___ a program window, it fills the entire screen.

17   When you ___Restore___ a maximized program window, the window is reduced to a
     size smaller than a full screen.

18   To ___drag___ an object, you click the object and continue to hold the mouse button
     down as you move the mouse.

19   A(n) ___Icon___ is a small picture that represents an object.

20   Right-clicking an object will open that object's ___menue___.

21   The Windows ___help___ system provides on-screen information about the program
     you are using.

22   To close the Start menu after you've accidentally opened it, you click the ___Start___
     button.

review questions

MULTIPLE CHOICE

*Select the letter of the **one** best answer.*

23 **When you click a program button on the taskbar:**

 a the Start menu appears

 b the program window is redisplayed

 c nothing happens

 d the program begins running

24 **To click an object, a right-handed person would use:**

 a the left mouse button

 b the right mouse button

 c the center mouse button, if the mouse has three buttons

 d any mouse button

25 **The short description that appears when you point at an object on the screen is called:**

 a a definition

 b a ToolTip

 c Help

 d an icon

26 **To start a Windows accessory program such as WordPad or Paint, you click the Start button, and then you:**

 a click Accessories

 b click Programs

 c point to Accessories

 d point to Programs

review questions

27 **If there are three program buttons on the taskbar, then you know:**

   a all three programs are running

   b three programs are active, but only one program is running

   c at least two programs have been minimized

   d two of the programs must be closed immediately, before you get into trouble

28 **The Windows feature that allows you to work on more than one program at a time is called:**

   a multiprogramming

   b windowing

   c multitasking

   d multirunning

29 **The three buttons in the right corner of a program title bar are collectively called:**

   a program buttons

   b title buttons

   c bar buttons

   d sizing buttons

30 **When a program window is a predetermined size that is smaller than a full screen, that window is:**

   a normalized

   b maximized

   c minimized

   d restored

31 **To move a window to a new position on the screen, you:**

   a drag its title bar

   b pull an edge

   c click Window, then click Move

   d restart the program

32 **Which of the following is not a tab in Windows Help?**

  a Contents

  b Definitions

  c Index

  d Find

33 **In a Help window, clicking a word that is underlined and colored green will cause:**

  a the Help window for that topic to appear

  b a definition of the word to appear

  c the Help system to close

  d a program to start

MATCHING

Select the letter from the right column that correctly matches each item in the left column.

34 🔲

35 ▭

36 Start

37 ▶

38 ☒

39 ⬒

40 ▨

41 ↔

a The button you click to maximize a program window

b The typical pointer shape

c The button you click to restore a program window

d The button you click to close a program

e One possible pointer shape for resizing a window

f Indicates that a menu option has a submenu

g The button you click to minimize a program window

h The button you click to gain access to Windows programs and documents

review questions

SHORT ANSWER

Use a separate sheet of paper to write out your answers to the following questions.

42 What is multitasking, and what role do taskbar buttons play in multitasking?

43 What is the difference between clicking and right-clicking? When would you right-click an object?

44 What are sizing buttons, where are they located, and what are they used for?

45 When you start a program, what two clues do you see on the screen that indicate the program has started?

46 Explain the differences among the Contents tab, the Index tab, and the Find tab in the Windows Help system.

Projects

These Projects are designed to help you review and develop the skills you learned in Tutorial 1. Complete each Project using the Microsoft Windows software. You should not need to use the e-Course software to complete the Projects.

If you've forgotten some of the skills you need to complete the Projects, refer to the Task Reference.

REVIEW SKILLS

1 Using the Start Menu

In this tutorial you learned how to use the Start menu. Open the Start menu and then write out your answers to the following questions. Close the Start menu when you've completed the questions.

    a   Which options on the Start menu lead to a submenu?

    b   What are the three options on the Settings submenu?

    c   How many options appear on the Programs submenu?

    d   How many options on the Programs submenu lead to another submenu?

    e   Looking at the Programs submenu, can you determine any logic behind the ordering of the options?

projects

2 Starting a Program and Manipulating a Program Window

Suppose you want to use the Paint program to draw an organizational chart. In this tutorial, you learned how to start Paint. For this Project, start Paint, maximize the Paint window (if necessary), and then write out your answers to the following questions:

    a What are the two visual clues that tell you Paint has started?

    b What are the two visual clues that tell you the Paint window is maximized?

    c What is the shape of the pointer when it's positioned on the Paint title bar?

    d To what shape does the pointer change when you move it into the workspace?

    e Which Windows control do you use to exit Paint?

3 Running Two Programs and Switching Between Them

In this tutorial you learned how Windows allows you to multitask by running more than one program at a time. Start Calculator, start Paint, maximize the Paint window (if necessary), and then write out your answers to the following questions. Exit both Paint and Calculator after you've completed the questions.

    a What program(s) are now running?

    b What program(s) are now active? How can you tell?

    c How many program buttons appear on the taskbar?

    d Can you maximize or restore the Calculator window? Why or why not?

    e How does the desktop change when you minimize the Calculator window?

    f How does the desktop change when you now minimize the Paint window?

    g How does the desktop change when you switch to Calculator?

4 Resizing Windows

In this tutorial you learned how to resize a program window. Start Paint and then restore the Paint window (if necessary). Write out your answers to the questions.

a What are the approximate dimensions of the current Paint window? (You don't need to use a ruler; simply estimate the dimensions.)

b What happens when you drag the right edge of the Paint window to the left in order to make the window as narrow as possible? Approximately how wide is the resulting window?

c What happens when you drag the top edge of the Paint window down to make the window as short as possible?

d What are the approximate dimensions of the Paint window after you've maximized it and then restored it again?

e Drag a corner of the Paint window to resize it to the original dimensions you noted in question **a** above.

5 Right-Clicking to Open an Object's Menu

In this tutorial you learned to right-click an object to open the object's shortcut menu. Complete the following steps and then write out your answers to the following questions.

a What options do you see when you right-click the Start button? Which option is bolded?

b How many options do you see when you right-click the My Computer icon? Which option is bolded?

c When you click the Open option on the My Computer shortcut menu, what is the label for the icon that appears in the My Computer window?

projects

6   Using Windows Help

In this tutorial you learned how to use the Windows Help system. In this Project, you'll use that system and learn some additional features that it provides. Start Windows Help and then click the Index tab. Write out your answers to the following questions:

a   How many characters of the word "desktop" do you need to type before that topic is highlighted in the lower window?

b   What appears when you click the Display button with "desktop" highlighted?

c   What happens when you click the topic that mentions the background of your desktop, and then click the Display button?

d   How many terms in the current Help window have definitions? How can you tell?

e   What is the definition of the term "Wallpaper"?

f   What appears when you click the ■ button at the bottom of the Help window? (If necessary, maximize the window so you can see the button.)

7   Improving Mouse Skills With a Game

Required: Solitaire

Windows includes several games, which you can play to sharpen your pointing, clicking, double-clicking, and dragging mouse skills. Click the Start button, point to Programs, and then point to Accessories. Is Games one of the menu options on your Accessories submenu? If not, then no games are installed on your system, and you cannot complete this Project. If Games is an option, point to Games. Then write out your answers to the following questions:

a   What games are listed on the Games submenu?

b   Click Solitaire. The Solitaire window contains all the standard parts of a program window except a toolbar. What are the other standard program window features? Find them in the Solitaire window.

c   Play a game of Solitaire. (Click Help on the Solitaire menu bar if you are unsure how to play.) If you have played the card version of Solitaire before, how did this computer version compare? If you had never played Solitaire before, what did you like most about this computer game?

8 Minimizing, Maximizing, Restoring, and Redisplaying Windows

You used the sizing buttons in the online Steps. In this Project, you'll experiment with maximizing, restoring, minimizing, and redisplaying to discover the significance, if any, of the order of these operations. Start WordPad, and then experiment with maximizing, minimizing, restoring, and redisplaying the WordPad window, in all possible sequences. Write out your answers to the following questions.

a Which sequences were not possible? (For example, you can't redisplay a window immediately after maximizing it.)

b When you redisplay a minimized window, is the window always redisplayed to a maximized state, or always redisplayed to a minimized state; or does the size of the redisplayed window vary? If the size of the redisplayed window varies, what determines the redisplayed size?

9 Using the Microsoft Windows Tutorial
Required: Windows 10-minute Tour

Windows includes an online tutorial you can use to review what you've learned and to pick up some new tips for using Windows. (Note: This tutorial is not available in Windows NT.) If the tutorial is not installed on your computer, a message will ask you to insert the Windows installation CD-ROM disk. If you are in a computer lab, check with your technical support person. If you are using your own computer, once you insert the installation CD-ROM, you can proceed.

Start Windows Help, and then click the Contents tab, if necessary. Click "Tour: Ten minutes to using Windows," and then click the Display button. Click the Starting a Program button, and then follow the tour directions. Write out your answers to the following questions.

a What are the names of the four programs on the Programs submenu in the tutorial?

b Click the Switching Windows button, and then follow the tour directions. What picture appears in the Paint window?

c Click the Using Help button, and then follow the tour directions. What does the tutorial say is the fastest way to find a topic?

projects

10 Using Windows Help Animations

The Windows Help System includes several animations, which you can watch to review what you've learned and to pick up some new tips. Start Windows Help and then click the Index tab, if necessary. Type "basic skills" and then click the Display button. (If "basic skills" is not one of the topics displayed in the large list box, then you can't complete this Project.) Write out your answers to the following questions.

    a Click the Moving windows button, and then follow the directions. What is the title of the window used in the animation?

    b Click the Sizing windows button, and then follow the directions. Which three edges or corners are used in the sizing animation?

    c Click the Closing windows button, and then follow the directions. What technique is used to open the icon in the animation?

    d Click the Switching between windows button, and then follow the directions. What is the first line of text in the WordPad document window?

BUILD SKILLS

11 Using WordPad's Help

You learned to use Windows Help in the online steps. Most Windows programs, including WordPad, also provide Help specific to that program. In this Project, you'll use WordPad Help to learn some handy features for creating WordPad documents. Start WordPad. Click Help on the WordPad menu bar, then click Help Topics. Use WordPad Help to answer these questions:

    a How can you correct a mistake?

    b How do you center text?

    c How do you set tab stops?

projects

12 Using Calculator's Help

You learned to use Windows Help in the online Steps. Most Windows programs, including Calculator, also provide Help specific to that program. In this Project, you'll use Calculator Help to learn how to use some of the Calculator features.

Start Calculator. Click View on the Calculator menu bar, then click Scientific. Click Help on the Calculator menu bar, then click Help Topics. Read the first topic under Tips and Tricks on the Contents tab, and then use the method described to answer the following questions:

a   What does the **n!** button do?

b   What does the **x^y** button do?

c   What does the **PI** button do?

Switch to the Index tab in the Calculator Help System window, and then answer the following questions:

d   What four number systems are available?

e   What four operators are used in simple (standard) calculations?

13 Starting a New Program and Viewing ToolTips
Required: Microsoft Excel

In this Project, you'll start a program you've never used before, and view the ToolTips for several buttons. Click the Start button, point to Programs, then click Microsoft Excel. Maximize the Excel window, if necessary. Write out your answers to the following questions:

a   What is the ToolTip for the button?

b   What is the ToolTip for the **$** button?

c   What is the ToolTip for the **%** button?

d   What is the ToolTip for the **Σ** button?

projects

14 Running Multiple Programs, Moving Windows, and Passing Information from One Program to Another

Sometimes it's handy to copy information from one application into another. In this Project you will do this. Start WordPad. Start Calculator. Switch to WordPad, then restore the WordPad window, if necessary. Move the WordPad window to the upper-left corner of your desktop. Move the Calculator window to the lower-right corner of the desktop. Write out your answers to the following questions:

a What final result do you get when you use the Calculator to compute 650.25/4, and then take the square root of that quotient?

b What happens when you click Edit and click Copy on the Calculator menu bar, and then click Edit and click Paste on the WordPad menu bar?

15 Investigating the Office Shortcut Bar

Locate the Office Shortcut Bar on your desktop. The Office Shortcut Bar is a set of buttons that appears either along the top edge or on the right side of the desktop. The leftmost or topmost area in the Office Shortcut Bar contains a square made up of four colored squares. (If the Office Shortcut Bar doesn't appear on your desktop, you can't complete this Project.) Write out your answers to the following questions:

a What ToolTip is displayed for each button on the Office Shortcut Bar?

b What's the title of the window that appears when you click the Answer Wizard button? How many tabs are in that window?

c Click the Cancel button to close the window. What appears when you click the square containing the four colored squares in the Office Shortcut Bar?

EXPLORE

16 Starting Programs Using the Start Button Open Command

Write out your answers to the following questions:

a Right-click the Start button, then click Open. What window appears? How many icons appear in that window?

b Open the Programs icon. What window now appears?

c Open the Accessories icon. What window now appears?

d Open the Paint icon. What now appears?

e Exit Paint. Which windows, if any, are now visible on the desktop?

projects

17 Exploring the Date/Time Control

In this Project, you'll explore the Date/Time control, which is located at the far right of the taskbar. Right-click the Date/Time control, then click Adjust Date/Time. Then write out your answers to questions a through d.

  a What is the title of the window that appears?

  b How many tabs are in that window, and what are the names of these tabs?

  c What appears in the right portion of the current tab?

  d What option appears at the bottom of the Time Zone tab?

18 Exploring the Title Bar Icon

In this Project, you'll explore the icon that appears at the far left of a program title bar. Start WordPad, then maximize the WordPad window, if necessary. Write out your answers to questions a through e.

  a What appears when you right-click the 🖼 icon?

  b Does clicking "Minimize" produce the same result as clicking the ▬ button?

  c When you click the 🖼 icon while the WordPad window is maximized, which options appear in black text?

  d Restore the WordPad window. When you now click the 🖼 icon, which options appear in black text?

  e What can you deduce from the color of an option's text?

19 Exploring the Date/Time Control Tile Options

In this Project you'll investigate the tile options on the Date/Time control shortcut menu. Start WordPad, then maximize the WordPad window, if necessary. Start Paint, then maximize the Paint window if necessary. Write out your answers to questions a through e.

  a Right-click the Date/Time control, then click Tile Vertically. Describe how your desktop currently appears.

  b Right-click the Date/Time control, then click Undo Tile. How does the desktop change?

  c Right-click the Date/Time control, then click Tile Horizontally. Describe how your desktop appears.

projects

d Right-click the Date/Time control, then click Undo Tile. How does the desktop change?

e Right-click the Date/Time control, then click Minimize All Windows. What happens?

20 Using the Desktop Shortcut Menu and the Recycle Bin

One of the icons on your Windows desktop is the Recycle Bin, which acts like a trash basket for documents you no longer want. In this Project, you'll use the desktop shortcut menu to create a document, and then you'll delete the document by dragging it to the Recycle Bin icon. Right-click an open area of the desktop to display the desktop shortcut menu. Write out your answers to questions a through e.

a How many options appear on the shortcut menu?

b Which of these options lead to a submenu?

c Point to New, then click Bitmap image. What is the label for the new icon that appears on your desktop?

d Open the new icon. What program starts?

e Exit the program, without saving changes. Drag the new icon to the Recycle Bin icon. What happens when you release the mouse button?

INVESTIGATE

21 Smooth Operators

You learned in the e-SSentials chapter that Windows is the most popular operating system for today's personal computers. In this Project, you'll attempt to determine if this statement is true for a small sample of computer users in your area.

a Prepare a short questionnaire (4 to 6 questions) that you will use to interview a personal computer user. The questions should help you to determine the specific operating system used on a particular personal computer, how long that operating system has been used, the level of user satisfaction, and so on.

b Use your questionnaire to interview five individuals who own or use a personal computer.

c Write a report. Page 1 should provide your results and conclusions. Page 2 of your report should be the questionnaire. Pages 3 through 7 should be the five filled-in questionnaires from your five interviews.

22 Let's Do Windows

Assume you own a personal computer that doesn't currently use the Microsoft Windows operating system, and that you plan to purchase Windows. In this Project, you'll investigate retail sources for the Microsoft Windows operating system.

a Look through computer magazine ads, visit computer stores, or search the Internet to locate five sources from which you could purchase the Windows operating system software.

b Write a report that compares the prices, claims, suggested minimum computer requirements, and additional services offered (if any) for the five sources.

23 Personal Computer Purchase

Suppose that you plan to buy a personal computer to use at home. In this Project, you'll investigate sources and prices for purchasing a personal computer.

a Determine a minimum set of system requirements—operating system, speed, monitor type and size, memory, peripheral equipment, and so on. (Hint: You can use computer magazine ads to help you determine typical requirements.) Then prepare a one-page requirements checklist and make five copies of that checklist.

b Look through computer magazine ads, visit computer stores, or search the Internet to locate sources from which you could purchase personal computers. Find five sources for a computer that meets or exceeds your requirements, and fill out your requirements checklist for each.

c Write a report that compares the prices, terms, and support services for your five sources. Then decide which of the five you would purchase, and justify your decision.

projects

24 A History of Microcomputer Operating Systems

You can better appreciate the features of the Windows operating system if you know a little bit about the history of microcomputer operating systems.

a Visit a library and look through books and the magazine archives to learn about the history of development for microcomputer operating systems.

b Write a two-page paper discussing the history of microcomputer operating systems; point out each notable developmental step and explain its significance. Be sure to include the people and institutions that played significant roles in this history.

25 Watch Out Madison Avenue!

Computer games represent a large segment of the computer software industry. If you visit any computer software store, you'll find many shelves filled with computer games; similarly, many of the ads in computer magazines are for computer games. In this Project, you'll create a computer game ad.

a Look through computer magazines and study the ads for computer games.

b Make up a new computer game that you think might appeal to game players, and then create an ad to promote sales of that game.

Microsoft Windows

Tutorial 2: Windows Programs

Tutorial 2

Windows Programs

Walking Through Windows

You've now mastered the basic Microsoft Windows skills and know how to start a program. In this tutorial, you'll learn the general skills you need for working in a program—any program—in the Windows environment.

Projects

In the Tutorial 2 Projects, you'll review the new skills you've learned, and extend those skills using Microsoft programs such as Word, Excel, and PowerPoint. You'll also capture screen images, paint a picture, learn three new Help techniques, and learn how to use keyboard alternatives to the mouse.

If you're not assigned Projects 12, 13, 16, 17, or 18, you might want to at least read these Projects or, better yet, work through them. In Projects 12 and 13, you'll learn how to capture and print a screen image. Projects 16, 17, and 18 will show you more about using the Help button in a program, the Help button in a dialog box, and the Answer Wizard, respectively—all valuable techniques for receiving assistance as you work.

WHAT'S ONLINE

1 Use Program Menus
- Open and Close a Menu
- Select a Menu Option
- Select from Submenu Options
- … to Dialog Boxes
- Grayed-Out Menu Options
- Toggle Check Marks

2 Scrolling

3 Select from a List
- Use a Simple List Box
- Use a Drop-Down List Box

4 Use Text Boxes
- Enter Text in a Text Box
- Edit Text in a Text Box
- Use Spin Bars

5 Use Option Buttons and Check Boxes
- Use Option Buttons
- Use Check Boxes

6 Use Toolbar Shortcuts
- Use Toolbar Tools
- Cut and Paste

Walking Through Windows

Okay, so you finished the first Windows tutorial. Bet you were feeling pretty proud of yourself—as well you should! Bet you also couldn't wait to show off your new knowledge. Hope you didn't do anything silly like trying to turn conversations to computer topics just so you could drop terms like "operating system," "desktop," "multitasking," and "icons"? You did? Oh, we know just what happened next. The conversation took twists you hadn't expected and strange new words started flying all around and over your head, right? Maybe you heard terms like "command buttons," "toggle," "scroll," "spin bar," "radio buttons," and "toolbar," and you were lost.

Don't despair! Have you already looked at the Table of Contents for Windows Tutorial 2? Well, you'll learn every one of those new terms in the online steps for this tutorial as you learn to work with menus, dialog boxes, and toolbars. Are you ready? Let's go!

Review Questions

FILL-IN-THE-BLANKS

Fill in the blank with the correct word or phrase.

1   In a program that runs in Windows, _____ provide an easy way for you to locate and select program commands.

2   A program's menu bar is typically located beneath the _____ bar.

3   If a ▶ appears to the right of a menu option, pointing to that option will open a _____.

4   If an **...** appears to the right of a menu option, clicking that option will open a _____.

5   A(n) _____ is a special window in which you enter or select specifications for how you want a task carried out.

6   A dialog box will always have at least two _____ buttons.

7   Inactive menu options are shown in _____ type.

8   A(n) _____ switch is a menu option that can be on or off.

9   You _____ in order to move a portion of an image into the visible area of the screen or window.

10   As you scroll, the _____ moves a proportionate distance within the scroll bar.

11   A(n) _____ is a dialog box control that displays a vertical column of choices.

12   A(n) _____ list box initially displays only one choice.

13   To see the additional choices in a drop-down list box, you click the _____.

review questions

14 You can type information in a(n) _____ in a dialog box.

15 The _____ is the flashing vertical line that indicates the current typing position.

16 When you delete text using the Backspace key, characters to the _____ of the insertion point are deleted.

17 When you delete text using the Delete key, characters to the _____ of the insertion point are deleted.

18 To replace existing text, you _____ the text and then type the replacement text.

19 A(n) _____ is a special type of text box used to change a numeric setting.

20 _____, also called radio buttons, allow you to select *one* option from a set of options.

21 A(n) _____ is a small square box that contains a check mark when the option it represents is selected.

22 A(n) _____ is a collection of icons that provide menu command shortcuts.

MULTIPLE CHOICE

*Select the letter of the **one** best answer.*

23 **To open a program menu, you:**

   a point to the menu name on the menu bar

   b click the menu name on the menu bar

   c right-click the menu name on the menu bar

   d double-click the menu name on the menu bar

24 **Which of the following is not a Windows menu convention?**

   a ellipsis

   b check mark

   c check box

   d graying-out

25 Selecting a simple menu option:

a   results in an immediate action   c   opens a submenu

b   opens a dialog box   d   opens a menu

26 To close a dialog box without taking any action, you would typically click the:

a   OK button   c   taskbar

b   Cancel button   d   dialog box title bar

27 When you click a menu option that appears in gray type:

a   the menu closes

b   a submenu appears

c   nothing happens

d   an error message appears

28 When a menu toggle switch is "on":

a   the corresponding menu option appears in gray type

b   clicking that menu option has no effect

c   a check mark appears in front of the menu option

d   all of the above

29 The active options on a menu are those that:

a   have a check mark

b   appear in black type

c   use menu conventions

d   must be double-clicked to take effect

30 Which of the following is *not* a scrolling control?

a   scroll box   c   scroll button

b   scroll bar   d   scroll arrow

31 You can scroll most rapidly by dragging the:

a   scroll box   c   scroll button

b   scroll bar   d   scroll arrow

review questions

32 **You can tell that a drop-down list box is not a text box by the:**

  a box title

  b scrolling controls on the right

  c list box arrow on the right

  d none of the above; you can't know for sure until you click the box

33 **Which of the following might include scrolling controls:**

  a list box

  b drop-down list box

  c both a and b

  d neither a nor b

MATCHING

Select the letter from the right column that correctly matches each item in the left column.

34 ⊙   **a** Cut button

35 📋   **b** Selected option button

36 | **c** Ellipsis

37 ✂   **d** Insertion point

38 ...   **e** Selected check box

39 ☑   **f** Paste button

SHORT ANSWER

Use a separate sheet of paper to write out your answers to the following questions.

40 Explain the components of a scrollbar and how you would use each.

41 Describe how you remove, replace, and add text in a text box.

42 Describe the process you use to move text by cutting and pasting.

Projects

These Projects are designed to help you review and develop the skills you learned in Tutorial 2. Complete each Project using the Microsoft Windows software. You should not need to use the e-Course software to complete the Projects.

If you've forgotten some of the skills you need to complete the Projects, refer to the Task Reference.

1 Using Menus and Menu Conventions
Required: Microsoft Excel

You can review your menu and menu convention skills using any Windows program. In this Project, you'll use the Excel program. Write out your answers to questions a through i.

    a Start Excel. (Microsoft Excel is an option on the Programs submenu.) How many menu names appear on the Excel menu bar?

Starting with the first menu on the left, open menus as needed to locate b through e.

    b What is the first simple menu option and on which menu does it appear?

    c What is the first menu option that leads to a submenu?

    d What is the first menu option that leads to a dialog box?

    e What is the first grayed-out menu option?

    f How many Data menu options are simple options?

    g How many Data menu options lead to a submenu?

    h How many Data menu options lead to a dialog box?

    i How many Data menu options are grayed-out?

projects

2 Scrolling

You'll use the Windows Help system to practice and test your scrolling skills. Start Windows Help. Click the Index tab, if necessary. Scroll the large list box using all three scrolling techniques. Scroll as necessary to answer these questions. Write out your answers to questions a through d.

   a How many subtopics follow the topic heading "quitting"?

   b What topic precedes "Internet"?

   c How many subtopics follow the topic heading "naming"?

   d What kind of scrolling can't you practice in the current window?

3 Using Text Boxes

The Index tab of the Windows Help system includes a text box. In this Project, you'll use the Windows Help system to practice and test your text box skills. Write out your answers to questions a through d.

   a Start Windows Help. Click the Index tab, if necessary, and then type "clearing" in the text box near the top of the window. How many subtopics appear under the "clearing" topic in the list box?

   b Highlight the "r" in "clearing," then type n. What topic is now highlighted in the list box?

   c Highlight the "ean" in "cleaning," then type os. What topic is highlighted in the list box, and how many subtopics appear under that topic?

   d Without repositioning the insertion point, press the Backspace key once, press the Delete key three times, then type ck. What topic is now highlighted in the list box?

4   Identifying and Using Page Setup Dialog Box Controls

Suppose you wanted to check the page setup specifications for a Paint picture. The Page Setup dialog box contains a number of dialog box controls. Start Paint. Click File on the Paint menu bar, then click Page Setup to open the Page Setup dialog box. Write out your answers to questions a through f.

a   What types of dialog box controls, and how many of each, do you see in the Page Setup dialog box?

b   How many command buttons are there in the Page Setup dialog box?

c   Based on the label on the rightmost command button, what would you expect to see if you clicked that button? Why?

d   How many choices are there in the Source drop-down list box?

e   Change the left margin value to 3". How does the dialog box change to reflect the new left margin value?

f   Change the Orientation to Landscape. Where is the large margin now located in the dialog box sample?

5   Identifying and Using Print Dialog Box Controls
Required: Microsoft Word

Suppose you wanted to print a Word document. The Print dialog box contains a number of dialog box controls. Start Word. Click File on the Word menu bar, then click Print to open the Print dialog box. Write out your answers to questions a through k.

a   What types of dialog box controls, and how many of each, do you see in the Print dialog box?

b   How many command buttons are there in the Print dialog box?

c   Change the Number of copies value to 3. Toggle the Collate check box. Click the Pages option button in the Page range section of the dialog box. Where is the insertion point now located?

d   Type 1, 3, 5-10. Highlight the characters from the first comma through the 5, then press the Delete key. What is now displayed in the Pages text box?

e   Click the Print what list box arrow. How many choices are available in the drop-down list?

f   Does the drop-down list include scrolling controls?

projects

g Click Annotations in the drop-down list. How did the settings in the Page range section of the dialog box change?

h Notice the ... following "Options" on the command button in the lower-right corner of the dialog box. What do you expect would happen if you clicked that command button?

i Click the Options button. How many grayed-out check boxes do you see?

j How many active (i.e. not grayed-out) check boxes do you see?

k How many of the active check boxes contain check marks?

APPLY SKILLS

6   Compare WordPad Toolbar Buttons and Menu Commands

The online Steps told you that a toolbar button, which can be activated by a single click, is more convenient than a menu. In this Project, you'll verify this statement by comparing several toolbar buttons and their corresponding menu command sequences. Start WordPad. Write out your answer to the question:

a For each button or drop-down list box on the two WordPad toolbars, what is the ToolTip and the comparable menu and menu option? In several cases, you'll have to open a dialog box to verify that the menu option provides comparable results. Some of the toolbar buttons and menu options are inactive (grayed-out), but you can still read the ToolTips and menu options.

7   Compare Microsoft Word Toolbar Buttons and Menu Commands   Required: Microsoft Word

The online Steps told you that a toolbar button is more convenient to use than a menu because the toolbar button can be activated by a single click. In this Project, you'll verify this statement by comparing several toolbar buttons and their corresponding menu command sequences. Start Word. Type your name, then press the Enter key. Highlight the line containing your name. Locate the toolbar button whose ToolTip is "Copy," click that button, position the insertion point in the blank line below your name, then click the toolbar button whose ToolTip is "Paste" three or four times. Write out your answers to questions a through d.

a Highlight one occurrence of your name, locate the button whose ToolTip is "Bullets," click that button, then click in an empty area of the Word workspace to remove the highlight. How has that occurrence of your name changed in appearance?

b Highlight another occurrence of your name. Experiment to determine the menu commands necessary to produce the same result as clicking the Bullets toolbar button. (Hint: Try the Format menu.) What is the equivalent menu command sequence?

c Click the toolbar button whose ToolTip is "Print Preview." Briefly describe what appears. Then click the Close button in the Print Preview toolbar.

d Determine the sequence of menu commands needed to produce the equivalent of clicking the Print Preview button. What is that sequence of the commands?

8   Comparing Menu Bars, Menus, and Toolbars
Required: Microsoft Word

Word and WordPad are both word processing programs, so you might expect that the menu bar, the various menu options, and the toolbars would be similar for the two programs. In this Project, you'll compare Word and WordPad menu bars, menu options, and toolbars. Start Word, then start WordPad. Switch between the two programs as needed to answer the following questions.

a What menu names appear on both the Word and the WordPad menu bars?

b Do those same menus appear in the same order?

c What menu names appear only on the Word menu bar?

d What menu names appear only on the WordPad menu bar?

e Note the menu options in WordPad's Format menu. Which option does not appear in Word's Format menu? Which menu option in Word's Format menu do you suspect might be comparable to the WordPad Format menu option?

f How many of Word's Format menu options do not appear in WordPad's Format menu?

g Note the menu options in WordPad's Insert menu. Do these options appear in Word's Insert menu?

h How many buttons appear on a WordPad toolbar but do not appear on a Word toolbar? What are the ToolTips for those buttons?

i Based on their menus, menu options, and toolbars, which of the two programs do you believe is probably more flexible and powerful?

projects

9 Identifying Dialog Box Controls
Required: Microsoft PowerPoint

You can test your knowledge of dialog box controls using any Windows program. In this Project, you'll use the PowerPoint program. Start PowerPoint. If you see the Tip of the Day window, click the OK button. When the dialog box titled "PowerPoint" appears, select the Blank Presentation option, then click the OK button. Then click the OK button in the New Slide dialog box. Click Format on the PowerPoint menu bar, then click Slide Layout. Answer the following questions about the Slide Layout dialog box. Write out your answers to questions a through j.

   a   How many command buttons does the dialog box contain?

   b   What type of dialog box control (list box, drop-down list box, text box, spin bar, option button, or check box) appears?

   c   Are all the different slide layout options in view? How do you know?

   d   How many different slide layout options are there?

   e   Which of the slide layout options is currently selected?

Click Insert on the menu bar, then click Clip Art. Answer the following questions about the dialog box that appears, then click the Close button when done.

   f   What is the dialog box title?

   g   How many command buttons does the dialog box contain?

   h   Without clicking any of the command buttons, can you predict if any command buttons lead to another dialog box? If so, which command buttons?

   i   What's the last category in the Categories list box?

   j   What's the second picture in the Signs category?

projects

10 Comparing Word and Excel Menus and Toolbars
Required: Microsoft Word and Microsoft Excel

In the online Steps you read that you can apply the knowledge you gain from using one Windows program to other Windows programs. If that is true, you should be able to find common elements in two programs that are both Windows programs but that both accomplish very different tasks, such as Word, a word processing program, and Excel, a spreadsheet program. Start Word. Start Excel. In Word, click View on the menu bar, click Toolbars, then make sure the Standard and the Formatting toolbars are displayed. Repeat for Excel. Switch between the two programs as needed to answer the following questions.

a What menu names appear on both the Word and the Excel menu bars?

b Do the menus that appear on both menu bars appear in the same order?

c What menu name appears only on the Word menu bar?

d What menu name appears only on the Excel menu bar?

e Note the menu options in the Format menu in both Word and Excel. How many options appear on both menus, and what are those options?

f Compare the Standard toolbars for the two programs. (The Standard toolbar is the one with the ▢ New button on the far left.) Are the first ten buttons the same or different?

g Are the corresponding ToolTips for those ten buttons exactly the same, somewhat different, or completely different? If different, how do they differ?

h Consider Excel's Formatting toolbar, which has two drop-down list boxes followed by a series of buttons. How many of those list boxes or buttons also appear on the Word Formatting toolbar?

i Considering what you've just learned about Word's and Excel's menus and toolbars, would you agree or disagree with the claim that learning to use one Windows program helps you to subsequently learn to use another Windows program? Justify your answer.

projects

11 Using Text Box Skills in WordPad

In the online Steps you learned how to position the insertion point and how to remove, replace, and insert text in a text box. You can use those same skills in a word processing program such as WordPad.

Start WordPad. Type your name, press the Enter key, then type the following paragraph exactly as it appears here:

> To format a paragraph, click within the you want to format, then click View, then click Paragraph, then choose the alignment and indents you want.

Replace the word "View" with the word "Format." Positioning the insertion point as needed, remove the first two occurrences of the word "then." Position the insertion point at the end of the first occurrence of the word "the," then insert a space and the word "paragraph". Replace the first comma (,) with a colon (:). Click the toolbar button whose ToolTip is "Print" to print a copy of your finished document. Exit WordPad; click the No button when asked if you want to save changes.

12 Capturing a Screen Image and Pasting It into Paint

Suppose you wanted a printed copy of the Windows desktop. In this Project, you'll use Windows Help to learn how to capture a screen. Then you'll paste the captured image into Paint and print the result. Use Windows Help to find out how to capture window or screen images and how to paste a captured image into a document, then exit Windows Help.

Using what you learned in Help, capture the entire desktop screen image.

Start Paint. As you learned from Windows Help, paste the image into Paint. (Click the Yes button if asked if you want the bitmap enlarged.)

Now to print the image in Landscape mode (sideways), click File on the Paint menu bar, click Page Setup, then change the Orientation to Landscape. Next print the image.

13 Capturing and Examining Screen Images

In this Project, you'll use WordPad Help to learn how to capture a screen and insert the captured image into WordPad.

Use WordPad Help to learn how to capture an image of the entire screen and how to paste the image into a document, then exit WordPad Help. (Note: If that topic is not available in your WordPad Help System, then use the Windows Help System to learn about capturing screen images.)

Now you need to capture an image of the WordPad Page Setup dialog box. To do this locate the Page Setup option on a WordPad menu, and open the Page Setup dialog box. Capture the current screen image. Close the Page Setup dialog box.

Paste the image into WordPad.

To print a copy of the captured screen image, click the toolbar button whose ToolTip is "Print." On your printout, draw arrows and labels to identify each of the dialog box controls by type.

14 Using Text Box Skills in PowerPoint
Required: Microsoft PowerPoint

In the online Steps, you learned how to position the insertion point and how to remove, replace, and insert text in a text box. You can use those same skills in other programs, including PowerPoint. Complete the following Steps.

1: Start **PowerPoint**. If you see the Tip of the Day window, click the **OK** button. When the dialog box titled "PowerPoint" appears, select the **Blank Presentation** option, then click the **OK** button. Click the **OK** button in the New Slide dialog box.

2: Click inside the box labeled "Click to add title," then type the following:

Hersh Industries, Incorporated

3: Click inside the box labeled "Click to add sub-title," then type the following:

A company for the future

4: Delete the comma and the word "Incorporated."

5: Insert the word "International" between "Hersh" and "Industries."

6: Change "Hersh" to "Hersch."

7: Replace the first three words in the subtitle with the words "Looking to."

8: Position the insertion point after the final letter in "future," press the **Enter** key, type **by**, press the **spacebar**, then type your name.

9: Click the 🖨 button to print a copy of your finished product.

15 Using Help to Learn Paint Skills

In this Project, you'll use the Paint Help system to learn how to use the Paint program and its tools and menus. Your goal is to create and print a picture that looks like the following danger sign.

Use Paint Help to learn how to draw rectangles and ellipses, how to enter text in a picture, how to undo changes, and how to print a picture. Draw the sign using rectangles, ellipses, and text as shown above. Print your picture.

EXPLORE

16 Using a Program's Help Button

Required: Microsoft Excel

Suppose you were working in a program (Excel, for example), and you weren't sure of the purpose of a feature in the program window. If the feature is a button, its ToolTip will tell you the button name, but nothing more. What if the feature you're unsure of isn't a button? In this project, you'll use the Help button, an additional Help technique available in some Windows programs. Start Excel, then maximize the Excel window if necessary. Write out your answers to questions a through g.

a What is the ToolTip for the ⬛ button?

Repeat the following sequence as necessary to answer the questions: Click the ⬛ button, click any part of the Excel screen for which you want information, read the displayed information, then click the information box to close it.

b What name is given to the numbers along the left side of the window?

c What name is given to the row of letters ("A," "B," "C," and so on)?

d What name is given to the bar that appears along the right side of the Excel window?

e What name is given to "Sheet1," "Sheet2," and so on, which are located near the bottom of the Excel window?

f What name is given to the bar immediately above the taskbar?

g Clicking the ⬛ button displays or hides what object?

projects

17 Using the Help Button in a Dialog Box

When you're working in a program, you might encounter a dialog box you've never seen before. What do you do if you're unsure of the significance of a particular dialog box item? How can you specify an appropriate choice if you don't know the impact of a particular choice? In this Project, you'll use the Help button, an additional Help technique available in Windows dialog boxes. You'll use a Help system dialog box, but the technique works for any dialog box. Start Windows Help, then click the Contents tab. Repeat the following sequence as necessary to answer the questions: Click the [?] button, click any part of the Help System window for which you want information, read the displayed information, then click the information box to close it. Write out your answers to questions a through f.

    a How does Help tell you to close a book?

    b What does the Cancel button do?

    c What information will print if you've selected a book before you click the Print button?

Switch to the Find tab, then use the [?] button to answer the following questions.

    d What does an ellipsis indicate when it appears in the middle area?

    e What information is displayed in the box to the right of the box giving the number of topics found, and how would you change that information?

    f What is the purpose of the Rebuild button?

18 Using the Answer Wizard

Required: Microsoft Excel

Many Microsoft programs include a Help system feature called the Answer Wizard. When you use the Answer Wizard, you pose a question in your own words; the Answer Wizard then determines the type of assistance you need and displays a list of Help topics to answer your question. In this Project, you'll explore Excel's Answer Wizard. Start Excel. Click Help on the Excel menu bar, then click Answer Wizard. Write out your answers to questions a through d.

    Type "display toolbars" then click the Search button. Display the "Display or hide toolbars" topic, then follow the directions.

    a What menu was opened?

    b What menu option was selected?

    c How many toolbars does Excel have?

d Close the dialog box. Start the Answer Wizard again, type "sort a column", then click the Search button. Display the "Sort rows in descending order by one column" topic. As a result the Answer Wizard displays an information box telling you about a particular button. What is the name of that button and on what toolbar is it located?

19 Using the Keyboard to Open and Close Menus

When you are entering text in a document, both hands are on the keyboard. If you use the mouse to open a menu, you have to move one hand from the keyboard to the mouse and then back again. To save time and trouble, you can use the keyboard to open and close menus. In this Project, you'll investigate the use of key combinations to open and close menus. Start WordPad. Write out your answers to questions a through i.

a Notice that one letter in each menu name on the menu bar is underlined. Which letter is underlined in "File"? In "Edit"? In "Format"?

b Hold down the Alt key as you press the E key, then release both keys. (This is called using a key combination and is abbreviated as Alt+E.) What happens?

c Press the Alt key only. What happens?

d Press Alt+I. (Remember: this does not mean to press the plus key (+); it means to hold down the Alt key and press the I key, then release both keys.) What happens?

e Press the right arrow key several times. What happens each time you press the right arrow key?

f Press the left arrow key several times. What happens each time you press the left arrow key?

g Press the down arrow key several times. What happens each time you press the down arrow key?

h Use the arrow keys to highlight the Bullet Style option on the Format menu, then press the Enter key. What appears in the WordPad workspace?

i Notice that the first letter of the menu name isn't always underlined. Why is the "o" rather than the "F" underlined in the Format menu name?

projects

20 Using the Keyboard to Select a Menu Option

When you are entering text in a document, both hands are on the keyboard. If you use the mouse to open a menu and select a menu option, you have to move one hand from the keyboard to the mouse and then back again. To save time and trouble, you can use the keyboard to select menu commands. In this Project, you'll investigate the use of key combinations and shortcut keys to select menu commands. Start WordPad and open the View menu. Write out your answers to questions a through g.

    a   What letter is underlined in the View menu name?

    b   What letter is underlined in the Ruler menu option?

    c   Click Ruler. How has the WordPad window changed?

    d   Hold down the Alt key as you first press and release the V key and then press and release the R key; then release the Alt key. (This is called typing a "key combination." This particular key combination is abbreviated as Alt+V+R.) How has the WordPad window changed?

    e   Press Alt+O+B. What appears in the WordPad workspace?

    f   Open the File menu. What appears to the right of the New option?

    g   Close the File menu. Hold down the Ctrl key as you press the N key, then release both keys. (This key combination is called a "shortcut key" and is abbreviated as Ctrl+N.) What happens?

INVESTIGATE

21 Tools of the Trade

The online Steps included the statement that a toolbar button is more convenient to use than a menu. In this Project, you'll investigate to determine if Windows program users more often use toolbar buttons or the equivalent menu commands.

    a   Prepare a short questionnaire (4 to 6 questions) that you will use to interview a Windows user. The questions should help you to determine if a person is more likely to use a toolbar button or a menu command in general as well as in certain specific instances (such as cutting and pasting).

    b   Use your questionnaire to interview five people who use the Windows operating system.

c   Write a report based on your questionnaires and interviews. Page 1 of your report should be a narrative telling your results and conclusions. Page 2 should be the questionnaire. Pages 3 through 7 should be the five filled-in questionnaires from your five interviews.

22   Making the Most of Your Internet Browser

The program you use to browse the Internet is likely to include a menu bar and one or more toolbars. To become a more efficient Internet user, you should know the various menu options available to you and the purpose of all toolbar buttons.

a   Start your Internet browser, and make note of all the menu names and the options in each.

b   For each toolbar button: capture or sketch the toolbar button, and determine its purpose.

c   Write a two- to four-page report that presents your findings. Include all the toolbars and menu names with their accompanying options, their purposes, and your sketches. Include an analysis of how much of the browser's tools and menus you actually used before doing this Project. How will this Project change the way you use your browser?

23   Adopt a Computer Pioneer

Learning about computer pioneers and the early years of computer development will enable you to better understand and appreciate the current computer environment. In this Project, you'll investigate an important computer pioneer.

a   Visit a library or browse the Internet to learn about one of the following people:

- John V. Atanasoff
- Lady Ada Lovelace Byron
- John von Neumann
- Grace Hopper

b   Write a paper of at least two pages discussing the pioneer you selected and his/her role in the development of computer technology. At the end of the report, list two questions you would ask this pioneer if you had the chance.

projects

24 Windows Shopping

Windows and Windows NT are related operating systems. You're using one of those two in this e-Course. In this Project, you'll investigate both operating systems and learn the differences between them.

Look through computer magazine articles and ads, visit computer stores, or search the Internet to learn about the Windows and Windows NT operating systems. Write an article (approximately 500 words) that could be printed in your school paper or company newsletter. The article should discuss the two operating systems, clarify their similarities and differences, and explain under what circumstances each is appropriately used.

25 Menus by Design

Think of a specific application for which a computerized program might be helpful. Possible examples include: a household inventory system, a club membership roster, a personal address book, or an instructor's grading system.

   a Using the menu bars for programs with which you're already familiar as a rough guide, design a menu bar for the application.

   b For each menu name on your menu bar, list several realistic and useful menu options.

   c Designate at least three of your menu options as realistic candidates for toolbar buttons. Sketch how these buttons might look.

Microsoft Windows

Tutorial 3: Managing Files

Tutorial 3

Managing Files

Walking Through Windows

Wouldn't you like to apply the Microsoft Windows knowledge and skills you've gained in a practical, realistic way? Good! Then you can help Brenda Collins organize and manage her computer files.

Projects

In the Tutorial 3 Projects, you'll review and build on the skills you learned in the tutorial. You'll also discover how to do wildcard finds, find files based on dates, and find files containing specific text. Finally, you'll make a backup copy of all the files on a floppy disk, select and work with multiple files in Explorer, and use the Documents option on the Start menu.

If you're not assigned Projects 6, 11, 12, 13, 14, 15, 17, 18, 19, or 20, you might want to at least read these Projects or, better yet, work through them, because they contain some additional valuable information on working with files and getting the most out of Windows Explorer and the Windows Find feature. In Project 6, you'll learn to make a backup copy of a file within the same folder; Project 17 teaches you how to make a backup copy of an entire disk. In Project 11, you'll learn how to change the order of the Explorer Contents pane list. Projects 12, 13, 15, 19, and 20 give you practice with additional options of the Find feature. In Project 14, you'll learn how to select multiple files for copying, moving, or deleting. Project 18 introduces the Documents option on the Start menu, a useful shortcut to your current files.

WHAT'S ONLINE

1 Make a Project Disk

2 Explore Files and Folders
- Change Drives
- Arrange Explorer Panes
- Folders and Files
- Expand the Disk Hierarchy
- Open a Folder
- Create and Rename a Folder
- Collapse the Disk Hierarchy

3 Delete and Rename Files
- Delete a File
- Rename a File

4 Move and Copy Files
- Move Files
- Copy Files

5 Find Files

6 Make Project Disks

Walking Through Windows

You've already learned a lot about working in the Windows operating system. You know how to start a program, use the program's menus and toolbars, and exit the program. You're familiar with all different types of dialog box controls. And you've learned a lot of new terminology.

Your friend Brenda Collins is a young single mother who works part-time and is attending Weaver College part-time to complete her masters degree. She is also secretary of the Hike Club, a Weaver organization that sponsors hiking excursions, fund raising events, and equipment sales. Brenda doesn't own a computer; instead she uses the computers in the lab at Weaver, to which all students have access. When she was an undergraduate, Brenda worked with earlier, quite different, versions of Windows.

You've impressed Brenda with your knowledge of the current Windows operating system, so she asks you to help her with her files. You readily agree to help her *before* you know the whole story. Then she tells you that all her files are on a single disk. She thinks the files should be organized in some way, but she doesn't know how to do that.

You panic. You don't know how to organize, move, and copy disk files. Brenda says she thinks she needs to use folders under the root directory, and you joke to yourself that this sounds like a terrible dental procedure.

Well, you're not quite ready to help Brenda yet, but you will be as soon as you finish Tutorial 3. Brenda is depending on you, so let's get going on Windows Tutorial 3!

Review Questions

Fill in the blank with the correct word or phrase.

1 The _____ procedure will erase all files on a disk.

2 You can use the Windows _____ program to learn what's on a disk.

3 The _____ pane of the Exploring window shows a hierarchy of all the drives, folders, and files on your computer.

4 The _____ pane of the Exploring window displays detailed information about folders and files.

5 A(n) _____ is an organizational structure used to group files.

6 A(n) _____ is a named collection of data stored on a floppy disk or hard disk.

7 The main directory of a disk is called the _____ directory.

8 A file _____ is the 3-characters suffix indicating the program used to create it.

9 When you _____ a file, the file is removed from the disk directory and the space the file occupied is freed up.

10 If you delete a file from a hard disk, the file doesn't completely disappear but instead is held in the _____.

11 You _____ a file to change its filename.

12 When you moved a file in Windows Explorer, you opened the file's shortcut menu and then selected the _____ option.

13 When you _____ a file, you create a duplicate of the file.

review questions

14 You use the _____ feature, which is activated from the Start menu, to locate a file.

MULTIPLE CHOICE

*Select the letter of the **one** best answer.*

15 **The first steps for quick formatting a disk are:**

a click ![Start], then click Format

b open My Computer, open the drive's shortcut menu, then click Format

c start Windows Explorer, click File, then click Format

d click ![Start], click File, then click Format

16 **Which of the following is not part of the Exploring window?**

a panes

b menu bar

c tabs

d status bar

17 **The hierarchy of all drives, folders, and files on your computer can be seen in:**

a the All Folders pane

b the Contents pane

c the Files pane

d the Find window

18 **All the folders and files in the active folder or drive are displayed in the:**

a All Folders pane

b Contents pane

c Files pane

d Find window

19 Which of the following is *not* a column heading in the Contents pane?

   a Type

   b Program

   c Size

   d Name

20 In the Exploring window, the icon indicates a:

   a file

   b folder

   c floppy disk

   d bitmap image

21 In the Exploring window, you can tell the type of a file by the:

   a icon following the filename in the Contents pane

   b corresponding entry in the Type column

   c corresponding entry in the Program column

   d icon preceding the filename in the All Folders pane

22 The main directory of a disk is called the:

   a major directory

   b level 1 directory

   c folder directory

   d root directory

23 To open a folder in the All Folders pane, you:

   a click the folder name

   b right-click the folder name, then click Open

   c click Folder, then click the folder name in the displayed list

   d none of the above; you can't open a folder in the All Folders pane

review questions

24 A folder can also be called a:

a file

b superfile

c subdirectory

d drive

25 If a hierarchy for a particular drive or folder is collapsed, then:

a none of the subdirectories in that drive or folder appear in the All Folders pane

b all of the subdirectories in that drive or folder appear in the All Folders pane

c none of the folders or files in that drive or folder appear in the Contents pane

d the files, but not the folders, in that drive or folder appear in the Contents pane

26 A filename in Windows:

a must be 8 characters long

b may be up to 300 characters long

c may not contain a ? or a :

d may not contain numbers

27 If a ⊞ appears to the left of an icon in the All Folders pane, then you know:

a the hierarchy for that icon is expanded

b the hierarchy for that icon is collapsed

c that icon contains no subdirectories

d that icon contains no files

28 When you delete a folder:

a all the files and folders within that folder are also deleted

b the files, but not the folders, within that folder are also deleted

c the folders, but not the files, within that folder are also deleted

d only the folder is deleted; the files and folders it contained are not deleted

29 To move a file in the Exploring window, you open the file's shortcut menu and then click:

a the Delete option

b the Move option

c the Copy option

d the Cut option

30 **When you use the Find feature to locate a file by name:**

  a the first file with that name is displayed

  b the last file with that name is displayed

  c every file with that name is displayed

  d at most one file will be found, because filenames must be unique

MATCHING

Select a letter from the right column that correctly matches each item in the left column.

31 ⊞

32 ✛

33 📁

34 ⊟

35 \

36 /

37 [icon]

a The character that separates folder names in a path

b A character that is not allowed in a filename

c Click this icon to expand a hierarchy

d Icon that indicates a bitmap image file

e Click this icon to collapse a hierarchy

f Column resizing pointer shape

g Folder icon

review questions

Use a separate sheet of paper to write out your answers to the following questions.

38 Briefly describe how to quick format a disk. What is the purpose of a quick format?

39 List the steps you would complete to learn the names of every folder on a particular disk.

40 Describe how you would move a file from one folder to another in Windows Explorer. How would the process differ if you wanted to copy, rather than move, the file?

41 Specifically describe the steps you would follow to rename a file. In your description change the name of a file from "Initial Version" to "Final Version".

Projects

These Projects are designed to help you review and develop the skills you learned in Tutorial 3. Complete each Project using the Microsoft Windows software. You should not need to use the e-Course software to complete the Projects.

You'll need a Project Disk for most of the Projects. If you haven't already done so, complete the Steps in Topic 6 of Tutorial 3 to make the Project Disks you'll need.

If you've forgotten some of the skills you need to complete the Projects, refer to the Task Reference.

REVIEW SKILLS

1   Finding Files   Required: Windows 10-minute Tour

Windows includes an online Tutorial you can use to review what you've learned about finding files. (Note: This tour is not available in Windows NT.)

Start Windows Help, then click the Contents tab, if necessary. Click "Tour: Ten minutes to using Windows," then click the Display button. Click the Finding a File button, then follow the tour's directions. Answer the following questions:

   a   What was the name of the first file you found?

   b   In what folder was the first file located?

   c   What was the name of the second file you looked for?

   d   Was the attempt to find the second file successful?

projects

2   Exploring Brenda's Disk   Required: Project Disk #2

Project Disk #2 is on Brenda's disk. You'll now explore that disk to find out what files it contains. Insert the disk labeled "Project Disk #2" in drive A. Start Windows Explorer, and maximize the Exploring window, if necessary; then select 3½ Floppy [A:] in the All Folders pane. Answer the following questions:

    a   How many files are in the root directory?

    b   Which of the files in the root directory is the largest, and how large is that file?

    c   What's the complete path to the file named "Schedule?"

    d   How many files are Microsoft Excel Worksheet files, and what are their names?

3   Moving Files on Brenda's Disk
Required: Project Disk #2

All the files on Brenda's disk are in the root directory. In this Project, you'll begin to organize Brenda's disk by creating a folder and moving documents into that folder. Insert the disk labeled "Project Disk #2" in drive A. Start Windows Explorer, and maximize the Exploring window, if necessary; then select 3½ Floppy [A:] in the All Folders pane.

Create a new folder within the root directory, then name the folder "Letters."

Move the file named "Mom&Dad" to the Letters folder.

Move the file named "Sarah" to the Letters folder.

Move the Microsoft Word document file named "Flyer" to the Letters folder. Answer the following questions:

    a   How many objects are now in the root directory, and what is their total size? (Hint: Use the status bar to answer this question.)

    b   How many objects are now in the Letters folder, and what is their total size?

    c   What's the name and size of the largest file in the root directory?

    d   What's the name and type of the smallest file in the Letters folder?

4 Organizing a Disk Required: Project Disk #3

All the files on Project Disk #3 are in the root directory. You'll now begin to organize that disk by creating new folders and moving files into those folders.

Insert the disk labeled "Project Disk #3" in drive A. Start Windows Explorer, and maximize the Exploring window, if necessary; then select 3½ Floppy [A:] in the All Folders pane.

Create two new folders within the root directory, naming one of the folders "Taxes" and the other "Medical." Create a new folder within the Medical folder, then name the new folder "Letters."

Move the file named "Dentist" to the Letters folder. Move the file named "Doctor" to the Letters folder. Move the three files with "Tax" in their filename to the Taxes folder. Answer the following questions:

a How many objects are now in the root directory, and what is their total size? (Hint: Use the status bar to answer this question.)

b What is the total size of the files in the Taxes folder?

c What's the name and size of the largest file in the root directory?

d What's the name and type of the smallest file in the Letters folder?

5 Copying Files on Brenda's Disk
Required: Project Disk #2

In Tutorial 3 you selected the Details option on the View menu the first time you started Windows Explorer. You can choose three other options for displaying files in the Contents pane. In this Project, you'll work with large icons as you copy files on Brenda's disk.

Insert the disk labeled "Project Disk #2" in drive A. Start Windows Explorer, and maximize the Exploring window, if necessary; then select 3½ Floppy [A:] in the All Folders pane. Select the Large Icons option on the View menu.

a How did the display in the Contents pane change?

b What information is no longer displayed?

projects

    c   Create a new folder within the root directory, then name the folder "Hike Club." Copy the file named "Outing" into the Hike Club folder. Copy the file named "HikePres" into the Hike Club folder, then rename the copy as "Hiking Presentation." Which of the files in the Hike Club folder is the largest? (Hint: Open each file's shortcut menu, select Properties, then note the file size on the General tab.) Then select the Details option on the View menu.

APPLY SKILLS

6   Copying a File within a Folder

Required: Project Disk #2

In Tutorial 3 you copied and moved files from one folder into another folder. Suppose you wanted to create a copy of a file within the same folder, perhaps as a backup. Can you do that?

    Insert the disk labeled "Project Disk #2" in drive A. Start Windows Explorer, and maximize the Exploring window, if necessary; then select 3½ Floppy [A:] in the All Folders pane. Copy the file named "Logo" from the root directory into the root directory.

    a   What is the name of the copied file?

    b   Why is the name different? Then rename the copy as "Logo.bak."

7   Moving Files Within the Contents Pane

Required: Project Disk #2

When you moved files in Tutorial 3, you always moved a file from the Contents pane to a folder or drive in the All Folders pane. In this Project, you'll work completely within the Contents pane.

    Insert the disk labeled "Project Disk #2" in drive A. Start Windows Explorer, and maximize the Exploring window, if necessary; then select 3½ Floppy [A:] in the All Folders pane.

    Create a new folder within the root directory, then name the folder "Weaver." Move the file named "Schedule" into the Weaver folder icon that appears in the Contents pane.

    a   Open the shortcut menu for the Weaver folder in the Contents pane, then click Explore. What information about the Schedule file can you now see in the Exploring window? Be specific.

b Select drive A in the All Folders pane, open the shortcut menu for the Weaver folder in the Contents pane, then click Open. What now appears?

c What information about the Schedule file is now displayed?

8 Moving and Copying Files Using Drag-and-Drop
Required: Project Disk #3

You used shortcut menus in Tutorial 3 to move and copy files. In this Project, you'll use a drag-and-drop technique.

Insert the disk labeled "Project Disk #3" in drive A. Start Windows Explorer, and maximize the Exploring window, if necessary; then select 3½ Floppy [A:] in the All Folders pane. Create a new folder within the root directory, then name the folder "Correspondence." Expand all hierarchies on drive A.

a Use the right mouse button to drag the file named "Letter1" to the Correspondence folder in the All Folders pane, releasing the mouse button when the Correspondence folder is highlighted. What now appears?

b Select the Move Here option. Use the right mouse button to drag the file named "Letter3" to the Correspondence folder in the All Folders pane, releasing the mouse button when that folder is highlighted. Select the Copy Here option. Repeat these preceding steps for each remaining file in the root directory with "Letter" in its filename.

c How many files are now in the Correspondence folder and, according to the status bar display, what is their total size?

d What's the largest file in the Correspondence folder? The smallest?

9 Formatting a Disk   Required: Project Disk #1

In Tutorial 3 you did a quick format to erase all the files and folders on a disk. Actually, a quick format erases only the disk's file allocation table (FAT), in which the locations of files are stored. Because the FAT is empty, the disk *appears* empty to the computer. In this Project, you'll do a full disk format, in which the magnetic particles on the disk surface are rearranged, thus truly erasing all the files on the disk.

Insert the disk labeled "Project Disk #1" in drive A. Open the My Computer icon, open the shortcut menu for drive A, and then click Format. Set Capacity = 1.44 Mb (3.5"). For Windows 95, set format type = Full and make sure the Display summary when finished check box contains a check mark. For Windows NT, make sure the Quick Format check box does *not* contain a check mark.

projects

a Did the full format seem to take significantly less time, significantly more time, or about the same time as a quick format?

For Windows 95 use the Format Results dialog box to answer Questions b through e. For Windows NT, open the shortcut menu for drive A, click Properties, and then answer Question b only.

b How many bytes of total disk space are on the disk?

c How many bytes are used by system files?

d How many bytes are in bad sectors?

e What is the serial number of the disk?

10 Refreshing the Contents Pane

Required: Project Disk #2

The information that appears in the Contents pane of the Exploring window might not always be up-to-date, so you might occasionally need to use the Refresh option on the View menu.

Insert the disk labeled "Project Disk #2" in drive A. Start Windows Explorer, and maximize the Exploring window, if necessary; then select 3½ Floppy [A:] in the All Folders pane.

Copy the file named "Logo"(a bitmap file) to the root directory. Rename the copy of the file as "LogoX."

a What's the size of the Logo file?

b What's the size of the LogoX file?

c Open the shortcut menu for the LogoX file, then click Open. Position the insertion point over the blue dot at the center of the right side of the picture. When the pointer changes to ↔, drag to the right to widen the picture by an inch or so. Save the current version of the file. Use the taskbar to switch to the Exploring window.

d How large is the LogoX file now?

e Click View on the menu bar, then click Refresh. How does the Contents pane display change?

f How large is the LogoX file now? Delete the LogoX file.

BUILD SKILLS

11 Organizing the Contents Pane

Required: Project Disk #4

In all the work you've done so far in Explorer, the files in the Contents pane have always appeared in alphabetical order. In this Project, you'll change the file display order.

Insert the disk labeled "Project Disk #4" in drive A. Start Windows Explorer, and maximize the Exploring window, if necessary; then select 3½ Floppy [A:] in the All Folders pane.

   a   What's the first file listed in the Contents pane?

   b   Click the Name column heading. In what order are the files now listed?

   c   Click the Size column heading. In what order are the files now listed?

   d   Click the Size column heading again. In what order are the files now listed?

   e   What's the largest file in the root directory?

   f   What are the smallest files?

   g   Click the Type column heading. In what order are the files now listed?

   h   Click the Modified column heading. In what order are the files now listed?

   i   What's the name of the oldest file?

12 Finding Files   Required: Project Disk #4

Suppose you wanted to locate all files created during a given time period. Or maybe you want to find all small files. In this Project, you'll use some of the additional options of the Windows Find feature.

Insert the disk labeled "Project Disk #4" in drive A. Click [Start], point to Find, then click Files or Folders. Click the Look in [▼], then select drive A. Click the Date Modified tab in the Find dialog box. Click the between option button, specify the time period from 12/1/97 to 12/31/97, then click the Find Now button.

   a   How many files were found?

   b   What are the paths for each file?

projects

    c Click the Advanced tab in the Find dialog box. Click the Size is ▼, then select the at most option. Enter 20 in the spin bar, then click the Find Now button. How many files were found?

    d What are the filenames and file sizes of the found files?

13 Finding Files by Type   Required: Project Disk #4

Suppose you wanted to find all the bitmap files in all of the folders on a particular disk. In this Project, you'll learn an additional option of the Windows Find feature.

Insert the disk labeled "Project Disk #4" in drive A.

Click [Start], point to Find, then click Files or Folders. Click the Look in ▼, then select drive A.

Click the Advanced tab in the Find dialog box. Click the Of Type ▼, click Bitmap Image, then click the Find Now button.

    a How many files were found?

    b What are the paths for each file?

14 Selecting Multiple Files   Required: Project Disk #4

In Tutorial 3 you moved, copied, and deleted several files—one file at a time. Suppose you wanted to perform an operation on three files in a folder *at the same time*. In this Project, you'll learn how to select and work with more than one file at a time.

Insert the disk labeled "Project Disk #4" in drive A. Start Windows Explorer, and maximize the Exploring window, if necessary; then select 3½ Floppy [A:] in the All Folders pane.

Use Windows Help to learn how to select multiple files and folders.

    a What technique is described in the first paragraph for selecting multiple files?

Use that technique to select these three files: Andrews, Harper, and Jones. With the pointer positioned over one of the three highlighted filenames, click the right-mouse button to open the shortcut menu, then select the Copy option. Paste the selected files into the root directory. If the three file copies don't appear consecutively in the Contents pane, click the Name column heading. Select the first of the three file copies, then hold down the Shift key as you click the last of the three file copies.

b What files are now selected and highlighted?

c With the pointer positioned over one of the three highlighted filenames, open the shortcut menu, then select the Delete option. What is the name of the window that appears?

d What question is asked? Click the Yes button.

15 Working With Found Files — Project Disk #4

In Tutorial 3, you opened a file in the Find window. In this Project, you'll move a file using the Find window.

Insert the disk labeled "Project Disk #4" in drive A. Start Windows Explorer, maximize the Exploring window, if necessary, then select 3½ Floppy [A:] in the All Folders pane.

Create a new folder within the root directory, then name the folder "Customers." Expand all hierarchies on drive A.

a Click ▌Start▐, point to Find, then click Files or Folders. Find the file named "Klein" on drive A. What's the path for the file that was found?

b Drag the Find window to the right so that you can see the All Folders pane of the Exploring window. Open the shortcut menu for the file in the Find window. From the menu options listed, which of the following operations do you think you could perform on the file: cut, copy, rename, delete, open?

c Select the Cut option. Open the shortcut menu for the Customers folder in the All Folders pane, then select the Paste option. Close the Find window. What files are now in the Advertising folder?

d How many files must there have been in the Advertising folder when you started this Project? How do you know?

projects

16 Exploring Using My Computer
Required: Windows 10-minute Tour

In Tutorial 3, you explored the contents of a disk using the Explorer. In this Project, you'll use the Windows tour to learn how to explore a disk using My Computer. (Note: This tour is not available in Windows NT.)

Start Windows Help, then click the Contents tab. Click Tour: Ten minutes to using Windows, then click the Display button. Click the Exploring Your Disk button, then follow the tour's directions.

   a   What was the name of the first folder you opened?

   b   What three files are contained in that first folder?

   c   What files are in the Reports folder?

17 Copy a Floppy   Required: Project Disks #1 and #2

Before you do any more work on Brenda's disk, you decide to make a backup copy of her entire disk for safety's sake. In this Project, you'll copy Project Disk #2 to Project Disk #1. That second disk need not be blank.

   a   Locate the Windows Help information for "Copying disks." What are the three steps to make a copy of a floppy disk?

Insert the disk labeled "Project Disk #2" in drive A. Open the My Computer icon, then make a copy of Project Disk #2 from drive A to drive A. Place Project Disk #1 in the drive when you are prompted to insert the second disk. When the copy procedure is completed, close the dialog box and close My Computer.

   b   Start Windows Explorer, and maximize the Exploring window, if necessary; then select 3½ Floppy [A:] in the All Folders pane. Expand all hierarchies on drive A. How many folders are on the disk, and what are the folder names?

   c   How many files are in the root directory?

   d   What are the names of the files in the root directory?

projects

18 Using the Start Menu Documents Option

Any Project Disk

Windows provides an easy way for you to open files that are recently created or saved. Insert any one of your Project Disks in drive A. Start Paint, and use the Pencil tool to write your first name in the Paint workspace.

Click File on the Paint menu bar, then click Save As to open the Save As dialog box.

Type your first and last name in the File name text box, click the Save in ▼, select drive A, then click the Save button.

Exit Paint.

Click [Start], then point to Documents.

  a What appears on your screen?

  b What type of entities are its entries?

  c Click the occurrence of your name. What happens?

19 Wildcard Finds   Required: Project Disk #4

The Windows Find feature allows you to use the wildcard characters * and ? in file and folder name searches. A ? stands for any one character, and a * stands for zero or more characters of any kind. For example, if you specify the name "lo?e," then any file or folder named "love," "lone," "lore," and so on, would be located. If you specify "i??o*," then any file or folder whose name starts with an "i" and whose fourth letter is "o" would be located; possible examples include "IDIO," "income," and "In Out Status."

Insert the disk labeled "Project Disk #4" in drive A. Click [Start], point to Find, then click Files or Folders.

Change a dialog box setting so that the disk in drive A will be searched.

  a Enter appropriate text in the Named text box so that all files or folders starting with the letter "a" will be found, then click the Find Now button. Which files and folders were found?

  b Enter appropriate text in the Named text box so that all files or folders whose name ends with an "r" will be found, then click the Find Now button. Which files were found?

c   Enter appropriate text in the Named text box so that all files or folders containing an "e" as the third letter of the name will be found, then click the Find Now button. Which files were found?

20 Finding Files Containing Text

Required: Project Disk #2

Suppose you've forgotten the name you used when you saved a file of important information. With the Windows Find feature, you can search for files containing some specific text string. You'll use that feature to find all the files on Brenda's disk that contain her name.

Insert the disk labeled "Project Disk #2" in drive A. Click **Start**, point to Find, then click Files or Folders.

Change a dialog box setting so that the disk in drive A will be searched.

a   Click the Advanced tab, type Brenda in the Containing text box, then click the Find Now button. How many files were found?

b   Click in the text box after "Brenda," press the spacebar, type Collins, then click the Find Now button. How many files were found?

INVESTIGATE

21 Software Usage: What and How Often

Thousands of programs, or software packages, exist that run in the Windows environment. In this Project, you'll investigate software usage to determine which types of programs and which specific programs are used most often.

a   Prepare a short questionnaire (four to six questions) that you will use to interview a Windows user. The questions should help you to determine which types of programs (word processing, spreadsheet, and so on) and which specific programs (Word, WordPerfect, and so on) a person uses most often.

b   Use your questionnaire to interview five people who use the Windows operating system.

c   Write a one page paper reporting your results and conclusions. Page 2 of your report should be the questionnaire. Pages 3 through 7 should be the five filled-in questionnaires from your five interviews.

projects

22 How Much is that Software in the Window?

Suppose that you have, or plan to buy, a personal computer to use at home. In this Project, you'll investigate software packages that you would find useful or fun to have.

a Look through computer magazine ads, visit computer stores, or search the Internet to determine five Windows-compatible software packages that you'd like to own.

b For each of the software packages you've selected:

- Determine the system requirements—memory, equipment, and so on.

- Explain why you selected that particular package.

- How much money would you need to purchase all five of these programs? Be sure to include tax and any shipping costs if applicable.

- Do you think this cost is reasonable? Why or why not?

23 Computer Pioneers: How Far We've Come

Learning about computer pioneers will enable you to better understand and appreciate the current computer environment. In this Project, you'll investigate an important computer pioneer.

a Visit a library or browse the Internet to learn about one of the following people:

- Bill Gates
- Ted Hoff
- Mitch Kapor
- Sandra Kurzig

b Write a paper of at least two pages discussing the pioneer you selected and his/her role in the development of computer technology. At the end of the report, list two questions you would ask this pioneer if you had the chance.

projects

24 Computers in Film: Two Thumbs Up?

Rent and view a movie in which a computer figures prominently. Some of the many films you might consider are *2001: A Space Odyssey, Mission Impossible, The Net,* or *WarGames.*

a What part did the computer play in the movie? How significant a role did it play? Was the computer a hero or a villain? Why?

b How believable was the computer activity in the movie? Were there any scenes involving the computer that you felt were especially realistic or unrealistic? Choose one of these scenes, describe it, and explain why you chose it.

c What influences, positive and negative, do you feel the movie would have on a person unfamiliar with computers?

25 Computers in Everyday Life

Some people claim that computers are entering every aspect of our life. For this Project, look for surprising uses for computers—instances where a few years ago you might not have thought a computer would be useful or relevant. After you've found five examples, decide in each case if you think the addition of computer technology has been advantageous or intrusive. Then use your imagination to predict a possible future use for computers in everyday life. Write a two-page paper that presents your findings and justifies your conclusions.

Answers to Odd-Numbered Review Questions

Tutorial 1

1 Windows

3 mouse

5 pointing

7 menu

9 submenu

11 multitasking

13 sizing

15 redisplay

17 restore

19 icon

21 Help

answers

23 b

25 b

27 a

29 d

31 a

33 b

MATCHING

35 g

37 f

39 c

41 e

answers

SHORT ANSWER

43 When you click an object, you click with the left mouse button. To right-click an object, you click with the right mouse button. You would right-click an object when you want to open the object's shortcut menu. (Note: For left-handed mouse users who have changed the Control Panel mouse settings, the left and right mouse buttons exchange roles.)

45 When you start a program, the program window appears on the screen, and a button for that program appears on the taskbar.

answers

Tutorial 2

FILL-IN-THE-BLANKS

1 menus

3 submenu

5 dialog box

7 gray

9 scroll

11 list box

13 list box arrow

15 insertion point

17 right

19 spin bar

21 check box

MULTIPLE CHOICE

23 b

25 a

27 c

29 b

31 a

33 c

answers

MATCHING

35 f

37 a

39 e

SHORT ANSWER

41 You can remove text in a text box in one of three ways:

- Position the insertion point at the far left of the text to be deleted, and then repeatedly press the Delete key.

- Position the insertion point at the far right of the text to be deleted, and then repeatedly press the Backspace key.

- Highlight the text to be removed, and then press the Delete key.

You can replace text in a text box by highlighting the text to be replaced and then typing the replacement text. To add text, you position the insertion point where you want the text added, and then type the new text.

answers

Tutorial 3

1   quick format

3   All Folders

5   folder

7   root

9   delete (or erase)

11   rename

13   copy

answers

MULTIPLE CHOICE

15 b

17 a

19 b

21 b

23 a

25 a

27 b

29 d

MATCHING

31 c

33 g

35 a

37 d

answers

39 To learn the names of every folder on a disk:

1. Insert the disk in tho disk drive.

2. Start Windows Explorer.

3. Switch to the appropriate drive.

4. Click the plus box to the left of the drive icon to expand the hierarchy one level.

5. If a plus box appears to the left of a folder name, click that plus box.

6. Repeat Step 5 until no more plus boxes appear. The disk's hierarchy is now completely expanded, and all the folders on the disk appear in the All Folders pane.

41 To change a filename from "Initial Version" to "Final Version:"

1. Start Windows Explorer.

2. Switch drives, expand hierarchies, and open folders as necessary so that the file named "Initial Version" appears in the Contents pane.

3. Right-click that filename, then click Rename on the shortcut menu.

4. Highlight just the word "Initial."

5. Type "Final".

6. Press the Enter key.

Word Processing e-SSentials

Documents are an integral part of our society and culture. Historical documents such as the Declaration of Independence and the U.S. Constitution promote social and political philosophies. Literary documents, such as *To Kill a Mockingbird* and *War and Peace* record the issues and dilemmas facing societies and cultures. Fiction entertains. Weekly magazines and daily newspapers provide information on current events. Contracts record agreements for corporations and individuals.

Today, we take documents and literacy for granted. But in the 1400s, few people in the world could read or write, and access to documents was limited. Until Johann Gutenberg invented the moveable type printing press in 1448, scribes produced manuscripts by copying them by hand—a slow, time-intensive, costly process. After 1448, the printing press made it easy to produce and distribute books, magazines, newspapers, pamphlets, and newsletters.

Figure 1 *Personal printing devices.*

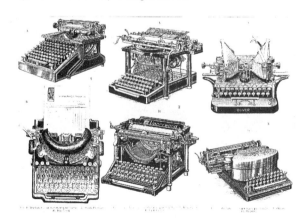

The printing press was a technological leap forward of great magnitude, but even smaller changes in technology had profound effects on document production. The quill pen was inconvenient because it required the writer to pause every few words to dip the pen into an inkwell. Fountain pens, ball-point pens, and felt-tip pens provided writers with more free-flowing writing tools. The pencil and erasable ink were notable innovations for providing writers with editing capabilities. The typewriter became what might now be called a personal printing device and enabled individuals to produce professional-looking documents without using an expensive printing press (Figure 1).

overview

For most of today's document production tasks, computers with document production software have replaced pencils with chewed-up erasers, smudgy ball-point pens, and clacking typewriters.

WHAT IS DOCUMENT PRODUCTION SOFTWARE?

Document production software includes word processing software, desktop publishing software, e-mail editors, and software that helps you create home pages and hypertext documents for the Internet's World Wide Web.

Today, it seems that everyone uses computers to produce documents. Using computers, college students write research papers, elementary school students write short essays, secretaries write memos, grandmothers write thank-you notes, executives write corporate reports, job-hunters produce resumes, novelists write books, reporters write news stories, and the list goes on. Should you use a computer for your writing? Check out some good and bad reasons in Figure 2.

Figure 2 *Using a computer for your writing—good and bad reasons.*

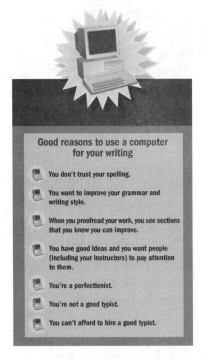

Good reasons to use a computer for your writing

- You don't trust your spelling.
- You want to improve your grammar and writing style.
- When you proofread your work, you see sections that you know you can improve.
- You have good ideas and you want people (including your instructors) to pay attention to them.
- You're a perfectionist.
- You're not a good typist.
- You can't afford to hire a good typist.

Bad reasons to use a computer for your writing

- You never get started until the last minute.
- You're too lazy to proofread your document.
- You want to "borrow" your roommate's report from last semester.
- You hope your readers will be so impressed with your graphics and layout that they don't read what you have written.

Typically, creating a document requires several steps. To begin, you type the text using a word processor. Next, you edit the document until you are satisfied with the content and writing style. Then, you might use the word processing software to format and print the document. Alternatively, you might transfer your document to desktop publishing software to complete the layout and printing.

WHAT ARE SOME ADVANTAGES OF USING DOCUMENT PRODUCTION SOFTWARE?

Document production software has a variety of features that help you create documents easily, for example in-line spell checking, word wrap, and alternative symbol sets.

When you use document production software, correcting typing and spelling errors is easy. Some word processing software features **in-line spell checking** that checks the spelling of each word as you type, as shown in Figure 3.

Figure 3 *In-line spell check.*

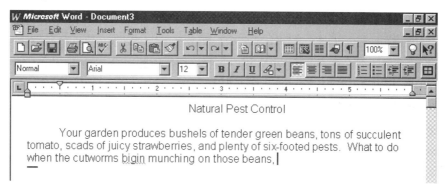

Writing instructors suggest that you can produce better documents faster if you just let your words flow. Word processors make it easy to let your ideas flow because they automatically handle many of the tasks that distracted writers who used typewriters. For example, you don't need to worry about typing off the edge of the paper. With document production software, a feature called **word wrap** takes care of where to break lines. Imagine that the sentences in your document are ribbons of text and word wrap bends the ribbons. Changing margins just means bending the ribbon in different places. Even after you have typed an entire document, adjusting the size of your right, left, top, and bottom margins is simple.

In a global society, communication increasingly involves multiple languages and their alphabets. Most document production software includes **alternative symbol sets** that provide symbols other than those you see on the keyboard. Using these alternative symbol sets, you can insert the Japanese Yen symbol ¥ or the British pound sign £. Also available are foreign language characters with umlauts and accent marks such as ä and é. It is not efficient to use special symbols for an entire document. So, if you're writing a letter or paper in Greek, for example, use the foreign language version of your document production software.

overview

Computers have been blamed for releasing a truckload of poor quality documents into circulation. To anyone who reads electronic mail it soon becomes painfully clear that many literate people still have trouble with spelling and grammar. Some observers characterize the material exchanged in online discussions and newsgroups as crude, silly, uninformed, and self-serving.

This criticism implies that instead of helping writers, computers have somehow lowered literary standards. But, people—not computers—create documents. Spelling errors, grammatical blunders, incoherent arguments, and unverified assertions are more attributable to human fallibility than to some computer-sponsored plot to subvert literature as we know it.

When used skillfully, computerized document production tools can help you improve the quality of your writing. With such tools, it is easy to edit the first draft of your document to refine its overall structure, then zero in to make detailed improvements to your sentence structure and word usage.

Is it necessary to use document production software to improve your writing? In many situations your writing is a reflection of your organizational skills, your creativity, your level of education, and your ability to think coherently. Your admission to graduate school might depend on the creativity and grammatical accuracy of the biographical essay required as part of the application process. Getting a job might depend on the spelling and phrasing of your resume and cover letter. Keeping your job might depend on the accuracy and structure of your written reports. In today's competitive world, it is important to take advantage of every opportunity, including the opportunity to fine-tune your writing with the assistance of document production software.

HOW CAN I USE BLOCK OPERATIONS AND AN OUTLINER TO IMPROVE MY ORGANIZATION?

Using document production tools, you can easily insert text, cut sections of text, and move entire paragraphs or pages to improve the structure and logical flow of a document. In document production terminology, sections of your document are referred to as **blocks**. Deleting blocks and moving blocks are sometimes referred to as **block operations**.

Although document production software simplifies block operations, you first need to decide how to rearrange your document for a more effective progression of ideas. Some writers find that the limited amount of text displayed on the screen prevents them from getting a good look at the overall flow of ideas throughout the document. One solution is to use the outline feature of your software.

An **outliner** helps you develop a document as a hierarchy of headings and subheadings. This WorkText, for example, is structured into chapters, sections, and subsections. When you create a hierarchical document you "tag" each heading to identify whether it starts a chapter, section, or subsection. To get an overall view of the document your software can show only the chapter headings. Or, to view the structure in more detail, the outliner can display the chapter headings and the section headings. When you move a heading in outline view, the outliner automatically moves all its subheadings and paragraphs.

ARE THERE TRICKS I CAN USE TO FIND THE RIGHT WORDS?

Once you have taken care of the overall structure of your document, you can turn to the details of word usage, spelling, and grammar. Your software's **thesaurus** can help you find more descriptive words to clarify and enliven your writing.

Some writers know that they tend to overuse certain words or use them incorrectly. For instance, you might tend to overuse the word "however." If you have specific writing problems such as this, you might use the **search feature** to hunt for all the occurrences of your problem word. For each occurrence, you can decide to leave it or revise it. Another feature, **search and replace**, is handy if you want to substitute one word or phrase for another. For example, after you finish the first draft of a short story, you might decide to change its location. Use search and replace to change every occurrence of "Texas" to "New Mexico." In non-fiction writing, clever use of search and replace can help you use terminology consistently to increase the clarity of your explanations.

WILL A SPELL CHECKER MAKE UP FOR MY POOR SPELLING SKILLS?

Now, what about spelling? A document with spelling errors reflects poorly on the writer. Most document production software, including newer e-mail editors, has some type of spell check feature. An in-line spell check shows you errors as you type. A less sophisticated, but equally useful, spell check looks through your entire document any time you activate it. You would generally use this type of spell check when you have completed your first draft, then again just before you print it. To activate spell check such as the one shown in operation in Figure 4, you select it from a menu or click a button.

Figure 4 A spell check in operation.

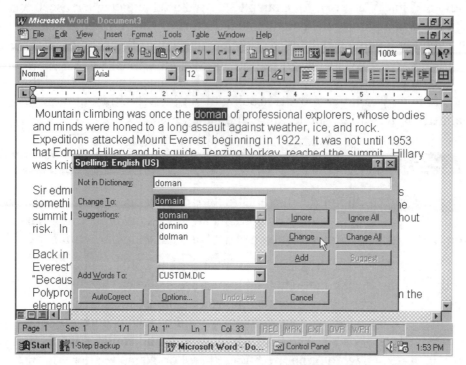

Don't depend on a spell checker to proofread your document. A spell check works by looking for each word from your document in a list called a **dictionary**. If the word from your document is in the dictionary, the spell check considers the word correctly spelled. If the word is not in the dictionary, the word is counted as misspelled. Sounds okay, right? But, suppose your document contains a reference to the city of "Negaunee." This word is not in the dictionary, so the spell check considers it misspelled. It might even suggest that you change the word to "negate"—a word that does appear in the dictionary. Because they are not in the dictionary, proper nouns and scientific, medical, and technical words are likely to be flagged as misspelled, even if you have spelled them correctly. If you plan to use such words often, you can add them to the dictionary. If you frequently use technical words, you should check to see if special technical dictionaries are available for your document production software. By installing a medical dictionary, for example, your spell checker would know the spelling of medical terms.

Now suppose that your document contains the phrase "a pear of shoes." Although you meant to use "pair," not "pear," the spell check will not catch your mistake because "pear" is a valid word in the dictionary. Your spell check won't help if you have trouble deciding whether to use "there" or "their," "its" or "it's," "too" or "to." Remember, then, that a spell check will not substitute for a thorough proofread.

WILL A GRAMMAR CHECKER FIX MY WRITING THE SAME WAY A SPELLING CHECKER FIXES MY SPELLING?

All languages are complex. Many linguists characterize English, for example, as having an exception to every rule. Which is grammatically correct: "Did the plot turn out *like* you expected?" or "Did the plot turn out *as* you expected?" You can clear up many grammatical questions by using a **grammar checker**, a feature of most word processors that coaches you on correct sentence structure and word usage. Think of a grammar checker as an assistant that will proofread your document, point out potential trouble spots, and suggest alternatives. If English is your second language, a grammar checker might be especially helpful.

A grammar checker will not change your document for you. Instead it points out possible problems, suggests alternate words or phrases, and gives you the option of making changes. For example, if a document contains the sentence, "Did the plot turn out like you expected?" a grammar check might point out that you should consider using "as" instead of "like," but you have to decide whether to actually make the change. Refer to Figure 5.

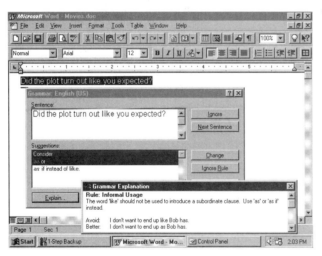

Figure 5 *A grammar checker suggests a change.*

Although "like" is not wrong in this context, it is a more casual usage. If your English professor is a traditionalist, it would be a good idea to follow the grammar checker's recommendation and substitute the word "as." But, if you're writing an article for a casual newsletter, you might decide to use "like."

HOW DO I CREATE A GREAT LOOKING DOCUMENT?

Today's document production software provides you tools to produce professionally formatted and illustrated documents. When you create documents, you'll want to take advantage of formatting tools such as document templates, wizards, fonts, styles, borders, and clip art. But be aware that computerized document production provides you with a tool, not a crutch. A document that looks

"cool" will not disguise poor writing. So, before you focus on how your document looks, make sure its contents is well organized and well written.

A **document template** is a preformatted document into which you type your text. Most document production software encourages you to select a template before you type the text for your first draft. These templates were created by professionals so your document can have a professional look. If you don't select a template, the software will select one for you—usually a plain template suitable for letters and reports. Format settings such as margins, line spacing, heading fonts, and type size have all been set up for you. Figure 6 shows some of the document templates typically available with today's word processing software.

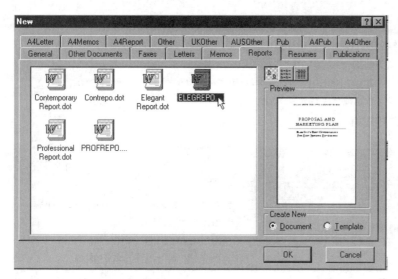

Figure 6 Document templates.

You might wonder if selecting a template before you begin to type contradicts the conventional advice to ignore formatting issues for your first draft. In practice, you'll want to select a template and perhaps format your headings as you type. You can postpone the rest of your formatting activities until you're satisfied with the content.

Some software goes a step further than templates by furnishing you with **document wizards** that not only provide you with a document format, but also take you step by step through the process of entering the text for a wide variety of documents. A wizard and a template are not the same thing. A *template* simply provides you with preset formats for a document. A *wizard* is a feature that coaches you step by step through the process of entering the text of your document.

One popular word processor has wizards for:

resumes	tables	memos
agendas	fax cover sheets	newsletters
award certificates	business letters	legal documents

Check out the templates and wizards provided by your software before you struggle with creating your own formats. For example, to create an entry-level resume, you might find it easy to use a resume wizard like the one shown in Figure 7.

Figure 7 *Entry-level resume wizard.*

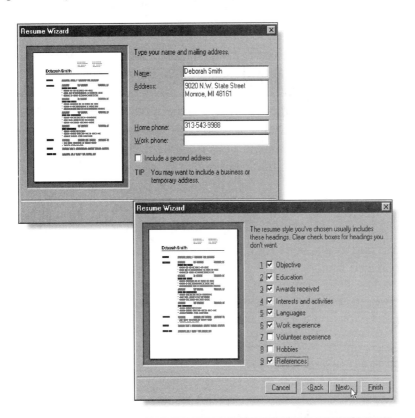

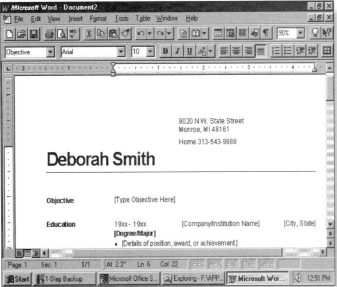

overview

The **font** you select has a major impact on the look of your document. Fonts are designed by typesetters and artists. Each font is given a name. Your document production software generally supplies you with many fonts. If you want even more variety, you can purchase and install additional font collections.

Typeset fonts such as Times New Roman and Arial make your document look formal and professionally produced. But don't get too carried away with fonts. You should select, at maximum, three fonts to use in your document. You can vary these three fonts by adding italics and boldface and changing the size of the font.

Research studies show that serif fonts are easier to read on the printed page, whereas sans serif fonts are easier to read on the computer screen. In addition, a kerned font is easier to read than a monospaced font. Figure 8 shows you the difference between a serif and a sans serif font, and the difference between a kerned font and a monospaced font.

Figure 8 *Serifs and kerning*

Each character of a monospaced font takes up the same amount of space.	`Wow, look at this!`
A kerned font provides a wider space for wide letters such as "w," but reduces the amount of space allotted to narrow letters such as "t."	Wow, look at this!
A serif font has small embellishments called "serifs" on the ends of the lines that form the characters.	**Wow, look at this!**
A sans serif font lacks serifs.	Wow, look at this!

In addition to selecting fonts, you can manipulate the look of your document by adjusting the line spacing, margins, indents, tabs, borders, and frames. Figure 9 takes a brief look at why you might use some of these format options.

Figure 9 *Using formatting options.*

- Additional space makes a document easier to read. Larger **margins** and **double-spacing** generate white space, make your document appear less dense, and make reading seem easier.

- **Justification** defines how the letters and words are spaced across each line. Typeset documents are often **fully justified** so the text on the right margin as well as on the left margin is aligned evenly. Your document will look more formal if it is fully justified than if it has a **ragged right margin**.

- When summarizing information, listing information, or even typing your answers to homework questions, your points will stand out if you use **hanging indents**, **bulleted lists**, or **numbered lists**.

- **Columns** enhance readability and **tables** organize data. In document production terminology, columns generally mean newspaper-style layout. Tables arrange data in a grid of rows and columns. Instead of trying to arrange columns or tables using the Tab key and space bar, consider using your software's automatic table feature or column format.

- To add visual interest to your documents, incorporate borders, rules, and graphics. A **border** is a box around text—usually around a title, heading, or table. A **rule** is a line, usually positioned under text. Graphics are pictures and illustrations. **Clip art** collections provide hundreds of images that you have permission to use in non-commercial works. You can also find graphics on the Internet. With the right equipment, you can scan pictures from books and magazines. Just be sure you check for permission before you use any graphic in your documents. Pictures on the Internet, in magazines, and in computer programs are often copyrighted. Using them without permission is not legal.

HOW CAN I AUTOMATE DOCUMENT PRODUCTION TASKS?

Computers are expert at repetitive tasks such as counting, numbering, searching, and duplicating. Document production software makes clever use of these computer talents to automate many of the repetitive tasks associated with document production. Automating such tasks saves time and increases productivity. Let's look briefly at a few of the more useful tasks of this type.

As you edit a document and change its format, you might remove large sections of text, reducing the page count. Or, your instructor or publisher might insist that you double space the document, doubling the page count. It makes sense, then, to let the software take care of numbering your pages. **Automatic page numbering**, sometimes called **pagination**, means the computer automatically numbers and renumbers the pages as you edit and format your document.

You usually tell your software to include page numbers in a header or footer. A **header** is text that automatically appears in the top margin of every page. A **footer** is text that appears in the bottom margin of every page. Headers and footers help identify the document and make your documents look more like published works. Look at a page in this book. It has a footer. Published books will often have either a header, a footer, or both on each page. Your documents can easily have these professional elements. A simple footer might be the word "Page, " followed by the current page number. For identification purposes, you might put your name in the header of your documents.

overview

IS THERE A TOOL THAT WILL HELP ME MAKE SURE MY WRITING IS SUITED TO THE AUDIENCE?

Most grammar checkers have built in **readability formulas** that count the number of words in each sentence and the number of syllables per word. As you write, you can use readability formulas to target your writing to your audience. The longer your sentences and words, the higher the reading level required to understand your writing. Most writers aim for a seventh or eighth grade reading level on documents for the general public.

HOW CAN I KEEP TRACK OF FOOTNOTES AND A TABLE OF CONTENTS?

Scholarly documents often require **footnotes** that contain citations for works mentioned in the text. As you revise your text, the footnotes need to stay associated with their source in the text and must be numbered sequentially. Your document production software includes footnoting facilities that correctly position and number the footnotes even if you move blocks of text. Need end notes instead of footnotes? Your software can gather your citations at the end of your document and print them in order of their appearance in the document or in alphabetical order. Some word processors even have wizards that help you enter your citations in the correct format depending on whether they are books or magazine articles.

Longer documents benefit from a **table of contents** and an **index**. Because of document production technology, many people have come to expect that all documents, not just those created by professional publishers, have indexes and tables of contents. Most document production software will automatically generate an index and table of contents, then automatically update them as you edit your document.

CAN I USE THE SOFTWARE TO CREATE FORM LETTERS AND MASS MAILINGS?

Sometimes, you might want to send out the same material to many people, for example an advertising mass mailing or a mass mailing of resumes. Other times, you might want to reuse the same material in many different documents, for example standard product descriptions or contract clauses. Two word processing features—boilerplating and mail merge—can help you automate these types of tasks.

Mail merge automates the process of producing customized documents such as letters and advertising flyers. You might use mail merge to send out application letters when you're searching for a job. To set up a mail merge, you create a document with specially marked "blanks" and a file of information that goes in the blanks each time the document is printed. Your document production software will merge the document and the information.

Boilerplating refers to the process of merging standard paragraphs to create a new document. Law offices frequently use boilerplating to draw up legal documents such as contracts, wills, and divorces.

HOW DO I FORMAT MY DOCUMENT FOR PUBLISHING ON THE WORLD WIDE WEB?

One of the most significant effects of computerized document production came as a somewhat unexpected surprise. The development of a worldwide data communications network has created amazing opportunities for **electronic publishing**. It's old fashioned to think of a computer as just a place to store information before it is committed to paper. Once a document is in electronic format, why not keep it there? Electronic documents are easy to send, store, and manipulate. Today virtually anyone can post a document on the World Wide Web, send an e-mail message, or participate in online discussion groups. The power of the printed word seems to be evolving into the power of the electronically published word (Figure 10).

Figure 10 *The power of the electronic word.*

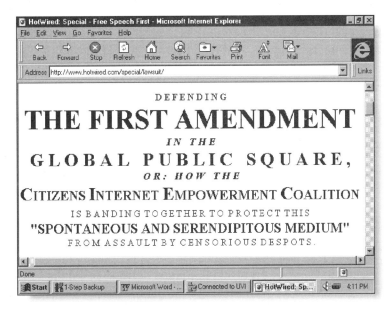

overview

Many of the documents that zap through the airways were created using a simple word processor or e-mail editor. However, one of the most popular means of electronic publishing, the World Wide Web, requires documents to be specially formatted using HTML. HTML stands for **hypertext markup language**. An HTML document contains special codes such as <i> for italics or <img src = "surprise.gif"> to display a graphic. Many word processors and desktop publishers can automatically generate an HTML formatted document from any document that's been entered and stored.

Another effect of computerized document production is the emergence of what some experts are calling a new literary form. Traditionally, narrative works such as novels and essays follow a linear structure. To read such a work, you start at the beginning and proceed page by page to the end. In the process of writing traditional narrative, the author makes many decisions—what to include, the order of events, and so on. Now, however, electronic documents called **hypertext** can be read starting at any "page." Links connect non-adjacent sections of documents and might even connect to a different document entirely. Navigating these linked documents becomes the responsibility of the reader. With readers proceeding in different ways through a document, authors may lose a good deal of control over what readers experience. Historian Shelby Foote comments, "There's no telling what's going to come of this. Maybe a new kind of literature."

HOW DO I KNOW WHICH DOCUMENT PRODUCTION SOFTWARE IS RIGHT FOR ME?

In a consumer society, the name of the game is "variety." Consumers who shop for document production technology have a dazzling variety of hardware and software options. To get the right product and stay within your budget, you should be aware of the major product categories.

Word processing technology includes inexpensive electronic typewriters, personal word processors, and microcomputers. Of the three word processing technologies, only the microcomputer will also support sophisticated desktop publishing. Should you purchase desktop publishing software in addition to a word processing software? If you generally work with text that flows sequentially through a document, a word processor should be adequate. If you answer yes to any of the items on the list below, you should consider supplementing your word processor with desktop publishing software:

- Do you frequently work on brochures, newsletters, or books?

- Do you want precise control over the placement of graphics on the page?

- Are you are working with a variety of graphics formats such as Gif, Jpg, Bmp, Pcx, and Tif?

- Do you need to deal with text in "chunks," for example, by continuing a story on page 5?

- Do you want irregular shaped areas of text or text that flows around irregularly shaped graphics?

- Do you need color separation capability to produce full-color output?

- Will your documents be printed by a professional printing house?

The top-selling word processing software packages are Microsoft Word, Corel's WordPerfect, and Lotus Word Pro. You might also consider Microsoft Works or ClarisWorks, integrated software that includes a word processor, spreadsheet, database, and drawing package. Popular desktop publishing software packages include Adobe Pagemaker and QuarkXPress. For simpler desktop publishing projects, check out Microsoft Publisher. These products are shown in Figure 11.

Figure 11 Document production software.

CheckPoint _____

1   The spread of literacy went hand-in-hand with technological developments, culminating in today's use of computers and _____ software.

2   True or false? Automatic features like word wrap and in-line spell checking make it harder to let your ideas flow because they are distracting.

3   You can globalize your documents by inserting letters and symbols from foreign alphabets, referred to as _____.

4   True or false? The spell check feature of word processing software would alert you if you accidentally used the word "see" instead of "sea" when referring to a large body of water.

5   A(n) _____ provides preset formats for a document, whereas a(n) _____ is a feature that coaches you step by step through the process of entering text.

6   _____ can help you target your writing to your audience.

7   One of the most significant effects of computerized document production has been to encourage _____ publishing.

8   Documents that are posted on the World Wide Web must be in _____ format.

9   True or false? If your document requires precise placement of graphics, columns, text flowing around graphics, or full-color output, you should consider using desktop publishing software instead of word processing software.

10 The three major types of word processing technology are _____, _____, and _____.

Microsoft Word

Tutorial 1: Word Basics

Tutorial 1

Word Basics

Retail Clothing Trends

Today's casual lifestyles have changed the way people dress outside of work as well as what is worn in the workplace. Successful clothing manufacturers must not only respond to trends but, more importantly, anticipate them. Are you curious about the inner workings of such a company? In this tutorial, you'll get to peek at some of the memos, letters, planning documents, and press releases prepared by employees of Dakota Jeans Company, Inc.

Doing the e-Thing

You'll find out how to get started with the e-Course software tutorials. This is an easy way to learn how to use computer software.

Projects

In the Tutorial 1 Projects, you'll practice and improve your newly learned Word skills as you edit existing memos, flyers, and letters; add a footer to a document; create new documents; use Word's Help facility; use the Memo Wizard; and design your own flyer.

WHAT'S ONLINE

Disks

If you'd like to keep track of your progress, you should have a blank formatted disk ready when you begin the online Steps for Tutorial 1. As you log in, the e-Course software will create a **Tracking Disk** for you. The Tracking Disk will keep a record of the length of time you spend on each e-Course session and your scores on the CheckPoint questions you answer online. If your instructor will collect your Tracking Disk for grading, make sure you have a backup copy! You should have a second formatted disk to use as a **Project Disk**. You'll find out how to make and use your Project Disk when you get to the Projects section of the WorkText.

Retail Clothing Trends

What would you think if you worked in a large office building in a major U.S. city and one of your colleagues came to work wearing jeans and a tee shirt? At some businesses 10 or even 15 years ago, this might have been grounds for firing—not following the dreaded company dress code. But today things are different.

"Business casual" is a trend that has evolved in the 90s. The executives in charge today are the baby boomers who grew up in blue jeans. Nine out of ten U.S. companies allow casual dress on specially designated days, and 33 percent of companies allow business casual every day!

Relaxed, comfortable, natural, and easy-care—that's what the consumer of the 90s seeks in clothing for both work and play. And this trend at work has spurred the U.S. retail clothing industry. Today's clothing designers and retail buyers have shifted their approach. Retail stores such as The Gap, The Limited, and Structure have appeared. Department stores have increased their private label casual lines. Some of the high-end fashion designers—previously beyond the reach of the typical consumer—have created casual clothing lines with more affordable prices. Companies that produce jeans and overalls are expanding and experiencing record profits.

In this tutorial, you'll work with documents created by employees of one company that has benefited from the business casual trend—Dakota Jeans Company, Inc. You'll learn the basic skills you need in Microsoft Word to view and make simple changes to documents. Here are some of the things you'll do:

- Start and exit the Word software

- Scroll through a document to view all of its pages

- Enter text into a document and use word wrap

- Correct typing and spelling mistakes

- Rename and save documents on your own disks

- Print documents

GET STARTED ONLINE WITH e-COURSE

The e-Course software is designed to teach you how to use the Microsoft Word word processing software. The first time you use the e-Course software, you'll probably want to set up a Tracking Disk, which keeps track of your progress and your CheckPoint scores. Now, it's time to use your computer.

To start the e-Course software and set up a Tracking Disk:

1: Label a formatted disk "Tracking Disk" and place it in the disk drive. (This step is optional, but if you do not insert a disk, you will not have an electronic record of your progress.)

2: Start your computer, then click the **Start** button.

3: Point to **Programs**.

4: Point to **e-Course**.

5: Click **e-Course Word**.

6: If you see the message "The tracking file was not found on drive A," click the button labeled "Copy the tracking database to a disk in drive A." This will copy some files onto your disk, and then display the Login window.

➔ If you're in a computer lab and e-Course is not on the Programs menu, ask your technical support person how to start the e-Course software. If you're using your own computer, you must install the e-Course software before you use it. Refer to the TechTalk section of this WorkText.

The first time you log in, e-Course asks you to enter your name and other information that automatically appears on your CheckPoint reports. This information is stored on your Tracking Disk, so you won't have to enter it the next time you log in.

To log in the first time:

1: On the Login screen, fill in the blanks with your **first name**, **last name**, **course section**, and **student number**. If you don't know your course section or student number, just type anything—you can change it later.

2: Click the **OK** button. In a few seconds, you should see the e-Course Welcome screen.

scenario

At the e-Course Welcome screen, you can print your Task Reference. The Task Reference will help refresh your memory about how to do the tasks you learn in the tutorials.

To print the Task Reference:

1: Click **Task Reference** on the Welcome screen menu bar.

2: Click **View/Print Task Reference**.

3: After the Task Reference appears, click **File** on the menu bar, then click **Print**.

4: When the printout is complete, click **File** again, then click **Exit**.

e-Course is easy to use. After the short e-Course Introductory Tour, you'll be ready to use all the e-Course features.

To start the e-Course Introductory Tour:

1: Click the **Introductory Tour** button on the Welcome screen.

2: Follow the instructions on the screen to navigate through the tour.

After you've finished the Introductory Tour, it's time to get started on Tutorial 1!

To start Tutorial 1:

1: Click **Tutorials** on the menu bar at the top of the Welcome screen.

2: Point to **Tutorial 1**.

3: Click a topic—you should begin with Topic 1.

Review Questions

Fill in the blank with the correct word or phrase.

1   Microsoft _____ is word processing software that helps you produce memos, letters, and reports.

2   The _____ is the large rectangle that displays the Word software.

3   The _____ is the smaller rectangle within the Word window that displays a document.

4   The _____ is a blinking vertical bar that indicates where the next character you type will appear in the document.

5   The _____ is a small horizontal bar that indicates the end of the document.

6   The three _____ are used to control the size of the document window.

7   The _____ controls and displays the tab and margin settings for a document.

8   You use the _____ to select normal, outline, or page layout view.

9   _____ are located along the bottom and right side of the document window.

10   The _____ displays information about your location in the document.

11   The _____ contains the names of Word's menus.

12   The _____ provides helpful hints about using Word more efficiently.

13   _____ are rows of buttons that provide you with menu shortcuts.

14   A(n) _____ identifies a button's name and displays a brief description of the button's function on the status bar.

15 Word automatically adds the _____ extension to your document filenames.

16 _____ view shows how your document will look on the printed page while allowing you to create and edit your document.

17 _____ view enables you to quickly move, copy, and reorganize blocks of text.

18 _____ view is the best all-purpose view for typing, editing, and formatting text.

19 _____ are symbols that appear on the screen but do not show up on your printed document.

20 When you're entering several lines of text in a document, Word's _____ feature automatically moves you to the beginning of the next line when you reach the end of the current line.

21 Text that is _____ appears as white letters on a black background.

22 The _____ button on the Standard toolbar reverses the last change you made.

23 Text that is printed at the top of every page of a document is called a(n) _____.

MULTIPLE CHOICE

*Select the letter of the **one** best answer.*

24 When you're writing, you'll usually want the Word window:

a minimized

b maximized

c restored

d hidden

25 To maximize the *document* window in a maximized Word window, you click:

a the ⊡ button on the Word title bar

b the ◻ button on the Word title bar

c the ⊡ button on the Word menu bar

d the ◻ button on the Word menu bar

26 The two Word toolbars you'll use most frequently are the:

a Standard and Microsoft toolbars

b Ruler and Formatting toolbars

c Formatting and Standard toolbars

d Microsoft and Formatting toolbars

27 You won't often want to display the Office Assistant because:

a it causes Word to run more slowly

b it reduces the screen space available for your document

c the tips it displays are rarely useful

d it increases the disk space required to store your document

28 Which of the following is *not* one of Word's views?

a normal

b draft

c outline

d page layout

29 **Word's Document View buttons are located:**

   a in the lower-left corner of the Word window

   b in the lower-right corner of the Word window

   c in the upper-left corner of the document window

   d in the lower-left corner of the document window

30 **To close a document but leave the Word window open, you click the:**

   a top ☒ button   **c** leftmost ☒ button

   b lower ☒ button   **d** rightmost ☒ button

31 **To move the insertion point a short distance within your document, it's most efficient to use the:**

   a scroll box   **c** scroll arrows

   b arrow keys   **d** Page Down or Page Up keys

32 **Which of the following is not one of Word's nonprinting characters?**

   a ¶ (end of paragraph mark)

   b · (space between words mark)

   c × (end of line mark)

   d → (tab mark)

33 **To show or hide nonprinting characters, you click the:**

   a [¶] button

   b [🖨] button

   c [📄] button

   d [NP] button

review questions

34 **You can easily remove existing text by first selecting it and then pressing the:**

   a Remove key

   b Erase key

   c Delete key

   d Enter key

MATCHING

Select the letter from the right column that correctly matches each item in the left column.

35 w.wwwww

36

37 error

38 error

39

   a normal text

   b click to display or hide the TipWizard

   c indicates a word not in Word's dictionary

   d click to see how your document will look when printed

   e selected text

review questions

Use a separate sheet of paper to write out your answers to the following questions.

40 In the online Steps, you learned you should check window settings whenever you start Word. What are the four steps in that process? What is the advantage of checking window settings?

41 How do Word's document views differ from one another? When is each appropriate?

42 What kinds of assistance can Word's AutoCorrect provide as you create a document? What kinds of mistakes will AutoCorrect not detect?

43 How do you save a file to a new location or with a new name? How do you save a file with the same name on the same disk?

Projects

These Projects are designed to help you review and develop the skills you learned in Tutorial 1. Complete each Project using Microsoft Word. *If you have not yet made the Project Disk for Tutorial 1, start the e-Course software, click Project Disk on the e-Course Welcome screen menu bar, and follow the instructions on the screen.*

If you've forgotten some of the skills you need to complete the Projects, refer to the Task Reference.

REVIEW SKILLS

1   Congratulations   File: Award.doc

In the online Steps, you leaned how to open, modify, and print a document. In this project, you'll review those skills without the assistance of the online Steps. If you've forgotten how to do the skills, refer to your Task Reference.

Open the Award document from your Project Disk. Change the date at the top of the letter to today's date, and then change the name at the bottom of the letter to your name. Following the word "on" at the beginning of the second line of the second paragraph within the body of the letter, insert a date two weeks from today followed by the text "at Palmer's Restaurant and Tavern". Print the document and then close it without saving changes.

2   Help Wanted   File: Wanted.doc

In the online Steps, you learned how to put your name in the document header and how to use AutoCorrect to fix spelling errors. In this Project, you'll review those skills without the assistance of the online Steps. If you've forgotten how to do the skills, refer to your Task Reference.

Open the Wanted document from your Project Disk. Put your name in a document header. Then use AutoCorrect to correct all marked spelling errors. (Do not change names.) Print the document and then close it without saving changes.

3   Dakota Belts   File: Market.doc

In the online Steps, you learned how to delete and insert text and how to save a document. In this Project, you'll review those skills as you put the finishing touches on a Dakota Jeans Company memo.

projects

Open the Market document from your Project Disk. Insert your name and the title "Product Manager" after the "From:" heading in the memo. In the body of the memo, the first sentence in the fourth paragraph repeats information from earlier in the memo; delete the entire first sentence in the fourth paragraph. At the end of the memo, add a blank line and then type "Thanks for your input on this project.". Save the document without changing the filename, and then print the document.

4 Past Performances   File: Closet.doc

In the online Steps, you learned how to preview a document. In this Project, you'll first edit a document to insert text, learning a Word AutoFormat trick in the process. You'll then preview the document and print using a button on the Print Preview toolbar.

Open the Closet document from your Project Disk. Position the insertion point between the "s" and "n" in "Performancesnow." Type two hyphens immediately followed by the word "an" (no space between the second hyphen and the "an"). Watch the screen as you press the spacebar to insert a space after the word "an".

they become **a** What happened to the two dashes when you pressed the spacebar?

b Type "upscale consignment shop--is" and then press the spacebar. Save the document without changing the filename, and then preview the document. What feature can you see on the document in the Preview window that wasn't visible when you viewed the document in normal view?

c Print the document by clicking the 🖨 Print button on the Print Preview toolbar. Does that button produce the same results as the 🖨 Print button on the Standard toolbar in the Word window?

5 I'm the One   File: Job.doc

You might have already sent your resume to a company in hopes of being hired. The cover letter that accompanies the resume introduces you and attempts to convey how your education or experience makes you an ideal candidate for the job. Further, this cover letter can demonstrate your ability to write clearly and logically. In this Project, you'll edit a cover letter to improve it.

Open the Job document from your Project Disk. Read the letter, and take special notice of the first paragraph in the body of the letter. Replace that first paragraph with a single, simple sentence that more clearly and succinctly states the purpose of the letter. Replace both occurrences of Lisa's name with your own, and replace her address with your address. Save the document without changing the filename, and then print the document.

6 See It Now   File: Idea.doc

In the online Steps, you learned that normal view is the best all-purpose view for typing, editing, and formatting text. In this Project, you'll compare what you can see in normal view with what you can see in page layout view.

Open the Idea document from your Project Disk and then switch to normal view, if necessary. Create a document header that contains your name followed by two tabs and then today's date. As you type the date, note its location. Scroll through the document to see it all. Switch to page layout view, and then scroll through the document again to see it all. Next, preview the document. If you can't discern details in the document image, click the document in the Print Preview window to magnify the image. Click the document a second time to return to an unmagnified view.

a Where is the date located within the header?

b What three document features could you see in page layout view that you could not see in normal view?

c Are the three document features you saw in page layout view also visible in the Print Preview window?

7 The Lineup   File: Proposal.doc

You can use the Tab key in Word to align or indent text. In this Project, you'll use the Tab key to left-align the names in a memo distribution list as well as the text following the memo headers.

Open the Proposal document from your Project Disk, then show nonprinting characters, if necessary. Position the insertion point immediately to the left of the "L" in "Larry Clifton" in the distribution list, and then press the Tab key. For each of the remaining names in the distribution list, position the insertion point to the left of the name, and then press the Tab key. All names in that list are now aligned.

Position the insertion point after the space following "DATE:", press the Tab key, and then enter today's date. Use the Tab key to align the text following the headings in the next three lines, producing memo headings aligned as shown below. (Your date will be different.) Save the document without changing the filename, and then print the document.

DATE:	02/17/98
TO:	Product Development Distribution
FROM:	Marcia Feltcroft
SUBJECT:	Standard Format for Product Proposals

Text following headings is left-aligned.

projects

8 Celebrate!

Suppose your company has won an award and you are writing a memo to your employees announcing the news and inviting them to help you celebrate. In this Project, you'll create, save, and print such a memo.

Start Word. Then enter text as needed to create a memo that looks like the one shown below:

To: All employees
From: Mary Blackwell
Date: February 18, 1998
Re: Let's celebrate our award!

Thanks to all your hard work this past year on various community projects and on expanding our business, we have won the 1997 J. Arthur Davis Award for New Business Excellence.

I've been invited to attend the annual Small Business luncheon on March 26, 1998, to accept the award, and I will do so on behalf of all of us.

Receiving this award is a real feather in all of our caps, and I think it is something worth celebrating. I would like to plan a potluck family dinner for 6 p.m. on Saturday, March 7, or Saturday, March 14.

Please let me know as soon as possible which date will work out best for you and how many people, including yourself, will be coming. Once we have chosen the time and know how many people will attend, we can work on the menu.

Look over your memo and make any necessary corrections or adjustments. Save the document as Hurrah on your Project Disk, and then print the document.

9   It's Up To You   File: Code.doc

So far, as you've worked through the online Steps and Projects, you've had explicit instructions on how to save your documents. Now is your chance to make your own decisions about saving.

Open the Code document from your Project Disk. In the second paragraph in the memo body, replace the last two words and the comma preceding them with "when appropriate". Locate and correct the misspelled word in the last paragraph. Save your modified document, but don't overwrite the old document. Answer the following questions about how you accomplished the task:

   a   Did you use the Save button or the Save As option from the File menu?

   b   What name did you use for your modified document?

   c   On which disk did you store the modified document?

   d   If you now closed the document, would you expect to have to respond to a message asking if you want to save changes? Why or why not?

10 Footloose!   File: Sanchez.doc

In the online Steps, you added a document header with text that is printed at the top of every page. In this Project, you'll add a footer, which is text that is printed at the bottom of every page.

Open the Sanchez document from your Project Disk.

To create a footer:

1: Click **View** on the menu bar, and then click **Header and Footer**.

2: Click the ▣ **Switch Between Header and Footer** button on the Header and Footer toolbar.

3: Create a footer as follows:

- Type **The Dakota Dazzler**
- Press the **Tab** key two times.
- Type **Page**
- Press the **spacebar**.
- Click the ▣ **Page Numbers** button on the Header and Footer toolbar to insert automatically generated page numbers in the footer.
- Click the **Close** button on the Header and Footer toolbar.

Save the document without changing the filename. Print the document. (Don't forget to look at the footer of your printed document.)

BUILD SKILLS

11 Word Toolbars

In the online Steps, you learned a setup procedure that made sure the Standard and Formatting toolbars were displayed. Word has additional toolbars you can display if you need them. In this Project, you'll learn what toolbars are available, how to display them, and how to hide them.

To display or hide toolbars:

1: Click **View** on the menu bar.

2: Click **Toolbars**.

3: Click the name of a toolbar to add or remove a check mark. Those toolbars with check marks will be displayed; toolbars without check marks will be hidden from view.

projects

To complete this Project, use the View menu to display all the toolbars. If the toolbars become stacked on top of each other, drag the title bars to move them. Next, point to each toolbar button and read its ScreenTip. For each of the descriptions below, indicate the name of the toolbar it describes. When you're finished, hide all but the Standard and Formatting toolbars, and then exit Word.

a   The _____ toolbar lets you add lines around part or all of an object.

b   The _____ toolbar provides one-button access to other Microsoft programs.

c   The _____ toolbar lets you add shapes and lines to a document.

d   The _____ toolbar provides tips about more efficient ways to accomplish tasks.

e   The _____ toolbar lets you add, delete, sort, and find records.

f   The _____ toolbar provides tools for form design.

12 AutoCorrect

In the online Steps, you learned that Word's AutoCorrect feature capitalizes the first word in a sentence when you forget to do so. You also learned that AutoCorrect will automatically correct common spelling errors, such as "adn" for "and", or "teh" for "the". In this Project, you'll learn about other tasks that AutoCorrect can handle.

Start Word, click Tools on the menu bar, and then click AutoCorrect to open the AutoCorrect dialog box.

a   According to the set of check boxes in the top portion of the dialog box, what other types of corrections can AutoCorrect make?

b   If you type ":-)", what will AutoCorrect do?

c   If you type "detente", what will AutoCorrect do?

Use the following Steps to locate and delete the AutoCorrect entry that changes "occurence" to "occurrence".

To delete an existing AutoCorrect replacement entry:

1: Use the scroll bar to locate the entry in the list box in the bottom portion of the dialog box.

2: Click the entry to select it, and then click the ⬚ Delete ⬚ button.

3: Click the **OK** button to close the dialog box.

    d Type "The first occurence of neckties can be traced to the Thirty Years War." Did AutoCorrect recognize the misspelled word? Did AutoCorrect replace the misspelled word?

Use the following Steps to add an AutoCorrect entry to replace "occurence" with "occurrence".

To add an AutoCorrect replacement entry:

1: Open the AutoCorrect dialog box.

2: Type the misspelled word in the *Replace* text box, press the **Tab** key, type the correctly spelled word in the *With* text box, and then click the Add button.

3: Click the **OK** button to close the dialog box.

    a Click the OK button to close the dialog box. Type "The first occurence of neckties can be traced to the Thirty Years War." Did AutoCorrect recognize the misspelled word? Did AutoCorrect replace the misspelled word?

13 Help: Wizards and Assistants

Microsoft Word includes a Help facility that provides how-to information about Word features and procedures. One of the most popular ways to access the Help facility is to use an "agent," such as the Office Assistant. To use a help agent, you simply type in a question. The agent looks through the Help facility, then shows you a list of topics likely to contain relevant information. You can look at one or more of these topics until you find the information you need. Let's see how this works.

Suppose you accidentally deleted something you didn't want to delete, and now you can't remember how to undo a change.

To use Word's Help agent to learn about undoing changes:

1: Click **Help** on the menu bar.

2: Click **Microsoft Word Help**.

3: In the box that appears, type **How do I undo a change?**

4: Click the **Search** button, and Help displays a list of relevant topics.

5: Click **Undo mistakes**.

projects

6: Read the information that appears, then click the **Help Topics** button.

Now that you know how to use Word's help agent, write out your answers to the following questions:

  a Suppose you decide your document would look better if the first line in each paragraph was indented. How do you indent a paragraph?

  b How do you return to a previous editing location in a document?

  c Suppose you'd like the fraction 1/2 to appear as ½ when you type it into your document. Will Word will automatically format a fraction?

  d Suppose you decide after previewing a document that the page margins should be changed. How do you set page margins?

(14) Help: Contents

You can access Word's extensive Help facility in several ways. For example, Contents Help is arranged as a series of online books, with each book covering a topic. Opening a book reveals a list of related topics that you can open to select a particular page of information.

Suppose you'd like to learn more about previewing a document, and you wonder if you can make changes to a document in the Print Preview window.

To use Contents Help to learn about editing while previewing:

1: Click **Help** on the menu bar, click **Contents and Index**, and then click the **Contents** tab. You'll now see a list of Help "books."

2: Locate the book called **Printing**, click that book, and then click the **Open** button. A subsidiary list of Help books appears under the open Printing book. Click the **Previewing a Document Before Printing** book, and then click the **Open** button.

3: Display the page called **Edit text in print preview** by clicking it and then clicking the **Display** button. Read through the information about editing text in print preview, and notice the underlined text. You can click an underlined word or phrase to see its definition.

4: Click **print preview** to see its definition. To hide the definition, click it.

5: To return to the list of books, click the **Help Topics** button. Close any open books by clicking the book and then clicking the Close button.

Now that you know how to use Contents Help, write out your answers to the following questions:

  a How can you save all open documents at the same time?

  b When you're typing text, how do you type the international character ñ in the word "señor"?

c When you save a document, you must provide Word with a name for the file. Are there any letters, numbers, or symbols that you cannot use when naming a file?

15 ScreenTips

Microsoft Word offers a feature called ScreenTips, which provides helpful information about dialog box buttons and options. Let's see how this works.

To view a ScreenTip:

1: To view the ScreenTip for an item in a dialog box, click the [?] button in the upper-right corner of the dialog box.

2: Click the item for which you want help. The ScreenTip appears.

3: Read the ScreenTip information, and then click the ScreenTip to hide it.

Now that you know how to view ScreenTips, you can use them. Click Format on the menu bar, and then click Font to open the Font dialog box. View ScreenTips as needed to answer the following questions:

a What is the purpose of the Color list box in the dialog box? What color is represented by "Auto"?

b What is the purpose of the Hidden option?

c What's a Strikethrough?

Close the Font dialog box. Click File on the menu bar, and then click Page Setup to open the Page Setup dialog box. Use ScreenTips to answer the following questions:

d On the Margin tab, what's the purpose of the Mirror Margins option?

e On the Paper Size tab, what's the purpose of the Landscape option?

f On the Layout tab, what's the purpose of the Different First Page option?

EXPLORE

16 Page Orientation   File: Magazine.doc

You've been asked to check a mock-up for a magazine ad for Dakota Jeans. In this Project, you'll learn how to change a document's page orientation.

Open the Magazine document from your Project Disk. Preview the document, and inspect the ad mock-up. If you can't discern details in the document image, click

projects

the document in the Print Preview window to magnify the image. Click the
document a second time to return to an unmagnified view.

a How many pages is the document?

b Suppose you want to change the orientation of the ad. Click File on the
menu bar, click Page Setup to open the Page Setup dialog box, and then
click the Paper Size tab to select it. What are the two options in the
Orientation section of the dialog box?

c Click Landscape. How did the sample in the Preview section of the dialog
box change?

d Click the OK button to close the dialog box. Examine the ad mock-up
again. What effect has changing the orientation had on the image in the
Print Preview window?

e How many pages is the document now?

17 Additional Navigating Skills   File: Ties.doc

In the online Steps, you learned how to navigate a Word document using the scroll
bars and the arrow keys. In this Project, you'll learn some additional navigation
techniques. Open the Ties document from your Project Disk. Write your answers to
the following questions:

a Scroll until the first paragraph under the "Fabric" heading (located on page
2) is visible. Position the insertion point in the middle of that paragraph.
Make a mental note of the first line visible at the top of the screen, and then
press the Page Up key. By how much did the displayed portion of the
document shift when you pressed the Page Up key? Did the insertion point
move as well?

b Note the last visible line on the screen, and then press the Page Down key.
By how much did the displayed portion of the document shift when you
pressed the Page Down key? Did the insertion point move as well?

c Experiment with pressing the Home key and the End key. Does the display
shift when you press the Home key? When you press the End key? To
where does the insertion point move when you press the Home key? When
you press the End key?

d Hold down the Ctrl key while you press the Page Up key; then release both
keys. (This is called pressing a key combination, and it is abbreviated as
Ctrl+Page Up.) Then try pressing Ctrl+Page Down. To where does the
insertion point move when you press Ctrl+Page Up? When you press
Ctrl+Page Down?

e Experiment with the two key combinations Ctrl+left arrow and Ctrl+right arrow. To where does the insertion point move when you press Ctrl+left arrow? When you press Ctrl+right arrow?

f Experiment with the two key combinations Ctrl+up arrow and Ctrl+down arrow. To where does the insertion point move when you press Ctrl+up arrow? When you press Ctrl+down arrow?

g Experiment with the two key combinations Ctrl+Home and Ctrl+End. To where does the insertion point move when you press Ctrl+Home? When you press Ctrl+End?

18 Use the Memo Wizard and Create a Subdirectory

Word includes several document wizards that ask questions and then use your answers to automatically lay out and format a document such as a newsletter, resume, or memo. In this Project, you'll use the Memo Wizard to create a memo and then you'll save the memo in a new folder on your Project Disk.

Start Word, click File on the menu bar, click New, and then click the MEMOS tab.

To use the Memo Wizard to create a memo:

1: Click the **Memo Wizard** icon to select it, make sure the **Document** option button is selected, and then click the **OK** button. The Memo Wizard window appears, displaying the first Memo Wizard screen.

2: Respond to prompts on the Memo Wizard screens to specify the following information. Click the **Next** button to move to the next screen or the **Back** button to return to a previous screen, as necessary.

- Style = **Contemporary**
- Title = **memorandum**
- Include only the following header items: **Date**, **From**, **Subject**, and **To**. Type your name following "From".
- Include no Cc, no separate page for distribution list, no closing items, no header items for subsequent pages, and no footer items.

3: When you reach the last screen, click the **Finish** button. Close the Office Assistant if it appears. After a few moments, a memo created to your specification appears.

4: Clicking in the locations indicated in the memo, edit the memo as follows:

- Send the memo to **Dana Richlieu** and **Chhaya Rajupur**.
- Type **Planning meeting location change** as the subject.

projects

- Write a sentence or two as the memo text informing the memo recipients that the monthly planning meeting scheduled for 10:00 a.m. next Tuesday (include the date) has been moved to Conference Room 218.

You'll now save the completed memo on your Project Disk, in a new folder (also known as a subdirectory) called MyMemos.

To create a new folder and save a file:

1: Click **File** on the menu bar, and then click **Save**. Because you haven't previously saved this file, the Save As dialog box appears.

2: Make sure the *Save in* box contains the location of your Project Disk.

3: Click the ⬜ **Create New Folder** button. The New Folder dialog box appears.

4: Type **MyMemos**, and then click the **OK** button to close the New Folder dialog box. The folder MyMemos is created and now appears in the file list of your Project Disk.

5: Click **MyMemos** in the list, and then click the **Open** button.

6: Type an appropriate name for this memo in the *File name* box, and then click the **Save** button.

Print the memo.

19 Using Help About Microsoft Word

Microsoft has published several versions of Word. Each version is numbered; examples include Microsoft Word version 5.0, Microsoft Word for Windows 95 version 7.0, and Microsoft Word 97. You can use the Help menu's About Microsoft Word to find out which version you're using. Help About also provides a handy way to find out about your computer system specifications; this information is likely to be requested by your technical support person if your system is not performing correctly.

To access Help About:

1: Click **Help** on the Word menu bar, then click **About Microsoft Word**.

2: Read the information provided, and make a note of which version of Word you're using.

3: Click the **System Info** button. A window with two sections appears.

4: Make sure **System** is selected in the left section. The information in the right window provides you with information on your computer's operating system processor type, memory, and so on.

   a   Write the item label and value for the first five items in the right window.

20 Document Properties   File: Ties.doc

Word's Properties window can provide you with useful information about the current document. In this Project, you'll explore the Properties window.

   Open the Ties document from your Project Disk.

To explore Word's Properties window:

1: Click **File** on the menu bar, and then click **Properties**. The Ties.doc Properties window appears.

2: Click the **General** tab, if necessary. Read the information displayed.

3: Click the **Statistics** tab, and read the information displayed there.

   a   What is the size of the document?

   b   When was the document created?

   c   How many words does the document contain?

   d   How many characters does the document contain?

INVESTIGATE

21 What a Deal!

Suppose you plan to have a garage sale to sell some items (clothing, tools, appliances, your jigsaw puzzle collection, or whatever) you no longer need. You've decided to post notices all around the neighborhood—on the bulletin boards in stores and churches, on light poles, in your yard—announcing your sale. Sketch a design for an eye-catching flyer/poster that you could create using Word. Be sure to include all the necessary information (what, when, where). Feel free to use color, but restrict any art work to simple lines and shapes.

22 Web Shopping

Did you know that all kinds of stores advertise on the Web? Suppose you wanted to buy some authentic Western wear—boots, a hat, and a belt—to wear with your new Dakota Jeans Company jeans. For this Project, you'll search the Web looking for sources from which you could purchase authentic Western wear. Find at least three

projects

sites that sell one or more of the items mentioned, and write a report about what you found. Be sure to include the URLs of the sites you found in your report. Your instructor will give you specific details about the length and format of the report.

23 Publish Or Process

Have you ever heard the term "desktop publishing?" If so, have you wondered how desktop publishing differs from word processing? For this Project, you'll use the resources in your library and/or on the Internet to research desktop publishing.

After you've completed your research, write a two-page article about word processing and desktop publishing. Be sure to point out the similarities as well as the differences between these two processes, and clarify when each is appropriate.

24 Levi Who?

Perhaps more than any other product, blue jeans signify "America" throughout the world. A truly original American product, blue jeans have an interesting history. For this Project, you'll use the resources in your library and/or on the Internet to research the history of blue jeans. Who invented them? When? Why? Why denim? Why those rivets?

After you have completed your research, write a paper that presents the information you found. Your instructor will provide you with specifications for length and format.

25 Tell Me About It

Make an appointment with someone who uses word processing software at home or for business. Be sure you clearly state the purpose of your visit, and receive permission to conduct an interview.

To prepare for the interview, compose a list of questions. Here are some suggestions, but do not use only these questions:

    a How long have you used word processing software?

    b How did you learn to use it?

    c What word processing software are you using now?

    d What features do you like best or use most often?

    e For what kinds of projects do you use your word processing software?

After the interview, write up your findings as if you were writing a magazine article. Your article might be in the format of an interview; or, you might choose to write a narrative in which you summarize and paraphrase the interviewee. Your instructor will provide you with specifications for the article's length and format.

Microsoft Word

Tutorial 2: Develop and Edit Documents

Tutorial 2

Develop and Edit Documents

Coffee by the Book

Close your eyes and think back to the last time you visited a retail bookstore. Try to picture the scene in your mind, imagine the feel of a book in your hands, listen to the sounds in your memory, smell the smells…. Did you suddenly remember the distinctive aroma of freshly brewed coffee? Yes, many retail bookstores now also sell coffee within the store. In this tutorial you'll learn about one such bookstore—Novel-Tea & Coffee.

Projects

In the Tutorial 2 Projects, you'll work with a broad selection of documents—letters, flyers, schedules, menus, outlines, and newsletter articles—as you expand your knowledge and skills for developing and editing documents. Specifically, you'll learn additional text selection techniques, you'll work in outline view, and you'll use the additional options and features of the Thesaurus, the Grammar Checker, the Find command, and the Replace command.

   If you're not assigned Projects 9, 11, 12, 13, 14, 16, 17, or 18, you might want to at least read these Projects or, better yet, work through them. Project 9 deals with techniques for selecting text, some of which you may find handy. Projects 11 and 12 deal with the advanced options of the Find command. The advanced options of the Replace command are used in Projects 13 and 14. In Project 16 you'll create an outline, and in Project 17 you'll edit an existing outline. The Grammar Checker's readability statistics—handy statistics for evaluating how easy your documents are to read and understand—are introduced in Project 18.

WHAT'S ONLINE

1 Select Text
- Select a Line or a Paragraph
- Select a Block of Text

2 Move and Copy Text
- Drag and Drop Text
- Cut and Paste Text
- Copy and Paste Text

3 Switch Between Documents
- List Open Documents
- Switch Between Open Documents
- View Two Document Windows
- Transfer Data Between Documents

4 Find and Replace Text
- Find Text
- Find and Replace Text

5 Use Word's Thesaurus

6 Use the Grammar Checker
- Set Grammar-Check Options

Coffee by the Book

You can't think of one without the other—bread and butter, eggs and bacon, cake and ice cream. And now there's a new inseparable pair: coffee and books. Coffee and books? That's right, coffee and books are today's dynamic marketing duo for a profitable business and for a new social scene.

America's favorite establishments that serve coffee have changed over time. You just have to look at TV sitcoms over the last 20 years or so. After all, TV shows do reflect what's hot and what's not! Diners of the 1970s found people drinking black coffee served by a woman with an apron, short skirt, and teased hair. Remember the hit TV show "Alice"? Alice, Flo, and Vera served the regulars as they sipped coffee, read the local newspaper, and ate a full breakfast of bacon, eggs, and toast. Then came "Seinfeld" with the popular lunch-time hangout. Picture the vinyl booth where Jerry, Elaine, George, and Kramer exchange advice and make plans over coffee. And how about the coffee house where "Friends" get together and romances blossom, or the *Buy the Book* bookstore owned by "Ellen"?

Are you ready to join those who value reflection and relaxation in a quiet, comfortable atmosphere? Imagine sipping your favorite coffee or tea as you survey the latest best sellers, and then settling on an oversized sofa to enjoy your selection. While providing you with a variety of books, magazines, and music for your reading and listening pleasure, today's bookstores can also offer you a cup of your favorite specialty coffee or tea. You can sip on cappuccino (decaf, please) as you bite into a biscotti and enjoy poetry by Browning.

In this tutorial, you'll work with documents created by employees of one company that combines the popularity of bookstores and coffee houses—Novel-Tea & Coffee. You'll learn the skills you need to develop and refine the content of your documents. Here are some of the things you'll do:

- Move or copy text from one location in your document to another location or document.

- Find occurrences of specific text in your document.

- Replace existing text in your document with revised text.

- Use Word's Thesaurus to help you with word selection or replacement.

- Use Word's Grammar Checker to help you refine your grammar.

Review Questions

Fill in the blank with the correct word or phrase.

1   The steps for many word processing tasks can be summarized as "_____, then do."

2   You can select all the text in a document using the Select All option on the _____ menu.

3   The _____ method for moving text is appropriate only if you need to move a small section of text a short distance within a document.

4   When you click the _____ button, the selected text is removed from the document and placed on the Clipboard.

5   When you click the _____ button, the selected text is placed on the Clipboard, but is *not* removed from the document.

6   When you click the Paste button, a copy of the contents of the _____ is transferred into the document at the current insertion point location.

7   A list of all open Word documents appears at the bottom of the _____ menu.

8   In the list of open Word documents, the active document is indicated by a(n) _____.

9   When you click the _____ option on the Window menu, all open Word documents appear, each in its own window.

10 When more than one document appears in the Word window, the _____ document is the one with the highlighted title bar.

11 Word's _____ command conducts a search of your document for specific words, phrases, formatting, or special symbols.

review questions

12 Word's _____ command conducts a search of your document for specific words, phrases, formatting, or special symbols, and then substitutes replacement text for one or more occurrences of the search text.

13 Word's _____ contains a list of words and their synonyms and antonyms.

MULTIPLE CHOICE

Select the letter of the **one** *best answer.*

14 **Which of the following techniques can you use to select a word?**

   a Click the word.

   b Double-click the word.

   c Click in the left margin next to the word.

   d Double-click in the left margin next to the word.

15 **Which of the following techniques can you use to select a line?**

   a Click the line.

   b Double-click the line.

   c Click in the left margin next to the line.

   d Double-click in the left margin next to the line.

16 **Which of the following techniques can you use to select a paragraph?**

   a Click the paragraph.

   b Double-click the paragraph.

   c Click in the left margin next to the paragraph.

   d Double-click in the left margin next to the paragraph.

17 **When selecting a block of text using the keyboard, which key do you hold down as you press arrow keys?**

   a Ins key

   b Shift key

   c Ctrl key

   d Alt key

18 **How many Word documents can be open at one time?**

   a one

   b two

   c 255

   d as many as your computer's memory can handle

19 **How many Word documents can be active at a time?**

   a one

   b two

   c 255

   d as many as your computer's memory can handle

20 **To switch between open Word documents, you:**

   a click a button on the taskbar

   b select an option on the View menu

   c click a document in the File menu file list

   d click a document in the Window menu file list

21 **When more than one document is visible in the Word document window, the documents are said to be:**

   a stacked

   b tiled

   c heaped

   d arranged

22 **The easiest way to locate a good synonym for a particular word in your document is to use Word's:**

   a Thesaurus

   b Dictionary

   c Lexicon

   d Grammar Checker

23 **To search your document for syntax and style errors, you would use Word's:**

   a Thesaurus

   b Dictionary

   c Lexicon

   d Grammar Checker

24 **Which of the following is *not* one of the styles you can specify for the Grammar Checker?**

   a Casual

   b Business

   c Government

   d Custom

25 **When the business writing style is selected, which of the following will the Grammar Checker flag?**

   a jargon

   b contractions

   c subject-verb disagreements

   d all of the above

MATCHING

Select the letter from the right column that correctly matches each item in the left column.

26   ⌖

a Word feature that searches for occurrences of specified text

27   I

b selected text

28   **Find**

c insertion point shape during a drag and drop operation

29   **Thesaurus**

d move box pointer

30   ⫶

e Word feature that finds occurrences of specified text and lets you define substitution text

31   text

f typical pointer shape when the pointer is positioned in the Word window

32   **Grammar Checker**

g normal insertion point shape

33 |

h Word feature that checks text for syntax errors

34   ⬈

i normal text

35   **Replace**

j Word feature that offers synonyms

36   text

k pointer shape when the pointer is positioned in the left margin of a document

review questions

Use a separate sheet of paper to write out your answers to the following questions.

37 Selecting text is an important skill in Word. Describe an efficient technique for selecting each of the following:

- a word
- a block of text
- a line
- a paragraph
- the entire document

38 Describe two techniques for moving text within a document.

39 List the steps you would use to place a copy of some specific document text in another part of your document.

40 What is tiling and why would you use it? How do you tile all open documents? How do you switch between tiled documents?

Projects

These Projects are designed to help you review and develop the skills you learned in Tutorial 2. Complete each Project using Microsoft Word. *If you have not yet made the Project Disk for Tutorial 2, start the e-Course software, click Project Disk on the e-Course Welcome screen menu bar, and follow the instructions on the screen.*

If you've forgotten some of the skills you need to complete the Projects, refer to the Task Reference.

REVIEW SKILLS

1   The Price Is Right   File: Prices.doc

In the past, Novel-Tea & Coffee has sporadically mailed notices of various kinds to the customers on its mailing list. The manager of the Nashua, New Hampshire store has now decided to initiate a monthly newsletter to publicize book sales, limited offers, special events, and so on. The newsletter will also print short, informative articles about tea and coffee, various book genres, particular authors, and so on. All employees will be encouraged to contribute articles. Suppose that you're an employee at Novel-Tea & Coffee. Because you're learning to use Word, you've been asked to help edit the articles.

Your first assignment is to edit a document that lists the various beverages sold at the store, along with their prices. In the process, you'll review your text moving skills.

Open the Prices document from your Project Disk. Use cut and paste to put the list of 19 coffee flavors in alphabetical order. Scroll the document so you can see the list of seven tea varieties, then use drag and drop text to alphabetize the list of tea varieties. Save the document without changing the filename, and print the document.

2   Ah, Poetry   File: Reading.doc

Novel-Tea & Coffee stores regularly hold special events, such as poetry readings, at their store. The assistant manager of the Nashua, New Hampshire store has drafted a form letter to send to the invited poets to participate at the next reading. She has asked you to customize the letter for each of the individual recipients. In this Project, you'll review your text copying, pasting, and replacing skills.

Open the Reading document from your Project Disk. Read the document, noticing the place where the addressee's name and address must be inserted and the two places where you need to replace "{first name}" with the addressee's first name. Select the "[Name, address here]" paragraph, and then type the following three lines:

> **Ingrid Hanssen**
> **87 Heritage Road**
> **Grantham, NH 01863**

Select the first name only from the name and address you just typed, and then click the 📋 Copy button on the Standard toolbar. Select the first occurrence of "{first name}," and then click the 📋 Paste button on the Standard toolbar. Select the second occurrence of "{first name}," and then click the 📋 Paste button on the Standard toolbar. Print the letter.

Now begin to prepare the document for a second addressee by replacing the three name and address lines you previously inserted with the following:

> **Dwight Sobieski**
> **P.O. Box 130**
> **Ripton, NH 01877-0130**

Copy the first name from the text you just typed, and then replace the two occurrences of the first addressee's first name with the current addressee's first name by pasting. Print this second version of the letter, and then close the document without saving changes.

3   It's Berry Good!   File: JanDrink.doc

Some of the Novel-Tea & Coffee stores have decided to spotlight one particular drink each month—most often a rich concoction of coffee and other delicious ingredients. In this Project, you'll open the document describing January's featured drink and use Word's Find feature.

a   Open the JanDrink document from your Project Disk and read through this document. Click Edit on the menu bar, and then click Find. Make sure the Search box shows All, and that all check boxes are blank. Find every occurrence of the text string "berry" in the document. How many occurrences were found?

b   Did the Find command locate the capitalized word "Berry?" Did it locate the text "berry" in the word "blackberry?" Did it locate the word "berries?"

c   Find every occurrence of the text string "berr" in the document. How many occurrences were found? Is this number different than your answer for Question a? If so, why?

4   Nuts!   File: FebDrink.doc

Each month Novel-Tea & Coffee features a particular tea or coffee drink. You've been asked to edit the newsletter article announcing and describing February's featured drink. Unfortunately, the article writer mistakenly called the drink pecan café supreme rather than almond café supreme. In this Project, you'll review your skills with the Replace command, which you learned to use in the online Steps.

Open the FebDrink document from your Project Disk. Read the document, taking notice of every occurrence of the text strings "pecan" or "Pecan".

a   How often does the text string "pecan" appear?

b   How often does "Pecan" appear?

c   Click Edit on the menu bar, and then click Replace. Make sure that none of the five option boxes in the dialog box contains a check mark. What is the label on the first option box?

d   Find and replace all occurrences of "pecan" in the document with "almond". According to the Message box that appears, how many replacements were made?

e   Did the Replace operation replace both "pecan" and "Pecan"?

Save the document without changing the filename.

5   What's the Good Word?   File: Kudos.doc

Each month Novel-Tea & Coffee presents an Employee of the Month Customer Service Award to an outstanding employee in one of its stores. You've been asked to edit the newsletter article announcing the latest winner. In this Project, you'll review your skills with Word's Thesaurus, which you learned to use in the online Steps.

Open the Kudos document from your Project Disk. Locate and click the word "approachable" in the third paragraph, and then read the sentence containing that word. Click Tools on the menu bar, and then click Thesaurus. Look through the list of possible synonyms, scrolling to see the entire list. Click "accessible" in the list, and then click the Replace button.

Sometimes you can use the Thesaurus to find a synonym for a phrase. In that case, you need to select the entire phrase before using the Thesaurus. Locate and select the words "get there" in that same paragraph. Use the Thesaurus to find synonyms for the words "get there." Look through the suggestion list, click "arrive," and then click the Replace button.

The word "founding" in the next paragraph isn't the best word choice. Use the Thesaurus for "founding" and replace it with a word you think is more suitable.

Save the document without changing the filename, and then print the document.

APPLY SKILLS

6   Watch that Fat Intake   File: FatGrams.doc

You learned to use the Grammar Checker in the online Steps. In this Project, you'll review those skills as you check the grammar in an article written for the Novel-Tea & Coffee newsletter. You'll also learn a new way to set the writing style and spelling options, and you'll change the document itself during the grammar check.

Open the FatGrams document from your Project Disk. Click Tools on the menu bar, click Options to open the Options dialog box, and then click the Spelling & Grammar tab. Click Formal in the Writing Style list box, if necessary.

Make sure that the Show Readability Statistics check box is blank, and then click the OK button to close the dialog box.

Start the Grammar Checker. Ignore all suggestions (if any) until the Grammar Checker points out the passive voice in the second sentence ("…you may be asked about the calories…"). You'll change the sentence to eliminate the passive voice. To do this, click in the document to make it active, select the words "you may be asked", type "customers may ask you", and then click the Resume button in the dialog box to continue checking grammar.

Ignore all suggestions until the Grammar Checker points out the subject-verb agreement problem in the sentence containing "…a typical one-ounce chocolate bar contain…". The Grammar Checker's suggestion is suitable, so click the Change button to accept the suggested change.

Ignore all suggestions (if any) until the Grammar Checker flags the word "Hopefully" in the last sentence. The suggestion offered in the dialog box is inappropriate, so you'll make your own change. Select the word "Hopefully" in the document and then type "We hope". Then close the Grammar Checker.

Save the document without changing the filename, and print the document.

7   It's Too Delicious!   File: MarDrink.doc

The person who wrote the newsletter article announcing Novel-Tea & Coffee's featured drink for March is stuck on the word "delicious." In this Project, you'll use the Thesaurus to help you choose synonyms for "delicious."

Open the MarDrink document from your Project Disk. Read the document, taking notice of every occurrence of the word "delicious". Use the Thesaurus to choose a different synonym replacement for any occurrence of the word "delicious". (Hint: You can click any word in the list of synonyms, and then click the Look Up button to display additional synonyms.)

Repeat these replacements until only one occurrence of "delicious" remains in the document. Save the document without changing the filename, and then print it.

8   Drink Up   Files: Menu97.doc and Menu98.doc

In the online Steps, you learned how to view two document windows at the same time. In this Project, you'll compare the 1997 beverage menu to the 1998 beverage menu.

Open the Menu97 and Menu98 documents from your Project Disk. Arrange all the open documents. Scroll one or both documents as needed to answer Questions a through h.

a   What coffee flavors offered in 1997 do not appear in the 1998 menu?

b   What 1998 coffee styles did not appear on the 1997 menu?

c   Did the price of a medium espresso increase or decrease from 1997 to 1998? By how much?

d   What tea varieties offered in 1997 do not appear in the 1998 menu?

e   Did the prices change for any of the "other beverages" items from 1997 to 1998? If so, which items?

f   What new "other beverages" item is offered in 1998?

g   Describe the appearance of the Menu98 document window title bar when the Menu97 document is active.

h   While the Menu98 document is active, can you close the Menu97 document? Why or why not?

9   Let's Be Selective   File: Coffee.doc

In the online Steps, you learned to select a word by double-clicking it, to select a block of text by dragging over the text, and to select a line or a paragraph by moving the pointer into the left margin of the document and then clicking or double-clicking, respectively. You also learned to select a block of text by holding down the Shift key while using the arrow keys, and to select the entire document using the Select All command on the Edit menu.

In this Project, you'll review those skills and also learn some additional selection techniques as you work on a newsletter article about what makes a great cup of coffee.

Open the Coffee document from your Project Disk. Remember to deselect any selected text as you start each question.

a   Select the first line in the body of the article. Move the pointer into the left margin next to the second line in the article, and then hold down the mouse button as you move the pointer straight down until it is next to the fourth line. What text units are selected?

b   Select the second paragraph in the body of the article. Move the insertion point into the third paragraph, and then triple-click the mouse button. (Triple-clicking is like double-clicking, except you click the left mouse button three times.) What text unit is selected?

c   You've selected text using a click-and-drag technique, in which you click and hold down the mouse button as you drag the mouse. Now you'll try a double-click-and-drag technique. First practice double-clicking a word without releasing the mouse button after the second click. That is, do not complete the second click but instead continue to hold the mouse button down. What shape is the pointer immediately after you simply double-click a word? What shape is the pointer if you continue to hold the mouse pointer down after the second click of a double-click?

d   Using a double-click-and-drag technique, double-click the word "wondering," hold down the mouse button, drag the mouse to the right until the pointer is positioned over the word "quality," and then release the mouse button. What happened as you dragged the mouse to the right? What text units are selected?

e   Move the pointer into the left margin next to the first paragraph in the article, and then double-click-and-drag as you move the pointer straight down until it is next to the third paragraph. What text units are selected?

f   Move the pointer into the left margin next to the second paragraph in the article, and then triple-click. What text is selected?

g Press and hold down the Ctrl key as you click in any sentence. What text unit is now selected?

h Click anywhere in the document, and then press and hold down the Shift key as you click anywhere else in the document. What text is now selected?

10 Long Live the King
Files: KingBook.doc and KingName.doc

Some Novel-Tea & Coffee customers are so eager to read books by their favorite author that they want to know the moment his or her latest book is available. As a service to its customers, the Nashua, New Hampshire Novel-Tea & Coffee store maintains mailing lists for every requested book or author. Suppose that the latest Stephen King novel is now available, and you've been asked to send a notification to each person on the King mailing list. In this Project, you'll open two documents and copy text from one document to another.

Open the KingBook and KingName documents from your Project Disk and arrange all the open documents.

Select and copy the first three-line name/address set from the KingName document, and then paste it in the KingBook document to replace the second of the three empty paragraphs between the date and the salutation. Print the KingBook document.

Select and copy the second three-line name/address set from the KingName document, and then paste it in the KingBook document to replace the previous name/address set. Print this version of the KingBook document.

BUILD SKILLS

11 Additional Find Options   File: JanDrink.doc

In the online Steps, you used Word's Find command to locate simple text strings. In this Project, you'll learn how to use several options in the Find dialog box: Match Case, Find Whole Words Only, Sounds Like, and Find All Word Forms.

Open the JanDrink document from your Project Disk. Click Edit on the menu bar, and then click Find. Make sure the Search box shows All, and that all check boxes are blank.

a Find every occurrence of the text string "berry" in the document. What occurrences were found?

b Repeat the Find operation, but this time make sure the Match Case check box contains a check mark and all other check boxes are blank. What occurrences were found?

c Repeat the Find operation, but this time make sure the Match Case and the Find Whole Words Only check boxes both contain a check mark and all other check boxes are blank. What occurrences were found?

d Repeat the Find operation, but this time make sure the Find Whole Words Only check box contains a check mark and all other check boxes are blank. What occurrences were found?

e Repeat the Find operation, but this time make sure the Find All Word Forms check box contains a check mark and all other check boxes are blank. What occurrences were found?

f Move the insertion point to the end of the document, and type "Barry, bury, barely, bary, beery, bore". Then Repeat the Find operation, but this time make sure the Sounds Like check box contains a check mark and all other check boxes are blank. What occurrences were found?

12 Advanced Find Features   File: Menu98.doc

Suppose you have a lengthy Word document in which you need to quickly find all italicized words. Or perhaps you want to locate all the digits in the document, or all occurrences of some particular special character, such as a tab. In this Project, you'll learn how to use the advanced features of the Find command.

Open the Menu98 document from your Project Disk. Click Edit on the menu bar, and then click Find. Make sure the Search box shows All, and that all check boxes are blank.

a Find all occurrences of the text string "ar" in the document. Do not close the Find dialog box when you are through. How many occurrences of "ar" were found?

b Next you'll change the search so that only occurrences of "ar" that are bolded will be located. (Bold is a format characteristic associated with font.) Click the More button. In the Find dialog box, notice that the area immediately beneath the Find What box is currently blank. Click the Format button, and then click Font in the list that appears to open the Find Font dialog box. Click Bold in the Font Style list box, and then click the OK button to close the Find Font dialog box. What now appears in the area immediately beneath the Find What box?

c Repeatedly press the Find Next button to find all occurrences of the bolded text string "ar" in the document. How many occurrences were found? When you've found all occurrences, click the No Formatting button to clear the Bold Format specification.

d To learn about the Use wildcards option, you'll use the Help button in the Find dialog box. Click the [?] Help button on the Find dialog box title bar, and then click Use wildcards. Read the displayed information, click the [»] button at the end of the information box to display an additional information window, and then read the additional information. If you wanted to find "late", "latte", "lattte", and so on, what text string should you type in the Find What text box?

e Close the information window and type your answer to Question d in the Find What text box. Make sure the Use wildcards check box contains a check mark and that all other check boxes are blank; then find all occurrences of your search criterion. Which words were found?

13 Replace Options   File: GoodTea.doc

The author of a tea brewing article written for the Novel-Tea & Coffee company newsletter mistakenly used the word "make" rather than "brew" throughout the article. In this Project, you'll edit that article, using one of the options in the Replace dialog box.

Open the GoodTea document from your Project Disk. Read through the article, taking special notice of instances where the word "make" or one of its word forms should be replaced by a word form of the word "brew."

a What other forms of the word "make" does the article contain?

b Are any of the forms of the word "make" capitalized?

c Are any of the forms of the word "make" used in a hyphenated phrase?

d Is there any occurrence of the word "make" or one of its forms that should not be replaced?

e Click Edit on the menu bar, and then click Replace. Make sure the Search box shows All, and that all check boxes are blank. Drag the Replace dialog box to the lower-right corner of the document window so that you can see as much of the document as possible. Type "make" in the Find What box, and then type "brew" in the Replace With box. Click the Find All Word Forms option so that a check mark appears in that check box. Are any of the options in the Replace dialog box now grayed out and thus unavailable? If so, which options?

Drag the Replace dialog box to the lower-right corner of the document window so that you can see as much of the document as possible. Click the Find Next button

projects

to locate an occurrence of a form of the word "make." Read the text around that highlighted occurrence to determine if the word should be replaced by a form of the word "brew." If so, click the Replace button; if not, click the Find Next button. Repeat this procedure until the entire document has been checked. Print the document.

On your printed document, underline every occurrence of a form of the words "make" or "brew."

14 More Replace Options   File: Flyer.doc

Suppose you have a lengthy Word document and that you need to quickly replace occurrences of some character string, but you want to replace only the occurrences that are bolded, or italicized, or otherwise formatted in some specific manner. Or perhaps you want to apply a formatting characteristic to all occurrences of some specific word.

In this Project, you'll edit a flyer announcing a workshop to be held at the Nashua Novel-Tea & Coffee store. In the process, you'll learn how to use the formatting specifications for the Replace command.

Open the Flyer document from your Project Disk, and read the flyer. Click each of the four occurrences of the word "healing" and note if the word is bolded, italicized, both, or neither. (Hint: Look at the Bold and the Italic buttons on the Standard toolbar; if the button appears pushed in, then that characteristic applies.)

a For each of the four occurrences of the word "healing," is the word bolded, italicized, both, or neither?

b Suppose you decide to replace the one occurrence of the word "healing" that is both bolded and italicized with another bold, but not italic word. Although you could easily do that directly, you'll use a feature of the Replace command to specify the format for the word to be replaced, and to specify the format for the replacement. Click Edit on the menu bar, and then click Replace. Make sure the Search box shows All and that all check boxes are blank. Type "healing" in the Find What box. Click the Format button, and then click Font in the list that appears to open the Find Font dialog box. Click Bold Italic in the Font Style list box, and then click the OK button to close the Find Font dialog box. What now appears in the area immediately beneath the Find What box?

c Type "Mind-Body" in the Replace With box. Repeat what you did in Question b above to specify the same format for the replacement text. Use the technique you learned in Question b to specify a bold (but not italic) format for the replacement text.

d Click the Replace All button. According to the message box that appears, how many replacements were made?

Save the document without changing the filename, and then print it.

15 Advanced Thesaurus Features   File: Workshop.doc

In the online Steps (and perhaps in Project 5), you used Word's Thesaurus to replace a word with one of its synonyms. In all cases, you found an acceptable synonym in the initial list of suggestions. In this Project, you'll learn what to do when none of the words in the initial suggestion list is suitable.

Open the Workshop document from your Project Disk.

Use the Thesaurus for the word "picture" in the second paragraph of the letter body.

Suppose you don't see a suitable synonym in the suggestion list in the middle of the Thesaurus dialog box. You should then check the list box labeled "Meanings" in the lower-left section of the dialog box. That Meanings list includes various senses for the word displayed in the Looked Up box. In this case, the Thesaurus recognizes four noun senses and one verb sense for the word "picture." The suggestion list currently displayed relates to the highlighted sense in the Meanings list. Perhaps the synonym you need relates to a different sense of the word.

Click each of the other words in the Meanings list, and look at the suggestion list for each. Then click "representation (noun)", which is the most appropriate of the senses in this case. Click "photograph" in the suggestion list, and then click the Look Up button. The new word, "photograph", is now listed in the Looked Up box, the senses listed in the Meanings list are two senses of the word "photograph", and the suggestion list now displays synonyms of the highlighted sense of that word.

In general, you would repeat these steps until you find a synonym you like in the suggestion list. In this case, however, the current suggestion list does contain a suitable synonym—"glossy". Click "glossy" in the suggestion list, and then click the Replace button.

Now you'll try the process for another word.

Locate the word "piece" in the fourth paragraph of the letter body, and then read that entire paragraph to get a clear understanding of the sense of the needed synonym. Then use the Thesaurus for the word "piece", continuing to refine meanings and select the best alternative until you find the word "feature" in the suggestion list. Then click "feature" and click the Replace button.

Print the revised version of the document.

projects

16 Outlining

In the online Steps in Tutorial 1, you were introduced to outline view—one of three options for viewing a document. In this Project, you'll work in outline view to begin to create an outline for an article you plan to write about coffee.

To create an outline:

1: Start Word, and then click the ▤ **Outline View** button in the lower-left corner of the Word window. Notice that a special Outline toolbar replaces the horizontal Ruler in outline view. A ▭ minus sign appears in the workspace, marking the location for the first outline item. The *Style* list box on the Standard toolbar shows "Heading 1," which is the style that corresponds to the highest outline level.

2: Type **Introduction**, and press the **Enter** key. Type **The History of Coffee**, and then press the **Enter** key again. You've now entered two items at the highest outline level.

Next you want to add four outline items subordinate to the "The History of Coffee" heading. If you started typing the first of those items now, it would appear at that same outline level as the two items you've already entered. Since this item will be subordinate, you need to first demote the current (third) line by one level.

3: Click the ➡ **Demote** button on the Outline toolbar.

Three things happened when you clicked the Demote Button. First, the ▭ in front of the second line changed to a ✛, which indicates a heading that has subordinate items. Second, the current (third) line is now indented to help visually indicate its subordinate status. Third, the style for the current line is changed to "Heading 2," which is the style associated with the second highest outline level. Now you can enter the four subordinate items.

4: Type **Trade** and then press the **Enter** key. Then add an outline entry at the current (second highest) outline level for each of the three remaining items—**Coffee Houses**, **Customs and Rituals** and **Facts and Myths**, pressing the **Enter** key after typing each item.

The next item you want to add to the outline should appear at the highest outline level. Before you add that item, you need to promote the current line so that it corresponds to the highest outline level.

5: Click the ⬅ **Promote** button on the Outline toolbar.

6: Type **Cultivation**, and then press the **Enter** key.

7: Using the techniques you used in Steps 3 and 4 above, enter these three outline items subordinate to the "Cultivation" heading:

- The Coffee Tree
- Coffee Classifications
- Coffees by Country

8: Save the document as **OutlineA** on your Project Disk.

9: Print the document.

17 More Outlining   File: OutlineB.doc

Suppose you're writing a report about coffee, and that you've created an initial outline and have typed some of the report body text. In this Project, you'll work in outline view to revise your outline.

Begin by opening the OutlineB document from your Project Disk, and then switch to normal view, if necessary. Scan the document; click on the various headings and note the style displayed in the Style list box on the Standard toolbar. Then switch to outline view.

Did you notice that the first heading, "Introduction," is at the wrong level? It's currently a second-level item, but should be a first-level item.

To revise an existing outline:

1: Click in the margin to the left of the word "Introduction" to select that item, and then click the [←] **Promote** button on the Outline toolbar.

Suppose you now decide that the entire "Cultivation" section should precede, rather than follow, the "Preparation" section. So you'll move that section.

2: Scroll the document so that the entire "Cultivation" section is visible, and then click in the margin left of the word "Cultivation" to select that item.

You want to move the entire "Cultivation" section, not just the single "Cultivation" item.

3: Double-click in the margin to the left of the word "Cultivation" to select that item and all its subordinate items.

4: Click the [↑] **Move Up** button on the Outline toolbar. The entire highlighted section moves up one position in the outline.

5: Click the [↑] **Move Up** button on the Outline toolbar a total of ten more times, so that the highlighted section follows the "Facts and Myths" item. Then click anywhere

projects

outside the highlighted text to remove the highlighting. The "Cultivation" and "Preparation" sections have now changed places.

6: Save the document without changing the filename.

7: Print the document.

18 Readability Statistics   File: Workshop.doc

Suppose someone criticized the articles you wrote or edited for the Novel-Tea & Coffee newsletter, saying they were too difficult for most people to understand. Would you have any defense to that charge? Is there any standardized way to measure the readability of written text?

Linguists have developed several readability statistics for evaluating written material to measure how easy it is to read and understand. Word's Grammar Checker can calculate and display several of those readability statistics, along with other useful information related to readability. In this Project, you'll use the Grammar Checker and display the readability statistics.

1: Open the **Workshop** document from your Project Disk. Click **Tools** on the menu bar, click **Options** to open the Options dialog box, and then click the **Grammar** tab.

2: Click **For Business Writing** in the list box, if necessary. Make sure that the *Show Readability Statistics* check box contains a check mark, and that the *Check Spelling* check box is blank, and then click the **OK** button to close the dialog box.

3: Select the indented paragraph (which begins "Robert Haskins…"), click **Tools** on the menu bar, and then click **Grammar**.

4: For each suggestion the Grammar Checker makes, click the **Ignore** button.

5: Click the **No** button when asked if you want to check the remainder of the document.

When the Grammar Check is complete, the Readability Statistics box is displayed. Fill in the blanks in the following table with the corresponding values displayed in that Readability Statistics box.

Counts:

   Words   _____

   Characters   _____

   Paragraphs   _____

   Sentences   _____

Averages:

Sentences per Paragraph	_____
Words per Sentence	_____
Characters per Word	_____
Readability:	
Passive Sentences	_____
Flesch Reading Ease	_____
Flisch-Kincaid Grade Level	_____

6: Click the **OK** button to close the *Readability Statistics* box.

7: Close the document without saving changes.

19 Using the Grammar Checker to Check Three Styles
File: Desserts.doc

In the online Steps, you learned that you can set the Grammar Checker to check your document using either a business, a casual, or a custom writing style. The specific grammar rules that Word uses to check for the business and casual styles are pre-selected; neither style checks all possible grammar rules. You select the grammar rules to be checked when you define a custom writing style. A fourth choice lets you check a document using *all* the grammar rules. In this Project, you'll check a business letter three times—first applying all rules, then using the business writing style, and then using the casual writing style.

On a sheet of paper, set up a table with two columns. Label the first column "Formal" and the second column "Casual".

Open the Desserts document from your Project Disk. Click Tools, click Options, and then click the Spelling & Grammar tab. You'll use a custom style first, so select a custom writing style option, click the Settings button, then make sure that every style and grammar option contains a check mark. Then close both open dialog boxes. Now check the grammar for the entire Desserts document. Click the Ignore button for every suggestion so that you don't change the document. Each time the Grammar Checker identifies a new problem type, label a new row in your table with a short description of the problem or the rule being applied.

Use the Options command on the Tools menu to select the Formal option. Click the Recheck Document button and then click the Yes button. Then check the grammar for the entire document again. Click the Ignore button for every suggestion. When the Grammar Checker identifies a problem, locate the

corresponding row in your table and place a check mark in the first column to indicate that the problem was checked when using that style.

Repeat the preceding paragraph using the casual option, placing a check mark in the "Casual" column to indicate that the problem was checked when using that style.

20 Splitting the Document Windows   File: Events.doc

Throughout the year, the Nashua Novel-Tea & Coffee store holds various events: poetry readings, book signings, workshops, and so on. In addition, book displays are periodically changed to promote sales of books related to the particular time of year. Suppose you've kept track of all the events and book displays for the current calendar year in a document you've named Events.

One day as you are updating the Events document, your boss mentions that the winter season seems to have many more events and book displays than the summer season, and that perhaps more events and book displays geared to children and teenagers should be presented during the summer. You decide to check the Events document to see if it's true that fewer events and book displays are held in summer.

Open the Events document from your Project Disk and scroll through the document to familiarize yourself with it.

To count the events and book displays for the winter months, you need to view the document for the months of January through March, plus December. The document is too long to view January and December simultaneously at the current magnification. If you decrease the Zoom Control percentage, the entire document could appear on the screen, but the print would be too small to read. The solution is to "split" the document window so that you can view two parts of the document simultaneously.

To split the document window:

1: Click **Window** on the menu bar, and then click **Split**. A horizontal bar that moves when you move the mouse appears in the document window. Move the bar so that it's a little less than halfway down the screen, and then click to set the position of the split bar.

2: Scroll the upper window so that the month of December is visible.

3: Scroll the lower window so that the months of January through March are visible.

   a How many different events or book displays occurred during the winter (December 22 through March 21)?

4: Scroll the lower window so that the months of June through September are visible.

b How many different events or book displays occurred during the summer (June 22 through September 23)?

5: To remove the split, click **Window** on the menu bar, and then click **Remove Split**.

21 Sidewalk Book Sale

The Nashua Novel-Tea & Coffee store plans to have a sidewalk book sale the week of May 18, 1998. To lure customers to the sale, the store will offer free samples of the month's featured coffee: cinnamon cappuccino. Your boss has asked you to design a half-page newspaper ad to promote the event.

Look through a newspaper and find three examples of store sale ads you think are effective and eye-catching. Using the best features from those ads as your inspiration, decide on a theme for the sidewalk sale, and then sketch a design for the Novel-Tea & Coffee sale ad. Create the text of the ad using Word. Be sure to include all the necessary information (what, when, where, why) in the ad. (You may invent a street address or location for the Novel-Tea & Coffee store.)

22 Going Shopping

Did you know that all kinds of stores advertise on the Web? Suppose you decided you wanted to buy two things: a book and some gourmet coffee. For this Project, you'll search the Web looking for sources from which you could purchase books or coffee.

Find at least three sites that sell books, and three sites that sell coffee. Select a specific book available from all three of your book sites, and determine the total price (cost plus tax and shipping) from each site. Then select some standard amount of a particular gourmet coffee available from all three of your coffee sites, and determine the total price for each site. Which showed more variability in price, the book or the coffee? Why do you think these variations occurred? Write a report of your findings. Be sure to include the URLs of the sites you found in your report. Your instructor will specify the length and other format requirements for the report.

23 My Word Processor Is Better Than Yours

What makes one word processor better than another? Ease of use? Number and quality of special features? Speed? A friendly user interface? The ability to interact with other software?

projects

Prepare a list of six to eight specific questions you'd ask someone who has used more than one word processor in order to determine which word processor he or she prefers and why. Then find a person who uses, or within the last two years has used, at least two different word processors and who is willing to take a few minutes to answer your questions. (Hint: If you have trouble finding such a person, try the instructors or other staff at your school or your place of business.)

After the interview, write up your findings as if you were writing a magazine article. Your article might be in the format of an interview; or, you might choose to write a narrative in which you summarize and paraphrase the interviewee. Your instructor will specify the length and format requirements of the magazine article.

24 Readability

An optional output from Word's Grammar Checker is a display of readability statistics, which you can use to evaluate whether or not a reader can easily read and understand your document.

Using the Word Help facility and the resources in your library and/or on the Internet, research the four readability measures that Word uses:

- Flesch Reading Ease
- Flesch-Kincaid Grade Level

After you've completed your research, write up your findings as if you were writing an article for a newsletter. Your instructor will specify the length and format of the article.

25 Fog Index

Word's Grammar Checker can calculate and display four readability statistics. The Fog Index is another often-used gauge for evaluating how easy written material is to read and comprehend. Using the resources in your library and/or on the Internet, learn about the Fog Index and how it is calculated. Then calculate the Fog Index for this paragraph.

Summarize your findings. Include the details of the Fog Index calculation you performed, and give the Fog Index evaluation as well as your own personal evaluation of the readability of the above paragraph.

Microsoft Word

Tutorial 3: Format Document Text and Tables

Tutorial 3

Format Document Text and Tables

Bring Your Work Home

What do you see when you picture yourself in your ideal job? Do you see yourself sitting at a large desk in an office in a skyscraper? Do you own a large wardrobe of suits and other expensive business attire? Are you working long hours at the office and then commuting home? This might have been your vision a few years ago—but not today! More and more people are working at home, and as you'll learn in this tutorial, a new trend is developing for home-based businesses—entrepreneurs who work at home, wear sweats while working, and don't commute.

Projects

In the Tutorial 3 Projects, you'll expand your knowledge and skills as you format a wide variety of documents. Specifically, you'll create bulleted lists with a custom bullet character; create numbered lists with alternative numbering schemes; add borders to text; insert, resize, and position clip art; prevent printing widows and orphans; layer text and graphics; and learn much more about working with tables, including selecting and adding rows and columns, centering, formatting, sorting, using AutoFit, and calculating.

If you're not assigned Projects 11, 12, 13, 16, 17 or 18, and 19, you might want to read these Projects or, better yet, work through them. Project 11 deals with borders. In Projects 12 and 16, you'll insert Microsoft clip-art pictures into your document. Projects 13 and 17 through 19 all deal with tables. You'll learn to format table text, change row height, center a table, and use AutoFit for adjusting the width of columns in Project 13. In Project 17, you'll add columns to a table and use Word's automatic calculation feature to calculate values for table cells. Project 18 is similar to Project 17, but deals with rows rather than columns. Sorting tables is introduced in Project 19.

Bring Your Work Home

More than 13 million people are doing it. Twenty-five million, if you count the part-timers. And most are successful—85 percent! What *are* these people doing? They are giving up the corporate world, long commutes to and from offices and factories, aggravating traffic, bad lunches, and the infamous boss's rule. They are managing their own businesses from their homes.

Types of home-based businesses range from consulting and human services to programming, accounting, sales, repairs, and the arts. Any skill or talent can become the basis for a new venture. Then, along with a little imagination and a lot of hard work, a home-based business can be very successful!

Why work from home? Working from your home offers flexibility, freedom, and control over your salary, hours, and work setting. You can also choose where, when, and with whom you work. The dream of becoming your own boss, coupled with the today's corporate downsizing, makes starting a home-based business a very attractive option.

Today, with technology linking computers, fax machines, and phones, isolation is a thing of the past. In fact, technology that includes telecommunications and the personal computer is the cornerstone for most home-based businesses. Inexpensive software can greatly assist with accounting, marketing, and scheduling. And many significant costs once associated with a small business are now greatly reduced—thanks to technology. For example, home-based business owners can now produce documents, brochures, and letters that were once only available as custom printing. Gone are the days when having your own business and working from home was a dream—today it's a reality for millions.

In this tutorial, you'll work with documents created by several home-based business owners and documents that describe home-based business trends. You'll learn the skills you need to format the text and paragraphs of your documents. Here are some of the things you'll do:

- Change font type and size
- Use bold, italics, and underlining
- Indent and align paragraphs
- Format bulleted and numbered lists
- Change paragraph line spacing
- Apply styles and templates
- Set tabs
- Format tables

Review Questions

Fill in the blank with the correct word or phrase.

1   A(n) _____ is any letter, digit, or special symbol.

2   A(n) _____ is a set of characters that has a certain design and shape.

3   The height of a font is measured in _____, of which there are 72 to an inch.

4   A(n) _____ is any unit of text that ends with a ¶.

5   To specify some paragraph formatting options, such as hanging indents or right indentation, you must use the Paragraph option on the _____ menu.

6   Paragraph _____ refers to how the lines of text are positioned horizontally between the left and right margins.

7   A(n) _____ is a small symbol used to add emphasis to a list item.

8   A(n) _____ is a set of formatting specifications, each of which has a name.

9   When you _____ a style, Word automatically updates all document text to which you have applied that style.

10   A(n) _____ is a set of predefined styles.

11   A(n) _____ adds space between the text and left margin, or between the text in one column and the text in another column.

12   A(n) _____ is an arrangement of information in horizontal rows and vertical columns.

13   In a table, the intersection of a row and column is called a(n) _____.

14   To move the insertion point to the next cell in a table, you press the _____ key.

MULTIPLE CHOICE

*Select the letter of the **one** best answer.*

---

15 All of the following are classifications of Word's formatting commands, *except*:

  a document-level   **c** character-level

  b page-level   **d** paragraph-level

---

16 Character-level formatting options include all of the following, *except*:

  a font style   **c** indentation

  b size   **d** color

---

17 To emphasize thoughts, ideas, words, or phrases, you can use any of the following, *except*:

  a accenting   **c** italicizing

  b bolding   **d** underlining

---

18 Word's Formatting toolbar includes style buttons for all of the following character-level formatting options, *except*:

  a underline   **c** bold

  b color   **d** italic

---

19 Paragraph-level formatting options include all of the following, *except*:

  a indentation   **c** margins

  b alignment   **d** line spacing

---

20 All of the following are paragraph indentation choices, *except*:

  a first-line indent   **c** hanging indent

  b last-line indent   **d** right indent

---

21 If the first line of a paragraph extends further left than the other lines in the paragraph, that paragraph is likely formatted with a:

  a first-line indent

  b last-line indent

  c hanging indent

  d left indent

22 If all lines after the first line in a paragraph extend further left than the first line, that paragraph is likely formatted with a:

a first-line indent

b right indent

c hanging indent

d left indent

23 Which of the following techniques will *not* work for indenting only the first line of a paragraph?

a dragging the first-line indent marker on the Ruler

b pressing the Tab key at the beginning of the paragraph

c clicking the [icon] Increase Indent button

d setting a First Line indentation value in the Paragraph dialog box

24 Which of the following techniques will *not* work for left-indenting an entire paragraph?

a dragging the small box at the left end of the Ruler

b pressing the Tab key at the beginning of the paragraph

c clicking the [icon] Increase Indent button

d setting a Left Indentation value in the Paragraph dialog box

25 Which of the following is *not* a paragraph alignment option?

a left-aligned

b right-aligned

c justified

d proportional

26 Every new Word document opens with which template?

a Standard

b Normal

c Letter

d Manual

27 Word's default tab settings:

a are located every quarter inch

b are located every half inch

c are located every inch

d depend upon the template

review questions

MATCHING

Select the letter from the right column that correctly matches each item in the left column.

28		**a** Align Left button
29		**b** Center button
30		**c** Left Tab alignment selector
31		**d** Insert Table button
32		**e** Justify button
33		**f** Numbering button
34		**g** Decimal Tab alignment selector
35		**h** Center Tab alignment selector
36		**i** Increase Indent button
37		**j** Decrease Indent button
38		**k** Bullets button
39		**l** Align Right button

review questions

Use a separate sheet of paper to write out your answers to the following questions.

40 Describe the four types of paragraph alignment in Word and explain how you can set or change a paragraph's alignment.

41 Explain how you can apply a style to a paragraph, and how you can redefine a paragraph style by example.

42 Describe specifically how you would set a left-aligned tab stop at the 2" mark and a centered tab stop at the 3.5" mark. How would you then delete the tab stop at the 2" mark?

43 Explain the process to create a table. How do you select a table?

Projects

These Projects are designed to help you review and develop the skills you learned in Tutorial 3. Complete each Project using Microsoft Word. *If you have not yet made the Project Disks for Tutorial 3, start the e-Course software, click Project Disk on the e-Course Welcome screen menu bar, and follow the instructions on the screen.*

If you've forgotten some of the skills you need to complete the Projects, refer to the Task Reference.

REVIEW SKILLS

1 Books and Bindings   File: Bindery.doc

In the online Steps, you learned how to apply simple character formatting. In this Project, you'll review those skills.

Suppose you've been asked to put the finishing touches on a letter written by the owner of a home-based book bindery business. Open the Bindery document from your Project Disk. Locate and italicize the following magazine and book titles: *Saturday Evening Post* (occurs twice), *The Golden Bough*, and *Complete Poems 1913-1962*.

Text to be emphasized, such as a company name, is often bolded and set in a different font. Change the font style for "Oxbridge Books and Bindings," located near the top of the letter, to bold, and change the font type to Lucida Blackletter. (If Lucida Blackletter isn't available, use Arial.)

Print the document and then close it without saving changes.

2 May I Quote You?   File: Freedom.doc

In the online Steps, you learned how to align paragraphs and how to use indentation and font type to emphasize certain paragraphs of text. In this Project, you'll review those skills.

Open the Freedom document from your Project Disk. Locate the paragraph that begins "Freedom of expression…", and then select that paragraph and the paragraph that follows it. Use the ⊞ Increase Indent button on the Formatting toolbar to indent the selected paragraphs to the 0.5" mark on the Ruler. Then right-indent the selected paragraphs by dragging the right-indent marker on the Ruler to the 5.25" mark.

projects

With those same two paragraphs still selected, change the font type to 11-point Arial.

Select the paragraph that begins "Freedom of expression…", and then change the paragraph alignment to Justified. Then select the next paragraph ("Concurring Opinion…") and change its alignment to Right.

Print the document and then close it without saving changes.

3   Dining in Style   File: Catering.doc

In the online Steps, you learned how to apply styles to a paragraph. In this Project, you'll review those skills.

Open the Catering document from your Project Disk. The Newsletter template is already attached to this document. Apply the style Title 1 to the "Sampling of Offerings" paragraph and the "Winter 1998" paragraph.

Apply the style Heading 1 to the following paragraphs: Appetizers, Specialty Breads, Soups, Salads, Entrees, Vegetables, Side Dishes, and Desserts. Then apply the style Heading 2 to the following paragraphs: Hot, Cold, Beef and Lamb, Chicken, and Fish and Seafood.

Delete all blank paragraphs following any paragraph with the Header 1 or Header 2 style.

Print the document and then close it without saving changes.

4   Endangered Species   File: Plover.doc

In the online Steps, you learned how to attach a template to an existing document and then manually apply styles. In this Project, you'll review those skills.

Open the Plover document from your Project Disk. This document is already formatted using styles from the Normal template. Attach the template Elegant Report to the document. Change the font size to 18 for the title "The Status of the Mountain Plover" located on page 1 of the document. On page 2 of the document, change the font size to 16 for that same title.

View the header, and then apply the style Header Base to both paragraphs in the header (labeled "Header - Section 2"). Click the [icon] Switch Between Header and Footer button on the Header and Footer toolbar to switch to the footer (labeled "Footer - Section 2"), and then delete the tab character in the footer so that the page number is centered.

Print the document and then close it without saving changes.

projects

5 Classy Glassy Letterhead　　　　　File: Glass.doc

In the online Steps, you learned how to use and set tabs to add space between text. In this Project, you'll review those skills.

Open the Glass document from your Project Disk. This letter was written by Mary Ann McCord, who is turning her hobby into a business. Suppose Mary Ann asks you to help her create a professional-looking letterhead. She's already done most of the work, but she needs your help in creating an information line.

Move the insertion point between the two blanks and the paragraph mark in the paragraph immediately below the horizontal line. Type the following four items in a single line, inserting a tab between each item:

Mary Ann McCord
835 Regent Road
Strathmore AB R8A 2S5
(403) 338-1005

With the insertion point still located in the line you just typed, set left-aligned tab stops at 1.75", 3.25", and 5".

Print the document and then close it without saving changes.

APPLY SKILLS

6 Ay, There's the Rub　　　　　File: Massage.doc

In the online Steps, you learned how to attach a template to an existing document, and how to redefine a style by example. You'll use both skills in this Project, as well as learn how to specify a nonstandard font size and how to indent using the Paragraph dialog box.

Open the Massage document from your Project Disk. This document is already formatted using styles from the Normal template. Attach the template Professional Report to the document. (If that template is not available on your computer, you cannot complete this Project.)

Select the first paragraph in the document, which currently has the Title style applied, and apply the style Title Cover.

Next you'll change the font size to 37, which is a nonstandard size that is not one of the choices in the Font Size list. Highlight the current value in the Font Size list box, type "37", and then press the Enter key.

Select the "Executive Summary" paragraph, which has the Heading 1 style, and change the font size to 16. Then redefine the Heading 1 style by example.

projects

Select the first paragraph following "Table of Contents." This paragraph ("The Business Venture…") has the TOC 1 style. Click Format on the menu bar, and then click Paragraph to open the Paragraph dialog box. Change the value in the Left box in the Indentation section to 0.75", and then click the OK button. Move the tab stop marker to the 5.25" mark on the Ruler. Then redefine the TOC 1 style by example.

Print the document and then close it without saving changes.

7   Say It With Flowers   File: Oliver.doc

Suppose you've been asked to help format an invoice for a home-based flower business. In this Project you'll define right-aligned and decimal-aligned tab stops, set a tab with a leader, and add today's date to the document.

Open the Oliver document from your Project Disk. Select all the text from the beginning of the line containing the words "Item" and "Cost" to the end of the document.

Set a right-aligned tab stop at 3" in the usual manner. With the text still selected, you'll now set a decimal-aligned tab stop with a dotted line leader using the Tabs dialog box.

To insert a tab stop with a leader:

1: Click **Format** on the menu bar, and then click **Tabs** to open the Tabs dialog box. The current 3" tab stop position is highlighted.

2: Type **4.5** to define a new tab position at the 4.5" mark, click **Decimal** in the Alignment section to specify a decimal alignment, and then click **2** in the Leader section to select a dotted line leader.

3: Click the **Set** button to set the new tab stop, and then click the **OK** button to close the Tabs dialog box.

Next you'll add today's date to the document.

To insert today's date:

1: Position the insertion point immediately left of the paragraph mark beneath the word "INVOICE."

2: Click **Insert** on the menu bar, and then click **Date and Time** to open the Date and Time dialog box.

3: Click the third option in the list, which displays the date in a "monthname day, year" format, and then click the **OK** button to close the dialog box.

Save the document as Flowers by Oliver on your Project Disk, and then print the document.

8 A Table for Pets   File: Pets.doc

Suppose you've been asked to help complete a letter for a home-based pet photography business. In this Project, you'll create a table, enter text in the table, and then use AutoFormat and center the table.

Open the Pets document from your Project Disk. Move the insertion point into the blank paragraph immediately above the paragraph that begins "I have also enclosed…", and then create a table with three columns and four rows.

Enter table text as shown here:

Category	Title	ID
Black & White Single	Dublin's Sweet Princess	PMF-1
Color Family Group	The Aaron Family	PMF-2
Color Action	Pete and Frisbee	PMF-3

Apply the List 8 AutoFormat to the entire table. As you do this make sure that only the Heading Rows option in the Apply Special Formats To section of the Table AutoFormat dialog box contains a check mark and that all the options in the Formats to Apply section *except* the Color option contain check marks.

To center the table, select the entire table (if necessary), click Table on the menu bar, click Cell Height and Width, and then click the Center option button in the Alignment section of the Row tab.

Print the document and then close it without saving changes.

9 Fishing with Bullets?   File: Fishing.doc

In the online Steps, you added bullets to a list, using a • (bullet) character. In this Project, you'll create a bulleted list, choosing a special character as the bullet.

Open the Fishing document from your Project Disk. Select the 3-item list following the "I provide:" line, and then add bullets.

Click Format on menu bar, click Bullets and Numbering to open the Bullets and Numbering dialog box, and then click the Bulleted tab if necessary. Note that you can change the bullet from a small dot to some other symbol by clicking one of the pictures and then clicking the OK button. In this case, however, you'll select another bullet character. Click the Customize button to open the Modify Bulleted List dialog box.

Click the Bullet button to open the Symbol dialog box. You'll want to choose a symbol in the Wingdings font, so select Wingdings in the Symbols From list box.

Click symbols until you find one you like, click the OK button to close the Symbol dialog box, then click the OK button to close the remaining dialog box. The list is now bulleted with the symbol you selected.

Now select the 3-item list following the "You provide:" line, and then open the Bullets and Numbering dialog box as before. The symbol you selected is now included in the Bullet Character display. Click that picture, and then click the OK button to close the dialog box. The second list is now bulleted with the same symbol.

Print the document and then close it without saving changes.

10 A Penny for Your Thoughts   File: Coins.doc

In the online Steps, you created a numbered list. In this Project, you'll create and modify two numbered lists. You'll also select a vertical block of text in order to apply formatting.

Open the Coins document from your Project Disk, and display nonprinting characters. Select the thirteen-item list labeled "MS-70" through "AG-3," indent the list to the 1.5" mark, and then add numbers to the list. Next you'll modify the numbered list to improve the alignment for the two-digit list numbers.

With the list still selected, click Format on the menu bar, click Bullets and Numbering to open the Bullets and Numbering dialog box, and then click the Customize button. Change the Number Position option to the Right, change the Aligned at value to 1.5", and change the Indent at value to 1.8". Then close the dialog box.

To the left of "Fine-12" in the tenth list item, type "F-12" and then press the Tab key. To the left of "Good-4" in the twelfth list item, type "G-4" and then press the Tab key.

Next you'll bold the grades in the list by selecting a vertical block of text. Move the insertion point immediately left of the "M" in "MS-70," press and hold the Alt key as you drag down and to the right to highlight the thirteen grades from "MS-70" through "AG-3," and then release the mouse button and the Alt key. The vertical block of grades should be highlighted, but not the vertical block of numbers nor the vertical block of explanations. Bold the highlighted text.

Select the four paragraphs following the paragraph that starts "I rated...", and then add numbers to the list. With the list still selected, click Format, click Bullets and Numbering to open the Bullets and Numbering dialog box, and select the appropriate sample to number the list with lowercase letters of the style a), b), and so on. Indent the list.

Preview the document. If the document requires two pages to print, make it fit on a single page by deleting one (or more) of the blank paragraphs above the name at the bottom of the document. Print the document and then close it without saving changes.

BUILD SKILLS

11 Add Borders   File: Research.doc

Word's Borders feature allows you to add a line to any side of a paragraph, graphic, or table. In this Project, you'll add a border to a paragraph, and also change the alignment for that paragraph.

Open the Research document from your Project Disk. Double-click in the left margin to select the indented paragraph that begins "The Wordsmithery…", and then justify the paragraph.

To add a border to a paragraph:

1: Display the Tables and Borders toolbar. Click the *Line Style* ▼, and then click the double-line style.

2: Click the *Line Weight* ▼, and then click **1½ pt**.

3: Click the ⊞ **Outside Border** button on that same toolbar, and then close the Tables and Borders toolbar.

Print the document and then close it without saving changes.

12 Insert Clip Art   File: Magician.doc

Many of the documents you've used in these Tutorials have included clip art. In this Project, you'll insert a piece of clip art from the Microsoft ClipArt Gallery, and resize and position it.

Open the Magician document from your Project Disk. Move the insertion point to the left of the middle of the three empty paragraphs.

To insert clip art:

1: Click **Insert** on the menu bar, and then click **Object** to open the Object dialog box. Click **Microsoft Clip Gallery**, and then click the **OK** button to open the Microsoft ClipArt Gallery dialog box.

2: Click **Entertainment** in the *Categories* list, click the picture of the top hat and wand, and then click the **Insert** button. The picture is now inserted in your document.

Next you'll size the clip art.

To make the clip art smaller:

1: Click the picture to select it, click **Format** on the menu bar, click **Picture** to open the Picture dialog box, and then click the **Size** tab.

2: Change both the *Width* and *Height* values to **3"**.

Drag the picture to the right to center it.

Print the document and then close it without saving changes.

13 Formatting a Table and Using the Drawing Toolbar
File: Children.doc

Suppose you've decided to improve the look of the Activity Schedule for your home-based child care business. In this Project, you'll learn how to select table cells, format table text, change row height, center a table, adjust column widths using AutoFit, add shading to cells, merge cells, and add and change cell borders. You'll also draw and modify lines and shapes.

Open the Children document from your Project Disk.

To select and format table cells:

1: The first change you want to make is to bold all the text in the first column of the table, so you'll need to select the first column. Move the insertion point anywhere in the first column of the table, click **Table** on the menu bar, and then click **Select Column**. The first column is now highlighted. Bold the selected column.

2: You'll now bold the entries in the first row. You can select a row using a technique similar to the one you just used to select a column, but let's use an alternative method. Move the insertion point into the left margin to the left of the first row, and then click. The first row is now highlighted. Bold the selected row. (Note: You'll have to click the

B Bold button twice; the first click unbolds the first cell.)

3: Now you'll change the font for all the unbolded cells in the table. Move the insertion point to the lower-left corner of the cell containing "Puzzles," click and drag to the last cell, which contains "Skits," and then release the mouse button. The 35 unbolded cells are now selected. Change the font for the selected cells to 10-point Arial.

4: Select the entire table, click **Table**, click **Cell Height and Width** to open the Cell Height and Width dialog box, and then click the **Row** tab (if necessary). You'll use this dialog box to change the row height, center the table, and use AutoFit to adjust the width of the columns. Click ▼ for *Height of Rows 1-8*, click **At Least**, and then change the *At* value from 12 pt to **18 pt**. Click the **Center** option button in the Alignment section to center the table. Click the **Column** tab, and then click **AutoFit** to make the columns only as wide as they need to be to display the text they contain.

5: Now you'll apply a border to all the table cells. (The gray cell outlines you see are gridlines that will not be printed; you can preview the document now to verify that the gridlines do not appear.) With the entire table still selected, click ▼ immediately to the right of the Borders button on the Formatting toolbar to display the borders palette, and then click the first button in the second row (the All Borders button).

Next you'll add a new first row to the table.

To add a new first row to the table:

1: Position the insertion point in the first cell in the table, click **Table** on the menu bar, and then click **Insert Rows**. One new row is added as the first table row.

Now you'll shade several cells using the Borders and Shading dialog box.

To shade cells:

1: Select only the first cell in the second row of the table (containing "ACTIVITIES").

2: Click **Format** on the menu bar, click **Borders and Shading** to open the Borders and Shading dialog box, and then click the **Shading** tab (if necessary). Click the gray box immediately below the black box in the Fill section to select a 15% gray shading, and then click the **OK** button to close the dialog box and apply the shading.

3: Select the cells in the second through sixth columns of the new first row, and then repeat Step 2 to shade those cells using the same 15% gray shading value.

You want the cells in row 1, columns 2 through 6, to contain a single centered label. So you'll merge those six cells, and then enter the label.

To merge cells and add a centered label:

1: If necessary, select the cells in the second through sixth columns of the new first row.

2: Click **Table** on the menu bar, and then click **Merge cells**. The six cells are now merged into a single cell, which is currently selected.

3: Click the ▤ **Center** button on the Formatting toolbar to center the text in the merged cell, and then type **DAY**

Now you'll complete the formatting of the table by changing a cell's borders.

To change a cell's borders:

1: Select the first cell in the first row.

2: Click ▼ immediately to the right of the Borders button on the Formatting toolbar to display the borders palette. Notice that all the buttons in the first row of the palette appear pushed in, indicating that a complete outside border is in effect, as well as top, bottom, left, and right borders. To delete a particular border, you click the appropriate button to deselect it.

3: Click the second button in the first row of the borders palette to remove the top border.

4: Repeat Steps 2 and 3, this time clicking the fourth button in the first row of the borders palette to remove the left border.

To add visual interest to the Activity Schedule, you'll now add several shapes and lines using the Drawing toolbar.

To draw and modify shapes:

1: Scroll to the top of the document.

2: Click the 🖌 **Drawing** button on the Standard toolbar to display the Drawing toolbar. Word switches to page layout view if that view is not already in effect.

3: Click the **AutoShapes** button on the Drawing toolbar, point to **Basic Shapes**, and then click the Can shape.

4: Position the pointer approximately 1" from the top of the page and ½" left of the center of the page, and then click and drag down to the right to create a cylinder approximately 1" wide and 1¼" tall.

5: Repeat Steps 3 and 4, but this time select the Isosceles Triangle shape (the third shape in the second row), and draw a triangle approximately the same size as the cylinder but slightly higher on the page and slightly overlapping the left portion of the cylinder.

6: Repeat Steps 3 and 4 again, but this time select the Rectangle shape (the first shape in the first row), and draw a square approximately the same size as the cylinder but slightly higher on the page and slightly overlapping the right portion of the cylinder.

7: Now you'll change the triangle and square into 3-D objects, and color all three shapes.

With the square still selected, click the 📦 **3-D** button on the Drawing toolbar to open the 3-D palette, then click the first sample in the palette. The square becomes a 3-D square.

8: Click the triangle to select it, then use the technique described in Step 7 to change the triangle to a 3-D triangle.

Now you'll color and reposition the three shapes.

To color and position shapes:

1: With the 3-D triangle still selected, click the ▾ immediately right of the 🪣 **Fill Color** button on the Drawing toolbar, and then click the bright red color sample in the displayed palette.

2: Click the 3-D square to select it, and then use the technique described in Step 1 to color it a bright blue.

3: Click the cylinder to select it, and then use the technique described in Step 1 to color the cylinder a bright yellow. Now you'll move the yellow cylinder in front of the other two shapes.

4: With the cylinder still selected, click the **Draw** button on the Drawing toolbar, point to **Order**, and then click **Bring to Front**. The complete cylinder is now visible.

5: To make a pleasing arrangement of shapes, resize and/or reposition any of the three shapes as you wish. To resize a shape, click the shape to select it, and then drag one of the corners. To reposition a shape, click the shape to select it, position the pointer over the center of the shape, and then drag the shape to a new position.

To complete the Activity Schedule, you'll now draw a line beneath the shapes.

To draw a line:

1: Click the ⬜ **Line** button on the Drawing toolbar. Position the pointer at the left margin of the document approximately halfway between the bottom of the cylinder and the top of the "Sedona Family Child Care" title, and then click and drag to the right margin to draw a straight line across the page.

2: With the line still selected, click the ≡ **Line Style** button on the Drawing toolbar, and then click the **4½ pt** double-line style.

3: If the line isn't colored black, click the ▾ immediately to the right of the 🖊 **Line Color** button, and then click the black color sample.

4: Click the 🔷 **Drawing** button on the Standard toolbar to hide the Drawing toolbar.

Save the document without saving the filename, print the document, and then close it.

14 Change Line Spacing, Create a Style, and Use AutoText   File: Cats.doc

Today you received a call from a friend who owns a home-based pet sitting service. She wants you to help her improve the appearance of a letter she has written to one of her customers. In this Project, you'll learn how to use the Format Painter, change line spacing using the spacing Before and spacing After options, create and apply a paragraph style, and use AutoText.

projects

Open the Cats document from your Project Disk. Notice that the two address lines as well as five words in the next-to-last paragraph appear in a different font than the rest of the letter. You'll use the Format Painter to apply the formatting of correctly-formatted text to the text that's in the wrong font.

To use the Format Painter:

1: Select the one-line addressee paragraph ("Mr. and Mrs. Hiro Watanabe"), and then click the **Format Painter** button on the Standard toolbar.

2: Click and drag in the left margin next to the two address lines to "paint" the format of the selected line onto the two address lines.

3: Select any correctly formatted word in the "Please let me know..." paragraph, and then click the **Format Painter** button on the Standard toolbar.

4: Click and drag over the words "anything else that your pets" to apply the format of the selected word onto those five words.

The letter is currently missing a closing. You'll add a closing by inserting one of Word's predefined AutoText entries.

To insert a Word AutoText entry:

1: Position the insertion point at the left of the next-to-last paragraph mark at the bottom of the letter.

2: Click **Insert** on the menu bar, point to **AutoText**, point to **Closing**, and then click **Sincerely**. That closing is added to the letter.

You'll need to add your name to two locations in the letter: in the last paragraph and in the heading area. You'll type your name in the last paragraph, and then use that name to create a user-defined AutoText entry. Then you can use that AutoText entry to insert your name in the heading area.

To create and apply a user-defined AutoText entry:

1: Position the insertion point at the left of the last paragraph mark in the letter, and then type your first and last name.

2: Select the name you just typed, but do not select the paragraph mark following your name. Click **Insert** on the menu bar, point to **AutoText**, and then click **New**.

3: Type **myname** as the name for the AutoText entry, and then click the **OK** button.

4: If necessary, switch to Page Layout view. Position the insertion point immediately to the left of the apostrophe in the heading area.

5: Type **myna**. Word recognizes "myna" as the start of an AutoText entry name and displays the corresponding AutoText entry in a small box above where you're typing. To accept the displayed AutoText entry, press **Enter**. Your name is now entered in the heading area.

If you use the same text frequently—such as your name or address or a company name—you can create an AutoText entry for that text. Then, to enter that text in a document, you only need to begin typing the appropriate AutoText entry name and then press the Enter key when Word displays the AutoText entry.

Now you'll vertically format the letter using spacing Before and spacing After options.

To specify spacing Before and/or spacing After:

1: Position the insertion point in the line containing the date, click **Format**, and then click **Paragraph** to open the Paragraph dialog box. In the Spacing section of the dialog box, change the *Before* value to **96 pt**, and change the *After* value to **12 pt**.

2: Repeat Step 1 for the salutation ("Dear..."), but change both the *Before* and *After* values to **18 pt**.

3: Repeat Step 1 for the closing ("Sincerely,"), but change the *Before* value to **6 pt** and the *After* value to **48 pt**.

4: Select the first paragraph in the body of the letter ("I am writing..."), and then format the selected paragraph to change the *After* value to **6 pt**.

Now you'll define a new style for that first paragraph, and then apply that style to other paragraphs in the letter.

To define and apply a new style:

1: With that first body paragraph still selected, click the **Style** box. The current style name, Normal, is now highlighted.

2: Type **MyNormal** as the name for the style currently applied to the selected paragraph, and then press **Enter**.

3: Select the last two paragraphs in the body of the letter ("Please let me know..." and "As we agreed..."). The Normal style is currently applied to those two paragraphs.

4: Click the *Style* ▼ and then click **MyNormal** in the style list to apply that style to the selected paragraphs.

projects

If you're not using your own personal computer, you should delete the myname AutoText entry you created earlier.

To delete an AutoText entry:

1: Click **Insert** on the menu bar, point to **AutoText**, and then click **AutoText**.

2: In the *Enter AutoText entries here* box, type **myname**, which is the name of the AutoText entry you want to delete.

3: Click the **Delete** button, and then click the **OK** button.

Save the document with the name Pet Sitting Service, and then print the document.

15 Take Care of Widows and Orphans
Files: PloverA.doc and PloverB.doc

The terms "widow" and "orphan" are both used to describe a line that is separated from its related text. A **widow** is a single, usually short, last line of a paragraph that appears alone at the top of a page. An **orphan** is the first line of a paragraph that appears alone at the bottom of a page. In this Project, you'll learn how to prevent widows and orphans in your documents.

Open the PloverA document from your Project Disk. Scroll so that you can see the bottom of page 1 and the top of page 2, and click anywhere in the paragraph following the "Status" heading. The last line of that paragraph is a widow, appearing alone at the top of page 2. (Note: Pagination is a function of the assigned printer. If you see more than one line at the top of page 2, try decreasing the bottom margin a tenth of an inch at a time until you create a widow. To decrease the bottom margin by a tenth of an inch, click File on the menu bar, click Page Setup, click the Margins tab, click the Bottom ⬇ one time, and then click the OK button.)

To eliminate a widow or orphan:

1: The option to eliminate a widow or orphan is a paragraph-level formatting option. Select the entire document, click **Format** on the menu bar, click **Paragraph**, and then click the **Line and Page Breaks** tab.

2: Click the **Widow/Orphan Control** check box to make a check mark appear, and then click the **OK** button.

Print the PloverA document and then close it without saving changes.

Next open the PloverB document from your Project Disk. Scroll so that you can see the bottom of page 1 and the top of page 2, and then click anywhere in the paragraph following the "Status" heading. The first line of that paragraph is an orphan, appearing alone at the bottom of page 1. (Note: To create an orphan on your computer, you may have to change the page setup to decrease the bottom margin by one or more tenths of an inch, using the procedure described earlier in this Project.)

Eliminate the orphan using the procedure described above. Print the PloverB document, and then close it without saving changes. Answer the following questions:

a What change did Word make to the PloverA document to eliminate the widow?

b What change did Word make to the PloverB document to eliminate the orphan?

EXPLORE

16 Layer a Drawing Object   File: Luggage.doc

Word's Drawing toolbar lets you create lines, boxes, circles and other objects in your document. You can then position the drawing objects in front of or behind the text in your document to create a layered effect.

The easiest way to layer text and a picture, such as a piece of clip art, in your document is to insert the picture in a text box you create using the Drawing toolbar. In this Project, you'll enhance a flyer for a home-based luggage repair business by layering a picture of a suitcase behind the business logo.

Open the Luggage document from your Project Disk, and switch to page layout view, if necessary.

To layer a drawing object in the document:

1: Display the Drawing toolbar.

2: Click the **Text Box** button on the Drawing toolbar, position the + pointer in the open area to the right of the five consecutive empty paragraphs, and then drag to draw a box approximately 1" square. Next you'll size and position the text box.

3: Click **Format** on the menu bar, and then click **Text Box**. Change settings on the Position tab, the Size tab, and the Text Box tab, in that order, so that both the *Horizontal* and *Vertical* positions are **2.75"** from **Page**, the *Height* is **2.5"**, the *Width* is **3.0"**, and the *Internal Margin* is **0**, and then click the **OK** button.

4: Click the **Line Color** button on the Drawing toolbar, and then click **No Line** at the top of the palette box that appears to ensure that the text box has no outline. Now you'll insert a picture into the text box.

projects

5: Click **Insert** on the menu bar, point to Picture and then click **From File** to open the Insert Picture dialog box. Change the drive in the *Look In* list box to your Project Disk, and then double-click **Luggage**. The picture is now inserted in your document, but it appears on top of the "We can handle it!" slogan. (If the picture isn't centered over the slogan, drag it into that position.)

6: Click **Draw** on the Drawing toolbar, point to **Order**, and then click **Send Behind Text**.

7: Click ⬛ to hide the Drawing toolbar.

Print the document, and then close it without saving changes.

17 Tables: Add Columns and Perform Calculations
File: SalesQ2.doc

In the online Steps, you learned how to create a table. In this Project you'll work with a quarterly sales report for a home-based health products distributor, adding columns to an existing table, and using Word to perform simple calculations in a table.

Open the SalesQ2 document from your Project Disk. The table needs three additional columns added to it: a first column for the sales representative names, a middle column for the month of May, and a final column for the quarterly totals by salesperson.

To insert and format columns:

1: To insert a column, you must first select the column to the right of the location where you want the column inserted. Move the insertion point anywhere in the April column of the table, click **Table** on the menu bar, and then click **Select Column** to select the first column. To insert a new column to the left of the selected column, click **Table**, and then click **Insert Columns**. A new first column is added to the table.

2: Repeat Step 1, but this time click in the June column to add a new column to the left of the June column.

3: To insert a column to the end of a table, you must first select the column of table end-of-row markers. Repeat Step 1, but this time click in the area to the right of the June column (right of the right table border) to add a new column to the end of the table. The table now contains five columns, with April data in the second column and June data in the fourth column.

4: The formatting for the paragraphs in the first column must be changed, so select the first column, click **Format** on the menu bar, click **Paragraph**, and then change the *Left Indent* value to **0.1"**, the *Right Indent* value to **0"**, and the *Alignment* to **Left**.

5: Enter the following information in the indicated rows and columns of the table:

	Column 1	Column 3	Column 5
Row 1	Salesperson	May	Total
Row 2	J. Davidson	5,500	
Row 3	M. Fontina	3,000	
Row 4	S. Jenkins	8,000	
Row 5	L. Michaelson	20,000	
Row 6	F. Ruth	14,500	
Row 7	Total		

6: Bold the word "Total" in the last row of the first column.

Now that you've inserted columns, formatted the table cells, and entered the data in the columns, you're ready to add calculated fields to the table.

To create calculated fields in a table:

1: For the value in the last row of the May column, you'd like a total of the five values in rows 2 through 6 of the May column. Click in that last cell in the May column, click **Table** on the menu bar, and then click **Formula** to open the Formula dialog box. The *Formula* text box contains "SUM(ABOVE)," which is the formula you want, so click the **OK** button. The calculated value 51,000 is now displayed in that cell.

2: For the value in the last row of the last column, you'd like a total of the three values to the left of that cell. Click in that cell, click **Table**, click **Formula**, note that the displayed formula is "SUM(LEFT)," which is the formula you want, and then click the **OK** button.

3: Repeat Step 2 for the cells in the sixth through second rows of the last column.

Save the document as Sales - Quarter 2, and then print the document.

18 Tables: Add Rows and Perform Calculations

File: SalesQ3.doc

In the online Steps, you learned how to create a table. In this Project, you'll work with a quarterly sales report for a home-based health products distributor, adding rows to an existing table, and using Word to perform simple calculations in a table.

Open the SalesQ3 document from your Project Disk. The table needs three additional rows added to it: a first row for column titles, a middle row for an additional salesperson, and a final row for the totals by month and the grand total.

projects

To insert rows in the table:

1: To insert a row, you must first move the insertion point into the row beneath the location where you want the row inserted. Move the insertion point anywhere in the first row of the table, click **Table** on the menu bar, and then click **Insert Rows**. A new first row is added to the table.

2: Repeat Step 1, but this time click in the row containing "F. Ruth" to add a new row above that row.

3: The procedure to add a row to the end of a table is different. Move the insertion point to the area to the right of the last cell (right of the right table border), and then press the **Tab** key. The table now contains eight rows, with rows 1, 6, and 8 currently empty.

4: Enter the following information in the indicated rows and columns of the table:

	Column 1	Column 2	Column 3	Column 4	Column 5
Row 1	Salesperson	July	August	September	Total
Row 6	C. O'Brien	0	1,250	2,400	
Row 8	Total				

5: Bold the word "Total" in the last row of the first column. Then select the entire first row (click in that first row, click **Table**, and click **Select Row**) and bold that row.

For the value in the last column of the new C. O'Brien row, you'd like a total of the three values to the left of that cell.

To add calculated fields to the table:

1: Click in the cell in row 6, column 5. Click **Table** on the menu bar, and then click **Formula** to open the Formula dialog box. The *Formula* text box contains "SUM(ABOVE)," which is *not* the formula you want. Edit the formula to change it to "SUM(LEFT)," and then click the **OK** button. The calculated value 3,650 is now displayed in that cell.

2: For the value in the cell in the July column and the last row of the table, you'd like a total of the six values above that cell. Click in that last cell in the July column, click **Table**, and then click **Formula** to open the Formula dialog box. The *Formula* text box contains "SUM(ABOVE)," which is the formula you want, so click the **OK** button. The calculated value 51,200 is now displayed in that cell.

3: Repeat Step 2 for the cells in the August, September, and Total columns of the last row.

Save the document as Sales - Quarter 3, then print the document.

19 Use Overtype Mode, Sort a Table, and Rotate Table Text   File: Lawns.doc

Greg Ropes is a youngster who mows his neighbors' lawns to earn his spending money. He has created a simple Word document containing a table with his customers' names and addresses, along with any special customer notes. Suppose he has asked you to help him correct a table entry and then present the table in various ways. In this Project, you'll learn how to correct text using Overtype mode and how to sort a table. You'll also add a column to the beginning of the table, merge cells, rotate text in a table cell, and center the rotated text.

Open the Lawns document from your Project Disk. The text in the last table cell is incorrect: "morning" should be "afternoon", and vice versa. Up to now, whenever you've typed new text in the middle of existing text, the new text has been *inserted*. When in Overtype mode, the old text is *replaced* by the new text, letter for letter. You can use Overtype mode with any document text, including table text.

To toggle Overtype mode and to correct text:

1: Look at the status bar at the bottom of the Word window. Each of the five indicators to the right of the line and column location information is currently dimmed. Press the **Insert** key. Notice that OVR now appears on the status bar in black type, indicating that you are now in Overtype mode. (If pressing the Insert key did not make the OVR in the status bar appear black, double-click OVR on the status bar.)

2: Position the insertion point immediately to the left of the first letter in the word "afternoon", and then type **morning**. Notice that the seven letters in "morning" have replaced the first seven letters in "afternoon".

3: Press the **Delete** key twice to delete the "on".

4: Position the insertion point immediately to the left of the first letter in the first occurrence of "morning", and then type **afterno**. If you now typed the remaining two letters in the word "afternoon", the "on" would replace the semicolon and blank space that you want to retain.

5: Press the **Insert** key. Notice that OVR on the status bar is once again dimmed. (If pressing the Insert key did not dim the OVR, double-click OVR on the status bar.)

6: Type **on**

Select the entire customer table. The rows in Greg's customer table are currently in no particular order. First you'll sort the table in ascending (alphabetical) order by customer name.

projects

To sort on the customer name field:

1: Click **Table** on the menu bar, and then click **Sort** to open the Sort dialog box. Word recognizes when your table includes a header row, such as this table does, and uses the column headings as the entries in the *Sort By* list box. (If your table did not contain a header row, the entries in that *Sort By* list box would be "Column 1," "Column 2," and so on.)

2: Make sure that **Name** is specified in the *Sort By* list box, **Text** is specified in the first *Type* list box, the **Ascending** option is selected, and in the My List Has section **Header Row** option is selected, and then click the **OK** button to sort the table. Notice that the header row remained as the first row—when you select the My List Has section Header Row option, the header row is not sorted with the other table rows.

Print the document, and then label the printout "ascending text sort on name". Next you'll sort the table on the address field. Select the table (if necessary).

To sort the table on the address field:

1: Click **Table** on the menu bar, and then click **Sort**. Select **Address** in the *Sort By* list box, and then click the **OK** button. Notice that all the addresses in the three-thousands sorted before those in the eight-hundreds; this is because you specified a Text sort and because the character 3 is less than the character 8. If you want the 800's to sort first, you must do a numeric sort.

2: Select the table (if necessary), click **Table**, and then click **Sort**. Select **Number** in the first *Type* list box, and then click the **OK** button.

Print the document, and then label the printout "ascending numeric sort on address."

You can also sort on multiple columns. Next you'll do an ascending text sort on name combined with a descending numeric sort on address.

To sort on multiple fields:

1: Select the table (if necessary), click **Table** on the menu bar, and then click **Sort**. Select **Name** in the *Sort By* list box, select **Text** in the first *Type* list box, select **Address** in the *Then By* list box, select **Number** in the second *Type* list box, click the second **Descending** option, and then click the **OK** button.

Before you print this latest sorted version of the document, you'll add a new column to the beginning of the table and merge some of the added cells.

To add a column and merge cells:

1: Move the insertion point anywhere in the first column of the table, click **Table** on the menu bar, and then click **Select Column** to select the first column. To insert a new column to the left of the selected column, click **Table**, and then click **Insert Columns**. A new first column is added to the table. Now you'll size that new column.

2: With the new column still selected, click **Table** on the menu bar, click **Cell Height and Width**, and then change the width of column 1 from 0.8" to **0.4"**. Now you'll merge eight of the cells in that column into a single cell.

3: Select only the eight cells in column 1, rows 2 through 8 (point to the cell in the second row in column 1, and then click and drag through the cell in the last row in column 1).

4: Click **Table** on the menu bar, and then click **Merge Cells**. The eight cells have now merged to become one large cell.

5: Type **Lawn Mowing**, press the **Enter** key, and then type **Customers**. Don't worry about word wrap.

Now you'll rotate the text in that merged cell.

To rotate and format table text:

1: Select the merged cell, click **Format** on the menu bar, and then click **Text Direction**.

2: Click the first of the two vertical samples in the Orientation section of the Text Direction – Table Cell dialog box, and then click the **OK** button to apply the change. The text in that cell is now oriented vertically rather than horizontally. Notice that the Align Left, Center, Align Right, and Justify buttons on the Formatting toolbar have changed in appearance to reflect the vertical orientation of the currently selected text.

3: With that cell still selected, bold the cell contents, and then center the cell contents by clicking the ⊞ **Center** button on the Formatting toolbar.

Print the document, and then label the printout "ascending text sort on name and descending number sort on address".

Close the document without saving changes.

20 Font Formatting Wrap-Up   File: Examples.doc

In the online Steps, you learned several font formatting commands, including font, font size, and font style (bold, italic, and underline). In this Project, you'll try all the other types of font formatting commands.

Open the Examples document from your Project Disk. This document consists of a title followed by twenty-four numbered lines.

To apply font formatting commands:

1: Select the word "strikethrough" in line 1, click **Format** on the menu bar, click **Font** to open the Font dialog box, and then click the **Font** tab (if necessary). Click the **Strikethrough** option in the Effects section to draw a line through the selected text, and then click the **OK** button to close the dialog box.

projects

2: Select the word "strikethrough" in line 2, open the Font dialog box, and then select the **Double strikethrough** option in the Effects section.

3: Select the word "superscript" in line 3, open the Font dialog box, and then select the **Superscript** option in the Effects section.

4: Select the word "subscript" in line 3, open the Font dialog box, and then select the **Subscript** option in the Effects section.

5: Select the word "shadow" in line 4, open the Font dialog box, and then select the **Shadow** option in the Effects section.

6: Select the word "outline" in line 5, open the Font dialog box, and then select the **Outline** option in the Effects section.

7: Select the words "embossed effect" in line 6, open the Font dialog box, and then select the **Emboss** option in the Effects section.

8: Select the words "engraved effect" in line 7, open the Font dialog box, and then select the **Engrave** option in the Effects section.

9: Notice that there are three capital letters in the text in line 8. Select that entire line, open the Font dialog box, and then select the **Small Caps** option in the Effect section. Notice that all letters are now capital letters, but that the three capitalized letters are taller than the other letters.

10: Select line 9, open the Font dialog box, and then select the **All caps** option in the Effects section. Notice that all letters are now capitalized and are the same height.

11: Hidden text is text, such as notes or comments that does not appear when the document is previewed or printed, but that can be seen in the open document. Select the word "hidden" in line 10, open the Font dialog box, and then select the **Hidden** option in the Effects section. Notice that the word now appears with a dotted underline. (If you can't see the word in the document, click Tools, click Options, click the View tab, and then make sure the All box in the Nonprinting Characters section contains a check mark.) Preview the document to verify that the word does not appear in the Print Preview window.

12: Select the word "red" in line 11, open the Font dialog box, click the *Color* 🔽, and then select the **Red** option.

13: Select the entire line 12, open the Font dialog box, click the **Character Spacing** tab, click the *Spacing* 🔽, and then click **Condensed**.

14: Select the entire line 13, open the Font dialog box, click the *Spacing* 🔽, click **Expanded**, and then change the By value from 1 pt to **3 pt**.

15: Select the last three words in line 14, open the Font dialog box, click the *Position* 🔽, and then click **Raised**.

16: Select the last three words in line 15, open the Font dialog box, click the *Position* 🔽, click **Lowered**, and then change the By value from 3 pt to **5 pt**.

17: Select the first four words in line 16, open the Font dialog box, click the **Font** tab, click the *Underline* ▾, and then click **Single**.

18: Select the first four words in line 17, open the Font dialog box, click the *Underline* ▾, and then click **Words only**.

19: Repeat Step 18 for lines 18 through 24, clicking the appropriate Underline option.

Print the document, and then close it without saving changes. Be sure to look at the printed document to check out all the various font formatting effects.

INVESTIGATE

21 I Can't Draw!

Suppose that you don't know how to use drawing or paint programs and have no artistic talent. Despite your lack of talent, you want to include drawings and graphics in various documents. For example, you know that a poster advertising your own business would be more eye-catching and effective with a graphic element; the same is true for business cards. Clip art, of course, will make up for your lack of talent. But is using clip art for your business literature legal? Don't copyright laws protect artistic works? Can you use art that you just happen to find? Use Internet and library resources to investigate copyright laws as they apply to clip art to answer these questions. Write a one- to two-page paper describing the copyright laws that apply to clip art, whether you need to pay a fee to use clip art, and the average price range that applies to clip art. Be sure to include your sources of information, whether books, magazine articles, or Internet articles. If your information comes from the Web, cite the URLs you used.

22 Tell Me About Clip Art

Make an appointment with someone who uses clip art along with word processing software, either at home or for business. Be sure you clearly state the purpose of your visit and receive permission to conduct an interview.

To prepare for the interview, compose a list of questions. Here are some suggestions, but do not use only these:

a How long have you been using clip art?

b What made decide to start using it?

c How did you learn to use it?

d What are your sources for finding clip art? Which source do you think is the best?

e Have you ever purchased a clip-art package? If so, why did you buy it instead of using what you can find for free?

projects

After the interview, summarize your findings as if you were writing a magazine article. Your article might be in the format of an interview; or you might choose to write a narrative in which you summarize and paraphrase the interviewee. Your instructor will give you guidelines for the article's length and format.

23 What Typeface Should I Wear Today?

Beatrice Ward once said, "Typefaces are the clothes that words wear." Use the library or Internet resources to investigate typography. Write a one- to two-page paper that explains what Beatrice Ward meant when she compared typefaces (fonts) to clothing. Is this a meaningful comparison? Be sure to include your sources of information, whether books, magazine articles, or Internet articles. If your information comes from the Web, include the relevant URLs in the paper.

24 Making the Right Impression

Pick three distinct jobs or careers that interest you. Choose a different font for your resume for each job or career and explain why that font is a good choice in each case. (Hint: Research and consider the emotional and perceptual impact of specific fonts.)

25 When the Help File Isn't Enough

No matter how good the online help that comes with a product, at some point most users have questions for which quick answers aren't available. And what if you haven't even been able to get the product to install correctly? Is there somewhere you can go for help when the Help file isn't enough? The answer to this question is "Yes, the Internet." All the major players in the word processing market—Microsoft (Word), Corel (WordPerfect), Lotus (WordPro)—have formal technical support areas on their Web sites.

Pick two word processing packages, and find their technical support sites. Write a two-page paper comparing and contrasting the technical support each company provides. Which technical support site do you think is the best? Why? (Hint: Microsoft's URL is http://www.microsoft.com; Corel's URL is http://www.corel.com; Lotus's URL is http://www.lotus.com.)

Microsoft Word

Tutorial 4: Format Pages of a Document

Tutorial 4

Format Pages of a Document

Lights, Camera, Action!

What would life be like without movies? From childhood, movies have entertained and educated us. Some may have frightened or disgusted us. Some of the best movies might even have inspired us. But mostly movies have made us think and dream. In this tutorial, you'll peek at many of the facets of the movie industry.

Projects

In the Tutorial 4 Projects, you'll practice the skills you learned in the online Steps and expand your knowledge as you format a variety of documents. Specifically, you'll change page orientation and margins, insert breaks, caption figures, create tables of contents and tables of figures, insert footnotes and endnotes, create envelopes and calling cards, insert fields, and format a document with columns.

If you're not assigned Projects 11, 12, 17, 19, and 20, you might want to read these Projects or, better yet, work through them. Project 11 deals with shrinking a document that's slightly too large for its page. In Project 12 you'll automatically create an envelope for a letter. Creating columns in a document is accomplished in Project 17. Project 19 introduces one of the special Word fields you can insert in a document. In Project 20 you'll sort various types of text.

Lights, Camera, Action!

Can you imagine a world without movies? Actually, the film industry began only about 100 years ago. And movies have evolved from Louis Lumiere's first film of moving trains in 1895 to Spielberg's spectacular use of special effects in the 1993 film, *Jurassic Park*. Today movies make us laugh and make us cry; they teach us, and often influence us. But above all, they entertain.

What would the typical Saturday night date be, if it were not for dinner and a movie? What would you do without Disney films on videotape to fascinate the kids when "nothing good" is on TV? Tired of all the TV news, talk shows, and sitcoms? Movies for the big screen, as well as made-for-TV movies, help. Whether it's a horror flick, a romance, a documentary, a comedy, or a drama, people of all ages include movie-watching as a favorite way to spend leisure time.

Movies have created Hollywood stars—respected and envied—who earn millions of dollars for each movie hit. Actors are the closest we get to having royalty. Watching the televised Academy Awards is as big an annual media event as watching the Super Bowl!

The way we watch movies has changed. Many remember going to a giant, ornate movie theater, complete with an intermission and ushers who showed people to seats. Drive-ins became the sensation with the popularity of the automobile in the 1950s. Later millions of Americans tuned in as the television became the most popular form of entertainment. While more than 30 million people saw the movie hit *Schindler's List* in theaters, double that number viewed the movie when shown on TV as a commercial-free presentation. Today's youth can't imagine anything but multiplex theaters to view the big screen, where there are more than ten movies from which to choose at any one time. And most recently, movie fans of all ages view all-time favorites, as well as recently released films, in their own home—thanks to the popularity of the VCR and video rentals.

In this tutorial, you'll work with poster and report documents centered around the Hollywood movie industry. You'll learn the skills you need to format the pages of your documents. Here are some of the things you'll do:

- Change the paper size
- Use portrait and landscape page orientation
- Change margins
- Insert section and page breaks
- Add page headers and footers
- Add footnotes and endnotes
- Generate a table of contents

Review Questions

Fill in the blank with the correct word or phrase.

1   The "sideways" page orientation, in which the paper is positioned so it is wider than it is tall, is called _____ orientation.

2   With _____ orientation, the paper is positioned so it is taller than it is wide.

3   A(n) _____ is the distance from the text to the edge of the paper.

4   To change the paper size setting, you use the _____ command on the File menu.

5   A(n) _____ forces the text that follows it onto a new page

6   A(n) _____ is a part of a document that you can format separately.

7   If you want the first page of a document to have different margins than the rest of the document, you should insert a(n) _____.

8   A(n) _____ is text that is printed at the bottom of every page.

9   Your document must be in _____ view when you're editing a header.

10 A(n) _____ is a horizontal line or border in a document.

11 The button that adds automatically numbered page numbers is located on the _____ toolbar.

12 _____ are remarks printed as a group on the last page of a document.

13 A(n) _____ is printed on the same page as the text it references.

14 When you compile a table of contents for a document, Word generates entries for text to which a _____ style is applied.

review questions

MULTIPLE CHOICE

*Select the letter of the **one** best answer.*

15 **Word's default paper size is:**

  a 8 x 11 inches

  b 8.5 x 11 inches

  c 8 x 14 inches

  d 8.5 x 14 inches

16 **Word's default page orientation is:**

  a picture

  b photo

  c portrait

  d landscape

17 **Which of the following would *not* allow you to fit more text on a line?**

  a decreasing the font size

  b decreasing the size of the right margin

  c condensing the font spacing

  d changing the page orientation to portrait

18 **In portrait orientation, the default left, right, top, and bottom margins are:**

  a 1.25", 1.25", 1", and 1", respectively

  b 1", 1", 1.25", and 1.25", respectively

  c 1.5", 1.5", 1", and 1", respectively

  d 1", 1", 1.5", and 1.5", respectively

19 **All of the following would force the text following the insertion point onto the next page, *except*:**

  a pressing the Enter key some number of times

  b inserting a continuous section break

  c inserting a page break

  d inserting a next-page section break

review questions

20 **Which of the following can have different values in the different sections in a document?**

   a page orientation   **c** paper size

   b margins   **d** all of the above

21 **Before typing text that you want centered in a header, you should:**

   a press the ▤ Center button

   b press the Tab key once

   c press the Tab key twice

   d insert sufficient spaces to move the insertion point to the center of the line

22 **Headers and footers are *not* visible:**

   a in normal view

   b in page layout view

   c in print preview

   d on a printed page

23 **If the footer line is 6 inches long, then default tab stops are set at:**

   a 0", 3", and 6"

   b 2", 4", and 6"

   c 3" and 6"

   d 0" and 6"

24 **To add an endnote, you use Word's:**

   a Endnote command on the Insert menu

   b Footnote command on the Insert menu

   c Endnote command on the Edit menu

   d Footnote command on the Edit menu

25 **To delete a footnote, you:**

   a must first delete the footnote text, and then delete the note number in the document

   b use an option on the same dialog box you used to add the footnote

   c must be in page layout view

   d select the note number, then press the Delete key

26 **If you used Word to compile a table of contents, which of the following is true?**

    a Page numbers might not appear.

    b The table of contents must be the second page of the document.

    c Only a single-level of topic levels is shown.

    d Word uses a standard TOC format that cannot be modified.

MATCHING

Select the letter from the right column that correctly matches each item in the left column.

27

    a footnote reference number

the greatest

Page 8

28

    b Page Numbers button

29

    c footer

    d footnote

30

    e Landscape orientation

31

32 AAAL[1]

    f Switch Between Header and Footer button

    g Top Border button

33 [1] American Aca

    h Portrait orientation

34

    i Borders button

35

review questions

Use a separate sheet of paper to write out your answers to the following questions.

36 Explain how you would instruct Word to vertically center a particular page of a document.

37 Compare a next-page section break to a page break. Describe a situation where each is appropriate.

38 How might the presence of sections in a document affect headers or footers?

39 Explain the process to add a footnote. Explain how to delete a footnote. Why is the automatic numbering feature important?

40 List the steps to insert a table of contents in a document. How does Word determine what to put in the table of contents?

Projects

These Projects are designed to help you review and develop the skills you learned in Tutorial 4. Complete each Project using Microsoft Word. *If you have not yet made the Project Disk for Tutorial 4, start the e-Course software, click Project Disk on the e-Course Welcome screen menu bar, and follow the instructions on the screen.*

If you've forgotten some of the skills you need to complete the Projects, refer to the Task Reference.

REVIEW SKILLS

1 Out of Order   File: Sign.doc

In the online Steps, you learned how to customize page-level document formatting by setting the page orientation and changing the margins, both of which you'll do in this Project. Suppose you work at a movie theater and that you've been asked to complete an out-of-order sign for the concession stand's popcorn machine.

Open the Sign document from your Project Disk, and then preview the document to verify that the document requires page-level formatting. Change the page orientation to Landscape, and then print the document.

Change the page orientation back to Portrait and then change margins so the left and right margins are both 0.75". Print the document, and then close it without saving changes.

2 Who's Albert Einstein?   File: Names.doc

In the online Steps, you learned how to insert a section break to create document sections that could be formatted independently. In this Project you'll edit a film magazine memo concerning movie stars' real names to divide the memo into several sections; then you'll apply font formatting and page-level margin formatting to two of the sections.

Open the Names document from your Project Disk. Insert four continuous section breaks, one at the beginning of the first "Celebrities Support AIDS" paragraph, and one at the beginning of each of the next three paragraphs.

projects

Select the first "Celebrities Support AIDS" paragraph, change the font to 10-point Arial, and then change the left and right margins for the selected section only to 1.75". Repeat for the second "Celebrities Support AIDS" paragraph.

Save the document without changing the filename, and then print the document.

3   The Golden Globes   File: GGlobes.doc

In the online Steps, you learned how to add headers and footers to your documents, how to center header or footer text, and how to include automatically generated page numbers. In this Project, you'll edit a film magazine article about the Golden Globe Awards, creating a footer with a centered page number; then you'll change the footer's font.

Open the GGlobes document from your Project Disk. Modify the footer to display the word "Page", followed by a space, followed by the page number, all centered in the footer line.

Select the footer line, and then change the font to 9-point Bookman Old Style.

Save the document without changing the filename, and then print the document.

4   Be-All and End-All   File: Essay.doc

In the online Steps, you added footnotes to a document. In this Project, you'll add endnotes to a student essay written for a college film class. The only difference between adding an endnote and a footnote is that you select the Endnote option rather than the Footnote option in the Insert section of the Footnote and Endnote dialog box.

Open the Essay document from your Project Disk, and then switch to page layout view (if necessary). Scroll the document so you can see the end of the second paragraph ("…and what they are made about."). Move the insertion point between the ending quotation mark and the paragraph mark, and then add an endnote with the following text:

"Biography of Steven Spielberg." Baseline's Encyclopedia of Film. [Online.] Available at http://www.cat.pdx.edu/~caseyh/horror/director/spielbio.html.

Move the insertion point to the right of the ending quotation mark in the line "…remember the personalities", which is at the bottom of the first page (or possibly the top of the second page), and then add an endnote with the following text:

"Interview with Steven Spielberg." [Reprinted online.] Available at http://smartlink.net/~deej7/bantha.htm. Original text appeared in Bantha Tracks, May 1981.

Insert a blank line between the two endnotes to improve readability. Save the document without changing the filename, and then print the document.

5   What's a Movie Without Popcorn?   File: Popcorn.doc

In the online Steps, you learned how to generate a table of contents for a document formatted with headings. In this Project, you'll create a table of contents for a report on the fat content of movie-theater popcorn.

Open the Popcorn document from your Project Disk, and then make sure that nonprinting characters are shown. You'll want to add the table of contents after the title page, on a page of its own. Move the insertion point to the left of the empty paragraph that follows the date on the title page, and then insert a page break.

Type "Table of Contents" at the top of page 2, and then press the Enter key. Apply the style Header to the "Table of Contents" line, change the font of that line to 16-point Arial, and then bold and center the line.

Select the empty paragraph that follows the "Table of Contents" line. Then insert a table of contents, making sure that the value in the Show Levels box is 2, so that all Heading 1 and Heading 2 paragraphs will appear in the table of contents.

Save the document without changing the filename, and then print the document.

APPLY SKILLS

6   A Foot in the Door   File: Winters.doc

In the online Steps, you learned how to add and delete footnotes. In this Project, you'll complete a biography of an up-and-coming actress by adding two footnotes, formatting text in a footnote, and moving a footnote.

Open the Winters document from your Project Disk, switch to page layout view (if necessary), and show nonprinting characters (if necessary).

First you'll add a footnote to the "1995 Forceful Stranger" entry in the Film Credits list. Move the insertion point between the last "r" in "Stranger" and the paragraph mark that follows it, and then add a footnote with the text "Retitled in video release as Montana Mountain Man." Select the three-word title you just typed and format it as italic.

Move the insertion point between the last "b" in "1995 Blonde Bomb" and the paragraph mark that follows it, and then add a footnote with the text "Released directly to video."

Now you'll move the first footnote so that it follows the last entry in the Film Credits list. Select the reference number 1 in the "1995 Forceful Stranger" entry by

projects

dragging over that reference mark. (If you have trouble seeing or selecting that reference number 1, change the Zoom Control value on the Standard toolbar to 200%.) Then click and drag to move the reference mark to the end of the "1993 The Man From Montana" entry. Notice that Word automatically renumbers the footnotes after the move.

Save the document without changing the filename, and then print the document.

7 Calling All Sandra Bullock Fans   File: Sandra.doc

In the online Steps, you learned how to change the vertical alignment of a section to center the section. In this Project, you'll create three copies of a film magazine quiz on Sandra Bullock's movie roles, each in its own section. Then you'll apply each of the three vertical alignment options, one per section.

Open the Sandra document from your Project Disk, and make sure that nonprinting characters are shown. Select the document, copy it, move the insertion point to the left of the last paragraph mark in the document, and then paste twice. Your document now contains three copies of the Sandra Bullock quiz.

Move the insertion point to the left of the second title ("Oh, Sandra!"), and then insert a next-page section break. Repeat for the third title. Now you'll assign a different vertical alignment option for each of the three sections.

Move the insertion point into the first section, click File on the menu bar, click Page Setup, and then click the Layout tab. Make sure the Apply To box contains "This Section" and that the Vertical Alignment box contains "Top". Repeat for the second section, except choose the "Center" option in the Vertical Alignment box. Repeat for the third section, this time choosing the "Justified" option in the Vertical Alignment box.

Print the document, and then close it without saving changes. Answer the following questions:

a   Did the position of the header text change for the different vertical alignment options?

b   Does the justified option for vertical alignment add space between lines in a paragraph, between paragraphs, or both?

c   What happened to the table when the justified option was selected?

8   Remember Drive-In Movies?   File: Drive-In.doc

Structured, formal documents often include tables and charts for which you can create captions. In this Project, you'll add captions to the chart and the tables in a report on the history of drive-in movie theaters.

Open the Drive-In document from your Project Disk. Scroll the document until you can see the chart, which is a bar chart with red bars that shows the number of drive-in theaters that existed in the United States for selected years between 1948 through 1987.

Click in the left margin next to the chart to select the chart, click Insert on the menu bar, and then click Caption to open the Caption dialog box. Type ":" (a colon), press the spacebar, and then type "Number of drive-ins by year". Make sure the Label box contains "Figure" and the Position box contains "Below Selected Item", and then click the OK button.

Scroll down until you can see the last table in the document (which has a header row plus five other rows), and then select the table. Insert a caption, again typing a colon, then inserting a space, and then typing "The 5 smallest drive-ins". Make sure the Label box contains "Table" and the Position box contains "Below Selected Item", and then click the OK button to close the Caption dialog box and insert the caption. Notice that tables are numbered independently from figures, and that this caption is for Table 1.

Scroll up to the other table, and then select the table. Insert a table caption below the selected item by typing a colon, pressing the spacebar, and then typing "The 8 largest drive-ins". Notice that Word has automatically numbered the caption for this first table in the document as table number 1.

Scroll down to the second table, and verify that its caption has changed to "Table 2". Print the document and then close it without saving changes.

9   Adding a Table of Figures   File: Theater.doc

In the online Steps, you added a table of contents to a structured, formal document. Such documents often include captioned figures (tables and charts). In this Project, you'll add a table of figures to a document with captioned figures, using a process similar to that for adding a table of contents.

Open the Theater document from your Project Disk, and then make sure that nonprinting characters are displayed. Scroll to the top of page 2, copy the "Table of Contents" line, paste at the next-to-last paragraph mark on that page, and then edit the pasted copy to change "Contents" to "Figures".

projects

Move the insertion point to the left of the first paragraph mark below the "Table of Figures" heading. Click Insert on the menu bar, click Index and Tables, and then click the Table of Figures tab. Make sure "Figure" is highlighted in the Caption Label box, and "From Template" is highlighted in the Formats box, and then click the OK button. The table of figures is added to the document, with one entry for each line in the document with the Caption style. Notice that the entries are indented, unlike the table of contents.

To format the table of figures to remove the indentation, click in the left margin to the left of the entry for Figure 1 to select the entire table of figures. Click Format on the menu bar, click Paragraph, and change the Left indentation value to "0". Click the Special ⏷, click (none), and then click the OK button.

Save the document without changing the filename, and then print the document.

10 Legal Matters   File: Festival.doc

Many printers can print on either letter-size paper (8½ x 11-inch) or legal-size paper (8½ x 14-inch). In this Project, you'll edit a Science Fiction Film Festival poster that is too long for letter-size paper, changing the paper size to Legal. You'll also condense the font for the two longest film names.

Open the Festival document from your Project Disk. Preview the document to verify that it does not fit on a single page. Click File on menu bar, click Page Setup to open the Page Setup dialog box, and then click the Paper Size tab. Click the Paper Size ⏷, click Legal 8 1/2 x 14 in. to select legal-size paper, and then click the OK button.

The films to be shown in the year-long film festival are listed in a two-column table. Scroll the document until the first row of the table is at the top of the screen. Notice that two films, *Close Encounters of the Third Kind* (1977) in the first column, and *Star Trek VI: Undiscovered Country* (1991) in the second column, require two lines to print. You'll condense the print slightly for both titles so that each will fit on a single line.

Select the *Close Encounters* title and year, and then click Format on the menu bar, click Font, and then click the Character Spacing tab. Click the Spacing ⏷, click Condensed, change the By value from 1 pt to 0.3 pt, and then click the OK button. Repeat for the *Star Trek VI* title and year.

If the paragraph "Weekly January 1, 2000 through January 1, 2001" near the top of the document doesn't fit on a single line, condense its font by 0.3 pt as well.

Preview the document to verify that it now fits on a single, long page and that each film prints on a single line. If one or more lines spill onto a second page, change the spacing before and after values to 0 pt for the "A Year of Favorite Films" and the "Weekly January 1, 2000 through January 1, 2001" paragraphs.

Save the document without changing the filename.

If your printer doesn't have legal paper, change the paper size to "Letter 8 1/2 x 11 in." Print the document (it will print on two pages if you've changed to letter-sized paper), and then close the document without saving changes.

BUILD SKILLS

11 Shrink to Fit   File: Sports.doc

Sometimes documents you create are slightly longer than a page when you'd like them to be no longer than a page. To make the document fit onto one page, you could go through it decreasing the font size of individual text items. Or, better yet, you could use a Word feature to do that process automatically. In this Project, you'll shrink a flyer announcing a movie theater festival of sports films so that it will fit on one page.

Open the Sports document from your Project Disk. Preview the document to verify that it is slightly longer than one page.

a What font and font size is the title (first) paragraph?

b What font and font size is the "Sports Festival" paragraph? What are the paragraph spacing before and after values for that paragraph?

c What font and font size are the movie title lines?

d What font and font size is the "And more!" paragraph?

Preview the document again, then click the Shrink to Fit button on the Print Preview toolbar. Save the document without changing the filename, and then print the document.

e What font size is the title (first) paragraph now?

f What font size is the "Sports Festival" paragraph now? Did the paragraph spacing before and after values change?

g What is the font size of the movie title lines?

h What font size is the "And more!" paragraph now?

projects

12 Word's Envelope Option   File: AMC.doc

When you've used Word to create a neat, attractive letter, it seems inconsistent to mail it in a hand-written envelope. In the early years of word processing, many people kept a typewriter on hand simply for addressing envelopes. In this Project, you'll use Word's envelope feature to automatically address an envelope for a letter written to the American Movie Classics channel.

To address and print an envelope:

1: Open the AMC document from your Project Disk. Click **Tools** on the menu bar, click **Envelopes and Labels** to open the Envelopes and Labels dialog box, and then click the **Envelopes** tab (if necessary). Notice that Word has automatically inserted the addressee from the letter into the *Delivery Address* box.

2: If you are working on your own computer, the *Return Address* box might already contain your name and address. Otherwise, that box probably contains computer identification information. You'll now temporarily replace the contents of that box. Select all the text in the *Return Address* box and then type the following:

> **Margaret Worthington**
>
> **5144 Lafferty Avenue**
>
> **Louisville KY 30417**

3: Assume your envelopes are 3 7/8 by 8 7/8 inches. Click the **Options** button, click the *Envelope Size* ▾, click **Size 9 (3 7/8 x 8 7/8 in)**, and then click the **OK** button.

4: Click the **Add to Document** button to add the envelope to the letter, and then click the **No** button when asked if you want to save the new return address as the default return address. Note that the envelope is added to the beginning of the document as page 0. Preview the document to check the envelope and letter.

5: Now you'll print just the envelope, using regular 8½ x 11-inch paper rather than an envelope. Click anywhere in the envelope, click **File** on the menu bar, click **Print**, click the **Current Page** option button, and then click the **OK** button. If a message box instructs you to "Please insert paper," click the **OK** button.

Close the document without saving changes.

13 Create a Custom Envelope

Sometimes you'll need to address an envelope for which you don't have a Word document letter, or you'll want to use an envelope that is a non-standard size. Suppose you want to use a 3½ x 6-inch envelope you have on hand to mail your entry to a movie trivia contest.

projects

To create a custom envelopes:

1: Start a new Word document, click **File** on the menu bar, click **Page Setup**, and then click the **Paper Size** tab. Click the *Paper Size* ▼, scroll to the bottom of the list, and then click **Custom Size**. Change the *Width* value to 6" and the *Height* value to 3.5".

2: Click the **Margins** tab, change all four margins to **0.5"**, and then click the **OK** button to apply all the changes.

3: Type your name, mailing address, and city, state, and zip code in the first three (or four) lines of the document. Then type the following addressee lines:

Movie Trivia Contest

P.O. Box 1053

Kansas City, Kansas 63125-1053

4: Select the return address lines and change the font to **12-point Arial**. Select the three addressee lines, change the font to **14-point Arial**, and increase the left indent to **1.5"**. Then select just the "Movie Trivia Contest" line, and format the paragraph to change the *Spacing Before* value to **54 pt**.

Save the document on your Project Disk with an appropriate name, and then preview the document to see how your envelope looks.

Change the paper size to "Letter 8 1/2 x 11 in.", print the envelope using regular 8½ x 11-inch paper, and then close the document without saving changes. Mark off a 3½ x 6-inch area on the printout to show the dimensions of the envelope.

14 Changing Page Numbers   File: StevenS.doc

In the online Steps, you created a footer with automatically generated page numbers for a simple document that wasn't divided into sections. In this Project, you'll edit a partially completed term paper on Steven Spielberg for a college film course; the document is already divided into three sections: the title page, the table of contents page, and the body of the report. You'll add a header that will appear only in the third section.

Open the StevenS document from your Project Disk. Move the insertion point so that it is positioned in the beginning of the third section of the document. (The section number is shown in the left portion of the status bar.)

Modify the header to create a right-justified header containing the word "Page" followed by a space, followed by the page number. Don't close the Header and Footer toolbar yet.

Notice that the header text box is titled "Header-Section 3" and that "Page 1" is currently displayed in the header text box. This matches the information in the status bar, which tells you you're on Page 1 of Section 3. This is actually the third page of the document (the title page is page 1, and the table of contents page is page 2), so you need to modify the page number field to display the correct value.

Click Insert on the menu bar, click Page Numbers to open the Page Numbers dialog box, and then click the Format button to open the Page Number Format dialog box. Make sure the Start At option is selected in the Page Numbering section, change the value in the box to 3, click the OK button to close the dialog box, and then click the OK button again to close the other dialog box and apply the change.

Close the Header and Footer toolbar. Notice that the information displayed in the status bar has changed to reflect the change you made to the page numbers. Then switch to page layout view to verify that the page numbers are correctly displayed on pages 3 through 5 of the document, and only on those pages.

Save the document without changing the filename, and then print the document.

15 Other Page Number Forms   File: Oscars.doc

In the online Steps you created a footer and inserted page numbers of the standard form (1, 2, 3…). Did you know that you can optionally number pages as A, B, C…, a, b, c…, I, II, III…, or i, ii, iii…? In this Project you'll edit a film magazine article to add a footer with inserted symbols and centered lowercase-letter page numbers.

Open the Oscars document from your Project Disk, and then switch to page layout view, if necessary.

To insert and format a page number of the form "— a —":

1: Click **View** on the menu bar, and then click **Header and Footer**. Click the ▦ **Switch between Header and Footer** button on the Header and Footer toolbar, and then press the **Tab** key. Now you'll insert a special character to precede the page number.

2: Click **Insert** on the menu bar, click **Symbol** to open the Symbol dialog box, and then click the **Special Characters** tab. Click the **Em Dash** character in the *Character* box, click the **Insert** button, and then click the **Close** button to close the Symbol dialog box.

3: Press the **spacebar** to add a space, and then click the ▦ **Page Number** button on the Header and Footer toolbar. Now you'll change the page number format.

4: Click **Insert**, click **Page Numbers** to open the Page Numbers dialog box, and then click the **Format** button. In the Page Number Format dialog box, click the *Number Format* ▼, click **a, b, c...**, click the **OK** button to close the dialog box, and then click the **OK** button to close the Page Numbers dialog box.

5: Move the insertion point immediately right of the page number, press the spacebar to add a space, click **Insert**, click **Symbol** to open the Symbol dialog box, click the **Insert** button, and then click the **Close** button to close the Symbol dialog box. The page number now appears as "— a —".

6: Select the entire footer line, and then change the font to 11-point Century Schoolbook.

7: Now you'll change the position of the footer line by changing the page setup. Click **File** on the menu bar, click **Page Setup**, click the **Margins** tab (if necessary), change the *Footer* value to **0.75"**, and then click the **OK** button.

Print the document and then close the document without saving changes.

EXPLORE

16 Create Business Cards   File: Camera.bmp

If you've ever had business cards printed, you know it can be costly, especially if you don't order a large quantity at once. Did you know that you can purchase high-quality, pre-cut business card stock at most office supply stores and that you can use Word to create your business cards? In this Project, you'll create a sheet of business cards for a movie cinematographer.

To create business cards:

1: Start a new Word document, make sure that nonprinting characters are showing, click **Tools** on the menu bar, click **Envelopes and Labels**, and then click the **Labels** tab.

2: Click the **Options** button, make sure the *Label Products* box contains "Avery Standard", and then select **5371 - Business Card** in the *Project Number* box. Note that the dialog box specifies that the cards are each 2" high by 3.5" wide, on an 8½ x 11-inch sheet. Click the **OK** button to close the Label Options dialog box, and then click the **New Document** button in the Envelopes and Labels dialog box. Word creates a table with five rows and two columns, with each cell the exact size of one of the business cards.

3: Select the table, change the font to **12-point Garamond**, and then format the paragraph to set the *Spacing Before* value to **0 pt**.

4: Move the insertion point to the left of the second paragraph mark in the first table cell. Press the **spacebar** twice, and then click **Insert** on the menu bar. Point to **Picture** and then click **From File** to open the Insert Picture dialog box. Change the entry in the *Look In* box to the location of your Project Disk, and then double-click **Camera**.

projects

5: Press the **spacebar** three times, type your name, press the **Enter** key, and then type the following information at the left margin. (Do *not* press the Enter key after typing the telephone number.)

Cinematographer

6422 Valley Road

North Hollywood CA 91608

(818) 555-1326

6: Select the last four lines of text you just typed and center them. Select your name and the line containing "Cinematographer" and bold the text. Then select just your name, and then change the font size to **14**. Finally, add or remove spaces in front of your name as needed so that your name is centered above "Cinematographer." One business card is now complete.

7: Move the pointer into the lower-left area of that first cell, click to select that cell, and then click the **Copy** button on the Standard toolbar.

8: For each of the remaining nine table cells, select the cell, and then click the **Paste** button on the Standard toolbar.

Preview the document, save it with an appropriate filename, then print the document on regular 8½ x 11-inch paper.

17 Creating Columns   File: NFRFilms.doc

Suppose you have some information in your document that you want to present in columns, perhaps to save space or to make the document more interesting or attractive. You could create a table with two columns and insert the information in the table. However, Word provides an easier way to create what it calls "newspaper columns": You select the material you want formatted in columns and then use the Columns option on the Format menu. In this Project, you'll edit a report on the National Film Registry and format the film lists in columns.

Open the NFRFilms document from your Project Disk and make sure that nonprinting characters are showing. Scroll through the document, noting that the twenty-five films selected for each of the eight years from 1989 through 1996 are listed beneath a year heading.

Select the 25 films beneath the 1989 heading. (Note: The easiest way to select a block of text is to click at the beginning of the block you want to select, scroll if necessary so you can see the end of the block you want to select, and then hold down the Shift key as you click at the end of the block.)

projects

To format text in columns:

1: Click **Format** on the menu bar, and then click **Columns** to open the Columns dialog box. Change the value in the *Number of Columns* box to **2**, and then notice how the picture in the Preview section of the dialog box changes to show the effect of putting the selected text in columns. By default, Word assigns a 0.5" spacing between the two columns; that value is acceptable in this case, so click the **OK** button to close the dialog box and create the columns. Notice that Word added continuous section breaks to the beginning and end of the selected material. Also notice that Word automatically wraps a paragraph longer than the column width (film 5. Dr. Strangelove…).

2: Switch to page layout view so you can see the columns. You'll do the remainder of this Project in page layout view. Because you're using default values for column size and spacing between columns, you can use the [icon] Columns button on the Standard toolbar as a shortcut for creating columns.

3: Select the block of 25 films beneath the "1990" heading, click the [icon] **Columns** button, and then click the second column in the box that appears below that button to format the selected text in two columns.

4: Repeat Step 3 for each of the remaining six sets of twenty-five films.

Notice that Word did not add a section break at the end of the 1996 (last) set of films, so the columns that were created are of unequal length. Move the insertion point to the end of the "25. Woodstock (1970)" entry, and then insert a continuous section break.

Each year heading and the 25 films for that year should appear together on a page. Starting at the beginning, go through the document and add page breaks where necessary.

Save the document without changing the filename, and then print the document.

18 Footnotes and Cross-References   File: Hitch.doc

Suppose you need to refer to the same footnote more than once in a document. You can use Word's cross-reference feature to accomplish this. In this Project, you'll edit a filmography of the movies that Alfred Hitchcock directed, adding footnotes and cross-references.

Open the Hitch document from your Project Disk, and then switch to page layout view if necessary.

You want to footnote the five films for which Alfred Hitchcock was nominated for an Academy Award for directing. The first of those films was 1940's *Rebecca*. Move the insertion point to the right of the "a" in "Rebecca," and then add a footnote with the footnote text "Academy Award directing nominee".

projects

The next film for which Hitchcock was nominated was 1944's *Lifeboat*. Rather than add another (identical) footnote for this film, you'll add a cross-reference to the earlier footnote.

To add a cross-reference to a footnote:

1: Move the insertion point to the right of the "t" in "Lifeboat," click **Insert** on the menu bar, and then click **Cross-reference** to open the Cross-reference dialog box. Click **Footnote** in the *Reference Type* box. Then click the note to which you want to refer in the *For Which* box to select it (if necessary; in this case only one footnote is listed, and it's already selected). Make sure "Footnote Number" is selected in the *Insert Reference To* box, click the **Insert** button, and then click the **Close** button.

2: You want the cross-reference mark to look like a footnote mark, so you need to format it. Select the cross-reference mark that was just added, click **Format** on the menu bar, click **Font**, click the **Font** tab (if necessary), click the **Superscript** option button in the Effects section of the Font dialog box, and then click the **OK** button.

You need to add the same cross-reference to three more films. The easiest way to accomplish this is with a copy-and-paste operation. Click the  Copy button on the Standard toolbar. Move the insertion point to the end of 1945's *Spellbound* title, and then click the Paste button; repeat the paste operation for 1954's *Rear Window* and 1960's *Psycho*.

Add a footnote with the text "Golden Globe directing nominee" to 1972's *Frenzy*. Then scroll to the top of the document. You decide the "aka" that appears in several film entries should be footnoted. Move the insertion point after the "aka" in the first film, and then add a footnote with the text "Aka: also known as".

Insert a page break at the beginning of the "1940s" paragraph so that paragraph and all the films for that decade will appear together on the same page. Notice that footnote number 2 is automatically moved from the first page to the second page because the footnoted text has moved to the second page.

Scroll the document so you can see all the films of the 1940s. Notice that the cross-reference on the films *Lifeboat* and *Spellbound* still show a "1" even though the footnote they cross-reference has been changed to footnote #2. Cross-references are updated in one of two ways: you can select each of the cross-references (or select the entire document) and then press the F9 key, or you can print the document, at which time Word automatically updates the cross-references.

Print the document. Notice that the cross-references are updated the moment you click the Print button.

Save the document without changing the filename, and then close the document.

19 Date Fields and Highlighting   File: Catalog.doc

Suppose you want to write a letter before you need it so that it's ready to go when it's time to print it. To save time when you print the letter, you can insert a date field that Word will automatically update when the document is printed. You can also highlight text to remind yourself of other information in the document that must be added or changed when you print. In this Project, you'll edit a letter to add a print date field and to highlight text.

Open the Catalog file from your Project Disk.

To add a print date field:

1: Move the insertion point to the beginning of the document (if necessary), click **Insert** on the menu bar, and then click **Field** to open the Field dialog box. Click **Date and Time** in the *Categories* box, and then click **PrintDate** in the *Field Names* box. Notice that the entry following "Field Codes" in the dialog box includes the text "Date-Time Picture," which indicates that the inserted field will include both the date and the time. You need to select a format that includes the date but not the time.

2: Click the **Options** button in the Field dialog box to open the Field Options dialog box. Click **MMMM d, yyyy** in the *Date-Time Formats* box, click the **Add to Field** button, click the **OK** button to close the Field Options dialog box, and then click the **OK** button to close the Field dialog box and add the print date field to your document. The field appears as "XXX 0, 0000" because the document hasn't been printed yet. Word will automatically insert the current date every time the document is printed.

Notice the "??" in the letter body. When the final copy of the letter is printed, you'll want to replace those question marks with an actual hours value. To remind yourself to update that text before final printing, you'll highlight the text.

To highlight text:

1: Select the two question marks, click the ▼ portion of the ✎ ▼ **Highlight** button on the Formatting toolbar, and then click the green block in the color palette box that appears.

Now replace the "X" that appears near the bottom of the letter with your name. Then scroll to the top of the document (if necessary), save the document without changing the filename, then print the document. Notice that Word replaces the

"XXX 0, 0000" with the current date when you click the 🖨 Print button

Close the document without saving changes.

projects

20 Sorting Text   File: NFR

If you did Project 19 in Tutorial 3, then you know how to use the Sort command on the Table menu to sort tables. (If you didn't do that Project, you might want to read through it now; or, you can use Help to learn about sorting columns in tables.) Did you know that you can use the sort command on the Table menu to sort text that's not in a table? In this Project, you'll sort a list of National Film Registry movies by title within year filmed.

Open the NFR document from your Project Disk. Notice that the 200 films selected for the National Film Registry between 1989 and 1996 are currently sorted by title. (In a text sort, numbers sort before letters, so *2001: A Space Odyssey* is the first title in the list.) The year that appears to the left of a film title is the year the film was made.

To sort text:

1: Select all the films, click **Table** on the menu bar, and then click **Sort Text** to open the Sort Text dialog box. Click the *Sort By* ▼, and then click **Field 1** to sort first on the year, which is the first field in the paragraphs to be sorted. Make sure **Number** is specified in the *Type* box in that same section of the dialog box. Click the **Descending** option button in that same section to sort the films from most recent to oldest.

2: Several films might have been made in any given year. You want the films for a particular year to be listed in alphabetical order, so you'll specify a secondary sort field. Click the *Then By* ▼, and then click **Field 2** to sort next on the film name, which is the second field in the paragraphs to be sorted. Make sure **Text** is specified in the *Type* box in that same section of the dialog box and that the **Ascending** option is also selected in that same section.

3: You want to sort all the paragraphs you selected, so make sure the **No Header Row** option is selected at the bottom of the dialog box, and then click the **OK** button to sort the text.

Preview the document and notice that it's already been formatted in columns. (If you don't know how to format text in columns, either read Project 17 in this tutorial or use Help to learn about creating newspaper-type columns.) If the document requires more than two pages, change the top margin (and/or bottom margin, if necessary) for the whole document, decreasing it by .1" at a time until the document fits onto two pages.

Print the document and then close it without saving changes. Check the printout and verify that the films were sorted from newest to oldest and that films appears in alphabetical order within a given year.

21 Create a Fax with Columns and a Watermark
File: MyFax.doc and Fax-Text.bmp

A fax document is essentially a regular Word document that you will fax to a recipient. To create a fax, you can use Word's Fax Wizard, which leads you through the steps for creating fax cover sheets and sending electronic faxes. Alternatively, you can create a document yourself; in which case, you should remember to include information about the sender and the recipient, either as a separate fax cover sheet or at the top of the first page of the document.

In this Project you'll complete a fax document that has been started, use both soft and nonbreaking hyphens, add and modify columns, and add a watermark.

Open the MyFax document from your Project Disk. Notice the heading table with recipient and sender information at the top of the document. First you'll complete that heading table.

To complete the fax heading information:

1: Type your name in the table cell to the right of the cell containing "From:".

2: Position the insertion point in the table cell to the right of the cell containing "Date:". Click **Insert** on the menu bar, click **Date and Time** to open the Date and Time dialog box, then click the first format in the list to insert today's date in a MM/DD/YY format.

The third line in the first paragraph of the body of the document is noticeably shorter than the other lines because the long word "comprehensive" will not fit on that third line. If you inserted a hyphen at a syllable break in that word, forming "compre-hensive", Word would split the word at the hyphen, placing "compre-" on the third line, and "hensive" at the beginning of the fourth line. However, that hyphen then becomes a part of the word. If you later add text earlier in that paragraph that changes the location of line breaks, the word would print on one line as "compre-hensive", including the hyphen. To avoid this, you should insert a "soft hyphen" in the word instead of a real hyphen. A soft hyphen is one that prints *only* if the word splits across a line.

To use a soft hyphen:

1: Position the insertion point between the "e" and "h" in "comprehensive," and then type Ctrl+hyphen (that is, hold down the Ctrl key while you press the hyphen key). Word splits the word between two lines, with "compre¬" appearing at the end of the first line. That "¬" symbol indicates a soft hyphen.

2: Preview the document to verify that the "¬" prints as a regular hyphen ("-").

projects

3: Insert the word "efficiently" at the end of the second sentence of that first paragraph ("… to do that efficiently."). Notice that "compre¬hensive" now appears on the fourth line.

4: Preview the document to verify that the "¬" in "compre¬hensive" does not print.

The movie title "Ben-Hur" in the second paragraph splits across two lines. If you'd prefer that hyphenated words in movie titles not split across lines, you should change the regular hyphen to a nonbreaking hyphen, which is a hyphen that prevents a hyphenated word or phrase from breaking if it falls at the end of a line.

To use nonbreaking hyphens:

1: Select the hyphen in "Ben-Hur," then replace that regular hyphen with a nonbreaking hyphen by typing Ctrl+Shift+hyphen (that is, hold down both the Ctrl and Shift keys while you press the hyphen key). That title now appears on a single line as "Ben–Hur," with the nonbreaking hyphen character appearing to be longer than a regular hyphen.

2: Preview the document to verify that the longer "–" in "Ben–Hur" will print as a normal hyphen.

3: Next you'll find and replace the regular hyphens in the rest of the document with nonbreaking hyphens. To do this click **Edit** on the menu bar, click **Replace** to open the Find and Replace dialog box, and then, if necessary, click the **More** button.

4: Type a regular hyphen ("-") in the *Find what* box, press the **Tab** key, click the **Special** button, click **Nonbreaking Hyphen** in the displayed list, and then click the **Replace All** button. Click the **OK** button when Word reports that it has made the changes, and then click the **Close** button to close the dialog box.

The document currently requires two pages. To save on the number of pages that must be faxed, you'll format the list of 59 movies at the end of the document into columns.

To format columns:

1: Select the alphabetical list of movie titles at the end of the document, from "Age-Old Friends" to "Two-Headed Spy, The" and then italicize the selected list.

2: With the list still selected, click the ▦ **Columns** button on the Standard toolbar, and then click the fourth column in the displayed palette to format the selected text in four columns. Four columns appears to be too many, as almost every movie title requires multiple lines to print.

3: Next you'll change the number of columns to three. With the list still selected, click the

▦ **Columns** button on the Standard toolbar, and then click the third column in the displayed palette to format the selected text in three columns. By default, Word has used ½" spacing between the columns.

4: You'll next decrease that spacing value. Click **Format** on the menu bar, and then click **Columns** to open the Columns dialog box.

5: Change the 0.5" spacing value for Col#1 to **0.3"**, click **Equal column width** to select that option, and then click the **OK** button to apply the changes. Now scroll to the end of the document and notice that Word has formatted the list in three columns, with the second column one line shorter than the first and third columns. (Don't worry if your column breaks are different; continue with these Steps.)

6: You'll now change those automatic column break positions by inserting a manual column break. Position the insertion point immediately to the left of the "*C*" in "*Court-Martial of Billy Mitchell, The*", click **Insert** on the menu bar, click **Break**, click **Column Break**, and then click the **OK** button to close the dialog box. The first column is now one line longer than the second column, which is two lines longer than the third column. The columns as Word originally split them were more appropriate, so you'll remove the column break you just added.

7: Click the ⟳ **Undo** button on the Standard toolbar. The list is now formatted as you want it.

Now you'll add two movies to the list.

To insert items in a columned list:

1: Add the following movies (with nonbreaking hyphens) at the appropriate location in the alphabetical columned list: ***Ex-Champ*** and ***Ex-Lady***. Notice that Word changes the automatic column breaks to adjust for the added entries. (Depending on the location of your automatic column breaks, there may be no change after you add the two entries.)

2: Italicize each of the three movie titles in the second paragraph.

To complete the fax, which now fits on a single page, you'll add a watermark. A **watermark** is any text or graphic that when printed appears either on top of or behind existing document text. To create a watermark in Word you inserted it into a header or a footer, but you can then position it anywhere on the page.

To insert a watermark:

1: Click **View** on the menu bar, and then click **Header and Footer** to open the Header and Footer dialog box. Now you'll insert a picture located on your Project Disk.

2: Click **Insert** on the menu bar, point to **Picture**, and then click **From File**. Then locate and insert the picture named **Fax-Text.bmp** on your Project Disk. You'll now format the picture to color it gray and position it behind the text. Click the picture to select it,

projects

click **Format** on the menu bar, click **Picture** to open the Picture dialog box, and then click the **Picture** tab, if necessary.

3: Click the *Color* ▼ in the Image control section, and then click **Watermark**. Click the **Wrapping** tab, click **None** in the Wrapping style section, and then click the **OK** button to close the dialog box. The picture is now colored gray and appears behind the text.

4: Drag the picture straight down so that the top of the picture coincides with the top of the columned list.

5: Close the Header and Footer toolbar.

Print the document, and then close it without saving changes.

22 Navigate With Go To and Create Alternating Pages
File: Nominees.doc

Suppose you're preparing to give a seminar on the Academy Awards, and you're currently working on a handout listing all nominees for all years for best picture, actress, and actor. The handout will have mirror margins and alternating headers and footers so that it can be bound along the left edge, like this WorkText is. Because the handout is a fairly long document (12 pages), navigating the document could be time-consuming. In this Project you'll learn how to go directly to a specific page, section or bookmark, and how to create mirror margins and alternating headers and footers.

Open the Nominees document from your Project Disk, and page through the document. Notice that some information is presented in columns; thus you know that the document is divided into sections. Word's Go To command allows you to move directly to a page, section, line, bookmark, comment, footnote, or endnote. You'll now use the Go To command to move to other pages and sections.

To go to a page or section:

1: If necessary, move the insertion point to the beginning of the document. Click **Edit** on the menu bar, and then click **Go To** to open the Go To dialog box. If Page is not highlighted in the *Go to what* list, click **Page**.

2: Click the **Next** button. Word moves the insertion point and the display to the top of the next page, which is page 2, as shown on the status bar. Whenever you want to go to the next page, section, or whatever, you only need to click the Next button.

3: To move some number of pages from the current location, you can specify a +n or -n (where "n" stands for "number") to move n pages forward or backward, respectively. To now move to page 5, you could specify a move of +3 pages from the current location. Click the **Enter page number** box, type **+3**, and then click the **Go To** button. The insertion point and display are moved to the top of page 5.

4: To move to a specific page, you type the page number. Click the **Enter page number** box, type **1**, and then click the **Go To** button. The insertion point and display are moved to the top of page 1, which is in the first section in the document.

5: Click **Section** in the *Go to what* list, and then click the **Next** button. The display shifts slightly, and the insertion point moves to the left of the "1996" in the first column. This point is the start of the document's second section.

6: Click the **Next** button, moving from section to section, until the display no longer shifts. You should have moved to four more sections, because the document has a total of six sections. You'll now move back three sections.

7: Click the **Enter section number** box, type **-3**, and then click the **Go To** button. The insertion point and display are moved to the top of page 5.

8: Click the **Close** button to close the Go To dialog box.

A **bookmark** is a location or selection of text that you name for reference purposes and that you can use for navigation. One bookmark named "Actress75" has already been defined in the document. Next you'll use and create bookmarks.

To use bookmarks:

1: Click **Edit** on the menu bar, and then click **Go To** to reopen the Go To dialog box.

2: Click **Bookmark** in the *Go to what* list, click the **Go To** button to move to the Actress75 bookmark, which is the name that appears in the *Enter bookmark name* list, and then click the **Close** button to close the dialog box. The display shifts and the insertion point is now positioned to the left of the "1975" above the list of the five best actress nominees for 1975.

Now you'll create bookmarks for 1975's actor nominee list and 1975's picture nominee list.

To create bookmarks:

1: Using the techniques you've learned, go to page 6, and then position the insertion point to the left of 1975 in the first column on that page.

2: Click **Insert** on the menu bar, click **Bookmark** to open the Bookmark dialog box, type **Actor75** to enter that name in the *Bookmark name* box, and then click the **Add** button. A bookmark named "Actor75" is now added to your document, located at the current insertion point location.

projects

3: Go to page 9, and then position the insertion point to the left of 1975 in the third column on that page. Then repeat Step 4, this time typing **Picture75** as the bookmark name.

4: Now you'll navigate the document using its three bookmarks. Click **Edit** on the menu bar, click **Go To** to reopen the Go To dialog box, and then click **Bookmark** in the *Go to what* list, if necessary.

5: Click the *Enter bookmark name* to display the list of bookmarks. Notice that three bookmark names appear in the list. Click one of the bookmark names, and then click the **Go To** button to move to that bookmark.

6: Repeat Step 5 two more times, selecting each of the other two bookmarks.

When you plan to print a document on both sides of the paper and then bind the document along its edge, like a book, you should define mirror margins for the document. With mirror margins, the inside margins of facing pages are the same width and the outside margins are the same width. Typically, the inside margins must be larger than the outside margins because part of the inside margin will be taken up by the binding. The Nominees document currently has equal 0.8" margins on the left and right. You'll now change the page setup to allow for mirror margins with an inside margin of 1" and an outside margin of 0.6".

To set mirror margins:

1: Click **File** on the menu bar, click **Page Setup**, and then click the **Margins** tab, if necessary.

2: Click **Mirror margins** to select that option.

3: Click the *Apply to* , and then click **Whole document**.

4: Change the *Inside* value to **1"**, change the *Outside* value to **0.6"**, and then click the **OK** button to close the dialog box and apply the changes.

5: Preview the document. The preview window shows page 1 alone, and then shows the remaining pages two at a time. With two pages showing in the preview window, notice that the left margins of the two pages are noticeably different sizes—the page on the left has a smaller left margin than the page on the right. (It's more difficult to notice the differences in right margin sizes because the document text doesn't align along the right margin.)

Now you'll add headers and footers to the document. Because you'll print this document like a book, you'll want the header and footer text to appear on the outside of the page. Word lets you define different odd and even page headers and footers.

To define odd and even page headers and footers:

1: Move the insertion point to the top of the first page of the document.

2: Click **View** on the menu bar, and then click **Header and Footer**.

3: Click the ⊡ **Page Setup** button on the Header and Footer toolbar to open the Page Setup dialog box, click the **Layout** tab, click **Different odd and even** to select that option, click the *Apply to* ▼, click **Whole document**, and then click the **OK** button to close the dialog box and apply the changes. The header box is now labeled "Odd Page Header - Section 1". On odd pages, you want the header and footer material to appear on the far right of the page.

4: Press the **Tab** key twice, type **Academy Award Nominees**, and then select and underline the three words you just typed.

5: Click the ⊡ **Switch Between Header and Footer** button on the Header and Footer toolbar.

6: Press the **Tab** key twice, type **Page**, press the **spacebar**, and then click the ⊡ **Insert Page Number** button on the Header and Footer toolbar.

7: Next you'll move to the even page footer and header, in which the text will be left-justified. Click the ⊡ **Show Next** button on the Header and Footer toolbar. Notice that the even page footer is already correctly defined and appropriately left-justified.

8: Click the ⊡ **Switch Between Header and Footer** button on the Header and Footer toolbar, and notice that the even page header is already correctly specified and appropriately left-justified.

9: Click the **Close** button on the Header and Footer toolbar.

Save the document on your Project Disk as Oscar Nominees.

Now you'll print just the first four pages of the document. If you are using a computer with a dedicated printer, you can print on both sides of the paper. First specify that you want to print pages 1-4 in the Pages box of the Page range section of the Print dialog box, and then select the Odd pages option in the Print box of that same dialog box. Pages 1 and 3 of the document will then be printed. Place those two printed pages in the paper feed tray, reopen the Print dialog box, again specify pages 1-4 in the Pages box, and then select the Even pages option in the Print box. Depending on your printer, you might have to click the Options button, and then click the Reverse print order option—check your printer documentation. If you do have to set that option, remember to set the Reverse print order option back to its original state after the pages are printed.

projects

If you are using a network printer, print pages 1-4 of the document. Then tape, paste, or staple the back of page 1 to the back of page 2; repeat for pages 3 and 4.

In either case, now stack the printed pages in the appropriate order and then staple along the left edge of page 1 to create a small "booklet."

23 Use Hyperlinks
Files: TopFilms.doc, Harrison.doc, and Top50.xls

A **hyperlink** is a graphic or colored underlined text in a document that you can click to jump to a destination on your hard disk, on a floppy disk, on a local intranet, or on the Internet, such as a page on the World Wide Web. In this Project you'll work with three related documents, creating and using hyperlinks from each document to each of the other two documents.

Open the TopFilms document on your Project Disk. You'll use the two red buttons at the bottom of the document for hyperlinks.

To create hyperlinks:

1: Click the red button on the left to select it, click **Insert** on the menu bar, and then click **Hyperlink**.

2: Click the **Browse** button at the top of the Hyperlink dialog box to open the Link to File dialog box, change the *Look in* entry to the location of your Project Disk, click **Top50.xls**, and then click the **OK** button to close the Link to File dialog box. The path to the Top50.xls file now appears in the text box at the top of the Hyperlink dialog box.

3: Click the **OK** button to create the hyperlink.

4: Repeat Steps 1 through 3, except click the red button on the right and link to the file named Harrison.doc.

5: Save, but do not close, the TopFilms document.

6: Position the pointer over the first red button; Word displays the path to your Top50.xls file. Then position the pointer over the second red button; Word displays the path to your Harrison.doc file.

7: Click the second red button. Word opens the Harrison.doc file.

Scroll to the bottom of the Harrison document. In this document you'll create hyperlinks using text rather than a graphic. Select the words "Current top-grossing movies" and then create a hyperlink to the file Top50.xls on your Project Disk, using the technique described above. When the hyperlink is created, notice that the text changes colors and is underlined.

Then select the words "Return to main page" and create a hyperlink to the file TopFilms.doc on your Project Disk. Save and print the file, but do not close, the current version of the Harrison document.

Click the "Current top-grossing movies" hyperlink in the Harrison document. Excel starts and the Top50.xls file opens. Scroll the Excel worksheet so that row 56 is visible. Again, you'll create hyperlinks using text. The process for creating hyperlinks in Excel is the same as in Word. Click cell B56, which contains "Return to main page", then create a hyperlink to the TopFilm.doc file on your Project Disk. Then click cell D56 (containing "Harrison Ford") and create a hyperlink to the Harrison.doc file on your Project Disk.

Save and print the Top50.xls document, but do not close it.

To test hyperlinks:

1: Click one of the two hyperlinks in the current document to jump to one of the other two files. If any hyperlink doesn't work correctly, select that hyperlink, click **Insert** on the menu bar, click **Hyperlink**, and then click the **Remove Link** button; then recreate the hyperlink as before.

2: Repeat Step 1 until you've tested all six hyperlinks.

3: Close the Harrison.doc and Top50.xls files, and then exit Excel.

Suppose you wanted to use the TopFilms.doc document, which is the current Word document, as a Web page. To do so, you must convert the file to HTML.

To convert a file to HTML:

1: Click **File** on the menu bar, click **Save as HTML**, and then save the file as **TopFilms.html** on your Project Disk. If a message box appears asking if you want to access the Internet for Web page authoring tools, click the **No** button.

2: Click the ¶ **Show/Hide** button, if necessary, so that nonprinting characters are not displayed.

When you save a Word document as a Web page, Word closes the document and then reopens it in HTML format. Word then displays the Web page in outline view, which is similar to the way it would appear in a Web browser.

If you do not have a Web browser installed on your computer, print the current document, exit Word, and skip the remainder of this project.

If you have a Web browser installed on your computer, you can use the Web Page Preview option to see *exactly* how the Web page would appear on your Web browser.

projects

To use Web Page Preview:

1: Click **File** on the menu bar, and then click **Web Page Preview**. (If that option is not available on the File menu, print the current document, exit Word, and skip the remainder of this Project.)

2: If your Web Browser has a print option (most likely located on the File menu), print the Web page.

3: Point to each of the two red buttons to verify that the hyperlinks are still operable. When you point to a hyperlink, the location associated with that hyperlink is displayed somewhere on the Web page, most likely in the status bar.

4: Close the Web Browser, close the Word document, and then exit Word.

As you learned at the beginning of this Project, a hyperlink can be either a graphic or text. A wide variety of graphics and text formats can be used for hyperlinks. Next you'll access the Microsoft Web site on the Internet to investigate the hyperlinks on that Web site. (If you do not have Internet access with your computer, your instructor will provide directions for completing this Project.)

To investigate hyperlink formats:

1: Access the Internet and go to the Microsoft Web site home page at http://www.microsoft.com.

2: Print the Microsoft home page.

3: Locate every hyperlink on this page by pointing to each object on the page. If an object you point to is a hyperlink, a location will appear somewhere on the Web page, most likely in the status bar. Then indicate every hyperlink on the printout of the Web page.

Suppose you wanted to know what materials Microsoft had to offer for support for Word for Windows.

To browse hyperlinks:

1: Use the hyperlinks on the various Microsoft Web pages to locate the Microsoft Word Support home page.

2: Print that Web page.

projects

24 Your Opinion Counts

Projects 17 and 20 in this Tutorial dealt with the National Film Registry. In conjunction with the National Film Preservation Act of 1988, the United States Library of Congress established the National Film Registry, which is dedicated to preserving films deemed "culturally, historically, or aesthetically important." Each year since 1989, 25 films have been selected for addition to the Registry.

Public nominations for the National Film Registry are welcomed. Nominations received by March 30 are considered for that year; nominations received after that date are considered the following year. Nominations should be sent to:

> National Film Registry
> Library of Congress
> Motion Picture, Broadcasting and Recorded Sound Division
> Washington DC 20540

A nominated film must meet two criteria:

1. The film must satisfy the National Film Preservation Board's evaluation of cultural, historic, or aesthetic significance.

2. The film must be at least 10 years old at the time of nomination.

Select a film that you believe should be considered for selection to the National Film Registry. Write a nomination letter explaining why you think the film is worthy of inclusion in the National Film Registry. Your instructor will provide you with specifications for the letter's length and format.

Note: Be sure to verify that your film is not already in the Registry. The file NFR.doc on your Project Disk contains an alphabetical listing of all films selected for the National Film Registry through 1996. Use the resources in the library or on the Internet to learn which films have been selected since 1996. (If you need help thinking of a deserving film or if you need to check the date of a film, the Internet Movie Database at http://us.imdb.com/ might be useful.)

25 Does Any One Know A Short Cut?

Sometimes it's easier to write a document if you have a good idea of how the final piece should look. If you're short on experience in an area—say, you've never seen a business plan or you're fresh out of ideas for how to structure your resume—is there anywhere you can turn for help? The answer is a resounding "Yes!" because of templates.

Select an area that interests you—business plans, public relations plans, marketing plans, resumes, or theses, for example. Use library resources, the Internet,

magazine articles and advertising, and Microsoft Word Help to learn how templates can help you create better documents faster and easier.

Write a one- to two-page paper that describes what you learned. Be sure to include a description of the major features of the type of template you investigated. Also include footnotes for all of your source material.

26 Giving Proper Credit

These days more and more information that appears on the Internet is not being published anywhere else. In college term papers, professional papers, and nonfiction writing, it is critical to let readers know the sources of your information. How do you construct a footnote or endnote for material whose source is online? In a one-page paper, describe the correct citation format for an e-zine article (an "e-zine" is an online-only magazine), a quotation from a Usenet newsgroup, and a white paper that you've downloaded from an FTP site. In your paper, be sure to include the source or sources you used to determine the correct citation formats.

27 Are There Any Guidelines Out There?

Throughout college and possibly throughout your career, you'll be called on to write many papers, both short and long. The format and style of these papers are critical to how they will be received. Wizards, templates, and help files can offer some assistance with structuring and formatting documents; but you'll need even more information to create an effective report, term paper, or thesis.

Select a type of document that interests you. Possible choices include business reports, science papers, term papers, theses or dissertations, newspaper articles, and magazine articles. In a one- to two-page paper describe three resources that provide style guidelines for creating that particular type of document.

28 By Design

How a document looks is almost as important as what a document says. Documents that do not follow the principles of graphic design are hard to read. Well-used graphic design elements help guide readers through the reading experience and enhance their comprehension and retention of written material.

Investigate the principles of document design, then write a one- to two-page paper that lists and explains 10 key principles of document design. Be sure to include correctly formatted endnotes for your source material.

Answers to Word Processing e-SSentials CheckPoint Questions

1 document production

2 False

3 alternative symbol sets

4 False

5 document template
  document wizard

6 Readability formulas

7 electronic

8 HTML

9 True

10 electronic typewriters
   personal word processors
   microcomputers

Answers to Odd-Numbered Review Questions

Tutorial 1

1   Word

3   document window

5   end mark

7   Ruler

9   scroll bars

11   menu bar

13   toolbars

15   .doc (or doc)

17   outline

19   nonprinting characters

21   selected (or highlighted)

23   header

answers

MULTIPLE CHOICE

25 d

27 b

29 a

31 b

33 a

MATCHING

35 c

37 e

39 b

answers

41 Page layout view shows how your document will look on the printed page while allowing you to create and edit your document. In page layout view, unlike other views, a vertical Ruler is displayed.

Outline view enables you to create and display a topic outline of your document so you can quickly move, copy, and reorganize blocks of text. In outline view, a special Outline toolbar replaces the horizontal Ruler.

Normal view is the best all-purpose view for typing, editing, and formatting text.

43 To rename and save a document, click File on the menu bar, and then click Save As to display the Save As dialog box. Then you specify disk or folder where you want to save the document in the Save in box, enter the new document name in the File name box, and then click the Save button.

To save a file with the same name on the same disk, you click the Save button on Word's Standard toolbar.

Tutorial 2

FILL-IN-THE-BLANKS

1 select

3 drag and drop

5 Copy

7 Window

9 Arrange All

11 Find

13 Thesaurus

MULTIPLE CHOICE

15 c

17 b

19 d

21 b

23 d

25 d

answers

27 f

29 j

31 b

33 g

35 e

SHORT ANSWER

37 To select a word, double-click the word.

To select a block of text, drag over the block of text.

To select a line, move the pointer into the left margin next to the line, and then click.

To select a paragraph, move the pointer into the left margin next to the paragraph, and then double-click.

To select the entire document, click Edit on the menu bar, and then click Select All.

39 To place a copy of some specific document text in another part of your document you would:

1. Select the text to be copied.

2. Click the Copy button on the Standard toolbar.

3. Move the insertion point to the document location where you want the text copied.

4. Click the Paste button on the Standard toolbar.

Tutorial 3

FILL-IN-THE-BLANKS

1 character

3 points

5 Format

7 bullet

9 redefine

11 tab

13 cell

MULTIPLE CHOICE

15 b

17 a

19 c

21 c

23 c

25 d

27 b

answers

MATCHING

29 g

31 j

33 h

35 i

37 c

39 k

SHORT ANSWER

41 To apply a style to a paragraph, select the paragraph, click the down arrow on the Style box on the Formatting toolbar, and then click the style you want to apply.

To redefine a paragraph style by example, select the paragraph to which the style you want to modify is applied, and then format the selected text. Click the down arrow on the Style box on the Formatting toolbar, and then click the style you want to modify. In the displayed Reapply Style dialog box, make sure the Redefine option button is selected, and then click the OK button.

43 To create a table, move the insertion point to the place where you want the table. Click Table on the menu bar, and then click Insert Table. Choose the number of columns, the number of rows, and (optionally) the column width, and then click the OK button.

To select a table, move the insertion point into the table, click Table on the menu bar, and then click Select Table.

Tutorial 4

FILL-IN-THE-BLANKS

1 landscape

3 margin

5 page break

7 section break

9 page layout view

11 Header and Footer

13 footnote

MULTIPLE CHOICE

15 b

17 d

19 b

21 b

23 c

25 d

MATCHING

27 i

29 g

31 b

33 d

35 e

SHORT ANSWER

37   A next-page section break and a page break are alike in that both force the text that follows to the next page. That's all a page break does, however, whereas a next-page section break also serves as a dividing line between sections.

If you want to force a page change within a series of logically related lines simply to improve the appearance or layout of a document, then you should use a page break.

If you want to define the start of a new portion of the document that is logically different than the preceding material, or that will require different page-level formatting than the preceding material, you should use a section break. If you want the new section to start at the top of a page, then the section break you add should be a next-page section break.

39   To add a footnote, you move the insertion point to a position immediately right of the text to be footnoted, click Insert on the menu bar, click Footnote, change dialog box settings as necessary, and then click the OK button. You then type the footnote text.

To delete a footnote, you select the reference mark in the text and then press the Delete key. The related footnote text is then automatically deleted.

If you've used the automatic footnote numbering feature to number your footnotes, then Word will automatically renumber all footnotes in the correct order when you move or delete a reference mark, saving you the trouble of doing it yourself.

Spreadsheet e-SSentials

Mathephobia /maθ(ə) ˈfəʊbɪə/ mathe after Fr *mathematiques* the abstract deductive science of number and quantity + phobia L f. Gk, f. `phobos` denoting fear, dislike, antipathy as in hope to never take another math class again.

The United States is one of the most technological societies on earth. The population's fear of math, therefore, is somewhat surprising. People with mathephobia hate to balance their checkbooks, calculate their tax returns, budget their expenses, or decide how to finance their retirement. For the mathephobic person, the words "story problem" produce headaches and indigestion.

Sensing financial opportunity, entrepreneurs have devised tools to ease the burden of making calculations. To date, the most ambitious of these tools—the computerized spreadsheet—is designed to help mathephobics as well as professional number crunchers such as accountants and financial planners.

Today an estimated 20 million people in the world use computerized spreadsheets. Certainly this software has had a major effect on the way people work with numbers. What's the big attraction? To answer this question, it's important to understand how spreadsheets work.

WHAT IS A SPREADSHEET?

A **spreadsheet** is a numerical model or representation of a real situation. For example, your checkbook register is a sort of spreadsheet because it is a numerical representation of the cash flow in and out of your bank account. One expert describes spreadsheets as "intuitive, natural, usable tools for financial analysis, business and mathematical modeling, decision making, simulation, and problem solving."

A spreadsheet can be written on paper and calculated manually, or it can be computerized. Computerized spreadsheets are usually referred to as **worksheets**.

Spreadsheet software is the computer tool you use to create a worksheet. Spreadsheet software makes it easy to enter numbers and indicate how you want them used in calculations. The computer automatically performs the calculations and displays the results.

For example, suppose you're planning a one-week trip to Mexico to see the Mayan ruins at Chichen Itza (Figure 1).

Figure 1 *Spreadsheet software can help you calculate the cost of a trip to see the ancient Mayan observatory Caracol at Chichen Itza.*

You're interested in the total cost of the trip. Using a spreadsheet, you can enter the cost of transportation, food, and lodging. Then, you can tell the computer to add these numbers together to give you a total. The computer performs the calculations and displays the results.

IS A SPREADSHEET BETTER THAN A HAND-HELD CALCULATOR?

A hand-held calculator might be useful for simple calculations, but it becomes less convenient as you deal with more numbers and as your calculations become more complex. For example, suppose your simple calculation for the Mexico trip becomes more complex because you've estimated your food expenses for each day and you must multiply by 7 before you total your expenses. Also, the cost of lodging is a per night rate and does not include the 10% room tax. Before you can total all the expenses, you must multiply the lodging cost by 6 and add on the 10% room tax.

Your calculation now contains multiple steps. Using your hand-held calculator, you have to use your calculator's memory functions or record the seven-day cost of food and lodging on paper for later use to calculate the total trip expense. Look at Figure 2 to visualize this process.

overview

Figure 2 *Using a hand-held calculator, you would need to multiply the daily food cost by 7, then write this number down. After making similar calculations for lodging and taxes, you would take the numbers you've written down, enter them in the calculator, and add them to obtain the total cost of the trip. Spreadsheet software would simplify this process.*

The biggest disadvantage of most calculators is that the numbers you enter are stored, but you can't see them. You can't see if they're accurate. You can't verify what you've entered so far. Also, it is difficult to change the numbers you've entered without starting the whole calculation over again.

If you use a spreadsheet instead of a calculator, all your numbers are visible on the screen, and they are easy to change. Spreadsheets have other advantages. You can print your results as a nicely formatted report, you can convert your numbers into a graph, and you can save your work and revise it later. You can easily incorporate your calculations and results into other electronic documents, post them as Web pages, and e-mail them to your colleagues. In addition, if you don't know exactly how to set up the formula for your calculation, you can use preprogrammed formulas provided by the spreadsheet software.

WHAT DOES A WORKSHEET LOOK LIKE?

Spreadsheet software displays a worksheet on the screen as a grid of **rows** and **columns**. Each column is lettered and each row is numbered. The intersection of a column and row is called a **cell**. Each cell has a unique **address** derived from its column and row location. For example, the upper-left cell in a worksheet is cell A1 because it is in column A of row 1.

A cell can contain a number, text, or a formula. A **number** is a value that you want to use in a calculation. **Text** is used for the worksheet title and for labels that identify the numbers. For example, suppose your worksheet contains the number 12,000,000. You could use text to identify this number as the "Size of television news audience." A **formula** tells the computer how to use the contents of cells in

calculations. You can use formulas to add, subtract, multiply and divide numbers. You can use more complex formulas to calculate statistical, financial, and mathematical functions (Figure 3).

Figure 3 *A typical worksheet displays numbers and text in a grid of rows and columns. Columns B and C contain numbers entered by the person who created the worksheet. Column D contains the results of calculations performed by the spreadsheet software.*

	A	B	C	D
1	**Ad Megabucks**			
2		Cost	Audience	Cost per 1,000 consumers
3	**Television** 30-second spot, network news	$65,000	12,000,000	$5.42
4	**Magazine** Full-page color ad, national weekly	$135,000	3,100,000	$43.55
5	**Newspaper** Full-page ad, midsize city	$31,000	514,000	$60.31
6	**World Wide Web** Online magazine one-month placement	$15,000	200,000	$75.00
7				

|◀ ◀ ▶ ▶|\ **Ad$$** / Graph / Notes / Sheet4 / Sheet5 / Sheet6 / She |

HOW DOES SPREADSHEET SOFTWARE WORK?

The value of spreadsheet software is the way it handles the numbers and formulas in a worksheet. Think of the worksheet as having two layers—the layer you see and a hidden layer underneath. The hidden layer can hold formulas, but the *result* of these formulas appears on the visible layer. Figure 4 shows how this works.

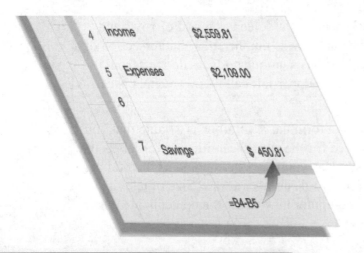

Figure 4 *The formula =B4-B5 works behind the scenes to tell the computer to subtract the number in cell B5 from the number in cell B4. The formula is located in cell B7, but what appears in cell B7 is not the formula but its results.*

Whenever you add or change something in a cell, the spreadsheet calculates all the formulas. This means that the results displayed on your worksheet always reflect the current figures contained in the cells.

Formulas can include numbers and references to other cells. This is what gives a spreadsheet such flexibility. If you have a formula that says "subtract the contents of cell B5 from the contents of B4," it doesn't matter what those cells contain. The result will be accurate even if you later change the contents of these cells. Using **cell references**, such as B5 and B4, you can create generic formulas that work no matter how many times you change the data in other cells.

HOW DO I CREATE A WORKSHEET?

Building a worksheet from scratch requires thought and planning so that you end up with an accurate and well-organized worksheet. When you create your own worksheets, use these seven steps as guidelines:

1: Determine the main purpose of the worksheet. Write down the purpose to make sure it is clear. For example, if you were going to make a worksheet for the Mexico trip, you might write, "The purpose of this worksheet is to calculate the total cost of a trip to Chichen Itza for one person next October."

2: List the information available to solve the problem. In the case of the Mexico trip, your list might include cost of airfare, number of days for the trip, daily lodging cost, the lodging tax percent, and daily food costs.

Consider which of your numbers might be variable. For example, if you're planning a trip to Mexico, the number of days you'll stay might depend on what you can afford. You can use the worksheet to compare the cost of a 5-day trip with that of a 7-day trip.

3: Make a list of the calculations you'll need. For example, your Mexico trip calculations include summing up the cost of food, lodging, and tax.

4: Enter numbers and labels in the cells. When you enter the numbers, make sure you put a descriptive label in an adjoining cell, usually to the left of the data. It's also a good idea to include a title at the top of the worksheet.

5: Enter the formulas.

6: Test the worksheet. There are various ways to do this that you'll learn about later, but the first question to ask yourself is "Do these results make sense?" If the results shown on the worksheet don't seem to be "in the ballpark" of what you expected, maybe you've made a typo when entering a formula. You'll need to check your numbers and formulas and make revisions until the worksheet produces correct results.

7: Save your worksheet.

overview

Figure 5 shows how the Mexico trip worksheet might look.

	A	B	C	D	E
1	Worksheet to calculate the total cost of a trip to Mexico				
2					
3	Created by:	Pat Graulich			
4	Latest revision:	March 12, 1997			
5					
6	Days	7			
7	Nights	6			
8					
9	Item	Cost	Total		
10	Airfare		649		
11	Lodging	75	450		
12	Lodging tax	0.1	45		
13	Food	45	315		
14	Total		1459		

Figure 5 *A worksheet to calculate the cost of a trip to Mexico might look like this. The worksheet has a title and all the numbers are labeled. The total, displayed in cell C14, seems to be "in the ballpark," indicating that the formulas are probably correct.*

WHAT IF I'M NOT SURE HOW TO SET UP THE WORKSHEET?

If you have trouble creating a worksheet from scratch, you might find a predefined template that meets your needs. A **template** is essentially a worksheet form created by professionals who have done all the formatting and formulas for you. If you decide to use a predefined template, you simply select the template you want, and then fill it in with your numbers. Microsoft Excel offers templates for the following tasks:

- tracking a household budget
- deciding on the best car lease option
- recording business expenses while you travel
- invoicing customers
- creating purchase orders
- calculating monthly loan payments
- creating a business plan
- providing customers with a sales quote
- tracking the time you work on various projects

WHAT IF I DON'T KNOW THE FORMULA FOR A CALCULATION?

You can enter your own formulas to specify how to carry out calculations. As another option, you can select a predefined formula called a **function**. Suppose you've got a research assignment, and you need to find the standard deviation of test scores for a school district. You can't find your old statistics text book. No problem. Your spreadsheet software has a built-in function to calculate standard deviations. You just enter the test scores in a series of cells and tell the computer to use the standard deviation function for the calculation. Most spreadsheet software includes hundreds of functions for mathematical, financial, and statistical calculations.

HOW DO I KNOW IF MY WORKSHEET IS PRODUCING CORRECT RESULTS?

The United States has more lawyers per capita than any other country in the world. In a society where lawsuits seem as common as weddings, it might be prudent to consider who is responsible for the accuracy of a spreadsheet. For example, who's fault is it when a project runs over budget because the formula to total the cost was not accurate?

In a well-publicized case, a company discovered that an incomplete worksheet formula resulted in a loss of more than one hundred thousand dollars. The company sued the spreadsheet software publisher, claiming that the software was faulty. The lawsuit was not successful. Responsibility for the accuracy of a worksheet lies with the person who creates it.

In a business situation, an error in a worksheet formula can cost a company hundreds of thousands of dollars. But even if the stakes are not that high for the worksheets you create, you should make an effort to verify the accuracy of your data and formulas. The prime directive of worksheet design is "Don't rely on your worksheet until you test it." Testing, called **auditing** in spreadsheet jargon, is important.

To test a worksheet, you can enter some test data for which you already know the result. For example, if you are designing a worksheet to calculate monthly payments for a car loan, you can use a loan table to find the actual payment for a $12,000 car at 8.5% interest on a three-year loan. Then you can enter this data into your worksheet and see if the result matches the payment specified in the loan table. Once you've verified that the results are accurate, you can enter the actual numbers for the car that you want to buy.

overview

Another test strategy is to enter simple data that you can figure out "in your head." For example, you might enter "1" for all the numbers on the Mexico worksheet and see if the total appears accurate.

More sophisticated tests are required for more complex worksheets. Most spreadsheet software includes **auditing features** to help you find references to empty cells, cells not referenced, and formulas that reference themselves, causing a never-ending calculating loop.

CAN I MODIFY MY WORKSHEETS?

Modifying the text, numbers, and formulas on a worksheet is as easy as using a word processor's insert and delete features. As soon as you enter new numbers in a worksheet, the computer recalculates all the formulas, keeping the results up-to-date. You can also modify the appearance of your worksheet using **formatting options** of your spreadsheet software, such as font size, font type, and background colors.

The formatting you use for a worksheet depends on your output plan. Worksheets that you intend to print might be formatted differently from worksheets that you intend to view only on the screen. Worksheets that you want to project for presentations often require a format different from printed worksheets.

HOW SHOULD I FORMAT WORKSHEETS FOR SCREEN VIEWING?

Worksheets for routine calculations that you're planning to view only on the screen are much handier to use if you can see all the information without scrolling, so try to place all the labels, numbers, and formulas on one screen. If necessary, you can make the columns narrow so that more of them fit on the screen. If you're creating a worksheet for your own use, there's probably no need to spend time making it look attractive.

ARE THERE SPECIAL FORMATTING CONSIDERATIONS FOR PRINTED WORKSHEETS?

If you are going to print your worksheet, you'll want to spend some time creating an attractive format (Figure 6). Use a larger font for the title, and consider italicizing or boldfacing important numbers and their labels. Your worksheet will look more polished if you omit the grid lines between rows and columns. As when you format documents with a word processor, maintain a liberal amount of white space on the page. However, don't try to skip every other row to give the appearance of double spacing. If you do this, you'll have trouble graphing the data.

	A	B	C	D	E
1	**Worksheet to calculate the total**				
2	**cost of a trip to Mexico**				
3	**Created by:**	Pat Graulich			
4	**Latest revision:**	March 12, 1997			
5					
6	**Days**	7			
7	**Nights**	6			
8					
9	**Item**	**Cost**	**Total**		
10	Airfare		$649.00		
11	Lodging	$75.00	$450.00		
12	Lodging tax	0.1	$45.00		
13	Food	$45.00	$315.00		
14	Total		*$1,459.00*		
15					

Sheet1 / Sheet2 / Sheet3 / Sheet4 / Sheet5 / Sheet6 /

Figure 6 *A large title font, boldface labels, and italicized totals increase the readability of this worksheet. For printing, you can eliminate the gridlines.*

Many printers do not have color capability, so on a printout, colors appear in shades and patterns of gray. Unfortunately if you used colors for the background and fonts of your worksheet, these colors might translate into similar gray shades that obscure labels and numbers. You might have to experiment with several color combinations to find one that looks good on the screen and also produces a legible printout.

WHAT IF I WANT TO USE A WORKSHEET FOR A PRESENTATION?

Spreadsheets for presentations must be legible when displayed by a projection device. Color and sizing can help legibility. You might consider a larger type size—one that can be easily seen from the back of the room in which you will project your worksheet. Scrolling is usually not desirable in a presentation situation, so try to fit the worksheet on one screen. You might have to eliminate the worksheet documentation to make room for the data and results that are important to your audience. Place your graphs on separate worksheets so you don't have to scroll to display them.

The use of color will make your presentation more interesting and help to highlight important data on the worksheet. When you use colors, remember that in a business situation red usually implies financial trouble—"in the red" means losing money.

	A	B	C
1	**MEXICO TRIP**		
2	Days	7	
3	Nights	6	
4	**Item**	**Daily Cost**	**Total**
5	Airfare		$649.00
6	Lodging	$75.00	$450.00
7	Lodging tax	10%	$45.00
8	Food	$45.00	$315.00
9	**Total**		**$1,459.00**

Figure 7 *The use of large fonts, color, and graphics are important for worksheets that you will project in a presentation. Here, the text colors for the title, headings, and total were selected to stand out against the background.*

CAN I MODIFY THE STRUCTURE OF A WORKSHEET?

In addition to formatting changes, you can also modify the structure of a worksheet by inserting rows and columns, deleting rows and columns, or moving the contents of cells to other cells. Many inexperienced spreadsheet users might hesitate to make such structural changes. Why? Suppose you've created a spreadsheet for the Mexico trip and have tested all its formulas. You decide to delete row 2, which is currently blank. All the labels, numbers, and formulas move up one row. But what's happened to that formula that used to sum up cells C10 through C13? Now those numbers have moved up to cells C9 through C12. Do you have to revise all the formulas on your worksheet? Happily, the answer is no.

When you insert, delete, or move cells, the spreadsheet software attempts to adjust your formulas so the cell references they contain are still accurate. It seems almost as if your spreadsheet has some "intelligence," but actually the spreadsheet is just adjusting the formulas relative to their original position as shown in Figure 8.

Figure 8 *When you delete a row on the worksheet, the data below that row moves up and the spreadsheet automatically adjusts the formulas.*

	C	D	E
1			
2			
3			
4			
5			
6			
7			
8			
9	Total		
10	649		
11	450		
12	45		
13	315		
14	1459		
15	▲		
16	The original formula is		
17	=C10+C11+C12+C13		
18			
19			

	C	D	E
1			
2			
3			
4			
5			
6			
7			
8	Total		
9	649		
10	450		
11	45		
12	315		
13	1459		
14			
15	▲		
16	After the data moves up,		
17	the revised formula is		
18	=C9+C10+C11+C12		
19			

What if you don't want the formula to change? You can define any reference in a formula as an absolute reference. An **absolute reference** never changes when you insert rows or copy or move formulas. Understanding when to use absolute references is one of the key aspects to developing spreadsheet design expertise.

IS THERE SUCH AS THING AS SPREADSHEET INTELLIGENCE?

When mainframe computers first made the headlines in the 1950s, they had an unsettling effect on the American public—and no wonder. Headlines dubbed these computers "Giant Brains," and journalists speculated how long it might be until computers "took over." The public was pacified when word spread that computers could only follow the instructions of their human programmers.

Fifty years have passed since the Giant Brain headlines appeared. Computer technology has improved to the point where it sometimes seems that computers do have some sort of intelligence—or at least they seem to anticipate what you want them to do. You'll run into some examples of this when you use spreadsheet software.

overview

An example that you'll recognize as soon as you begin to use spreadsheet software is its ability to distinguish between the data you're using for text and the data you're using for numbers. At first this might seem easy—text is letters and numbers are, well, numbers. But suppose that you want to enter a social security number in a cell. When you enter 375-80-9876 should the spreadsheet regard this as the subtraction formula 375 minus 80 minus 9876? Should the spreadsheet regard this as a single number 375809876 that can be used for mathematical operations? Or should the spreadsheet regard this as text that can not be mathematically manipulated? The answer is that your spreadsheet software will regard 375-80-9876 as text. If you think about this, you'll see that is correct. Even though we call these social security *numbers* we don't add, subtract, multiply, or divide them.

Shortcuts are another example of spreadsheet "intelligence." Spreadsheet software contains many handy shortcuts to help simplify the process of creating, editing, and formatting a worksheet. For example, **fill operations** continue a series you have started. Type "January" in one cell and "February" in the next, then use a fill operation and the spreadsheet will automatically enter the rest of the months in the next 10 cells. Fill operations also complete numerical sequences such as "1, 2, 3, 4.." or "1990, 1995, 2000…".

WHAT ABOUT GRAPHS AND CHARTS?

Spreadsheet software is characterized by its ability to easily create professional-looking graphs and charts. Did you ever draw graphs using graph paper and colored pencils? Remember the unsatisfactory results you got? With spreadsheet software it is simple to create an attractive pie graph that illustrates opinion poll data, a line graph that drives home the alarming increase in the national debt, or a bar graph that compares market share for U.S. and foreign automobile manufacturers (Figure 9).

Figure 9 *Ross Perot made extensive use of graphs to explain economic concepts during his bid for the United States presidency in 1992. It is likely that these graphs were produced using spreadsheet software.*

Graphs, as you know, provide a quick summary or overview of a set of data. Trends that might be difficult to detect in columns of figures come into focus when skillfully graphed. Graphs are an effective presentation tool because they are simple to understand and visually interesting. However, when you design graphs, you have a responsibility to your audience to create a visual representation of the truth. Although you might not intentionally design a graph to "lie" it is all too easy to design a graph that implies something other than the truth.

Figure 10 *Which graph shows a more dramatic increase in sales?*

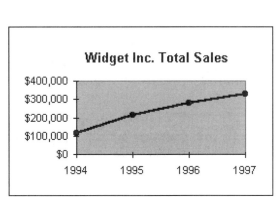

The sales figures represented by the graph on the right in Figure 10 certainly look better than those on the left. Examine these graphs closely. The sales figures on both graphs are the same, but by changing the shape of the graph, the trend in sales can look either pretty tame or very dramatic. When you design a graph, try to consider how the average person would interpret it, then make sure that interpretation coincides with reality.

ARE THERE GUIDELINES FOR CREATING EFFECTIVE GRAPHS?

Remember that the purpose of a graph is to quickly convey a summary of a set of data. Within two or three seconds, a graph should convey its main point, so the first rule of graphing is to "keep it simple." Here are some additional guidelines:

- Include a descriptive title that conveys the main point of the graph. A title such as "U.S. Camcorder Sales 1990-2000" is more descriptive than "Camcorders."

- Use line graphs to show changes over time. If the horizontal axis of your graph contains years, months or other dates, a line graph is probably more appropriate than a bar graph.

- Use bar graphs to show comparisons.

- It is best not to include too many bars on a graph because it can become difficult to pick out the major trends. If your bar graph has more than seven bars, you might consider using a different type of graph or consolidating some of the data to make fewer bars.

- Make sure you label the data. At minimum you should label the tick marks on the vertical and horizontal axes. On a pie chart you should label each wedge. On a bar graph you might also label each bar in addition to the horizontal axis labels.

- Use color or shading patterns to distinguish each set of data. Contrasting colors or patterns can provide emphasis and draw attention to certain aspects of a graph.

- Give your graph the 5-second test. Show your graph to a friend for five seconds, then hide it. Ask your friend to tell you about your graph and make sure your friend's impression is similar to what you intended.

IN WHAT SITUATIONS CAN I USE SPREADSHEET SOFTWARE?

Consider the general sorts of tasks that spreadsheet software supports. Spreadsheet software works well for recording and graphing data, for making calculations, and for constructing numerical models of the real world. The main advantage of spreadsheet software is the time it saves—once you create a worksheet, you can change your data without redoing all your calculations. In addition, worksheet data is stored in electronic format so it can be merged with word processing documents, posted on the Internet, or transmitted as part of an e-mail message.

Spreadsheet software is applicable in just about every profession. Educators use spreadsheets for grade books and analyzing test scores. Farmers use spreadsheets to keep track of crop yield, to calculate the amount of seed to purchase, and to estimate expenses and profits for the coming year. At home, spreadsheets help you balance your checkbook, keep track of household expenses, track your savings and investments, and calculate your taxes.

Entrepreneurs use spreadsheets to devise business plans. Corporate executives use spreadsheets to keep tabs on finances. Athletes use spreadsheets to track training programs and sports statistics. Contractors use spreadsheets to make bids on construction projects. Scientists use spreadsheets to analyze scientific data. The

overview

list goes on, and it shouldn't take you long to identify how you could use a spreadsheet in your career field.

WHAT ABOUT "WHAT-IF" ANALYSIS?

In his tongue-in-cheek book, *How to Claw Your Way to the Top*, Dave Barry defines a spreadsheet as "A kind of program that lets you sit at your desk and ask all kinds of neat 'what-if?' questions and generate thousands of numbers instead of actually working." These what-if questions are a key element of spreadsheet modeling.

Spreadsheet modeling means setting up numbers in a worksheet to describe a real-world situation. For example, spreadsheets are often used for business modeling. The worksheet data represents or describes the financial activities in a business—products sold, expenses for employees, rent, inventory and so forth. By looking at the numbers in such a business model, you can get an idea of its current profitability. You can also experiment with changing some of the numbers in the model to see how changes in business activities might affect profitability and other financial indicators. The process of setting up a model and experimenting with different numbers is often referred to as **what-if analysis**.

What-if analysis is certainly a useful tool. Imagine having answers to questions such as:

- What if I get an A on my next two economics exams? But what if I get Bs?

- What if I invest $100 a month in my retirement plan? But what if I invest $200 a month?

- What if our sales reps increase sales by 10%? But what if sales decline by 5%?

- What if I take out a 30-year mortgage at 8.5%? But what if I take out a 15-year mortgage at 7.75%?

Today's spreadsheet software includes features to simplify what-if analysis, but the basic procedure is to set up the numbers and labels for your model, then start plugging in different numbers to look at the result. For example, you can set up a model representing the money you'll invest in your retirement plan and showing how much you'll have accumulated by the time you retire. Suppose you enter 500 for the monthly investment amount and see that you'll have about $400,000 when you retire. Then you enter 700 and see that because of additional accumulated interest you can retire with a cool million. You'll find what-if analysis useful anytime you want to consider the results of alternative scenarios such as this.

overview

Computerized spreadsheet software was invented in 1978 by a Harvard Business School student, Dan Bricklin. Many computer historians believe that his software, called VisiCalc, not only launched a new genre of computer software, but put a rocket under the fledgling microcomputer industry and launched the Digital Age. Before the availability of VisiCalc, consumers couldn't think of much use for a personal computer. VisiCalc provided business people with a handy tool for making calculations without visiting a statistician or accountant.

VisiCalc contained all the basic elements of today's electronic spreadsheets—a screen-based grid of rows and columns, predefined functions, automatic calculations, and rudimentary "intelligence" for copying and replicating formulas.

VisiCalc's market dominance was supplanted by Lotus 1-2-3, which still remains one of the top-selling spreadsheets. Other popular spreadsheets include Microsoft Excel and Corel's Quattro Pro. You can purchase any one of these top-selling spreadsheets for less than $300. All three have similar features.

Another popular software option is Microsoft Works, which includes a spreadsheet, word processor, and database that you can purchase for less than $100. You give up some fancy features with low-cost integrated software, but had you given Microsoft Works to an early VisiCalc user, it would have seemed like a miraculously easy and feature-rich software package.

CheckPoint _____

1   List some of the advantages that spreadsheets have over hand-held calculators.

2   Why is it significant that spreadsheet formulas can contain references to other cells?

3   Most spreadsheet software includes hundreds of predefined formulas called _____ for mathematical, financial, and statistical calculations.

4   What design considerations should you remember when creating a worksheet that will be projected to an audience?

5   True or false? When you move or copy a cell, a spreadsheet typically adjusts any formulas in that cell relative to their original position. You must use an absolute reference if you don't want the formula to change.

6   True or false? The spreadsheet software publisher is responsible for the validity of the figures and formulas in your worksheets.

7   What are the advantages and potential disadvantages of using color for the background and fonts of a worksheet.

8   The process of setting up a model and experimenting with different numbers is often referred to as _____ analysis.

9   List three examples of worksheets that might be useful in your career field.

10   What effect did the first spreadsheet software have on the computer industry?

Microsoft Excel

Tutorial 1: Spreadsheet Basics

Tutorial 1

Spreadsheet Basics

WHAT'S INSIDE

Advertising Megabucks

TV, magazines, newspapers, and the Internet compete for customers, consumers, and sponsors. What's the cost of a typical TV ad? How many consumers watch it? You'll find the scoop here, and see how spreadsheet software helps you understand the true cost of advertising.

Doing the e-Thing

You'll find out how to get started with the e-Course instructional software. This is an easy way to learn how to use Microsoft Excel.

Projects

Tutorial 1 Projects include planning a trip to Disney World, buying a new Toyota Paseo, tabulating survey data on rap music censorship, and figuring out what you do with all your "spare" time.

1 Start Excel and Get Oriented
- Start Excel
- Get Oriented
- Get Help
- Exit Excel

2 Navigate a Workbook
- Display a Workbook
- Select a Worksheet
- Rows and Columns
- The Worksheet Pointer
- Activate Cells
- Scroll
- Close a Workbook

3 Text, Numbers, and Formulas
- Identify Worksheet Text
- Identify Worksheet Numbers
- Identify Worksheet Formulas

4 Enter Information and Fix Errors
- Enter Information
- Automatic Recalculation
- Fix Mistakes
- Fix Typos
- Edit Cell Contents
- Undo It
- Clear a Cell

5 Save, Rename, and Open Workbooks
- Rename and Save
- Save with the Same Name
- Open a Workbook

6 Print a Worksheet
- Print Preview
- Add Your Name to the Header
- Print Your Worksheet

Disks

If you would like to keep track of your progress, you should have a blank formatted disk ready when you begin the online Steps for Tutorial 1. As you log in, the e-Course software will create a **Tracking Disk** for you. The Tracking Disk will keep a record of the length of time you spend on each e-Course session and your scores on the CheckPoint questions you answer online. If your instructor will collect your Tracking Disk for grading, make sure you have a backup copy! You should have a second formatted disk to use as a **Project Disk**. You'll find out how to make and use your Project Disk when you get to the Projects section of the WorkText.

Advertising

Advertising is useful because it provides information about products and services. But ads also have a powerful effect on our culture. Those ad jingles that run through your head are as much a part of our national consciousness as our national anthem.

Companies spend top dollar to reach consumers through TV, magazines, newspapers, and radio. Now, advertisers are also invading the World Wide Web. Many Web magazines and search engines sell ad spots that appear when you access their Web sites. Currently, $15,000 will pay for one month's worth of Web ads. That sounds reasonable compared to the $135,000 an advertiser shells out for a full-page ad in a national U.S. magazine. However, the cost of an ad is not the only consideration.

Advertising must reach consumers—the more, the better. Advertisers usually consider not just the total ad price, but also the price of reaching each consumer. Is it more cost effective to spend $135,000 to reach a magazine's 3 million subscribers or to spend $15,000 to reach 200,000 Web surfers?

You can answer questions like this by doing a few calculations. Suppose you're interested in comparing the costs of different advertising media. You gather information on the cost of ads and how many consumers they'll reach:

Media	Ad Cost	Consumers
Television - 30-second spot on network news	$65,000	12 million
Magazine - full-page color in national weekly	$135,000	3.1 million
Newspaper - full-page ad, midsize city	$31,000	514,000
Web - one month in online magazine	$15,000	200,000

When entered in a worksheet, this data is easy to manipulate. You can use it for calculations. You can add to it, and you can modify it. As an added benefit, you can graph the data to create a visual summary. Now, let's get started online to see how spreadsheet software works.

GET STARTED ONLINE WITH e-COURSE

The e-Course software is designed to teach you how to use the Microsoft Excel spreadsheet software. The first time you use the e-Course software, you'll probably want to set up a Tracking Disk, which keeps track of your progress and your CheckPoint scores. Now it's time to use your computer.

To start the e-Course software and set up a Tracking Disk:

1: Label a formatted disk "Tracking Disk" and place it in the disk drive. (This step is optional, but if you do not insert a disk, you will not have an electronic record of your progress.)

2: Start your computer, then click the **Start** button.

3: Point to **Programs**.

4: Click **e-Course**.

5: Click **e-Course Excel**.

6: If you see a message saying "The tracking file was not found on drive A," click the button labeled "Copy the tracking database to a disk in drive A." This will copy some files onto your disk, and then display the Login window.

➔ If you're in a computer lab and e-Course is not on the Program menu, ask your technical support person how to start the e-Course software. If you're using your own computer, you must install the e-Course software before you use it. Refer to the TechTalk section in this WorkText.

The first time you log in, e-Course asks you to enter your name and other information that automatically appears on your CheckPoint reports. This information is stored on your Tracking Disk, so you won't have to enter it the next time you log in.

scenario

To log in the first time:

1: On the Login screen, fill in the blanks with your **first name**, **last name**, **course section**, and **student number**. If you don't know your course section or student number, just type anything—you can change it later.

2: Click the **OK** button. In a few seconds, you should see the e-Course Welcome screen.

At the e-Course Welcome screen, you can print your Task Reference. The Task Reference will help refresh your memory about how to do the tasks you learn in the tutorials.

To print out the Task Reference:

1: Click **Task Reference** on the Welcome screen menu bar.

2: Click **View/Print Task Reference**.

3: After the Task Reference appears, click **File** on the menu bar, then click **Print**.

4: When the printout is complete, click **File** again, then click **Exit**.

e-Course is easy to use. After the short e-Course Introductory tour, you'll be ready to use all the e-Course features.

To start the e-Course Introductory Tour:

1: Click the **Introductory Tour** button on the Welcome screen.

2: Follow the instructions on the screen to navigate through the tour.

When you've finished the Introductory Tour, it's time to get started on Tutorial 1!

To start Tutorial 1:

1: Click **Tutorials** on the menu bar at the top of the Welcome screen.

2: Point to **Tutorial 1**.

3: Click a Topic—you should begin with Topic 1.

Review Questions

FILL-IN-THE BLANKS

Fill in the blank with the correct word or phrase.

1   Excel is an example of a category of software referred to as _____ software.

2   _____ pop up when you rest the mouse pointer on a button on the Excel toolbar.

3   Excel stores your project in a file referred to as a(n) _____.

4   The filename for a workbook is displayed on the Excel _____ bar.

5   The tabs near the bottom of the screen contain the names for each _____.

6   It's a good idea to _____ your workbook, using one of the worksheets to record who created the workbook and when it was last modified.

7   The worksheet pointer appears in the shape of a(n) _____ when you are working with the grid.

8   The _____ bar shows the active cell and the contents of the active cell.

9   Because a worksheet has many more columns and rows than can fit on the screen, the _____ help you bring other parts of the worksheet into view.

10 Formulas begin with the _____ sign.

11 The _____ button is useful if you enter a number by mistake and want to restore the original value.

12 Suppose you're modifying a worksheet and your finger slips on the keyboard, pressing an unknown key and your worksheet gets "messed up." You should press the _____ key to see if you can get the spreadsheet back the way it was.

13 If you want to transport your worksheets, you'll probably want to save them on drive _____.

review questions

*Select the letter of the **one** best answer.*

---

14 **One of the main purposes of spreadsheet software is to:**

   a work with numbers and create graphs

   b improve your writing

   c help you collect and organize information

   d incorporate clip art into documents

---

15 **Which one of the following is not in the upper section of the Excel window?**

   a menu bar   **c** Formula bar

   b status bar   **d** Print Preview button

---

16 **Excel workbooks have the filename extension:**

   a .doc   **c** .xls

   b .exc   **d** .wbk

---

17 **On a worksheet, the intersection of a row and column is called a:**

   a cell   **c** workbook

   b pointer   **d** formula

---

18 **When you type a label or number into a cell and press the Enter key:**

   a a formula appears

   b you must press the Undo button to see the results

   c all the formulas on the worksheet automatically recalculate

   d you must click the mouse button before you can see what you have entered

---

19 **The cell in the upper-left corner of a worksheet is:**

   a 00   **c** A1

   b 1   **d** Start

---

20 **The worksheet cell with the dark border is referred to as the _____ cell.**

   a active   **c** interactive

   b dark   **d** border

---

21 Which one of the following worksheet entries is considered text?

  a 127   **c** 555-1212

  b -85   **d** .098

---

22 Suppose you want to create a worksheet that sums up the number of calories you consume each day. You read the label of the can of pop you just drank and see it has 160 calories. What should you enter into the cell of the worksheet?

  a 160 calories   **c** calories: 160

  b 160 cal.   **d** 160

---

23 Suppose you enter the cost of a $15,892.00 car in cell C15. The Formula bar will display this number as:

  a $15,892.00   **c** $15982.00

  b $15,982   **d** 15892

---

24 If you see P3 in a formula, it refers to:

  a the contents of cell P3

  b P*3

  c a special mathematical function for prime numbers

  d Pi

---

25 Which of the following keys can you use to fix typos before you press the Enter key?

  a Backspace   **c** Home

  b →   **d** Delete

---

26 If you're working on a standalone computer at home or at work, you'll probably save your workbooks on drive:

  a A   **c** C

  b B   **d** F

---

27 When you want to rename and save a workbook, you should use the:

  a Save button

  b Save As option on the File menu

  c Preview button

  d Rename menu

28 Suppose you open the Courier workbook and try to improve the appearance of a graph. After working on it for about an hour, you decide that the original graph was better than your revision. You close the workbook, but see a message asking if you want to save the changes. You should:

a click the No button

b click the Yes button

c go back into the worksheet and click the Undo button

d press the Esc key

MATCHING

Select the letter from the column on the right that correctly matches each item in the column on the left.

29

a The button you use to close Excel and close a workbook

30 A, B, C

b The Print Preview button

31

c The button you use to store your workbook on disk using its current name

32

d A formula

33 Save As

e Column identifiers

34 =B1+B2

f A pop-up label that tells you the function of a button

35 Chart

g The command you use to change the name of your workbook before you store it on disk

36

h Where Excel shows you which cell is active and shows you the active cell's contents

37 Formula bar

i The Undo button

38 ToolTips

j Excel terminology for a graph

SHORT ANSWER

Use a separate sheet of paper to write out your answers to the following questions.

39 Make up your own example of a workbook with four worksheets. What would each worksheet contain?

40 List three uses for a spreadsheet in business.

41 List the procedure you would follow to print the contents of your worksheet.

42 In your own words, describe what a spreadsheet program does.

43 Suppose you have a workbook that sums up your monthly household expenses. Currently, the number you have entered for food is $350. The workbook also contains a pie graph of this data. Describe what changes in the workbook when you enter $450 for food.

44 List as many ways as you know to move around on the worksheet.

45 How can you tell whether a cell contains a value or a formula?

46 When you make a typing mistake, the procedure you follow to correct the mistake depends on whether or not you have pressed the Enter key. Describe how you correct typing mistakes a) before you press the Enter key, and b) after you press the Enter key.

Projects

These Projects are designed to help you review and develop the skills you learned in Tutorial 1. Complete each Project using Microsoft Excel. You should not need to use the e-Course software to complete the Projects, except to create a Project Disk containing practice files. *If you have not yet made the Project Disk for Tutorial 1, start the e-Course software, click Project Disk on the e-Course Welcome screen menu bar, and follow the instructions on the screen.*

If you've forgotten some of the skills you need to complete these Projects, refer to the Task Reference.

REVIEW SKILLS

1 Advertising Megabucks   File: Ads.xls

In the online Steps you used the Ads workbook to learn how to open, navigate, modify, save, and print a workbook. In this Project, you'll review these skills without the assistance of the online steps. If you've forgotten how to do the skills, refer to your Task Reference.

Open the Ads workbook from your Project Disk. Scroll to cell U41 and clear the contents of that cell. In cell B5 enter "25,000". Check the new value in cell D5, then make sure the graph correctly reflects the changed data.

Rename and save this worksheet on your Project Disk under the new name Ad Megabucks.

Print the entire workbook after you put your name in the header. On your printout, circle all the cells that contain formulas.

2 Time Management   File: Time.xls

No one ever seems to have enough time. Time management helps us make effective use of "24 x 7" hours in a week. One of the first steps in time management is to figure out how you currently spend your time. The Time worksheet helps you do this.

projects

Suppose Jamie Curtin recorded her activities for a week. Transfer this information into the Time worksheet after zeroing out the current values. Put your name in the header, and then print only the worksheet containing the graph.

Activity	Average time per day
Studying	2 hours
Eat breakfast	20 minutes
Eat lunch	40 minutes
Eat dinner	1 hour 10 minutes
Attend class	4 hours
Commute	10 minutes each way
Shower, hair, etc.	30 minutes
Sleep	8 hours

3   Get a Jolt   File: Caffeine.xls

Many of the beverages you drink contain caffeine, but how much? The Caffeine workbook helps you calculate the amount of caffeine you consume based on the type and size of the drink. Open the Caffeine workbook. Print only the Caffeine Stats worksheet after you put your name in the header. Before you close the workbook, look at the cell contents. On your printout, write the formulas for cells C5 through C15.

4   Body Builders   File: Protein.xls

Protein stacking is one of the latest body building fads advertised in fitness magazines. The ads show impressive loss of body fat with accompanying photos of incredible "hard bodies." Is the data presented in the ads accurate?

projects

Suppose you found that the weight wasn't accurate. Enter the corrected data in the WEIGHT column. While you're at it, change the text in the WEEK column, so your worksheet looks like the one below. Put your name in the header and print only the Weight worksheet. Rename and save your worksheet as "Protein – Revised".

Stacking Protein to Lose Body Fat!

WEEK	WEIGHT (lbs)	LEAN BODY MASS (lbs)	BODY FAT
Week 1	180	163.6	9.1%
Week 4	189	177.5	6.1%
Week 8	186	178.0	4.3%
Week 12	181	176.0	2.8%
Week 16	178	173.5	2.5%

5 Rain, Snow, or Sleet   File: Courier.xls

The United States Postal Service (USPS) has become more aggressive in promoting its Priority Mail service. The USPS claims to have more trucks and cheaper rates than its competitors, UPS and FedEx. Some of these comparisons are presented in the Courier workbook.

Open the Courier workbook on your Project Disk. Suppose the USPS decreased Priority Mail rates to $2. Change the Priority Mail rate to $2. Put your name in the header and print only the worksheet that contains the graphs. Close your workbook without saving changes.

APPLY SKILLS

6 I'm Going to Disney World!   File: Disney.xls

One of your relatives is trying to create a workbook to calculate the cost of a trip to Disney World. Something seems to be wrong with some of the formulas.

Open the Disney worksheet from your Project Disk. Look at the formulas and their results to see if the results are what you expect. If necessary modify the formulas so they produce the correct result. *Remember that formulas begin with an = (equal sign)!*

After you've corrected the formulas, enter the following prices for the 4-day trip for two adults and two children. Print your results.

Final Prices for Disney Trip

Adult plane fare: $360 round trip

Child plane fare: $205 round trip

Parking: $5 per day

Hotel: $215 per room per night (the family will stay in one room)

Disney ticket for Adult: $30 per day

Disney ticket for Child: $21 per day

Food: $175 per day for the family

7   My Money   File: Budget.xls

Open the Budget worksheet from your Project Disk. Take a few minutes to study the Income/Expense worksheet. Notice which cells contain text, which contain numbers, and which contain formulas. Your goal for this Project is to modify this worksheet to reflect your own budget. (If some of the details are too personal, it's okay to make up some of the data.)

To modify the worksheet, you can change the labels and the numbers. Do not change the formulas. If the worksheet has extra lines that you don't need, clear the cells on those lines. For this Project, do not add extra lines. If you run out of space, you'll have to consolidate some of your budget categories.

Make sure you update the documentation sheet. Put your name in the header and print the entire workbook.

8   Save Options   File: Jobs.xls

So far, as you've worked through the online Steps and Projects, you've had explicit instruction on how to save your workbooks. Now is your chance to make your own decisions about this task.

Open the Jobs workbook from your Project Disk. Take a couple of minutes to study the worksheets so you understand the purpose of the workbook.

Change the December 1994 unemployment figure to 5.4%. Then, save your modified workbook, but don't overwrite the old one. Answer the following questions about how you accomplished this task:

a Did you use the Save button or the Save As option from the File menu?

b What name did you use for your modified workbook?

c On which disk did you store the modified workbook?

d As you were saving your workbook, did you have to respond to a message asking if you want to save changes?

9   A What-if Analysis   File: Toyota.xls

Suppose you've got your eye on a new car—a Toyota Paseo. Your dealer offers you $1,000 "cash back." You would have to take out a bank loan at 8.25%. As an alternative, your dealer offers you 4.9% dealer financing, but no cash back. Which deal is better?

The process of looking at alternatives is called "what-if" analysis. Spreadsheet software makes what-if analysis easy because it automatically recalculates each alternative as you enter it. To see how this works, open the Toyota workbook from your Project Disk. The cells at the top of the worksheet contain the data you'll change to look at each alternative. Enter the information for Alternative 1 ($1000 cash back, three-year loan at 8.25%), then print your results. Next, enter the information for Alternative 2 ($0 cash back, three-year loan at 4.9%), then print those results. After looking at the two printouts, circle the one for which the monthly payment is lowest.

10 Write Your Own Documentation   File: Rap.xls

As you learned in Tutorial 1, it is important to document your workbooks. Usually, the documentation is placed on a separate worksheet labeled "Notes" or "Documentation." The documentation should include the following information:

- name of the person who built the workbook

- the date when the workbook was created

- the date of the most recent modification

- a brief overview of the purpose of the workbook

- the source of the data

- explanation of formulas

The documentation is complete if it contains all the information a person would need to understand the workbook in its current form and to be able to successfully modify it.

Open the Rap workbook from your Project Disk. Suppose that one of your friends who is a journalist has asked 1,000 people, "Do you think Rap music should be censored by the government, by the record company, by the musicians, or not censored at all?" Your friend then created the Rap workbook containing the results of the survey. You offer to help verify that the data and formulas are correct. You decide to add the sample size. Enter the label "Sample size" in cell A11 and enter 1,000 in cell E11. You notice that your friend's documentation is incomplete. Complete the documentation to your satisfaction. Put your name in the documentation as the person who made the most recent modifications. Print the entire workbook.

BUILD SKILLS

11 Custom Headers and Footers   File: Grades.xls

In the online Steps, you learned how to add your name as a header in the upper-left corner of the page. Excel's custom headers and footers feature allows you to easily specify what your headers and footers contain and how they are formatted. In this Project, you'll learn how to use these additional features of the Header/Footer dialog box.

Open the Grades workbook from your Project Disk. Scroll to cell A58 and enter Test Notes. Click the Print Preview button, and then click the Setup button. Click the Header/Footer tab, and then click the Custom Header button. Study the instructions in the window to learn about all the options for headers and footers. To discover the function of the buttons, click the ☐? button in the upper-right corner of the dialog box, and then click each of the buttons. A pop-up window will explain how each button works.

Now, create a header for the Grades workbook that looks like this:

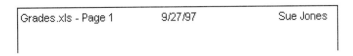

Remove the page number from the footer using the Custom Footer button. Print the worksheet.

projects

12 Page Setup Options
File: Profits.xls

In the online Steps you learned how to access Setup controls from the Print Preview window. You can also access these controls from the File menu. The Setup controls help you define the way the printed page will look. In this Project, you'll learn how to use some additional Setup controls.

Open the Profits workbook from your Project Disk. As you can see, this is a large worksheet—it's too large to fit on one page. It would be nice, however, to be able to print the entire worksheet on one page. To do this, use the Page Setup option on the File menu to open the Page Setup dialog box, then do the following Steps.

To use some additional Setup controls:

1: Use the **Page** tab to select **Landscape**.

2: Stay on the Page tab, and set the Scaling to Fit to 1 page.

3: On the **Margins** tab, choose to Center the worksheet horizontally and vertically.

Put your name in a header on the left side of the worksheet. Preview the worksheet to make sure it will all fit on one printed page, and then print the worksheet.

13 Edit Tab Labels
File: Jobs.xls

As you learned in the online Steps, worksheet tabs identify each of the worksheets in a workbook. To switch to a worksheet, you click its tab. You can easily change the worksheet tab labels. Try it with the file Jobs.xls.

To open the workbook Jobs.xls from your Project Disk:

1: To change the worksheet tab labels use the right mouse button to click the tab that's currently labeled **Rates**.

2: When the pop-up menu appears, click **Rename**.

3: Type **Unemployment** on the tab.

4: Press the **Enter** key.

When you've completed the Steps, the first tab should be labeled "Unemployment". Now change the Graph tab to "Trends". Change the Documentation tab to "Background". Save your revised workbook on your Project Disk as "Unemployment Trends".

Preview a printout of this workbook to make sure that the tab name appears as a header. Also add your name to the header on each worksheet. Print the entire workbook.

14 Toolbars   File: Jobs.xls

In the online Steps you used tools on the Standard toolbar, you saw the Formatting toolbar in the orientation animation, and you used the Formula bar to edit cell contents. Excel has additional toolbars that you can display if you need them. In this Project you'll learn what toolbars are available, how to display them, and how to hide them.

Open the Jobs workbook from your Project Disk. You won't make any changes to the file, so when you've completed this Project, close the workbook without saving it.

To display or hide toolbars:

1: Click **View** on the menu bar.

2: Click **Toolbars**.

3: Click the name of a toolbar to display or remove a check mark. Those toolbars with check marks will be displayed. Toolbars without check marks will be hidden from view.

To complete this Project, use the View menu to display all the toolbars. If the toolbars get stacked on top of each other, drag the title bars to move them. Next, point to each button on each toolbar and read its ToolTip. For each of the descriptions below, indicate the name of the toolbar it describes.

a How many toolbars are available? _____

b _____ is the toolbar that contains a Legend button.

c _____ is the toolbar you use to add shapes, lines, and shadows to a worksheet.

d _____ is the toolbar you use to add list boxes, spinners, and check boxes to create worksheets with automated data entry.

e _____ is the toolbar that helps you record a series of steps as a macro that you can later play back to automatically repeat the steps.

projects

15 Print Part of a Worksheet   File: Profits.xls

In the online Steps you learned that you can use the Print dialog box to print an entire workbook, an entire worksheet, or selected pages of a worksheet. What if you want to print only a selected section of a worksheet?

Suppose you're working with the Profits worksheet, and you decide that you want to print only the information about auto industry profits. Open the worksheet Profits.xls from your Project Disk and then complete the following Steps.

To print only a selected section of a worksheet:

1: Position the pointer on cell **B7**.

2: Hold down the mouse button and drag the pointer to cell **F11**. As a result, all the cells containing auto industry data should be "highlighted" with a dark background. Don't worry if the cell containing the word "Autos" does not appear highlighted.

3: Use the **Print Preview** button to set up a customized header containing your name.

4: Look at your print preview. It appears to show that the entire document will be printed, but you'll change that in the next Step.

5: Click the **Print** button on the Print Preview screen. As a result, you should see the Print dialog box.

6: On the Print dialog box, click **Selection**. Hint: Do not click Active sheet(s).

7: Click the **OK** button. Your printout should contain information about only auto industry profits.

EXPLORE

16 About Microsoft Excel

Microsoft has published several versions of Excel. Each version is numbered, for example Microsoft Excel version 5.0, Microsoft Excel for Windows 95 version 7.0, and Microsoft Excel 97. You can use the Help About menu to find out which version you're using. Help About also gives you a handy way to find out about your computer system specifications. Your technical support person might request this information if your system is not performing correctly.

To access Help About:

1: Click **Help** on the Excel menu bar, then click **About Microsoft Excel**.

2: Read the information provided to find out which version of Excel you're using.

3: Click the **System Info** button.

4: A window with two sections appears. Make sure **System** is selected in the left window. After a few seconds, the information that appears in the right window provides you with information on your computer's operating system processor type, memory, and so on.

Answer the following questions, then close the System Info window:

   a   What operating system is installed on your computer system?

   b   Which version of Windows is installed on your computer system?

   c   What type of processor does your computer have?

   d   How much physical memory does your computer have?

   e   Where is the TEMP directory located?

17 Help: Wizards and Assistants   File: Profit.xls

Microsoft Excel includes an extensive **Help facility** that provides how-to information about Excel features and procedures. One of the most popular ways to access the Help facility is using help "agents" such as the **Office Assistant**. To use these help agents, you simply type in a question. The agent looks through the Help facility, then shows you a list of any topics that might contain relevant information. You can look at one or more of these topics until you find the information you need. Let's see how this works.

Suppose you can't remember how to start a new workbook "from scratch."

To use Excel's Help facility to find out how to start a new workbook:

1: Open **Profit.xls** and click **Help** on the menu bar.

2: Click **Microsoft Excel Help**.

3: In the box that appears, type **How do I start a new workbook?**

4: Press the **Enter** key, and Help displays a list of relevant topics.

5: Click **Create a new workbook**.

6: Read through the Help window that appears. You might need to use the scroll bars to read all of the information.

7: Click the **Close** button to close the Help box.

Now that you know how to use Excel's Help facility, try to find the answers to the following questions and write out your answers:

projects

a When you want to discuss the printed layout of a worksheet, it would be advantageous to print the worksheet with its row and column headings so you could see the addresses of the cells that contain your data. Can you print the numbers and letters of the row and column headings for a worksheet? If so, how?

b Suppose you have a worksheet that you want to divide into two sections, with one section printed on each page. How do you insert a page break?

c What is the difference between *clearing* a cell and *deleting* a cell?

d Sometimes when you type a number in a cell, Excel displays ######## instead of the number you typed. What does ######## mean?

e When you save a workbook, you must provide Excel with a name for the file. Are there any letters, numbers, or symbols that you cannot use in filenames?

18 Help: Contents   File: Profit.xls

You can access Excel's extensive Help facility in numerous ways. If you're inclined to browse around looking for useful features or information that might help you streamline the procedures you use, then try Excel's Contents Help.

Contents Help is arranged as a series of online books. Each book covers a topic. Opening a book reveals a list of related topics, which you can open to select a particular page of information. Let's see how this works.

Suppose you're wondering what's the fastest way to create a graph, or "chart" as it is called in Excel terminology.

To use Contents Help to find out how to create a chart quickly:

1: Open the **Profit** workbook, then click **Help** on the Excel menu bar.

2: Click **Contents and Index**.

3: Click the **Contents** tab. A list of Help "books" appears.

4: Locate the book called **Working with Charts** and click it.

5: Click the **Open** button at the bottom of the Help Topics window.

6: Open the book called **Creating a Chart** by clicking it, and then clicking the **Open** button.

7: Now display the page called **Create a Chart** by clicking it, and then clicking the **Display** button. Finally, click the **Create a Chart** button.

8: Read through the information about creating a chart. Notice the underlined text. These are links to definitions. Click the **embedded chart** link to see its definition. To hide the definition, click it.

9: To return to the list of books, click the **Help Topics** button. Close the Creating a Chart book by clicking it and then clicking the `Close` button. Close Contents Help by clicking the **Cancel** button.

Now that you know how to use Contents Help, use it to find the answers to the following questions:

    a   What are the steps for printing cell gridlines?

    b   When you're entering data in a worksheet, how do you type ¢,£, ¥, and other characters for which there are no keys on the keyboard?

    c   When you enter data, you can enter text, numbers, and formulas. You already know that formulas begin with an = sign. But you wonder how Excel knows if you're entering numbers or text. Read in Contents Help about Entering Text and Entering Numbers. What are the rules that Excel uses to decide whether you're typing a number or text?

19 Workbook Properties   File: Caffeine.xls

The workbooks you used for Tutorial 1 had a separate worksheet devoted to documentation. On the documentation sheet, you would generally include information about who created the workbook, who modified it, the date of the last modification, the source of the data, and a description of the formulas. In addition you might want to maintain additional information about a workbook on a **property sheet**. For this Project, follow the Steps to explore some of the features of Excel's property sheets.

To explore Excel's property sheets:

1: Open the **Caffeine.xls** workbook from your Project Disk.

2: Click **File** on the menu bar, then click **Properties**. The Caffeine.xls Properties dialog box appears. The dialog box contains several tabs. Use these tabs to answer Questions a through e:

    a   How large is this workbook in bytes?

    b   What is the creation date listed on the Statistics tab?

    c   Who is listed as the workbook's author?

    d   How many worksheets, including blank worksheets, are in this workbook?

    e   Can you tell how many times this workbook has been edited?

projects

20 Design Your Own Worksheet

Suppose you were going to create your own worksheet and corresponding line or bar graph. First, think of a topic for your worksheet. Divide a piece of paper into rows and columns. Next, sketch a design for your worksheet on paper indicating the titles and labels. Show where you will enter your numbers. Also indicate the location of totals or other formulas.

On a separate piece of paper, sketch your graph. Provide a title for the graph and indicate the labels for the horizontal and vertical axes. Show how you visualize the lines or bars on your graph.

21 Spreadsheet Software History

Spreadsheet software has a colorful history, beginning with a spreadsheet pioneer named Dan Bricklin who invented VisiCalc, the first microcomputer spreadsheet software. Bricklin's company rocketed to success, then just as quickly it took a nosedive. What happened? You'll find out when you work on this Project.

Using the resources in your library and/or on the Internet, research the history of spreadsheet software. Discover who were the major spreadsheet software developers. What were the names of their products? Find out about the evolution of features supplied by spreadsheet software. See if you can determine how advances in microcomputer technology affected spreadsheet software and spreadsheet software publishers.

After you have completed your research, write an article that presents the information you found. Your instructor will provide you with specifications for length and format.

projects

22 The Great Spreadsheet Hunt

With the tremendous popularity of spreadsheets and the simplicity of creating graphs, you would expect to see them with some frequency in magazines and newspapers. For this Project, look for spreadsheet tables and graphs in current issues of magazines and newspapers. Photocopy at least five of each. Number your photocopies 1 through 5. On a separate sheet of paper, write a one-paragraph evaluation for each of the five photocopies. In your evaluation include characteristics you liked and you didn't like. Discuss what was effective or eye-catching. Identify elements that were distracting or misleading. Mention if titles and labels clearly described the data.

When you have completed your summary, apply what you've discovered to create a list of general principles for developing effective spreadsheets and a second list of principles for developing effective graphs. Submit your photocopies, your evaluation, and your lists of effective development principles.

23 Web Advertising

Tutorial 1 opened with a discussion of advertising in magazines, on television, in newspapers, and on the Web. Most of us are familiar with the first three, but might not have encountered (or paid attention to) advertising on the Web. For this Project, cruise the Web and look for ads. You might try *www.yahoo.com* to see examples of search engine advertising. Try *www.wired.com* for examples of ads in online magazines (called "zines"). Find two other sites with Web advertising. Write a one-page summary of what you found. Make sure you include the addresses of all the sites you visited.

projects

24 Interview with a Spreadsheet User

You might have read *Interview with a Vampire* or seen the movie. Now it's your turn to interview exotic creatures (spreadsheet users) and write up your findings. Make an appointment with someone who uses spreadsheets at home or for business. Make sure you clearly state the purpose of your visit and receive permission to conduct the interview.

To prepare for the interview, compose a list of questions. Here are some suggestions:

    a   How long have you used spreadsheet software?

    b   How did you learn how to use it?

    c   What software are you currently using?

    d   Which features do you like the best or use most often?

    e   For what kinds of projects do you use your spreadsheet software?

After the interview, write up your findings as if you were writing a magazine article. Your article might be in the format of an interview or a narrative in which you summarize and paraphrase the interviewee. Your instructor will provide you with specifications for length and format.

Microsoft Excel

Tutorial 2: Create Simple Worksheets

Tutorial 2

Create Simple Worksheets

Cellular Phones

Cellular phones or "cell phones" are everywhere. They're convenient, provide communications in emergencies, and help parents keep track of their children. But they're not cheap. Learn how to decipher your cell phone bill and check its accuracy as you learn to create spreadsheets "from scratch."

Review Questions

The Review Questions will help you assess whether you understand important concepts, such as absolute references, after you complete the online tutorial.

Projects

Tutorial 2 Projects include looking at gold price fluctuations, helping a used-car salesman come up with sticker prices, forecasting trends in highway violence, and auditing a rental report from the Oldies Video Club.

1 Start a Worksheet

- Label Tabs
- Enter the Title
- Enter Column Labels
- Align Labels
- Enter Numbers
- Fill Cells with a Series

2 Enter Simple Formulas

- Type a Formula
- Pointer Math
- Display and Print Formulas

3 Replicate and Copy Formulas

- Replicate a Formula
- Copy a Formula

4 Use Absolute References

- What Doesn't Work
- Create an Absolute Reference

5 Work With Excel Functions

- Use the Sum Button
- Use the Function Wizard

Disks

If you're using a **Tracking Disk**, remember to put it in the disk drive when you log into e-Course.

To complete the WorkText Projects, you'll need to create a **Project Disk**. Your Project Disk from Tutorial 1 might be getting full, so you should use a new, blank disk for your Tutorial 2 Projects.

Cellular Phones

All over the world, cellular phones are becoming indispensable communications links. People use these phones everywhere—while walking down the street, eating in restaurants, driving, and even grocery shopping. Cellular phones provide a cost-effective security measure for women driving alone. Commuters can put the time spent going between home and office to productive use. Soccer moms equip their children with cellular phones and beepers to keep in touch and keep track of their whereabouts.

The downside of cellular phones is the bill. Cellular phone companies charge a monthly rate, but they also charge for minutes of airtime. You use up airtime anytime you're connected—even if someone else initiates the call. So if your friend calls you and you talk for five minutes on your cellular phone, you'll be billed for five minutes of airtime. Airtime rates depend on the time of day. Your calls rack up **peak rate charges** during the day—usually between 7:00 a.m. and 7:00 p.m. Calls made at other times are charged at an **off-peak rate**.

As an incentive to use more airtime (and spend more money), cellular phone companies typically offer a variety of **rate plans**. A basic plan, called a Security plan, has a low monthly fee—usually about $10, but each minute of airtime is fairly expensive—perhaps as much as $1. Other plans are bundled with "free" minutes of airtime as shown in Figure 1.

Figure 1 *Typical U.S. cell phone rate plans.*

Plan	Monthly Access Fee	Peak Rate (per minute)	Off-Peak Rate (per minute)	Free Airtime (minutes)
Security Plan	$15	30¢	16¢	
Standard Plan	$29	30¢	16¢	60
Value Plan	$75	29¢	16¢	250
Volume Plan	$160	26¢	16¢	625
Volume Plus	$200	25¢	16¢	925

A rate sheet covers only local calls. Long distance charges are added for calls you make to phones outside of your local calling area. Unlike your good old land-based phone, a cellular phone is not wired into your wall. So, what if you take your cellular phone on a cross-country trip? Any time you call from outside your local area, a **roaming** charge is added to your bill.

With most cellular phone services, a simple phone call is not so simple when it comes time to total up the bill. Is the call included in the "free" minutes? Is it a peak or off-peak call? Is it a long distance call? Were you "roaming" when you made the call?

One essential survival skill for the twenty-first century just might be your ability to interpret your cellular phone bill! Take a quick look at a sample bill in Figure 2 (on the next page). Does it look accurate?

In Tutorial 2 you'll learn how to create a spreadsheet from scratch that will help you check the accuracy of your cellular phone bill. Essentially, you'll be creating a template that you could use every month, just by plugging in the peak and off-peak minutes.

It is valuable from time to time to check if your cellular phone plan is right for you. For example, if you're on the Security plan, but find yourself making about 10 minutes of calls every month, should you upgrade to the Standard plan? If you usually chat for about 300 minutes a month, would the Value plan be cheaper than the Standard plan? The process of examining different scenarios such as this is called **what-if analysis**. Spreadsheets are perfect for such analyses because you can easily plug in numbers for each of the different scenarios to compare costs.

GET STARTED ONLINE WITH e-COURSE

To learn about making spreadsheets from scratch, start e-Course and select Tutorial 2. If you're using a Tracking Disk, don't forget to put it in the disk drive before you log in.

Figure 2 A typical cellular phone bill.

CELLSERVICE-1

MONTHLY ACCOUNT SUMMARY

Bill Date: August 1, 1998   Page 1 of 1

Account: #88844444

Phone number: 888-123-4567

Plan: Standard

CURRENT CHARGES

Service charges

    Monthly Service Charge   29.00

Usage Charges

    Airtime Charges 102.00 79 peak, 23.0 off peak 15.38

    Roamer Charges   1.93

    Roamer Access Charges   2.50

TOTAL   48.81

Detail of Airtime charges for the period 7/01 thru 7/30/98

	Calls	Minutes	Rate	Charge
Incl. in plan	23	40	0.00	0.00
Free Peak	23	40	0.00	0.00
Peak-1	18	39	0.30	11.70
Off-Peak	22	23	0.16	3.68
Total Usage	63	102		15.38

Detail of Roamer Charges

C1(7) - Boston Non-Wireline

Date	Time	Number	City	St	Min	Air	Toll	Tax	Total
7/05	336P	809-111-2222	Atlanta	GA	2.0	1.70	0.08	0.15	1.93

Detail of Roamer Access Charges

Date	Type	Charge	Tax	Total
7/05	Daily	2.50	0.00	2.50

Review Questions

FILL-IN-THE BLANKS

Fill in the blank with the correct word or phrase.

1 When you're creating a workbook, you'll typically want to change the _____ labels to reflect the contents of each worksheet.

2 When you're using Excel and click the right mouse button, a(n) _____ menu pops up.

3 You typically enter the worksheet title in cell _____.

4 When you enter text in a cell, it is automatically _____ aligned.

5 When you enter a number in a cell, it is automatically _____ aligned.

6 Excel can automatically _____ a series of cells with a sequence of numbers or dates.

7 A worksheet _____ is similar to a mathematical equation because it uses arithmetic operators such as +, *, /, and -.

8 Suppose you enter =B5+B6 in cell B7. Cell B5 contains the number 10. Cell B6 contains 9. When you click cell B7 _____ appears in the Formula bar.

9 Suppose you enter =C1*C2 in cell C3. Cell C1 contains 5. Cell C2 contains 3. Excel displays _____ in cell C3.

10 To avoid typing in the wrong cell as you're entering a formula, it is often easier to use _____ math by using the arrow keys to select the cells you want included in the formula.

11 When you replicate or copy a formula, Excel changes the _____ cell references, such as B1 to B2, C1 to C2, and so on.

12 When you replicate a formula, you can use Excel's Fill Down command to place the new formulas in a series of _____ cells, such as D5, D6, D7 and D8.

13 Excel's built-in formulas such as SUM are called _____.

MULTIPLE CHOICE

*Select the letter of the **one** best answer.*

14 **When you first open a new workbook, the tab label for the first worksheet is:**

   a A1

   b Sheet1

   c the same as the workbook name

   d the same as the filename

15 **What happens if you enter a title for a worksheet in cell A1, but that title is wider than the cell?**

   a The title spills over into the next cell as long as that cell is blank.

   b Excel displays ######## to indicate that the cell was not wide enough.

   c Excel beeps a warning.

   d The title text turns red.

16 **Suppose you have a column of numbers under the column heading "Calls." You could make the worksheet easier to read if you:**

   a right-align the heading

   b left-align the heading

   c use a number for the heading

   d put an = in front of each number in the column

17 **When you enter a column of numbers, Excel typically aligns them on the right side of the cell. You should:**

   a left-justify them so they match any text in the same column

   b put an = in front of each number

   c skip a row between each number so they are easier to read

   d leave the numbers right-aligned

18 **An example of Excel's Fill Series command is:**

  a duplicating a formula from one cell into many other cells

  b making sure the cells are exactly wide enough to fit all the numbers in a series

  c completing a series of numbers, dates, or years, such as 1995, 1996, 1997, 1998

  d creating a series of similar worksheets, but each with a unique tab label

19 **All Excel formulas begin with:**

  a F

  b A1

  c =

  d SUM

20 **When you use the arrow keys to select the cells you want to include in a formula, it is called:**

  a pointer math

  b AutoFormat

  c interactive build

  d key selection

21 **If you want to see the formulas in the cells of a worksheet, instead of the results of those formulas, you must:**

  a select Formulas from the View menu

  b hold down the Ctrl key and press the ` key

  c select Formulas from the Print Preview menu

  d click the Shift View button on the Excel toolbar

22 **Which of the following is equivalent to the formula =B17+B18+B19+B20?**

  a =B17:B20

  b =B17*B20

  c TOT:B17:B20

  d =SUM(B17:B20)

23 **Which one of the following formulas contains an absolute reference:**

  a =SUM(B11:B19)   **c** =C4*.75

  b =B5*D11   **d** =$D$6*B1

24 **If you replicate a formula and some of the resulting cells contain #VALUE!, you probably:**

a need to use an absolute reference in the formula you're trying to replicate

b forgot to begin the formula with an −

c tried to copy the formula to nonadjacent cells

d used a ? instead of a $ for the absolute reference

25 **Suppose you have the formula =$D$5* E5 in cell F5. When you copy the formula into cell F6 what will the new formula be?**

a =$D$6*E6

b =D5*E6

c =$D$5*E6

d =$D$5*E5

26 **Suppose you want to enter a formula to calculate a standard deviation, but you can't remember the formula from your statistics course. You can use Excel's:**

a Sum button

b absolute references

c Function Wizard

d Statistics AutoFormat

27 **Which one of the following functions has its own button on the Excel toolbar?**

a AVERAGE

b SUM

c MINIMUM

d MAXIMUM

28 **Suppose you decide to create a worksheet to determine which cellular phone plan is best for you, depending on the average number of airtime minutes you use per month. You'll examine several scenarios. This is called:**

a what-if analysis

b the Function Wizard

c absolute referencing

d displaying formulas

MATCHING

Select the letter from the right column that correctly matches each item in the left column.

29	Σ	**a**	an error message that typically results when you replicate a formula that should have contained an absolute reference
30	$	**b**	a dollar value
31	f_x	**c**	the SUM button
32	#VALUE!	**d**	the keys you press to display formulas in the cells
33	$500.00	**e**	the button you use to create a new worksheet
34	Game 1, Game 2, Game 3	**f**	the symbol you use to create an absolute reference
35	A1, A2, A3, A4	**g**	a formula containing a relative reference
36	▯	**h**	the Function Wizard button
37	=D3*.75	**i**	a series
38	Control ` (Ctrl `)	**j**	adjacent cells

review questions

Use a separate sheet of paper to write out your answers to these questions.

39 Write a short paragraph that contrasts what happens to relative addresses and what happens to absolute addresses when you replicate a formula.

40 Sketch out a worksheet in which you would use an absolute reference. On your sketch, show the formulas each cell would contain.

41 There is a slight difference between a formula and a function. Use your own words to describe that difference.

42 Explain why you would want to display or print formulas instead of results for a worksheet.

43 Explain the difference between copying and replicating worksheet formulas.

44 List five different series that you might typically use in a worksheet.

45 Describe how you would use pointer math to enter the formula =C5*D2+B5 into cell A2.

Projects

These Projects are designed to help you review and develop the skills you learned in Tutorial 2. Complete each Project using Microsoft Excel. *If you have not yet made the Project Disk for Tutorial 2, start the e-Course software, click Project Disk on the e-Course Welcome screen menu bar, and follow the instructions on the screen.*

If you've forgotten some of the skills you need to complete these Projects, refer to the Task Reference.

REVIEW SKILLS

1   RetroTV Guide

Fans of the retro craze are channel surfing for classic TV shows from the 60s and 70s. Wouldn't they love a *RetroTV Guide*? In the online Steps, you learned how to enter text and numbers, as well as right-align the contents of cells. You can practice these skills by entering some information for this week's edition of *RetroTV Guide*.

Start a new workbook and change the Sheet1 tab label to RetroTV. Enter the title "Today on RetroTV" in cell A1. Enter the following information in columns A, B, and C:

	A	B	C
1	Today on RetroTV		
2	Program	Channel	Time
3	Adam 12	13	1:00 AM
4	Bewitched	52	1:00 AM
5	Dragnet	52	1:30 AM
6	Flipper	11	6:30 PM
7	I Spy	52	2:00 AM
8	Kojak	11	Midnight
9	Kung Fu	9	7:00 PM
10	Laugh In	52	1:00 AM
11	Rawhide	13	1:30 AM
12	That Girl	11	2:00 AM
13	Thin Man	7	1:00 AM

projects

Right-align the column labels "Channel" and "Time." Make two last-minute corrections: "Kung Fu is on channel 7" and "Kojak is on at 1:00 AM".

Put your name in the header, and then save the workbook on your Project Disk as "RetroTV Guide". Print the worksheet.

2   Personal Tales   File: Tales.xls

Looking for a unique gift? Personal Tales, Ltd. publishes a great collection of short stories—but you provide the name of the main character. Suppose you're looking for a gift for your friend, Bill Bertagnoli. You can call Personal Tales, order *Caribbean Tugboat*, and soon Bill will be reading about his adventures aboard a semi-seaworthy craft shuttling between Antigua and Cuba. Personal Tales, Ltd. is a small garage-run business that uses a spreadsheet to create customer invoices. Let's see how Excel works for this task.

Open the Tales workbook from your Project Disk. The workbook is designed so Tales employees can complete an invoice by filling in the cells that have a white background. However, the invoice does not yet contain any formulas, so it won't calculate the prices. Put your name and address in the Ship to section of the invoice.

Tales charges $2 shipping for each item in an order. In cell D11, enter the shipping formula "=C11*2". Replicate the formula for shipping through cell D15. In cell E11, enter the price formula "=B11*C11+D11". Replicate the formula for price through cell E15. In cell E17, use the SUM button to enter the formula to total cells E11 through E16. In cell E18, enter the formula for tax "=E17*.08". In cell E19, enter the formula for total "=E17+E18".

Rename and save the workbook on your Project Disk as "Worldly Invoice", and then print the entire worksheet. On your printout, circle all the cells that contain formulas.

3   People Multiplied   File: People.xls

In 1996 the world population was estimated to be 5.8 billion and growing at an annual rate of 1.5%. The country of Belize is an independent British commonwealth located in Central America. Its population in 1993 was 222,000. Suppose the population increases by .8% (.008) annually for the years 1994 through 2000. You can use a formula to predict the population through the year 2000.

Open the People workbook from your Project Disk.

Fill cells A3 through A10 with the years 1993 through 2000.

In cell B4, enter the formula "=B3*1.008" to calculate the population for 1994. Replicate this formula through cell B10.

Fill in the dates and annual population estimates through the year 2000 for Fiji and Iceland. Assume that the annual percent increase in population in these countries is the same as in Belize.

Save and rename the workbook on your Project Disk as "Population Increase", and then print the entire worksheet with your name in the header. Show the formulas, and then print your worksheet again in landscape orientation and scaled to fit on one page.

4   Donations   File:Djdoc.xls

Deejay Baby Doc gives benefit concerts throughout the state of California. Suppose she agrees to give 1% of gross ticket sales to the Red Cross and 3% of gross ticket sales to the Salvation Army. Complete the worksheet to determine how much she should give to the Red Cross and Salvation Army of each city.

Open the Djdoc workbook from your Project Disk. Notice that the donation percentages are located in cells A14 and B14.

In cell E4, enter the gross ticket sales formula "=C4*D4". Replicate the formula for gross ticket sales through cell E11.

In cell F4, enter the absolute reference formula to calculate the Red Cross donation "=E4*$A$14". Replicate this formula through cell F11.

Now enter the formula to calculate the donation to the Salvation Army.

Rename and save the workbook on your Project Disk as "Baby Doc Donations", and then print the entire worksheet. On your printout, circle the city that will receive the highest donation.

5   The Midas Touch   File: Gold.xls

On December 31, 1974, the U.S. federal government revised a 41-year restriction on the private ownership of gold. Activity increased in the worldwide gold market and prices reached a high of about $850 in 1980. What's happened since then? You can use some of the functions you learned in the online Steps to find the high and low prices of gold in the last 10 years, as well as the average price each year.

Open the Gold workbook from your Project Disk.

Use the Function Wizard in cell N3 to find the average price of gold in 1987. Replicate this formula through cell N12 to find the average price for each year.

projects

Look carefully at the results in cell N12 to make sure that Excel averaged only for the months January through July.

Use the Function Wizard in cell B14 to find the minimum gold price in the cells B3 through M12. Use the Function Wizard again to find the maximum price.

Rename and save the workbook on your Project Disk as "Gold Prices", and then print the entire worksheet. On your printout, write a short explanation about how Excel uses blank cells that are within the range of data you're averaging or finding minimums or maximums.

APPLY SKILLS

6   Eat at Joe's

Are you satisfied with the food and service in the restaurants where you eat? Six thousand people who participated in a USA TODAY/Penn State survey seemed generally satisfied with the restaurants they frequented, although some were disgruntled about slow service. Using the raw data from this survey, you can calculate percentages that provide a more meaningful summary of the survey results.

Create the worksheet shown here. In cell B11, enter the formula to calculate the percent of respondents who are satisfied with fast food restaurants. Hint: Divide the number in cell B5 by 6000. Copy this formula down and across so you have percentages for all the cells in the table.

	A	B	C	D
1	Restaurant Satisfaction Survey			
2				
3	Raw Data			
4	Type	Satisfied	Disgruntled	
5	Fast-food	4200	1740	
6	Casual	5460	540	
7	Fancy	5610	390	
8				
9	Percent			
10	Type	Satisfied	Disgruntled	
11	Fast food			
12	Casual			
13	Fancy			

To make it easier for users of this worksheet to interpret this data, you can format the cells to display the data as percentages.

To format cells as percentages:

1: Select the cells you want to format, in this case B11 through C13.

2: Right-click these selected cells and choose **Format Cells**. Click the **Number** tab. Click **Percentage** in the Category panel and set the decimal places to 2, then click the **OK** button.

To see how your worksheet will appear when printed, you can preview it.

To preview a worksheet:

1: Click the **Print Preview** button on the Standard toolbar. Notice that the title needs to be centered. After previewing the worksheet, click the **Close** button.

2: Center the title across cells A1 through C1 by selecting these cells and clicking the **Merge and Center** button on the Formatting toolbar.

3: Click **Setup** and put your name in the header. Print the worksheet. Save the workbook on your Project Disk as **Restaurant Survey**

7 Mango Air   File: Mango.xls

The marketing department of a new airline, Mango Air, is working with a consultant to find the most popular destinations within Central America and North Africa. You are given a list of countries and the number of passengers for each country. Your boss tells you to enter formulas in the worksheet to find the change in the number of passengers for each country between 1997 and 1998 and the total number of tourists for each region for 1997 and 1998.

Open the Mango workbook from your Project Disk. In previous Projects, you've been given the formulas you need to enter. For this Project, you'll need to determine the formulas yourself, so take a moment familiarize yourself with the location of the labels and numbers on the worksheet.

In cell B10, enter the formula to find the total number of passengers for Central America in 1997.

In cell C10, enter the formula to find the total number of passengers for Central America in 1998.

In cell D4, enter the formula to find the change in the number of passengers for Guatemala. Hint: Subtract the 1997 figure from the 1998 figure, so increased passenger traffic will be shown as a positive number, but a decrease will be shown as a negative number.

In cells D5 through D10, replicate the change formula.

projects

Perform the same calculations for North Africa as you did for Central America.

a Rename and save the workbook on your Project Disk as Mango Air Analysis. Print two versions of the worksheet—one showing results and one showing formulas (in landscape).

b On your worksheet, indicate in writing which country within Central America had the greatest increase in passengers.

c On your worksheet, indicate in writing which country within Central America had the greatest decrease in passengers.

d On your worksheet, indicate in writing which country within North Africa had the greatest increase in passengers.

e On your worksheet, indicate in writing which country within North Africa had the greatest decrease in passengers.

8   Out of Service   File: Aereo.xls

Aereo Groupo S.A. consists of Mango Air and Econo Air. The board of directors needs to discontinue air service to one country for each airline. The CEO has requested that you make this decision. To accomplish this task you must carefully follow the instructions below.

Open the Aereo workbook from your Project Disk. Familiarize yourself with the location of the labels and numbers so you will be able to create the formulas needed for calculations.

In cell B11, enter the formula to find the total number of flights for Mango Air. In cell D11, enter the formula to find the total number of flights for Econo Air. In cell B12, enter the formula to find the minimum number of flights for Mango Air. In cell D12, enter the formula to find the minimum number of flights for Econo Air. In column C, calculate the percentage of Mango Air flights that go to each country. In column E, calculate the percentage of Econo Air flights that go to each country. Hint: The percentage is the number of flights for a particular country divided by the total number of flights.

Rename and save the workbook on your Project Disk as "Out of Service", and then print two versions of the worksheet—one showing results, the other in landscape orientation showing formulas. On your printout, indicate the countries that you would recommend for discontinued service.

projects

9 Bordertown Beatnik

What would you do if you were a beatnik intellectual with no love life, stranded in a small town, and making minimum wage at a bookstore? Maybe you'd feed your mind with books! The Border Town Book Shop in El Paso, Texas offers its employees a discount on books. The amount of the discount depends on how many years the employee has worked at the book shop. Create the worksheet below that contains a list of books you want to purchase.

	A	B	C	D	E
1	Title	Price	Discount	You Pay	
2	Bad Seed	6.95			
3	Takedown	5.49			
4	Liar	4.99			
5	Vegas	5.95			
6	Mi Vida	7.95			
7					
8	Total				
9	Discount	0.1			

Enter the formulas to calculate the following:

- the discount or savings for each book at 10% (0.1) discount rate

- the amount you would pay for the discounted book

- the total cost for all books at retail prices

- the total savings for all books

- the amount you would pay for all the books at a discount

a   Save the worksheet on your Project Disk as "Beatnik Savings". Print two versions of the worksheet—one showing results and one showing formulas.

Next, modify the worksheet as necessary to answer questions b through f. Write your answers on your original results printout.

b   What is the discount on the book *Vegas* if the book shop offers you a 20% (.20) discount?

c   What is the discount on the book *Liar* if the book shop offers you a 17% (.17) discount?

d   What is the discount on the book *Mi Vida* if the book shop offers you a 5% (.05) discount?

e   What are your total savings if the book shop gives you a 7% (.07) discount on all the books?

f   What would be the total cost of all the books with a 22% (.22) discount?

projects

10 Cell Phone What-if

Using the information from the Rate Sheet and Monthly Account Summary provided in the scenario for this Tutorial on page EX 30, create a worksheet to select the plan that's best for you. You need to enter the number of peak minutes and the number of off-peak minutes you typically call per month. Then, you need to total up your monthly bill under each rate plan. Remember that under each plan you have a number of free minutes, but these only apply to calls made during peak times.

Create and test the worksheet, and then save the workbook on your Project Disk as "Cell Phone Analysis".

   a   Print the worksheet showing an analysis for each plan if you typically log 140 minutes of peak time and 20 minutes of off-peak time.

   b   Print a revised version of the worksheet showing the analysis for 40 peak minutes and 60 off-peak minutes.

On your printouts from a and b, circle the plan that is the best value.

BUILD SKILLS

11 Protein Bars & Worksheet Tabs   File: Muscle.xls

Muscles, Inc. is a nutritional supplement and protein bars distributor. Muscles has an Excel workbook containing worksheets with each protein bar's nutritional content. The sales staff at Muscles can use this workbook any time a customer calls to inquire about nutritional content of their products. As products change, product information needs to be updated in the workbook.

   In the online Steps, you learned how to change a tab label. In this Project, you'll learn how to delete tabs and how to copy data from one worksheet to another.

   Open the Muscle workbook from your Project Disk. Suppose that the Flex Bar is now produced by PowerBars International. Rename the Flex tab label to "Power".

   The Peanut Bar has very low sales and has been discontinued, so you need to delete the Peanut tab label and remove the worksheet associated with it.

To delete the tab label and remove the associated worksheet:

1: Click the **Peanut** tab.

2: Click **Edit** on the menu bar, then click **Delete Sheet**.

3: When you see the dialog box asking if you want to continue, click the **OK** button.

The company that makes the Panther Bar has a new protein bar called the Cheetah Bar, which has the same nutritional content as the Panther Bar. You want to create a new worksheet with the tab label "Cheetah" and then copy the nutritional content data from the Panther sheet.

To copy content from one worksheet to another:

1: Change the Sheet4 tab label **Cheetah**.

2: Click the **Panther** tab.

3: Highlight cells A1 through C10.

4: Click **Edit** on the menu bar, then click **Copy**.

5: Click the **Cheetah** tab.

6: Click cell **A1**.

7: Click **Edit**, then click **Paste**.

8: In cell A1, change "Panther" to **Cheetah**.

The company that makes the Power Bar has created the PowerPlus bar. Change the tab label for Sheet5 to "PowerPlus," then copy the data from the Power sheet to the PowerPlus sheet. On the PowerPlus worksheet, change Flex Bar to "PowerPlus bar". Then change the %RDA for Vitamin D to "80". Rename and save the workbook on your Project Disk as "Protein Bars", and then print the PowerPlus worksheet.

12 Honest Ernie's Order of Operations   File: Ernie.xls

Spreadsheets are a handy business tool for calculating prices, discounts, and profits. But as formulas become more complex, you're likely to run into the "order of operations" trap.

Open the Ernie workbook from your Project Disk. Look at the sticker price for the 72 Dodge Dart in column D. Try the calculation yourself on a piece of paper: Add $500 to $2500. Now add 10% ($300) to the result. Compare your results with the sticker price on the worksheet. Clearly something is wrong with the worksheet formula.

Excel follows the standard mathematical order of operations when it performs calculations. The order of operations specifies that all multiplication and division are performed first, and then addition and subtraction. In Honest Ernie's formula =Dealer Cost+Preparation Cost*Markup, the Preparation Cost is multiplied by the Markup first. But Excel is supposed to add the dealer cost and the preparation cost first. How can Honest Ernie make Excel do the calculation in the correct order?

projects

In cell D4, enter the formula "=(B4+C4)*$D$2". The parentheses tell Excel to add the contents of cells B4 and C4 before performing the multiplication. The results should be $3,300.00. Now replicate this formula in cells D5 through D11.

Suppose Ernie wants to know the sticker price if he marks up his costs by 115% (1.15). In cell E4, enter the formula to calculate the sticker price at 115% markup; then replicate this formula for all the cars.

Save the workbook on your Project Disk as "Updated Ernie". Print the entire worksheet after putting your name in the header.

13 Replicate Multiple Money Formulas   File: Money.xls

In the online Steps, you learned how to replicate one formula at a time. In this Project, you'll learn a shortcut to replicate multiple formulas in one step.

Suppose that this summer you plan to visit Canada, Britain, France, Germany, Switzerland, and Japan. You want to be a savvy backpacker so you look for the current currency exchange rates. The following exchange rates are listed at the Federal Reserve Web site:

British Pound	.61728
Japanese Yen	122.05
German Mark	1.6434
Canadian Dollar	1.3454
French Franc	5.5465
Swiss Franc	1.4255

Open the Money workbook from your Project Disk. Suppose you had already entered the formulas you needed to convert a U.S. $20 traveler's check into each of these foreign currencies. Look at the formulas in row 5. Now you want to adapt these formulas to calculate the exchange rates for traveler's checks in the amounts of $50, $100, $200, and $500. To do this you can replicate the formulas from cells B5 through G5 for all the traveler's check amounts.

To replicate the formulas:

1: Highlight cells B5 through G9.

2: Click **Edit** on the menu bar, point to **Fill**, and then click **Down**.

Now suppose you'd like to make similar calculations for the currencies of Italy, Spain, Hong Kong, and Taiwan. Create the formulas for the conversion of a U.S.

$20 traveler's check in row 13, and then replicate the formulas in one operation to calculate the rest of the traveler's check amounts. The exchange rates are:

Italian Lira	1669.20
Spanish Peseta	142.99
Hong Kong Dollar	7.7550
Taiwanese Dollar	27.610

Rename and save the workbook on your Project Disk as "Currency Exchange", and then print the entire worksheet after putting your name in the header.

14 Motorcycle Mama's PMT Function   File: Moto.xls

When you purchase a car or motorcycle, you usually take out a loan that you pay back in monthly installments. Excel's PMT function automatically calculates monthly payments for you based on the amount of the loan, the interest rate, and the pay-back period. The syntax for the PMT function is:

PMT (interest rate per period, number of payments, loan amount)

For example, to find the monthly interest on a $10,000, three-year loan at 9% (.09) interest, the PMT formula would be:

=PMT(.09/12,3*12,10000)

- .09/12 is the *interest rate per period* (the monthly interest rate equals the annual interest rate divided by 12 months).

- 3*12 is the total *number of payments* (the number of years of the loan multiplied by 12 months).

- 10,000 is the *loan amount*.

The Leather Neck Motorcycle shop, Mad Midget's Motorcycles, and Mama's Choppers offer three-year loans, but the interest rate varies by dealer and by the bike. Use the PMT function to calculate the monthly payment for each motorcycle.

To use the PMT function:

1: Open the **Moto** workbook from your Project Disk.

2: In cell D3, enter the formula containing the PMT function: **=PMT(C3/12,3*12,B3)**

3: Make sure the monthly payment for the Ducati is ($321.85). The parentheses indicate a negative number, or in this case, that it is a payment.

4: If the amount in cell D3 is correct, replicate the formula through cell D7.

projects

Next, you decide to see if the payments on a compact car would be more affordable. You find a dealer offering a four-year loan at 8% interest on a Saturn Sports Coupe that has a sticker price of $14,599. To find your monthly payment for this vehicle, enter the car loan information in row 10, and enter the payment formula in cell D10.

Rename and save the workbook on your Project Disk as "Chopper Payments". Put your name in the header. Print your worksheet and circle the vehicle that has the lowest monthly payment.

15 The IF Function Settles a Challenge   File: Slim.xls

The body builders at the local gym are arguing whether Slim Slurp or PowerPunch is the better body building supplement. The challenge is on! The gym manager created a worksheet that lists the percentage of the U.S. daily values (USDV) of sixteen essential vitamins and minerals, electrolytes, and trace elements in the two body-building supplements. The gym manager discovered that an IF function could automatically compare the USDVs for each nutrient and calculate which supplement has more.

The syntax of the IF function is:

> *=IF(logical test, value if true, value if false)*

The *logical test* is any value or expression that Excel evaluates as true or false. Some examples of expressions are B4>C4, B7<100, and B8<=999.

Suppose you want Excel to display a warning message if the nutrient content of Vitamin A is less than 50%; otherwise display the message "Value is at least 50%". You could use the formula:

> *=IF(B4<50%,"Value is less than 50%!", "Value is at least 50%")*

The gym manager decides to use the IF function to calculate whether the Slim Slurp product or the PowerPunch product contains the higher potency of each nutrient.

To use the IF function:

1: Open the **Slim** workbook from your Project Disk. Familiarize yourself with the location of the labels and numbers.

2: In cell D4, enter the IF function that indicates which product has the higher potency of Vitamin A: **=IF(B4>C4,"Slim Slurp","PowerPunch")**

3: Make sure the text **Slim Slurp** appears in cell D4.

4: If the text in cell D4 is correct, replicate this formula from cell D4 through cell D20.

The body builders also see that PowerPunch has a low USDV for several nutrients. Enter a formula using the IF function that prints "Low" if any PowerPunch nutrient falls below 75%, but if the value is at least 75%, it prints a blank. Hint: To print a blank, just put a space in between the quotation marks. Rename and save the workbook on your Project Disk as "Challenge Results". Put your name in the header and then print the entire worksheet. On your printout, circle the product that wins the challenge.

EXPLORE

16 Use the FORECAST Function   File: Chips.xls

The Highway Patrol has collected data on the number of highway violence incidents for the years 1990 through 1996. To prepare for the next two years, the Highway Patrol wants to predict how many violent incidents might occur in 1997 and in 1998. The information technology division of the Highway Patrol has suggested using the FORECAST function.

The FORECAST function looks at two sets of data. In this case, one set is the years and the other set is the number of incidents. You then need a target number. The target number in the first case will be 1997. The FORECAST function will calculate the expected number of incidents based on previous values.

The Syntax for the FORECAST function is:

$$=FORECAST(x, known\_y's, known\_x's)$$

- x is the data point for which you want to predict a value. In this example, you want to predict for 1997, located in cell A10.

- *known_y's* are the incidents for which you have actual data. The violent incidents are located in cells B3 through B9.

- *known_x's* are the actual data located in the same column as your x data point. These are the dates 1990 through 1996, located in cells A3 through A9.

To use the FORECAST function to predict the number of highway violence incidents for 1997:

1: Open the **Chips** workbook from your Project Disk.

2: In cell B10, enter the FORECAST function: **=FORECAST(A10,B3:B9,A3:A9)**

3: Make sure your forecast for 1997 is 1,951 incidents.

Now use the FORECAST function in cell B11 to predict the number of incidents for 1998. Rename and save the workbook on your Project Disk as "Violent

projects

Forecast". Print your worksheet in landscape orientation with your name in the header.

17 Help with the Auditing Toolbar   File: Bmovie.xls

According to film reviewer, Leonard Maltin, the 1958 movie *It! The Terror from Beyond Space* was the inspiration for the contemporary blockbuster, *Alien*. Old movies can be fun, and many video stores have a fairly good selection.

Suppose the Oldies Video Club discovers some errors in its Rental Report, which they produced using spreadsheet software. Let's see how Excel can help you check your worksheets so they don't contain embarrassing errors.

Excel's Auditing toolbar provides easy access to features that help you understand the relationship between cells on the worksheet and errors.

To explore the Auditing toolbar:

1: Open the **Bmovie** workbook from your Project Disk.

2: Click the **Tools** menu, point to **Auditing**, and then click **Show Auditing Toolbar**.

3: Use Help to explore the following auditing features of Excel:

- check and review data
- find cells referred to by a selected formula
- find formulas that refer to a selected cell
- find the source of errors

4: Close **Help**. Now use the Auditing toolbar to find the errors in the Bmovie Video Rental Report, and write out your answers to the following questions:

a Use the Trace Precedents button for cell B17. What is the range for this formula?

b Is the formula in cell B17 correct? Explain your answer. Use the Remove All Arrows button to remove the tracer arrows.

c Use the Trace Precedents button for cell D3. Which cells are used in this correct formula? Use the Remove All Arrows button to remove the tracer arrows.

d Which cells are used in the incorrect formula in cell D4?

e What should the correct formula for cell D4 be?

f Suppose you're thinking about moving the Subtotal formula to cell D8. Use the Trace Dependents button to determine which formulas use the results of the Subtotal formula in cell D13. Which formulas would you have to change if you moved the contents of cell D13 to cell D8?

g The error #VALUE! appears in cell C20. Use the Trace Error button to find the source of the error. What is the correct formula for cell C20? Hint: You might want to look in Help to find out what #VALUE! means.

h Examine the remaining formulas on the worksheet. Correct any formulas that do not produce the correct results. Rename and save this workbook on your Project Disk as "Trace Errors". Put your name in the header. Print two versions of the worksheet—one showing the formulas (in landscape, fit to 1 page) and one showing the results.

18 Use the Correlation Function   File: Leaders.xls

Calculating the degree of correlation between two variables results in a number between 0 and 1. A correlation of 0 indicates that there is no relationship between the variables. A correlation of 1 indicates that there is a perfect relationship between the variables. Usually a correlation falls somewhere in between 0 and 1. But the closer the correlation is to 1.00, the stronger the relationship between the variables.

A number representing the degree of correlation can have a positive sign (positive relationship) or a negative sign (negative relationship). A positive correlation means that those who score high on the first variable usually score high on the second variable also. It also means that those who score low on the first variable usually score low on the second variable.

To calculate the degree of correlation in Excel, you'll use the CORREL function. The syntax for the CORREL function is:

$$=CORREL(array1, array2)$$

- *array1* is a range of cells containing one set of values.
- *array2* is a range of cells containing another set of values.

Suppose someone has ranked 10 politicians from 10 different states on leadership, self-esteem, and communication skills; and suppose you want to know if there is a relationship between leadership ability ranks and self-esteem ranks.

To use Excel's correlation function:

1: Open the **Leaders** workbook from your Project Disk.

2: In cell C14, enter the CORREL function to calculate the correlation between leadership rank and self esteem rank: **=CORREL(B3:B12,C3:C12)**

projects

3: In cell D14, enter the formula to calculate the correlation between leadership rank and communication skills rank.

Rename and save the workbook on your Project Disk as Rank and Correlation. Print the worksheet with your name in the header. On your printout, write out the answers to Questions a through e:

a What is the degree of correlation between leadership and self-esteem?

b What does the number in cell C14 tell us about leadership ability and self-esteem rank?

c What is the degree of correlation between leadership rank and communication skills rank?

d What does the number in cell D14 tell us about leadership ability and communication skills?

e If you want to be a leader, would it preferable to have communication skills or high self-esteem? Explain your answer.

19 Create a Lookup Formula   File: Students.xls

Suppose you have a list of raw test scores and you want to assign letter grades based on a grading scale of some sort. Using Excel's VLOOKUP function, you can tell Excel to look at a raw score, and then to look at the grading scale and pick the correct letter grade.

The syntax for the VLOOKUP function is:

=VLOOKUP(lookup_value, table_array, col_index_num)

Using the test grades example:

- The *lookup_value* is the cell containing the raw score.
- The *table_array* is the location of the grading scale. Hint: Enter the entire range with absolute addresses: $D3$E15.
- The *col_index_num* is the offset in the grading scale. For example, if the grading scale contains scores in one column and letter grades in the next, the offset is 2.

Suppose a graduate assistant has entered the grading scale for the Introduction to Biology course into a worksheet. Open the Students workbook from your Project Disk. In cell C3, enter the VLOOKUP function to display the letter grade for Marty Molecule's final exam. Find the rest of the students' final exam grades using the VLOOKUP function.

Rename and save the workbook as "Grade Look-up" on your Project Disk. Put your name in the header and print the worksheet.

20 Explore Date Functions   File: Days.xls

This year you're determined to be better organized. So you have created a worksheet that automatically displays how many days until the fourth of July fireworks festival, how many days until you can dress up as the Hulk for Halloween, how many days until Christmas, how many days until New Years, and how many days until your birthday. Open the Days workbook from your Project Disk. You'll have to use Excel's online Help to find how to use the function that calculates the number of days between two dates.

When you have completed the worksheet, rename and save the workbook on your Project Disk as "Calculate Days". Print two versions of your worksheet—one version displaying the formulas (in landscape, fit to 1 page), and one version displaying the results.

INVESTIGATE

21 Spreadsheets vs. Tables

Spreadsheets are valuable tools because of their ability to perform calculations. But the row and column format tempts many people to also use spreadsheet software to create simple tables that do not involve any calculations. It isn't *wrong* to use spreadsheet software for creating tables, but a word processor is usually just as efficient for this task.

To examine this difference yourself, look in magazines and newspapers for three examples of simple tables, and three examples of spreadsheets that appear to have used calculations. Photocopy your examples and label each as a table or as a worksheet.

projects

22 Spreadsheet Software User Manuals

The trend today is to use online help to learn about or to review spreadsheet features. Most spreadsheet software, however, still includes a printed user manual. Also, if you look on the shelves of your local library or favorite bookstore, you'll probably see quite a collection of books about Excel and books about Microsoft Office, which include information about Excel.

For this Project, locate a book about Excel or Microsoft Office, and use it to answer the following questions:

   a   What is the title, author, publisher, and date of publication for the book?

   b   How many pages does the book contain specifically about Excel?

   c   Which version of Excel does the book cover?

   d   What are the titles of the Excel chapters?

   e   Is there an index?

   f   Which of the following spreadsheet topics are listed in the index?

      AutoFill
      Average
      ###
      Functions
      Landscape

      Aligning data in cells
      Absolute reference
      Lookup
      rename tabs

   g   Look for a description of how to perform a task such as Fill Down, Fill Series, or Copy. How helpful are the directions? Do they appear to be clear and easy to follow? Are numbers or bullets used to delineate each step in the task?

   h   How would you describe the use of graphics in the book?

   i   Do you think you would prefer to use a printed book or online help? Explain your answer.

23 Formula Syntax

In the online Steps, you learned how to use Excel's Function Wizard. Excel provides extensive help on each function that includes a description of the function, the function's syntax, some typical applications of the function, and some samples. To access help for a function, display the Office Assistant and then type the name of the function.

For this Project, create a mini-manual explaining how to use the IF, VLOOKUP, TODAY, GROWTH, LARGE, and COUNTA functions. For each function, specify its name and syntax. Then use your own words to describe what the function does and provide two examples of how to use it.

24 All About Microsoft

Microsoft Corporation, publisher of the Excel spreadsheet software, began as essentially a garage business, but has grown to be the world's largest software company. Suppose you are a computer industry analyst preparing an article about Microsoft for a popular computer magazine. Use your library and Internet resources to gather information about Microsoft. You'll probably want to look for answers to questions such as:

- Who is the CEO of Microsoft?
- Where is the company based?
- How many people are employed by Microsoft?
- In addition to Excel, what other software does Microsoft publish?
- What is the corporate culture at Microsoft?
- What are the employment opportunities at Microsoft?

After you have completed your research, write an article that presents the information you found. Your instructor will provide you with specifications for length and format for your report.

25 Cell Phone Info on the Web

The scenario for this Tutorial focused on cellular phones. The history, technology, and growth of cellular phones are rather interesting topics. Cellular phones are an example of modern technology taking off and becoming an integral part of our culture in a very few years. The Internet is a good source of information about the cellular phone phenomenon. Use your Internet resources to develop a report about any aspect of cellular phones you find interesting. For example, you might look at the growth of cellular phone use around the world. You could research improvements in cell phone technology or changes in rates.

Look for data to include in your report as a spreadsheet. For example, you might find per-minute rates for various countries that you could convert into U.S. dollars. Or you might be able to find historical data that you could use to forecast future trends.

Check with your instructor for the report's length and formatting requirements. Make sure you include a list of your Internet resources in your final report.

Microsoft Excel

Tutorial 3: Format a Worksheet

Tutorial 3

Format a Worksheet

WHAT'S INSIDE

Jackpot!

In this Tutorial, you will venture into the world of lotteries. Virtually every state and province sponsors a lottery with a huge jackpot. Isn't this gambling? Should it be illegal? Who gets the profits? You'll discover the answers to these questions and more as you read the scenario.

Doing the e-Thing

The focus of this Tutorial is formatting worksheets to make them more attractive, more meaningful, and more legible. As you modify the worksheets in the online Steps, keep an eye out for what looks good and what works so you can apply similar formats to the worksheets you create.

Projects

Tutorial 3 includes Projects that should be of interest to star gazers, car buffs, stock jocks, and entrepreneurs. You'll learn some shortcuts for changing font color and background colors on your worksheets. You'll also find out how to use styles to make formatting a breeze.

1 Apply AutoFormats

- AutoFormat a Worksheet
- Undo an AutoFormat

2 Work with Columns and Rows

- Change Column Width
- Change Row Height
- Insert a Column or Row
- Delete a Column or Row
- Sort Column Contents

3 Use the Formatting Toolbar

- Change the Font
- Change the Font Size
- Use the B, I, U Formatting Buttons

- Use the Alignment Buttons
- Center Across Columns
- Use the Number Style Buttons

4 Use the Format Cells Dialog Box

- Apply the General Format
- Apply Multiple Number Formats
- Change Font and Background Colors
- Add a Border

5 Finishing Touches

- Add Clip Art
- Check Spelling

Data Disks

If you're using a Tracking Disk, remember to put it in the disk drive before you log into e-Course. Your Project Disk from Tutorial 2 might be getting full, so you should use a new, blank disk for your Tutorial 3 Projects.

Jackpot!

Lotteries have a long and successful tradition of generating revenues for emperors, kings, countries, states, and provinces. Historians suspect that the first government-sponsored lottery was held in 1520 to raise money for the French treasury. In 1750 a U.S. lottery pulled in funds to finance buildings for what was then known as Yale College. Later, in 1777 the Continental Congress authorized a lottery to raise funds for the revolutionary army.

As public and private lotteries flourished, so did fraud and corruption. By the end of the 1800s, lotteries were outlawed in many countries. A notable exception was the Irish Hospital Sweepstakes, or "Irish Sweepstakes" as it is generally called. Established in 1930, the Irish Sweepstakes became wildly popular in the U.S. despite laws that prohibited importation of lottery tickets or their distribution through the U.S. Mail.

The first state to legalize a modern lottery was New Hampshire, which instituted a lottery in 1963 to raise revenues without increasing taxes. Many states followed and by 1990, forty-two states and all Canadian provinces were announcing winning numbers and raking in cash.

Lotteries are considered a form of gambling; in other words, they provide an opportunity to win a prize that is greater than the cost of the ticket and it takes no skill to win. The fact that gambling is outlawed in most states, except for state-run lotteries, might seem odd. Legalizing lotteries required some fancy footwork, but the formula in most states was the same—spend lottery revenues on education and a good cause receives funds without tax increases.

By looking at the summary in Figure 1 on the next page, you can see that in the state of Florida, a substantial amount of money is generated for education from lottery revenues. Although the worksheet in Figure 1 contains information about lottery revenues and expenses, it is a very plain worksheet and doesn't highlight any particular aspect of the data.

Figure 1 *Summary of Florida lottery revenues and expenses.*

DEPARTMENT OF THE LOTTERY			
Statements of Revenues, Expenses and Changes in Retained Earnings			
Years Ended June 30, 1994 and 1993 (in thousands)			
	1993	1994	Change
REVENUES	2132950	2162609	29659
EXPENSES	1294066	1312845	18779
INCOME FROM OPERATIONS	838884	849764	10880
TRANSFERS TO EDUCATION ENHANCEMENT TRUST FUND	850069	851005	936
RETAINED EARNINGS BEGINNING OF YEAR	17470	6285	-11185
RETAINED EARNINGS END OF YEAR	6285	5044	-1241
Source: Audited Financial Statements of the Department of the Lottery			

Suppose you wanted to make a point that a significant amount of the lottery profit was disbursed to education. You could use different font types, sizes, and styles along with shading and graphics to make a more visually attractive and informative worksheet like the one shown in Figure 2.

Figure 2 *An attractively formatted version of the Florida lottery report highlights the contributions to education.*

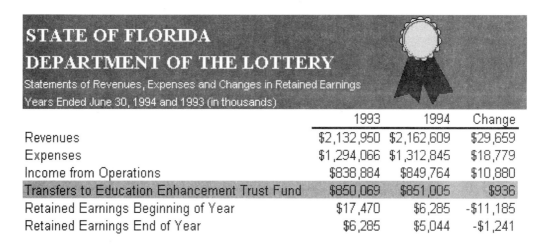

scenario

After you've read the Jackpot! scenario, it's time to go online and learn how to format Excel worksheets. If you're using a Tracking Disk, remember to put it in the disk drive. Start e-Course and select Tutorial 3.

Review Questions

FILL-IN-THE-BLANKS

Fill in the blank with the correct word or phrase.

1   _____ refers to the arrangement of data in the worksheet, but the _____ is the way the data in a cell appears.

2   Excel's _____ feature automatically formats selected cells to match a prepared design.

3   The _____ AutoFormats add $ signs to the first and last numbers in each section of a worksheet.

4   If you don't like an AutoFormat after you apply it, clicking the _____ button reapplies the original format to the worksheet.

5   It's a good idea to change the column _____ if one of the cells in the column contains ########.

6   When Excel can't display all the _____ that belongs in a cell, it uses the next cell if that cell is not blank.

7   Excel will _____ your data in ascending or descending order.

8   Excel's _____ toolbar contains controls for selecting fonts and font sizes, and buttons such as Bold, Italics, and Align Right.

9   Arial, Times New Roman, and Courier are examples of _____.

10 The _____ button slants each character in a font and is useful for drawing attention to totals and other important worksheet information.

11 The _____ format displays "plain" numbers without dollar signs, commas, or percents.

review questions

12 The _____ dialog box is handy if you want to apply multiple number formats to the contents of a cell.

13 A(n) _____ is a line that you can specify for the top, bottom, or sides of one or more cells.

14 A small pre-drawn graphic that you can use to decorate your spreadsheet is called _____.

15 True or False? Excel's spell checker flags words that are not in its dictionary and usually offers a list of correctly spelled alternatives. _____

MULTIPLE CHOICE

*Select the letter of the **one** best answer.*

16 To quickly format a worksheet using predefined format settings, you'd use:

   a the Function Wizard

   b Excel's AutoFormat feature

   c the Setup button on the Print Preview dialog box

   d the Zoom control on the Excel toolbar

17 Suppose you're creating a worksheet that shows financial data for your home-based business. To add $ signs to the cells containing numbers, you should use the:

   a Accounting 2 AutoFormat

   b Classic 2 AutoFormat

   c List 1 AutoFormat

   d Colorful 1 AutoFormat

18 When Excel displays ######## in a cell, it means that:

   a the formula in the cell contains an error

   b the text in the cell can't spill over into the next cell

   c the disk is full

   d the cell is not wide enough to display the number it contains

19 Which of the following would be the least effective way to emphasize the title of a worksheet?

a increase the row height

b bold the title text

c change the background color in the title area

d increase the column width

20 When you insert a row in a worksheet, what happens to the formulas in the rows that are renumbered?

a Excel automatically changes any relative references in those formulas.

b Excel deletes any formulas in those rows.

c Excel puts ######## in any cells that contain formulas you'll need to change.

d The formulas display incorrect results unless they contain absolute references.

21 Which one of the following is not an Excel font style button?

a Italics

b Arial

c Underline

d Bold

22 The buttons you can use to align the contents of cells include all of the following except:

a Center

b Align Right

c Center Vertically

d Center Across Columns

23 The Percent button changes .1 into:

a 100%

b 10%

c .1%

d .001%

24 Which one of the following would have been produced by applying the General format?

a 1600

b 1,600

c $1,600.00

d 1600.0

25 Excel displays eight small squares called _____ around clip art or other worksheet objects.

a markers

b clips

c handles

d selectors

review questions

26 **Does Excel's spell checker ever flag words that are correctly spelled?**

   a No. The spell checker would never flag a word unless it was misspelled.

   b Yes. Excel flags any word that is not in its dictionary, even though the word is spelled correctly.

   c Yes. Excel sometimes makes spelling errors.

   d Yes. There is a known bug in Excel's spell checker.

27 **Which one of the following formatting principles best applies to worksheets that you're designing for presentations?**

   a Skip every other line to provide lots of white space.

   b Use as many fonts as possible for visual interest.

   c Use large fonts so the information is easy to read from any row in the audience.

   d Use the Accounting 2 AutoFormat whenever possible.

28 **After applying an AutoFormat, you should examine the worksheet to make sure that:**

   a the column widths are acceptable.

   b the background color didn't spill over into neighboring cells.

   c the text and numbers in your worksheet remained the same.

   d the formulas didn't change.

29 **Suppose you're creating a worksheet that you'll distribute in printed format, but you're not sure if you'll have access to a color printer. What is the best rule about color?**

   a Use darker shades for background colors and text.

   b Pastel shades usually print best.

   c Use the Print Preview tool to see how your colors will translate into shades of gray.

   d Print the worksheet to make sure the colors you've selected don't blend together and obscure the data.

30 **Suppose you create a worksheet and enter "Club Hopping in New York" as the worksheet title in cell A1. You apply the Colorful 1 AutoFormat but notice that column A is now as wide as the title. What is your next best step to narrow column A?**

   a Double-click the dividing line between columns A and B.

   b Drag the dividing line between columns A and B to the left.

   c Use a different AutoFormat.

   d Click the Undo button.

review questions

MATCHING

Select the letter from the right column that correctly matches each item in the left column.

31 ########

a Center Across Columns button

32 [Z↓A↑ icon]

b Spelling button

33 [U icon]

c means that the cell is too narrow to display the number in the cell

34 [merge icon]

d Decimal Decrease button

35 [.00→.0 icon]

e a Sort button

36 [ABC✓ icon]

f changing row height

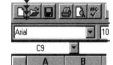

g Font Size control

37

38 [Top / Pennsylvania image]

h Align Right button

39 [10 dropdown image]

i the Formatting toolbar

40 [align icon]

j Underline button

review questions

Use a separate sheet of paper to write out your answers to the following questions.

41 List at least three format changes that AutoFormat makes to a worksheet.

42 Suppose you have a value in cell A3. Rows 5 and 6 contain formulas with absolute references to this cell, $A$3. Explain what happens to the absolute references if you insert a new row 2.

43 Explain how you ensure that when you sort cells, all the data in the neighboring cells is included in the sort.

44 Suppose you format a cell as currency, but then you realize that you don't want the $ sign in the cell. Explain how you would remove the $ sign.

45 Give an example of how you could use an outline border to enhance the readability of your worksheet.

Projects

These Projects are designed to help you review and develop the skills you learned in Tutorial 3. Complete each Project using Microsoft Excel. *If you have not yet made the Project Disk for Tutorial 3, start the e-Course software, click the Project Disk menu, and follow the instructions on the screen.*

If you've forgotten some of the skills you need to complete the Projects, refer to the Task Reference.

REVIEW SKILLS

1   Be Back in 2,400 Years   File: Comet.xls

In the spring of 1997, the comet Hale-Bopp blasted by earth, shedding a blazing trail of ice, gas, and dust. If you missed it, you're out of luck: it won't be back this way for about 2,400 years.

Comet watchers need to know where to point their telescopes and cameras. Directions such as "on February 9th, the comet will pass just southeast of the globular cluster M71" might point you to the neighborhood, but a table with data for right ascension and declination pinpoints the comet's position. Here's an opportunity to use a spreadsheet to create and format a simple table.

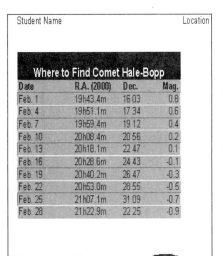

Date	R.A. (2000)	Dec.	Mag.
Feb. 1	19h43.4m	16 03	0.8
Feb. 4	19h51.1m	17 34	0.6
Feb. 7	19h59.4m	19 12	0.4
Feb. 10	20h08.4m	20 56	0.2
Feb. 13	20h18.1m	22 47	0.1
Feb. 16	20h28.6m	24 43	-0.1
Feb. 19	20h40.2m	26 47	-0.3
Feb. 22	20h53.0m	28 55	-0.5
Feb. 25	21h07.1m	31 09	-0.7
Feb. 28	21h22.9m	22 25	-0.9

Open the file Comet workbook from your Project Disk. AutoFormat the entire table using the style 3-D Effects 2. Center the title across columns A through D. Change the font color for the title to white and the background of the title to black. Change the title font size to 12. Adjust the column widths, row heights, and cell alignment to make the worksheet look like the one here. Put your name in the header and print the worksheet. Rename and save the workbook as "Comet Hale-Bopp".

projects

2   Lottery Financial Statements   File: Florida.xls

Many states use lotteries to supplement funding for education. How much of the lottery revenue actually makes it to schools? Florida publishes audited financial statements on the Web, detailing lottery revenues, expenses, and contributions to education. Open the Florida workbook from your Project Disk. This worksheet lost most of its formatting when it was transferred off the Web. In this Project, you'll format the Florida worksheet so it is easier to read.

AutoFormat cells A6 through C34 using the style Accounting 1. Change the font size in the two title rows to 12, boldface the titles, and change the title background color to light gray. Make the format in cell A14 match that of cell A6. In cells A3, A4, and A36, change the font size to 8.

Put your name in the header, and then print the worksheet. Rename and save the workbook as "Florida Lottery Report".

3   The Market Basket   File: Market.xls

Your local newspaper probably features a supermarket price comparison every few months. Someone from a consumer advocate group takes a shopping list to three or four markets and buys the products on the list. Our shopper went to a few markets and loaded up the shopping cart. Which store was the most expensive?

Open the Market workbook from your Project Disk. AutoFormat all the cells using the style Colorful 2. (Hint: Don't forget the totals in row 16.) Use Excel's auto column-width feature to increase the width of column A so you can read the entire label for each item. Use the Format Cells dialog box to format all the numbers as currency, making sure the cells are wide enough to display the currency values.

Sort the items with their corresponding prices in ascending alphabetical order. To make sure you've performed the sort correctly, your resulting list should begin with:

Caprisun juice   Case $11.99 $12.49 $11.59

Rename and save your workbook sheet as "Market Basket". Put your name in the header, and then print the worksheet. If you're using a dot-matrix or ink-jet printer, use the Setup dialog box to specify a black and white printout.

4   Deals on Wheels   File: Cars.xls

Shopping for a new car? What's the best deal you can expect to get? A professional shopper bargained with dealers for the best price on five compact sport utility vehicles. The data has been stored in the Cars workbook.

projects

Format the worksheet so it looks like the worksheet
...car clip art, select any image that you think is
...t. When you're satisfied with the format, put your
...the worksheet. Save the workbook as "Wheel Deals".

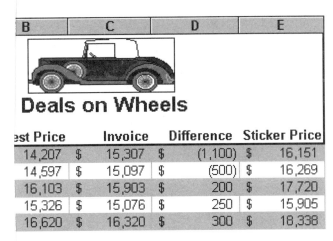

B	C	D	E
...est Price	**Invoice**	**Difference**	**Sticker Price**
14,207	$ 15,307	$ (1,100)	$ 16,151
14,597	$ 15,097	$ (500)	$ 16,269
16,103	$ 15,903	$ 200	$ 17,720
15,326	$ 15,076	$ 250	$ 15,905
16,620	$ 16,320	$ 300	$ 18,338

File: Luxury.xls

...car? Maybe you can afford to lease one, instead. One
...ertises three leasing plans. The plans differ by the
...igning fee, and the monthly payment. Is it better to pay
...onth?

...k from your Project Disk, and familiarize yourself
...ave to scroll to the right to see all the data.) Make the
...he worksheet:

...ply the Currency format to any cells that contain
... the number of decimal places to 0. Don't forget cell

...Percent format.

...General format.

...ow height to about ½ inch.

... size to 16, change font type to Times New Roman,
...lor to purple.

- Cells A2, D2, G2: Bold, italicize, and change the font color to purple.

- Cells A2 through I2: Add a thick border at the bottom of the cells.

- All cells: Make sure the columns are wide enough to display all text and numbers; then check the spelling.

In Class work 10:40-12:30

Start tutorial 3 with a "Tracking Mark" floppy disk
in the computer.
Complete e-course Excel 97 Tutorial 3 five topics.
Print Mark and Continue, then print a Report of your marks,
after that Create a Project disk for Tutorial 3

Steps to create a Project disk ONLY. Refer to page EX 12.
Start with a blank formatted floppy disk labeled "Project Disk"
Menus: Start, Tutorial & Manuals, e-Course Excel 97,
(Continue -- tracking data will not be save for this session).
Now enter information 1 TAB 1 TAB 1 TAB 1 TAB OK to bypass
e-course Login. DO NOT START A TUTORIAL IN THIS MANNER because
the marks will not be saved.

Excel Speadsheet Project Assignment 3 In Class Work
Page EX 72 P#2   1pt
Page EX 72 P#4   1pt
Page EX 73 P#5   1pt
Page EX 77 P#12   1pt

projects

When your format changes are complete, add your name to the header. Before you print the worksheet, use the Setup button to specify landscape orientation and fit the entire worksheet on one page. Save the workbook as "Leasing Options".

APPLY SKILLS

6 The Tao of the Dow

The Dow Jones industrial average was first published on May 26, 1886. On that day the average was 40.94. It took almost 90 years to reach 1000, but only 15 more years to reach the 2000 mark. Suppose you've gathered the following data on Dow Jones milestones:

Level	Date crossed	Size of move	Months to get there
1000	11/14/72	2,340%	1037
2000	1/8/87	100%	170
3000	4/17/91	50%	51
4000	2/23/95	33%	46
5000	11/21/95	25%	9
6000	10/14/96	20%	11
7000	2/13/97	17%	4

Enter this data into an Excel worksheet, adding the title "Dow Jones Milestones". Format the table so it is easy to read. Save the workbook as "Dow Tao". Print your worksheet, then annotate your printout by writing a description of the formats you used.

7   Rave Shades   File: Invoice.xls

A small business owner could use spreadsheet software to design an invoice form, which could be filled in and printed for each order. Suppose the owner of Rave Shades started to create such an invoice template and stored it as Invoice. In this Project, you'll work on perfecting the format for the invoice template.

Open the Invoice workbook from your Project Disk, and apply the following formats:

- Cells B6 through B11: Add a thick border to the bottom of these cells.
- Cells A1 through E15: Change the color of the background from none to white to eliminate the grid lines.

- Cells A13 through C15: Add a thick outline border, then add a thick underline border.
- Cells A16 through E16: Add a thick border to the bottom of the cells.
- Cells E25 and E28: Add a thick border to the top of the cells.
- Cells D5 and E5: Add a thick outline border.

After you make the format changes, fill out the invoice as if you bought item # 60665 Diesel Scud Sunglasses, at $69.95. Rename and save the workbook as "Rave Invoice". Print the invoice.

8 Parking, Taxis, and Limos   File: Mileage.xls

Suppose you travel for your job, and your employer reimburses you for your travel expenses. You're required to submit a travel expense report, so you've created an Excel worksheet that you can complete after each trip. Your template includes labels and formulas for the calculations, but no data because you fill in this data only after you return from a trip. The problem is that sometimes you forget and type numbers in cells that contain formulas. You decide to color in the work area with gray and then make the background color white for only the cells in which you're supposed to enter data.

Open the Mileage workbook from your Project Disk. Change the background color to gray for all the cells within the border area (cells A1 through F15). Change the background color to "none" in cells B2, D4, D7, D8, and D9.

Suppose you take a short trip, drive 125 miles and pay $10 for parking. Enter this information in the worksheet. Put your name in the header and then print the worksheet. Rename and save the workbook as "Mileage Template".

9 What Did You Watch that Night?   File: Nielsen.xls

Nielsen Media Research keeps track of the TV viewing habits of thousands of Americans. The ratings can make or break a TV show. Nielsen data includes:

- Viewers—the number of viewers in millions
- Rating—a rating point is 970,000 TV households
- Share—the percentage of sets in use
- Rank—the show with the highest share that week is ranked #1
- Last Week—the show's rank the previous week

Open the Nielsen workbook from your Project Disk. Sheet1 shows the Nielsen ratings for one day of the week. Format this worksheet to make it as legible as

projects

possible—you choose the formats you think look best. Rename the formatted workbook "Nielsen Ratings". Print the worksheet. Annotate your printout by writing a description of the formats you used and the cells in which you used them.

10 As Good as the Pros!

Look through magazines and newspapers for an example of a nicely formatted spreadsheet or table. When you find one that looks good, photocopy it (or if it is your own publication, tear it out). Using Excel, enter the data from your example and try to duplicate its format. Save your workbook and print your results. If your worksheet uses colors, but you're printing on a black and white printer, annotate your printout to indicate the colors you used. Turn in the example and your worksheet.

BUILD SKILLS

11 More Alignment Options   File: Miles.xls

In the online Steps, you learned how to align text right, left, centered, and centered across columns. Excel has some additional alignment options that come in handy from time to time.

Open the Miles workbook from your Project Disk. Increase the width of column A all the way to the right edge of column C (about 3 inches). The publication data for the studies in column A is still too wide to fit in the allocated width, so you need the text to wrap to the next line.

To keep the same width, but wrap the text to the next line:

1: Highlight cells A3 through A12.

2: Click **Format** on the menu bar, and then click **Cells**.

3: Click the **Alignment** tab.

4: Click the **Wrap Text** check box so it contains a check mark.

5: Click the **OK** button. As a result, the publication data for the studies wraps to the next line within the cell.

The headings for columns D, E, G, H, and I are much longer than the data in the cells. You can rotate this text 90 degrees.

To rotate the text orientation:

1: Click cell **D2**.

2: Click **Format**, and then click **Cells**.

3: Enter **90** in the *Degrees* box.

4: Click the **OK** button.

5: Decrease the width of column D.

Now that you know how to align text so it stretches vertically, do so for the column headings in E2, G2, H2, and I2. Don't forget to decrease the column width after you format these cells.

The title of the worksheet needs to stand out more. Increase the row height to about 1" and change the background color for cells A1 through I1 to light blue. Bold the title and increase the font size to 12. Now, suppose you'd like the title centered vertically in the row.

To center the title vertically:

1: Click cell **A1**.

2: Click **Format**, and then click **Cells**.

3: Click ▼ on the *Vertical* box, and then click **Center**.

4: Click the **OK** button.

Complete the format by right-aligning cells B2 and C2. Bold all of the column headings.

Rename and save the workbook as "Study Results". Put your name in the header and print the worksheet.

12 More Number Formats   Numbers.xls

Excel has a huge variety of number formats. To explore some of them, open the Numbers workbook from your Project Disk. Column A contains a description of an Excel number format. Column B contains a number so you can apply that format.

projects

To format a number in the General format:

1: Click cell **B3**.

2: Click **Format** on the menu bar, and then click **Cells**. If necessary, move the Format Cells dialog box to the right so you can see column A of the worksheet.

3: Click the **Number** tab.

4: Column A says to use the General format, so click **General**, and then click the **OK** button. The number changes to 56.3.

Now, follow a similar process to apply the format described in cell A4 to the number in cell B4, and so on through cell B18.

Next, compare the results of using the Currency format and the Accounting format.

To compare the Currency format with the Accounting format:

1: Highlight cells D7 through D10.

2: Click **Format**, click **Cells**, and then click **Accounting**.

3: Make sure to specify two decimal places.

4: Click the **OK** button and look at the results of the formatting.

5: Highlight cells E7 through E10.

6: Click **Format**, click **Cells**, and then click **Currency**.

7: Make sure to specify two decimal places.

8: Click the **OK** button and compare the two formats.

Now that your formatting is complete, rename and save the workbook as "Number Formats". Put your name in the header and print the worksheet. On your printout, describe the difference between the Accounting and Currency formats.

13 Fill and Font Shortcuts   File: Electric.xls

In the online Steps, you learned how to use the Font and Patterns tabs on the Format Cells dialog box. Excel provides shortcut buttons on the toolbar to change font and background colors. You'll find it quicker to use these shortcuts than the Font and Patterns tab.

projects

Open the Electric workbook from your Project Disk. Your task is to change the background color of the title and column headings to red. To do this, you'll use the Fill Color button.

To use the Color button to change the background color(s) in a workbook:

1: Highlight cells A1 through C2.

2: Click ▼ on the 🪣 ▼ **Fill Color** button. Excel displays a color palette.

3: Click the red color box on the color palette.

Next you'll use the Font Color button to change the color of the font to white.

To use the Font Color button to change the color of the title font to white:

1: Highlight cells A1 through C2.

2: Click ▼ on the A ▼ **Font Color** button. Excel displays a color palette.

3: Select the white color box on the color palette.

Row 13 has a dark blue background that obscures the data, so use the Font Color box to change the text color to white.

Spell check the worksheet before you rename it, and save the workbook as "Revised Electric". Put your name in the header, and print the worksheet. Check the colors to make sure that you can still read all the data.

14 Fonts on Your Computer   Winners.xls

Fonts vary from computer to computer, depending on the software that's installed. The standard Windows fonts include Arial and Times New Roman; other fonts can provide additional visual interest and convey a certain "attitude."

Open the Winners workbook from your Project Disk. Modify the format for the Feb 1 worksheet so it is more friendly and less formal. Here are some hints for achieving this effect, but use your own artistic judgment.

- Use more casual fonts—those that look like handwriting or block letters.
- Add additional white space by increasing some row heights or column widths.
- Move the graphic and enlarge it.
- Use the currency format, instead of the accounting format.

- Change the color of the fonts or backgrounds.

- Add borders.

When you've completed the formatting, rename and save your workbook as Winners with an Attitude. Put your name and date in the header, and then print the worksheet. Annotate your worksheet by indicating the names of the fonts you used in each cell.

15 Hide and Protect Cells   Ernie2.xls

In the online Steps you learned how to format cells to change the appearance of the information they contain. You can also format cells to hide them from view or prevent people from changing the contents.

Open the Ernie2 workbook from your Project Disk. Ernie doesn't want to show this sheet to his customers because it contains the amount that he pays for the cars. But if he hides column B, he can print the worksheet and use the sheet with customers in his sales presentations and price negotiations. All the calculations in the sheet will still work because the data is not deleted, only hidden.

To hide the cells in column B:

1: Highlight cells B4 through B12.

2: Click **Format** on the menu bar, click **Cells**, and then click the **Number** tab.

3: Click **Custom**, then delete whatever is in the *Type* box.

4: Type ;;; (three semicolons) in the *Type* box.

5: Click the **OK** button. Excel hides the data in the cells. (Hint: To see the data once again, you'd need to format the cells as currency.)

Now the cost data is hidden, but what if Ernie wants to protect the data and formulas on the worksheet so the only data that can be changed is the discount? First, he needs to format the discount cells as unlocked.

To unlock cells:

1: Highlight cells D4 through D12.

2: Click **Format**, click **Cells**, and then click the **Protection** tab.

3: Click the **Locked** check box to remove the check mark.

4: Click the **OK** button.

Now that the discount cells are formatted as unlocked, Ernie can protect the rest of the sheet to prevent changes from being made.

To protect the worksheet:

1: Click **Tools** on the menu bar, click **Protection**, then click **Protect Sheet**. Excel displays a dialog box that requests an optional password.

2: Do not enter a password, but click the **OK** button. Now the sheet is protected.

3: Try to enter some data in cell C6. Excel displays the message "Locked cells cannot be changed."

4: Click the **OK** button when you see this message. (Hint: To remove protection from the sheet, click Tools, click Protection, and then click Unprotect Sheet.)

5: Close the worksheet without saving your changes.

Now that you know how to hide cells, protect a sheet, and unprotect a sheet, use your own words to write a short description of the process that would allow you to change only cells B5 through B20 on a worksheet.

EXPLORE

16 Add Notes to Cells   File: Union.xls

Sometimes you might want to annotate the contents of cells. For example, you might create a form, but you can't be sure if the people who fill out the form will understand each of the items on the form. Open the Union workbook from your Project Disk. Notice the small red mark in cell B6. If you point to this mark, a comment appears in a beige box. Suppose you want to create a similar note or comment for cell C6.

To create a note or comment:

1: Click cell **C6**.

2: Click **Insert** on the menu bar.

3: Click **Comment**.

4: In the box provided, type **Amount billed for the services.**

5: Click any blank cell.

6: Point to the note to make sure it works.

projects

Add the following notes:

- Cell D6: Part of "Total Charges" not covered under the benefit plan.

- Cell E6: Part of "Total Charges" eligible for coverage.

- Cell F6: Portion of the "Covered Amount" that is not payable because it is being applied to a deductible.

- Cell H6: The percentage of the "Balance" which will be paid according to the benefit plan.

Put your name in the Patient Name blank. Rename and save the workbook as "Union Health Care".

To print the notes on your worksheet:

1: Click **File** on the menu bar, and then click **Page Setup**.

2: Click the **Sheet** tab.

3: Click ▼ on the *Comments* box, and then click **At end of sheet**.

4: Click the **OK** button.

5: Print your worksheet as usual. The notes should appear on page 2 .

17 Freeze Titles   File: Gargoyle.xls

When you're working with long worksheets, it's sometimes handy to prevent a section (called a "pane") of a worksheet from scrolling off the screen. For example, you might want to prevent the column headings from scrolling off the screen so you can see what belongs in each column.

Open the Gargoyle workbook from the Project Disk. Scroll down to the bottom of the worksheet, and note that the column headings scroll off the screen. This is a good example of when you would want to use the freeze pane command to keep column headings in view while you are scrolling through a worksheet.

To use the freeze pane command:

1: Scroll back to the top of the worksheet, and click any cell in row 3, the row just below the row you want to "freeze" on the screen.

2: Click **Window** on the menu bar, then click **Freeze Panes**.

3: Now you can scroll down to the bottom of the worksheet and the column headings will remain on the screen. (Hint: To unfreeze the panes, click Window, then click Unfreeze Panes.)

Now that the column labels are frozen, make the following changes:

- In cell G3, enter 3.00. Scroll down the worksheet, and enter 3.00 in the Shipping column for any products that have a price of less than 12.00.

- In row 9, change the price for the Le Petite Florentine Gargoyle to $18.95.

- In row 18, change the material for the Ancient Burden Gargoyle to Resin.

- In row 23, change the weight for the Chained Gargoyle of Turin to 17.

- In row 6, change the price for the Dwarf Corner Stone Gargoyle to $17.95.

Rename and save your workbook as "Gothic Reproductions". Put your name in the header and print the entire worksheet.

18 Explore AutoComplete   File: Convert.xls

Open the Convert workbook from your Project Disk. This partially-completed worksheet is designed to convert measurements from one scale to another.

Excel sometimes seems to fill in or complete cells on its own. This feature, called AutoComplete, works only if the AutoComplete setting is activated on your computer.

To activate AutoComplete:

1: Click **Tools** on the Excel menu bar, then click **Options**.

2: Click the **Edit** tab.

3: Make sure the check box for Enable AutoComplete for Cell Values contains a check mark.

4: Click the **OK** button.

Now that AutoComplete is activated, you can enter some text. As you enter text, you'll see that Excel tries to guess what you'd like entered in a cell, based on your previous entries. If Excel provides the text you want, you can accept it by pressing the Enter key. If the text is not want you want, just continue typing the correct text. Try it.

projects

To practice using AutoComplete:

1: Click cell **A4**.

2: Type the letter **a**

3: Notice that Excel completes the entry by putting "acres" in the cell. This is the text you want, so press the **Enter** key.

4: Click cell **B4**, type **miles, square**, then press the **Enter** key.

5: Click cell **A5**, and let Excel's AutoComplete feature help you enter "acres" again.

6: Click cell **B5**, then type the letter **m**. Excel guesses that you want the cell to contain "miles, square." However, we really want this cell to contain "meters, square."

7: Complete the entry by typing in the rest of the text you want in the cell, **eters, square**

8: Press the **Enter** key.

Now that you know how Excel's AutoComplete feature works, you can use it to complete the following table:

To convert from:	To:	Multiply by:	Number:
Acres	feet, square	43560.00	5
Acres	miles, square	.001562	8
Acres	meters, square	4046.856	3
Centimeters	inches	.3937	36
Centimeters	feet	.03281	80
Miles, square	kilometers, square	2.589998	12
Miles, statute	feet	5280	6
Miles, statute	miles, nautical	.8684	11
Miles, statute	meters	1609.334	3

After you enter the data for the table, create a formula in cell E3 to perform the conversion from acres to square feet. Create the formulas for the other conversions. Rename and save your workbook as "Convert Measurements". Put your name in the header and print the worksheet.

19 Explore Styles   File: Stocks2.xls

Excel borrows a feature from desktop publishing called **styles** that helps you to quickly define and apply formats to worksheet cells. Open the Stocks2 workbook from the Project Disk. Scroll down the worksheet and take a quick look at the data it contains.

Suppose you want to change the format of the category headings, "Autos," "Furnishings/Appliances," and so on. You'd like them to be in Times New Roman font, dark gray, and size 14. It would take a lot of time to change these three formats for each of the 11 categories. Excel offers you a shortcut using styles. You can define the attributes for a style such as the font style, font type, font color, and background. Once you have defined a style, you can apply all the format attributes in one operation.

To define a style for the category headings:

1: Click cell A1, click **Format** on the menu bar, then click **Style**.

2: In the box that contains "Normal," type **Heading**

3: Click the **Modify** button on the Style dialog box.

4: Click the **Font** tab.

5: Change the font to **Times New Roman**.

6: Change the font size to **14**.

7: Change the color to dark gray.

8: Click the **OK** button to return to the Style dialog box.

9: Click the **Add** button to add the style to the list, then click the **Close** button.

Now that you've created a style, you can apply it.

To apply the Heading style to cell A7:

1: Click cell **A7**.

2: Click **Format**, then click **Style**.

3: Change the contents of the *Style Name* box to **Heading**.

4: Click the **OK** button.

Now that you've applied the heading style to cell A7, you can do the same for the rest of the category headings.

projects

To apply the Heading style to the rest of the category headings:

1: Hold down the **Ctrl** (or Control) key while you click each of the cells in column A that contain a category heading.

2: Click **Format**, then click **Style**.

3: Change the contents of the *Style Name* box to **Heading**.

4: Click the **OK** button.

Now create a style called "Totals" that's size 12 Times New Roman, italics, and dark green. Apply this style to the cells in column A that contain "Total" labels.

Rename and save the workbook as "Second-Quarter Profits". Put your name in the header and print the worksheet.

20 Creating a Template

A **template** is worksheet "form" that contains labels and formulas, but no data. You'd create a template for spreadsheet tasks that you have to do repeatedly or periodically. An invoice, a tax form, or a time sheet would all be useful applications for templates.

Suppose you're a botanist who travels to several scientific conferences each year. Each time you travel, you're required to account for your expenses so you can be reimbursed. You have been writing the expense report by hand, but it involves some calculations, so you decide to create an Excel template to handle the task. You create a hand-written design for the template that looks like this:

Expense Report for (Your Name)
Date of departure
Return date
Total days traveled

	Per day	Total for the trip
Lodging		
Meals	$40	
Rental car		
Parking		
Conference fee		
Air fare		
Miscellaneous		

Total
Travel Advance
Total Due

To complete this Project, create a travel template that contains the information on your hand-written design and contains the formulas necessary to complete the calculations. (Hint: Get help on Excel's Date functions to find a formula or to calculate the number of days in a trip given the start and end dates.)

Test the template by entering the data for a trip. The total due is the Total minus the Travel Advance. Make sure you're satisfied with the way the numbers are formatted. Check carefully that the calculations are producing the correct results. When everything looks good, use the Edit, Clear Contents command to blank out the trip data, but keep the formulas.

Unlock only the cells on the template in which you'll enter data, and then protect the entire worksheet. (Hint: Refer to Project 15 or Help to find out how to unlock cells and protect a worksheet.)

Delete all headers and footers on the worksheet, and then save the workbook as Travel Template on your Project Disk. If you are using your own computer, you might want to look in Help to find out how to save a template in the Template folder on your hard disk.

Print the worksheet as a blank template with formulas displayed. Then fill in the template and print it showing some realistic trip data (without showing formulas). Your instructor might also collect your disk to check the cell locking.

21 Creating 3-D Objects

To enhance your worksheet presentation you can easily add three-dimensional objects. In this Project you'll practice creating a 3-D object.

To create a 3-D object:

1: Click the **New** button on the toolbar to create a new worksheet. Then click the **Drawing** button to display the drawing toolbar at the bottom of the screen.

2: To add three-dimensional effects to an object, you must first have an object, so create one by clicking the **AutoShapes** button. Choose **Stars and Banners**, then click the **Star** shape in the upper-right corner. The cursor changes to a crosshair.

3: Move the crosshair into the upper-left area of the worksheet. Drag down and to the right. Notice that a star forms. To keep the height to width ratio the same, press the **Shift** key.

4: Once you have drawn the star, release the mouse button. The star has sizing handles around it, which mean that it is selected. Click the **3-D** button on the Drawing toolbar. Experiment by applying different shapes to the star. You can also click the 3-D button and choose 3-D settings to display a toolbar with 3-D related options, including light, color, and depth.

projects

When you are finished experimenting, print a version of the worksheet that contains the 3-D star you like the best, and then close it.

INVESTIGATE

22 Design Principles

In Tutorial 3 you worked with many different worksheets. You've had a chance to improve their appearance by changing fonts, font size, font style, and font color. You've experimented with background colors and borders. You've looked at worksheets on the screen and as printouts. You might not be an expert yet, but you've certainly gained experience in what looks good, what works, and what doesn't work. Now its time to summarize your expertise.

For this Project, consider what you've learned about formatting worksheets and try to distill it into a brochure or poster called "Spreadsheet Design Guide." You'll probably want to focus on one type of output—for a presentation or for a printout. You might also want to consider creating some examples of good and bad designs to illustrate your points.

As a guideline, you should spend about 30 minutes outlining the points you want to make about good and bad formats. Spend another one or two hours creating some examples, then spend a final couple of hours putting your work into final format. Your instructor will give you other specific requirements for length and format.

23 Under the Hood

Now that you've worked with spreadsheets, you might wonder what goes on "under the hood"—what happens in the computer when it stores worksheet data and performs worksheet calculations. Does the computer store your data in some sort of matrix similar to what you see on the screen? If it doesn't do this, how would the computer locate the cells referenced in worksheet formulas?

For this Project, use your library and/or Internet resources to find out how spreadsheet software keeps track of all the data in a worksheet and performs calculations "under the hood." When you've completed your research, use your own words to report your findings. Your instructor will give you guidelines about length and format.

24 Spreadsheet Skills and Employment

Spreadsheet software is used almost everywhere in the business world and has found its way into the toolbox of many disciplines. Would spreadsheet expertise help you get a job?

For this Project, begin by studying position announcements in your career field. You might find these in newspapers, in professional journals, or on the Internet. Look carefully at the qualifications for positions in your field. How often is spreadsheet "know-how" mentioned? Are particular spreadsheets, such as Excel, Lotus 1-2-3, or Quattro Pro, specified? If spreadsheet expertise doesn't seem to figure into the qualifications for employment, can you make a hypothesis why this is so? Would you expect spreadsheet expertise to become more or less important in your career field?

Summarize your research findings in a one-page paper. Include some position announcements that support your findings, and don't forget to document your sources of information.

25 Find and Design Templates

In several of the Projects for Tutorial 3, you've had an opportunity to work with templates, those worksheet forms designed to be used and reused by filling in blanks. An invoice, travel report, and time sheet are some examples that might work well as Excel templates.

For this Project, collect five forms that you use at home, at work, at school, or as a consumer. Write a description of each form that evaluates its suitability for a spreadsheet template. Remember that templates should be used over and over again, and they should involve calculations. Also, be sure to consider how practical it would be to actually use the form as a template—who would fill it out, where would the data be stored, and would the data from a number of forms need to be somehow summarized.

When you have completed this Project, turn in your evaluations and the original forms that you evaluated.

projects

26 The Scoop on Lotteries

The popularity of modern lotteries in the U.S. and Canada raises some interesting questions. Who is the typical lottery player? What motivates a person to play the lottery? How much does an average player spend on the lottery per year? What are your chances of winning? Are certain numbers more likely to be winners? Is lottery software useful? Do you pay taxes on your winnings? What does the government do with lottery revenues? Is the government encouraging gambling by holding lotteries? Is that a good or bad thing to do?

For this Project, focus on two or three questions about lotteries that interest you. Use your library and/or Internet resources to find information related to your questions. Write a paper discussing your findings. Your instructor will provide additional guidelines about length and format. Don't forget to record and report your sources of information.

Microsoft Excel

Tutorial 4: Create Charts

Tutorial 4

Create Charts

Generation X

An Internet site describes Generation X as "grunge, gangsta, indie rock and film, cyberpunk, street fashion, extreme sports, political correctness and zines." Sometimes called "latchkey kids" or the "MTV generation," the 18 to 29-year olds of Generation X are finally emerging from the shadow of their Baby Boomer parents. What's the story about GenX? Find out inside.

Doing the e-Thing

It seems like you've got to use technology to get a McJob. In Tutorial 4 you'll learn how to make charts and graphs—that's a technology you can apply to reports, papers, and presentations.

Projects

Tutorial 4 Projects include creating picture charts, using charts to analyze what-if scenarios, creating test score histograms, and illustrating your data with maps.

Generation X

A Canadian author, Doug Coupland, coined the term "Generation X" in a book of the same name published in 1991. The book introduced X-isms such as "dumpster clocking" (the tendency to think of objects only in terms of the amount of time they'll take to decompose), "paper rabies" (hypersensitivity to littering), and "recurving" (taking a job that pays less, but puts you back on the learning curve).

Generation X follows the huge Baby Boomer blip on the population charts. Born between 1965 and 1981, GenXers grew up in households where both parents typically worked. TV was an inexpensive baby-sitter and so a GenXer typically logged close to 22,000 hours watching TV by age 18—twice the amount of time spent in school!

GenXers are finding a job market offering many low-paying service "McJobs." But a technological society also requires some employees with high-level skills to decipher instruction manuals, solve problems, and operate computers and complex machinery. These are the high-paying jobs, and to get them many turned to higher education. In 1992, for example, 54% of GenXers were enrolled in college, compared to 43% of the previous generation as shown in Figure 1.

Figure 1 *GenX flocks to college.*

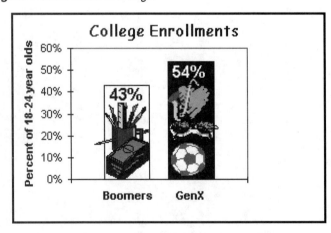

But there's trouble ahead. U.S. GenXers have discovered the unhappy fact that they'll pay about $550,000 into the social security fund over the course of their lifetime, but only get about $300,000 back in benefits when they retire. This is in contrast to Boomers who will contribute about $250,000, and can expect to receive about $290,000 in benefits. The chart in Figure 2 shows that only those people who are currently over 45 years old will receive more in social security benefits than they contributed.

Figure 2 *Social Security: Do you get what you pay for?*

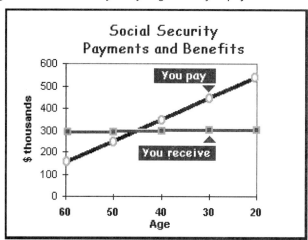

It's handy to have data on issues such as college enrollments and social security, but numbers are often easier to understand in graphical format. Spreadsheet software makes it easy to create graphs—called "charts" in Excel terminology.

To create a chart using Excel, you first begin with the data in the cells of a worksheet. You highlight the cells that you want to chart, and then you specify which cells contain information for labels and which cells contain the data that you want Excel to turn into the lines, bars, or pie slices on the chart. Excel's ChartWizard walks you through the steps for creating a chart—and that's the first thing you'll learn when you go online with Tutorial 4.

GET STARTED ONLINE WITH e-COURSE

If you're using a Tracking Disk, make sure you put it in the disk drive before you log into e-Course. After you've logged in, select Tutorial 4. Happy charting!

Review Questions

Fill in the blank with the correct word or phrase.

1   In Excel terminology, a graph is called a(n) _____.

2   Excel's _____ is a series of dialog boxes that takes you step by step through the process of creating a chart.

3   The cells in the worksheet that contain the data you want to chart is referred to as the _____.

4   A chart that represents data using vertical bars is called a(n) _____ chart.

5   A chart that represents data as wedges in a circle is referred to as a(n) _____ chart.

6   The _____ axis runs horizontally along the bottom of the chart.

7   Before you can move or change the size of a chart, you must click it to display the small squares called _____.

8   _____ are horizontal or vertical lines that extend from the tick marks on a chart to make it easier to estimate the numbers that correspond to the data points.

9   A chart _____ contains a key to the data that the chart displays.

10 The numbers such as 0, 10, 20, 30, 40 that identify the scale of the vertical axis are called _____.

11 Suppose you've created a pie chart and you want to display the percent for each slice. In Excel terminology, the percent is called a(n) _____.

12 If you would like to print a chart that is wider than it is tall, it would be best to select _____ orientation to tell Excel to print the chart sideways on the paper.

13 True or False? You can create charts on the same worksheet that contains the data you're charting, or on a different tab in the same workbook. _____.

review questions

MULTIPLE CHOICE

*Select the letter of the **one** best answer.*

---

14 **Suppose you're creating a chart using the ChartWizard. You see a dialog box containing =$A$3:$B$6. This is probably:**

   a the formula Excel uses to create percentages for the chart.

   b the data range for the chart.

   c the CHART function.

   d the location telling Excel where to put the new chart.

---

15 **Suppose you create a chart, but the labels for the x-axis seem to break onto two lines. Which one of the following is your best strategy to improve the appearance of these labels?**

   a Format the font for a smaller size.

   b Put a hyphen in the labels.

   c Increase the width of the cells that hold the label text.

   d Decrease the size of the chart.

---

16 **How do you highlight nonadjacent ranges for Excel to chart?**

   a Click the View on the menu bar, and then click Range.

   b Clear the contents of any cells in between the ranges.

   c Hold down the Ctrl (or Control) key while you highlight both ranges.

   d Type an & symbol in front of the row number and column letter.

---

17 **Once you've created a chart, is it possible to add additional data to the chart, such as an additional year's worth of data?**

   a Yes, you can modify the data range that Excel uses for the chart.

   b Yes, but you can, however, only modify the chart once.

   c No, but Excel will allow you to delete the current chart, but you must save the chart settings in a different workbook.

   d No, you would need to delete the current chart and recreate it from scratch.

18 **How does Excel know what to use as the title of a chart?**

   a Excel uses the contents of the first cell in the chart data range.

   b Excel uses the contents of the last cell in the chart data range.

   c Excel uses the contents of cell A1 as the chart title.

   d Excel requires you to type the text for the chart title.

19 **Which of the following chart types has a 3-D version?**

   a Bar

   b Column

   c Pie

   d All of the above

20 **Suppose the y-axis labels on your chart are in units of ten: 10, 20 , 30, 40 and so on. How would you change to units of 20?**

   a Highlight each of the numbers and type in the new value.

   b Format the axis to change the scale.

   c Increase the size of the font.

   d Change the numbers in the cells that were used for the y-axis labels.

21 **Suppose you've created a column chart, but you decide that a line would be better. What is your best course of action?**

   a Delete the chart and recreate the line chart from scratch.

   b Close the workbook without saving your changes and start the chart again.

   c Drag the bars of the chart to the right until they become lines.

   d Use the Chart Type button to convert the column chart to a line chart.

22 **How does Excel know what to put in the chart legend?**

   a Excel uses the labels from the first row or column for the chart legend.

   b Excel requires you to type in the text you want to use as the chart legend.

   c Excel generates the chart legend by computing averages of the data.

   d Excel uses any cells that contain text as the chart legend.

review questions

23 How does Excel decide what to use as the colors for chart objects?

   a Excel requires you to type in the color for each chart object when you start the ChartWizard.

   b Excel uses the color scheme you've used in the background of the cells in the worksheet.

   c Excel uses a standard color scheme for all charts, but you can change the colors by formatting the chart objects.

   d Excel uses whatever colors will look best on your printer.

24 If you don't have a color printer, how can you create the best visual differentiation between the chart bars that represent different data sets?

   a Use pastel colors.

   b Use patterns.

   c Use a dark border around each bar.

   d Use 3-D charts.

25 Excel provides you with all of the following options for printing charts, except:

   a Full page

   b Scale to fit page

   c Custom

   d Thumbnail

MATCHING

Select the letter from the right hand column that correctly matches each item in the left column.

26

   a specifies the chart range

27 =Trends!$A$3:$B$6

   b default chart type

28 Legend

   c helps select nonadjacent cells

29 Ctrl (or Control) key

   d starts the ChartWizard

30 Column

   e a box that identifies the patterns or colors assigned to the data series or categories in a chart

Create Charts EX 99

review questions

Use a separate sheet of paper to write out your answers to the following questions.

31 List five chart types from which you can select when you create Excel charts.

32 Describe how you enter and exit chart mode.

33 Explain why you might want to place a chart on a separate tab, instead of on the same tab that holds the data you're charting.

34 Explain the difference between data labels and data series.

35 Several of the worksheets you used in the Tutorial contained totals, but you did not chart the totals. Explain why.

Projects

These Projects are designed to help you review and develop the skills you learned in Tutorial 4. Complete each Project using Microsoft Excel. *If you have not yet made the Project Disk for Tutorial 4, start the e-Course software, click the Project Disk menu, and follow the instructions on the screen.*

If you've forgotten some of the skills you need to complete the Projects, refer to the Task Reference in the back of your WorkText.

REVIEW SKILLS

1   Chop Shop Stop   File: Alarm.xls

Some stolen cars are never seen again. They end up in a "chop shop" where they're disassembled and sold for parts. To stop car thieves, record numbers of auto owners are installing car alarms and other anti-theft devices.

Open the Alarm workbook from your Project Disk. The graph shows the increasing number of car thefts in one city. Make the following changes to the chart:

- Change the chart title to "Car Thefts Increase."

- Add data labels for the chart to show values.

- Change the chart type from a column chart to a line chart.

- Remove the legend.

- Bold the x-axis labels.

Rename and save the workbook as "Chop Shop Stop". Put your name in the header and print only the chart in portrait orientation, custom size, and centered horizontally.

2   Potato Chips vs. Peanut Brittle   File: Cheese.xls

The preferred snack of the kids, teens, and adults who participated in the Potato Chips vs. Peanut Brittle taste test was no surprise, but the chart summarizing the survey data needs a little work. Open the Cheese worksheet from your Project Disk, and take a quick look at the survey results. Click the Chart tab and make the following changes to the chart:

- Move the chart to the upper-left corner of the worksheet.
- Enlarge the chart so you can see all the data labels, including "kids," "teens," and "adults."
- Change the title from "Chez Cheese Products" to "Potato Chips vs. Peanut Brittle".
- Add gridlines to the chart.
- Remove the legend from the chart
- Change the color of the Potato Chips bars to light yellow.

Rename and save your workbook as "Taste Test". Put your name in the header, and then print the worksheet containing the chart in portrait orientation, centered horizontally on the page.

3   WigZine   File: Wig.xls

A "zine" is a magazine that is published and sold over the Internet. Open the Wig workbook from your Project Disk. The WigZine tab contains information about annual subscription sales from 1992 through 1996. Change the name of the Sheet2 tab to "Chart". Use the data from cells A3 through F4 of the WigZine tab to create the following chart:

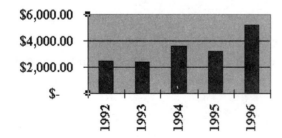

Make sure that on your chart:

- the major unit scale for the y-axis is 2000.
- the x-axis and y-axis labels use Times New Roman bold, font size 12.
- the chart title is "WigZine Sales."
- the legend has been removed.
- the bars are yellow.
- the title is Arial bold, font size 12.
- don't worry if the dates are not rotated 90 degrees.

Rename and save your workbook "WigZine Sales". Put your name in the header, and then print only the chart in portrait orientation, custom size and centered horizontally.

4   The Java Jolt   File: Caffeine.xls

In the online Steps, you learned how to select nonadjacent cells for the chart data range. This is a very handy skill, as you'll see in this Project. Open the Caffeine workbook from your Project Disk. Change the name of Sheet3 to "Chart" so you'll have a place to create a new chart. Use the data on the Caffeine Stats sheet to create the chart shown below. Add your name to the header then print only the chart in portrait orientation, sized to use the full page. Save the workbook as "Revised Caffeine".

Make sure that on your chart:

- all the x-axis labels are displayed.
- the data labels have been moved onto the bars.
- horizontal gridlines are displayed.
- the chart title "That Java Jolt" is positioned between gridlines 30 and 40.

- the chart title is Arial bold, font size 14.

- the chart bars are colored light yellow.

- the major unit on the z-axis (vertical axis) scale is 10.

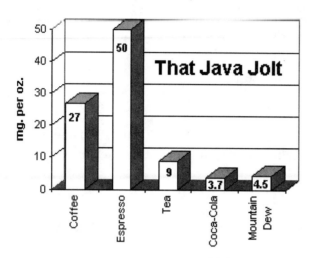

5   Why Not Spend It?   File: Survey.xls

Would you spend $60,000 for a car? Suppose you conducted a survey and asked people "If you had $60,000, would you buy a car, make a down payment on a house, or invest it?" You tabulate the data for men and women separately in a workbook called Survey.

Open the Survey workbook from your Project Disk, and take a look at the survey results. Create two 3-D pie charts on the same tab as the survey data. One pie chart should show the men's responses. The other pie chart should show the women's. Hint: You'll need to select nonadjacent ranges to construct the women's pie chart.

Make sure that:

- each chart has only three (not four) slices.

- the chart titles are "Men's Responses" and "Women's Responses."

- Excel displays the labels and percentages for each pie slice.

- use patterns to differentiate between the car, invest, and house slices.

- the slice that contains the highest percentage is pulled out from the pie.

Rename and save your workbook as "Survey Pie Charts". Put your name in the header, and then print the data table and chart on the same page in portrait orientation centered horizontally.

projects

APPLY SKILLS

6 Is It Hot in Balochistan?   File: Weather.xls

Open the Weather workbook from your Project Disk. The data in the Temperatures worksheet represents average high and low temperatures for each month in Balochistan province.

Look in Excel's online Help to get some pointers on selecting chart types. Be sure to check out the topic "Examples of chart types." As you're reading this information, think about the best chart type for the weather data.

On the Temperatures tab, create a chart that shows the average high temperatures for January through December, as well as the average low temperatures. Use your own judgment for font styles, font sizes, and chart colors. When the chart is complete, rename and save your workbook as Balochistan Weather. Put your name in the header and print the temperature data and chart on the same page. Use pen or pencil to annotate the printout to explain the design decisions you made about fonts, colors, and patterns.

7 Pink Floyd Fans   File: Pink.xls

The band Pink Floyd was popular in 1968, and its fans are still around in 1998. Suppose you collect some data on Pink Floyd Fan club members in the Midwest. Open the Pink workbook from your Project Disk. Suppose you would like to create a chart showing the trends in each state over the 30-year period, and on the same chart you'd like to show the trends in overall membership.

If you have not yet done so, use Excel's online Help to find information about selecting the best type of chart for your data. Look for the topic "Examples of chart types."

Select a chart type for the Pink Floyd data, and create a chart called "Pink Floyd Fans in the Midwest". You can create the chart on Sheet1 or Sheet2. Use your own judgment about fonts, font size, and chart colors.

When the chart is complete, rename and save your workbook as "Pink Floyd Midwest Fans". Put your name in the header, and print only the chart. Use pen or pencil to annotate the printout, explaining your design and print decisions.

projects

8   Chart Pro

Look for an example of an interesting chart in a magazine or newspaper. Photocopy the chart (or if it is your own publication, tear it out). Try to duplicate the chart using Excel. You'll need to first enter the data for the chart, and you might need to approximate the numbers by looking carefully at the chart.

As you try to duplicate the chart, consider the chart colors, font types and font sizes. Also be aware of titles, gridlines, x-axis labels, y-axis scale, and data labels. When your chart is complete, create a documentation tab to credit the source of the chart, and then save the workbook as "Chart Pro" on your Project Disk. Put your name in the header, and print the chart. Turn in your printout and the original chart from which it was derived.

9   Your Own Line Chart

Look in magazines, newspapers, or the Web for raw data that would be suitable for a line chart containing more than one line. Enter the data into an Excel workbook, and then create the chart on a separate tab. Use your own judgment about chart type, title, fonts, colors, and data labels. When the chart is complete, create a documentation tab to credit the source of the data, then save the workbook as "My Line Chart". Print the entire workbook. Annotate the chart page to explain your design decisions.

10 Your Own Pie Chart

Look in magazines, newspapers, or the Web for raw data that would be suitable for a pie chart. Enter the data into an Excel workbook, and then create the chart on a separate tab. Use your own judgment about chart type, title, fonts, colors, and data labels. When the chart is complete, create a documentation tab to credit the source of the data, and then save the workbook as "My Pie Chart" on your Project Disk. Print the entire workbook. Annotate the chart page to explain your design decisions.

BUILD SKILLS

11 Charts Convey Different Messages   File: Rap2.xls

In previous Tutorials, you might have looked at the data from a survey on rap music censorship. Over 1,000 people were surveyed, and their responses were categorized by age and sex.

Suppose you're particularly interested in the responses of males and females in the under 20-year old age group. Open the Rap2 workbook from your Project Disk, and make sure you're looking at the Column Chart tab. For this Project, you'll work with different column chart formats and pick the one most suited to the message you want to convey. The three messages are:

1. The percentage of males and females who believe that rap should be censored by the musicians or not at all is about equal. However, males and females hold different viewpoints about whether rap should be censored by the record companies or the government.

2. Females, as you might expect, don't always agree with males about rap censorship.

3. When the opinions of males and females are combined, it becomes clear that there is strong support for no censorship at all.

Right-click the chart and use the Chart Type dialog box to apply different column chart formats to the chart. Print out the chart that best conveys message 1. Then print out the chart that best conveys message 2. Finally, print the chart that best conveys message 3.

12 What Does This Chart Mean?   File: Mango2.xls

Charts are easy to make—so easy, in fact, that you can churn out a lot of meaningless charts, if you're not careful. In this Project, you'll try to interpret several charts and evaluate their usefulness. Open the Mango2 workbook from your Project Disk, and take a minute or two to study the data.

a Click the Chart A tab. Print the chart. On your printout, write a short description of what this chart shows and the message it conveys.

b Click the Chart B tab. This chart is the same as Chart A, except that Excel is charting the data as columns, instead of rows. Print the chart. On your printout, write a short description of what this chart shows.

projects

c Click the Chart C tab. Print this chart. The person who created this chart made a mistake. There are two symptoms of this mistake. Circle these symptoms on your printout, and explain the mistake made by the person who created the chart.

d After you have printed all three charts, put a star on the chart that you think is the most useful of the three. Next to the star, write a brief explanation of why you chose this chart.

13 Enhance a Line Chart   Chips.xls

In the online Steps, you worked briefly with line charts. In this Project, you'll learn how to enhance the appearance of a line chart by changing line color, line thickness, and data markers.

Open the Chips workbook from your Project Disk, and take a minute or two to study the data on the U.S. & CA tab. Click the Chart tab. The line chart contains one line representing U.S. highway violence and another line representing highway violence in Canada. The lines are not very distinctive, partly because they are too thin. You can change the thickness, color, and shape of the data markers on the line using the Format Data Series dialog box.

To format the U.S. line:

1: Click the chart so you can edit it.

2: Right-click the dark blue line representing U.S. incidents.

3: Click **Format Data Series**.

4: Click ▾ on the *Weight* box, then click the thickest line.

5: Click ▾ on the *Color* box, and then click the red color box.

6: Click ▾ on the *Style* box, and then click the circle.

7: Click the **OK** button. The revised chart line is thick, red, and has dark blue round data markers.

Now, use the technique you just learned to format the line for Canada as thick, black, and with pink triangular data markers.

Rename and save the workbook as "Chips Line Chart". Put your name in the header and print only the line chart in custom size, portrait orientation, and centered horizontally.

projects

14 Create A Chart Sheet   Act.xls

In the online Steps, you worked with charts that were embedded in a worksheet—that is, the charts were positioned in a regular worksheet containing rows and columns. Excel provides another way to deal with charts—they can have their own chart sheets on which no other data can appear. The advantage of a chart sheet is that the chart objects, such as fonts and bars, are proportioned more like the full-page printout of a chart. Another advantage is that the chart on the sheet is automatically selected when you select the chart sheet tab—you don't have to worry about selecting the chart or entering chart mode.

To create a chart tab:

1: Open the **ACT** workbook and highlight cells A2 through C9.

2: Click **Insert** on the Excel menu bar, then select **Chart**.

3: Use the ChartWizard to specify a line chart (format type 4) with the title "ACT Trends."

4: On the ChartWizard - Step 4 of 4 dialog box, click the **As New Sheet** option button.

5: Click the **Finish** button to display the completed chart sheet.

Now that you've created a chart sheet, answer questions a through g. When you've completed the questions, close the workbook without saving your changes.

   a What is the name of the chart sheet?

   b Can you change the name of a chart sheet? If so, how?

   c If you click View on the menu bar, and then click Zoom, what is the current custom zoom percentage?

   d If you click 25% and then click the OK button, what happens?

   e Can you move a chart on a chart sheet?

   f What happens if you click the View menu, and then click Sized with Window?

   g Can you close the workbook if the Chart tab is active, or do you have to select another tab before you can close the workbook?

15 Create a Picture Chart   Fruit.xls

Bar charts are nice, but you can make them more visually appealing by replacing the bars with a graphic. Open the Fruit workbook from your Project Disk, and click the Chart tab. The bar chart compares apple and grape production in the state of Washington over a six-year period. This graph would look much more appealing if the red bars were replaced by apple graphics and the purple bars were replaced by grape graphics.

projects

To replace the chart bars with graphics:

1: Click the **Crop data** tab to view the worksheet that contains the apple graphic.

2: Click the apple graphic so the small square handles appear.

3: Click the 📋 **Copy** button on the Excel toolbar.

4: Click the **Chart** tab to see the chart.

5: Right-click one of the red bars to display the shortcut menu.

6: Ignore the shortcut menu options, and instead click the 📋 **Paste** button on the Excel toolbar. Huge apples appear on the bars. You'll want to make the apples smaller.

7: Right-click one of the apples.

8: Click ▼ on the 🪣▼ **Fill Color** button, click **Fill Effects**, and then click the **Stack** option button.

9: Click the **OK** button to see the little apples stacked up the bar.

Now that you know how to add graphics to chart bars, add the grape graphic (from row 14 of the Crop data tab) to the purple bars. When you've completed the picture chart, rename and save the workbook as "Fruit Picture Chart". Put your name in the header and print the chart sheet in landscape orientation using the full page.

EXPLORE

16 What's Wrong with These Charts?   File: Edinc2.xls

Conventional wisdom says that income is related to education. Open the Edinc2 workbook from your Project Disk, and take a minute to study the data. The workbook also includes four charts. Put your name in the header and print each of the charts in custom size, portrait orientation, and centered horizontally.

Now look at each of the charts you've printed. The charts have formatting and conceptual problems that make them unacceptable. Identify as many problems as you can for each chart. On each chart printout, describe the problems you've identified.

17 Trendlines to the Future   File: Jobs.xls

Excel provides a way to project future trends based on historical and current data. Open the Jobs workbook from your Project Disk, and click the Graph tab. You'll see a line chart of monthly unemployment rates from August 1993 to December 1996. The trend seems to be downward, but there are also some upward "blips" in the data. You can use a trendline to smooth out the data and get a better look at trends.

To add a trendline to the chart:

1: Click the chart so you can edit it.

2: Right-click one of the points on the line to display the shortcut menu.

3: Click **Add Trendline** from the shortcut menu.

4: Using the **Type** tab, click the **Linear trend** box, then click the **OK** button.

This trend line seems to show that unemployment is decreasing steadily. If the trend continues, at some point in the future unemployment will be zero! That's not realistic, but just out of curiosity, let's have Excel project 5,000 days into the future to show us when we might expect to have zero unemployment.

To forecast the future trend:

1: Right-click the vertical axis to display the shortcut menu.

2: Click **Format Axis**.

3: Using the **Scale** tab, change the value in the Minimum box to **0**.

4: Click the **OK** button to see the chart plotted on a scale from 0.0% to 7.0%.

5: Right-click the thick black trendline on the chart.

projects

6: From the shortcut menu, click **Format Trendline**.

7: Using the **Options** tab, change the value in the *Forecast Forward* box to **5000**.

8: Click the **OK** button.

It looks like unemployment would reach zero sometime early in 2007. However, instead of unemployment reaching zero, it might be more realistic to suspect that it would level off at some point. Using what's called an exponential trend will provide you with a more realistic picture of the data.

To change the trend type to exponential:

1: Right-click the trendline.

2: Click **Format Trendline** from the shortcut menu.

3: Using the **Type** tab, click the **Exponential** box.

4: Click the **OK** button.

Now the trendline appears to gradually level off around at around 1.9% unemployment. Remember that this is just a statistical projection based on historical data—many of the economic indicators that affect unemployment are not included in the model.

Rename and save the workbook as "Job Trends". Put your name in the header, and print the chart in landscape orientation and sized to use the full page.

18 Charts Illustrate What-if Models   File: System.xls

In previous Tutorials, you learned that spreadsheets are valuable tools for analyzing different what-if scenarios. Rather than trying to decipher the numerical results of a what-if analysis, you can graph the data to get a clear visual picture of each scenario.

Suppose the kid with the neighborhood paper route is thinking of buying a new bicycle. A really great bike costs $357 and the bike shop is willing to take installment payments! With 74 customers on the paper route, how long would it take to pay for the bike? Would it help to expand the number of customers on the route? What if the publisher pays $.05 to deliver each paper?

projects

Open the System workbook from your Project Disk. Check out the following cells, so you understand what's going on in this worksheet:

- There are currently 74 customers on the route (cell B2).
- The publisher pays $.03 for each paper delivered (cell B3).
- In cell B5, a formula calculates the monthly income.
- In row 6, the monthly income accumulates—just like putting the money in a bank.
- Cell B7 contains the cost of the bike—it would be purchased in January.
- Row 8 contains cumulative costs, including tune-ups in April and June.
- According to the graph, the cumulative income (blue line) grows steadily.
- The cumulative costs (pink line) increase very slightly.
- The break-even point is where the blue line crosses the pink line (in June)— the bike will be paid for.

By changing the numbers on the sheet to reflect different scenarios, the graph will change. Try each of these scenarios:

1. Suppose the bike goes on sale for $325 dollars—will that make a difference in the time it takes to pay for it? Enter "325" in cell B7, and then look at the graph. The blue line crosses the pink line in May instead of June, so that's the break-even point. Click the ◄ button on the Excel toolbar to get back to the original scenario.

2. Now what if in February, the income per paper increases to $.05? In cell C3, enter ".05", and then duplicate the value through cell J3. This scenario is even better than the bike sale! It looks like the break-even point is in April.

3. What if, in addition to the income increase, the number of customers increases to 80 in February? Enter "80" in cell C2, and then duplicate the value through cell J2. The graph shows that this makes a small difference in the break-even date.

4. Finally, with such great potential, what about buying a more expensive bike? Enter "$579" in cell B7 to see the results of this scenario.

projects

Now that you know how to use a chart to illustrate what-if scenarios, click the Computer Payback tab. Create a chart that shows the relationship between the cumulative savings and the cumulative costs, and print it showing the current scenario. Manipulate the data to answer questions a through e. You don't need to print the chart for each scenario, just write your answers on the original printout.

a In the original scenario, when would the computer be paid for—in what year is the break-even point?

b Suppose the development cost in year 1 was $480 thousand. When would the system be paid for?

c Suppose that with the original development cost ($280) the cost of operating the system in year 2 was only $1,200 thousand? How does that affect the break-even point?

d Would it have much effect on the scenario in c if the year 2 development costs increased to $127 thousand?

e What if the costs of operating the current system were $100 thousand less per year than the cost currently shown on the sheet? How would that affect the break-even point in the previous scenario?

19 Create a Histogram   File: Sea.xls

A histogram is a summary of frequencies within categories. For example, a histogram could show the frequency of exam scores in various grade categories— how many students scored 90 to 100%, how many scored 80 to 89%, and so on. Excel includes a **histogram analysis tool** that makes it easy to create a histogram.

Open the Sea workbook from your Project Disk. The data shows test scores for 40 people. In a typical test situation, you would expect most people to score somewhere between 70 and 80. Are the scores in the Sea workbook typical? Or is there evidence of some grade inflation? In this Project, you'll create a histogram from this data to show how many people scored in each the following categories:

less than 50	70-79
50-59	80-89
60-69	90-100

Before you can create a histogram, you should make sure that Excel's Data Analysis Toolpak is available.

To activate the Histogram Analysis Toolpak:

1: Click **Tools** on the Excel menu bar.

2: If the Tools menu contains an option called Data Analysis, press the **Esc** key and skip to Step 1 in the next set of Steps.

3: If the Tools menu does not contain the Data Analysis option, click **Add-ins**.

4: Click **Analysis ToolPak**, then click the **OK** button.

➔ If the Analysis ToolPak is not on the menu, ask your technical support person for some help. You cannot proceed with this Project until the Toolpak is available.

Now that the Data Analysis Toolpak is available, you can start the histogram. You'll need to supply Excel with three pieces of information about how to build the histogram. Before you start the histogram, study the worksheet so you'll be able to supply this information.

First, you'll need to tell Excel where to find the scores for the Input Range, so look at the data to locate the range of cells that contains the scores (D4 through D43).

Next, you'll need to indicate the Bin Range or categories you want Excel to use for the test scores. These are the Score Ranges in cells F4 through F8. The 50 category is for scores 50 and under.

Finally, you'll need to tell Excel the Output Range—where to put the histogram. Excel can begin the histogram in cell A45, below the existing data.

To create the histogram:

1: Click **Tools** on the menu bar, and then click **Data Analysis** to display the Analysis Tools dialog box.

2: Click **Histogram** from in the Analysis Tools list, and then click the **OK** button.

3: Click the **Input Range** box, then enter **$D$4:$D$43** as the input range.

4: Click the **Bin Range** box, then enter **$F$4:$F$8**.

5: Click the **Output Range** option button, and then enter **A45** in the *Output Range* box.

6: Make sure that only the Chart Output check box contains a check—the other square check boxes should be empty.

projects

7: Click the **OK** button. Excel creates the histogram. You might need to make the histogram larger so the labels are readable.

➔ If you need to revise your histogram, you must re-generate it. To do this, click Tools, click Data Analysis, click Histogram, and then click the OK button. Revise the information in the Histogram dialog box, and then click the OK button. To respond to the message "Histogram - output range will overwrite existing data," click the OK button.

8: Save the workbook as **SEA Histogram**

9: To print the histogram, click it, and then continue the print process as usual. Put your name in the header, and then print the histogram in landscape orientation using the full page.

Now that you've created and printed the histogram, take a moment to analyze it. On the back of your printout, write the answers to the following questions:

    a In which category were the score frequencies the highest?

    b In which category were the score frequencies the lowest?

    c Does this histogram coincide with a typical distribution of test scores, where the greatest number of scores falls between 70 and 80?

    d Would you say that the people who took this test scored higher or lower than expected?

20 Mapping and Moving a Range   File: Asylum.xls

Excel provides a mapping feature that helps you display data on maps of countries and states. Any time a worksheet contains data categorized by country or state, consider using the mapping feature to visually represent that data. The mapping feature has many twists and turns, so check Excel's online Help if you use mapping after completing this Project. The mapping feature is not part of the basic Excel installation, although it is included in the Excel software. If you begin this Project and discover that mapping is not installed on your computer, check with your technical support person.

In response to political, social, and economic upheavals, people seek asylum in more stable countries. Data for asylum applications in Western Europe has been gathered in the Asylum workbook. In this Project, you'll create a map to show the number of applications in each country during 1990.

To begin the map:

1: Open the **Asylum** workbook from your Project Disk. You realize that you should put the average number of applications on a separate worksheet. Highlight cells A3 through A15. Click **Insert**, point to **Name**, and click **Design**. In the **Names in Workbook** text box, type **Countries**. Repeat the process to assign cells G3 through G15 the name **Average**. This assigns names to both the ranges.

2: To copy the country names to the second worksheet, press **F5** (Go To), select **Countries**, and click the **OK** button. This highlights the range named Countries. Click the **Copy** button on the toolbar. Click the **Sheet2** tab and click cell **A1**. Click the **Paste** button. The Countries range is still selected on the Applications worksheet. Press **Esc** to turn off the selection. Widen Column A so that it contains all of the country names. Press **F5** (Go To) again, and double-click **Average**. The Average range is highlighted. Click the **Cut** button to begin to move the data to the second worksheet. Click the **Sheet2** tab and click cell **B1**. Click the **Paste** button. Press **Esc** again to turn off the selection. You have now copied the range named Countries and moved the range named Average onto the second worksheet. Double-click the **Worksheet2** tab and rename it **Average**. Click the **Applications** tab and delete Column G.

3: Press **F5** again and double-click **Countries** to highlight the range. Highlight the data for 1990 in column B (cells A3 through B15).

4: Click **Insert** on the Excel menu bar, then click **Map**. The plus-shaped pointer indicates that you need to specify the location for the map.

5: Use the scroll bar to scroll down until you can see cell A19.

6: Hold down the mouse button and drag a large rectangle over cells A19 through F35.

➜ If you see a message that mapping is not installed, click the OK button and contact your technical support person. You can't continue with this Project until mapping is installed.

7: If the Multiple Maps Available dialog box appears, click **Europe Countries**, and then click the **OK** button. Excel draws a map and uses gray shades to indicate the number of asylum applications for each country.

Your screen now contains a basic map, the Mapping toolbar, and the Microsoft Map Control dialog box. In the next set of Steps, you'll close the Map Control dialog box and zoom in on the map so it shows only the countries in Western Europe.

To zoom in on Western Europe:

1: Click ⊠ on the Map Control dialog box to close it.

2: Click ▼ on the Zoom control box, and then click **250%**. Click the ■ **Center Map** button.

3: Click **France** or **Germany** on the map (one of the dark gray countries). Now it is easier to see the countries in Western Europe.

4: Drag the box containing the title "Europe" to the upper left corner of the graph.

If the legend in the lower-right corner of the map looks like ▆ – ☐ Column B , you should expand it to show the values for each of the gray shades.

To expand the legend (only if the legend is not expanded):

1: Right-click the legend to display the shortcut menu.

2: Click **Compact** to remove the check mark.

3: If the legend covers some of the countries you want to display, enlarge the rectangle that holds the map by dragging the map border.

It would be helpful to have the names of the countries appear on the map. You'll use the Map Labels button on the Mapping toolbar to do this.

To add the country names to the map:

1: Click the [Map Labels icon] **Map Labels** button on the Mapping toolbar.

2: If the Map Labels dialog box appears, click **Map feature names**, and then click the **OK** button.

3: Move the pointer over France and the name of the country appears.

4: Position the country name in the middle of the country, then click to anchor the name in that position.

5: Position the pointer over Spain, and click to anchor it.

6: Add the rest of the country names to the map.

7: If you need to reposition a country name after you anchor it, click the 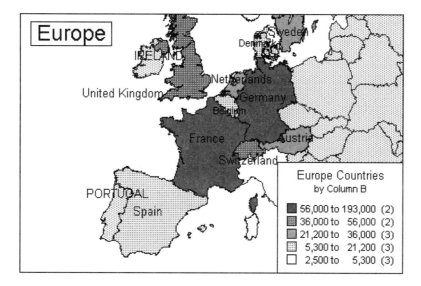 button on the Mapping toolbar, and then use the pointer to drag the country name to its new location. Your completed map should look like this:

When your map is complete, rename and save the workbook as "Western Europe Map". Put your name in the header. Print the worksheet showing the original data table and the map you just created.

projects

21 Selecting the Right Chart Type

In Tutorial 4 you learned how to create and edit a variety of charts. To some extent, creating the chart is the easy part—the hard part is understanding the information that you want to present in the chart and selecting the chart type that best presents the information.

Use Excel's online Help, Internet resources, books, or any other resources you have available to complete the following:

a Suppose that your company spends $148,000 per year on advertising. Of the total advertising budget, $42,000 is spent on local newspaper ads, $12,000 on yellow page ads, $56,000 on television ads, and $38,000 on radio ads. You have been asked to create a chart that shows the relative amount of money spent on each type of advertising and that calls particular attention to the amount of money spent on television ads. Write a one-paragraph description of the type of chart that you would use and why you would use that type of chart in this situation. Draw a rough sketch showing how the chart would look.

b Your boss showed your chart to the president of the company. He liked it so much, that he now wants you to create a chart that compares advertising expenditures for each of the three branch offices. The chart has to include the total advertising expenditure and the amount allocated to newspaper ads, yellow page ads, television ads, and radio ads for each branch office. Write a one-paragraph description of the type of chart that you would use and why you would use that type of chart in this situation. Draw a rough sketch showing how the chart would look.

22 Specialty Charts

In Tutorial 4 you worked with the most common chart types—column, bar, line, and pie charts—in both 2-D and 3-D versions. These basic chart types can be used to present information in most situations. However, there are situations in which you must use specialized chart types to effectively present certain types of information. Search through newspapers, magazines, or other materials to find an example of a chart that is not a column, bar, line, or pie chart. Photocopy the chart, then write a one-paragraph description of the type of chart and the purpose of the chart. Indicate why you think a specialized chart was used instead of one of the more common chart types.

23 Truth in Charting

Sometimes there is a thin line between editing a chart to more clearly present information and editing a chart to create a misleading picture of the data.

Suppose that the national sales manager has created a chart showing sales for each branch of your company during 1996 and 1997 as shown in Chart A below.

Chart A

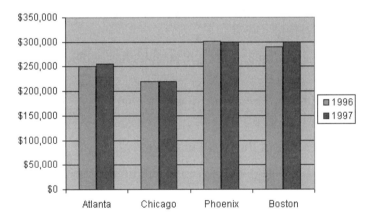

projects

The manager of the Phoenix branch modified the chart as shown in Chart B below.

Chart B

Sales by Branch

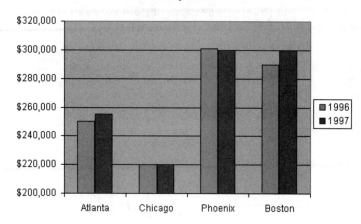

Examine both charts, and then write your answers to the following:

a Is the branch with the best sales the same in both charts?

b Is the branch with the worst sales the same in both charts?

c Which chart appears to show more differential between the sales for each branch?

d If you were the manager of the Chicago branch, which chart would you prefer? Why?

e If you were the manager of the Atlanta branch, which chart would you prefer? Why?

f What accounts for the difference in the two charts?

g Which chart do you think is a more accurate representation of the data? Why?

24 Chart Design

In Tutorial 4 you worked with a variety of charts and chart formatting options. Assume that you have been asked to give a brief presentation summarizing some important Do's and Don'ts for charting.

Make a list of ten principles of effective chart design and ten chart design pitfalls. Your instructor might provide guidelines on the format for your presentation. Instead of a simple written list, you might create a poster, presentation slides, or a tri-fold brochure. In addition, your instructor might require you to provide sample charts to illustrate your Do's and Don'ts.

25 Generation X

Members of Generation X face some distinct political and social issues in the years ahead. As Baby Boomers enter retirement age, demands on programs such as social security increase. Further, when Baby Boomers retire, there are likely to be fewer working adults to pay the taxes necessary to fund social security and medical programs. Some analysts foresee a future in which inter-generational issues such as social security play a much larger role in national politics.

Use the Internet or your library to find additional information about one social issue facing Generation X in the years ahead. Look for data that helps you understand the trends—changes in income levels, changes in the pool of social security funds, population growth, and so on.

Based on the data you find, write a two-paragraph summary of the issue, and create a chart to graphically depict the data.

Answers to Spreadsheet e-SSentials CheckPoint Questions

1 Spreadsheets show the numbers you're working with in a grid of rows and columns, rather than in the small window of a calculator. It is easier to change the numbers in a spreadsheet after you have entered them. You can print your results in a professional format. You can easily create a graph of your data. Because a spreadsheet is in electronic format, you can transfer the data into other programs, such as a word processor, and you can transmit the data electronically via e-mail or post it on a Web page.

2 Because spreadsheet formulas can contain references to other cells, the formulas are "generic." Therefore, the data used in the cells referred to by the formulas can be changed, and the spreadsheet will recalculate the formula using the new data.

3 functions

4 Spreadsheets that will be projected for an audience should be easy to read, so you would usually use large fonts and make use of colors for text and backgrounds. In addition, you might add a graphic for visual interest. Documentation and graphs should be placed on separate worksheets.

5 True

6 False. The person who creates a spreadsheet is responsible for its accuracy. Therefore it is important to audit any worksheets you create before you depend on their results.

7 The biggest disadvantage would be making sure that the colors did not turn into similar gray shades when printed.

8 what-if

9 If you need a clue to this question, look in magazines and journals for your career field. Many tables and most graphs in these publications are created using spreadsheet software.

10 The first spreadsheet, VisiCalc, created interest in using personal computers for business and launched the digital age.

Answers to Odd-Numbered Review Questions

Tutorial 1

1   spreadsheet

3   workbook

5   worksheet

7   plus sign

9   scroll bars

11 Undo

13 A or (A:)

answers

15	a
17	b
19	c
21	c
23	d
25	a
27	b

answers

29 b

31 a

33 g

35 j

37 h

answers

39 Your students were asked to make up their own example of a workbook with four worksheets and explain what each worksheet would contain. Answers will vary. The two important grading criteria are:
The workbook should contain numbers
Each workbook should involve some calculations, rather than just table data

41 First, click the Print Preview button. Then click the Page Setup button to add a header. Click the Print button. Check the setting in the Print dialog box. Click the OK button to print.

43 When you change $250 to $450, the total for monthly household expenses increased by $200. The section of the pie chart for food gets larger.

44 Click the cell to make it the active cell, then look at the contents of the Formula bar. If the cell contents shown on the Formula bar begin with an equal sign, the the cell contains a formula.

answers

Tutorial 2

FILL-IN-THE-BLANKS

1 tab

3 A1

5 right

7 formula

9 15

11 relative

13 functions

MULTIPLE CHOICE

15 a

17 d

19 c

21 b

23 d

25 c

27 b

answers

29 c

31 h

33 b

35 j

37 g

SHORT ANSWER

39 When you replicate a formula, Excel changes the relative addresses. For example, if you replicate a formula down to adjacent cells, Excel increases the row number in each subsequent formula. So, for example, cell reference D5 becomes D6. Absolute addresses are not changed when a formula is replicated. If you copy a formula containing cell reference $C$5, the new formula will also contain $C$5. Absolute addresses are important when you want to refer to a value, such as a percentage or tax rate that is located in one cell.

41 A formula is the entire expression that begins with the equal sign (=). A function, though it is defined as a "built-in formula" can be incorporated into longer formulas. Therefore, you might think of a function as a building block for a formula.

43 You replicate a formula when you want the new formulas in adjacent cells. You copy a formula when you want the new formula to appear in cells that are not adjacent to the cell that contains the original formula.

45 First, click cell A2 and type = (an equal sign). Use the arrow keys to move the cell pointer to cell C5 and type * (an asterisk). Use the arrow keys to move to cell D2, and type + (a plus sign). Use the arrow keys to move to B5, and then press the Enter key.

answers

Tutorial 3

1 Layout, format

3 Accounting

5 width

7 sort

9 fonts

11 General

13 border

15 True

MULTIPLE CHOICE

17 a

19 d

21 b

23 b

25 c

27 c

29 d

answers

MATCHING

31 c

33 j

35 d

37 i

39 g

SHORT ANSWER

41 Answers should include any three of the following: change column widths, format numbers, apply borders, change font and background color, align cell contents.

43 When you sort cells, make sure you highlight all the rows and columns that contain the data you want to sort. Do not just select column A if the data in columns B and C "belongs to" the data in column A—select all three columns before you sort.

45 An outline border would make a title stand out; it could bracket the entire worksheet, or define an area of the worksheet.

Tutorial 4

FILL-IN-THE-BLANKS

1 chart

3 data range

5 pie

7 handles

9 legend

11 data label

13 true

MULTIPLE CHOICE

15 a

17 a

19 d

21 d

23 c

25 d

answers

MATCHING

27 a

29 c

SHORT ANSWER

31 Any five of the following: area, bar, column, line, pie, scatter, donut, radar.

33 When the chart is on a separate tab, you don't have to scroll to view it.

35 The totals would change the scale of the chart because they are much larger than the rest of the data. Also, the totals are a different category of data—rather than "raw" data, the totals are summary data so they would not belong on the same chart.

Database e-SSentials

Sometime in the middle of this century our industrial society began to evolve into an information society. The way we live has changed in many ways. We more frequently interact with information, we enter careers connected to information management, we increasingly attach a cash value to information, we tend to depend on information, and we are becoming aware of the potential problems that can occur when information is misused.

The Information Age is fueled by an explosion of data collected and generated by individuals, corporations, and government agencies. Some experts estimate that the amount of information doubles every year. This information is stored in an uncountable number of databases, most of them computerized. In the course of an ordinary day, you're likely to interact with more than one of these databases. It's pretty clear, then, that understanding and using databases is an important skill for living in the Information Age.

WHAT IS A DATABASE?

The term "database" is a slippery thing. In this chapter, we'll focus on the popular rendition of databases, using a broad, non-technical definition. We'll define a **database** as a collection of information stored on one or more computers.

In most of this chapter, we'll be focusing on database management software that's designed to create and manipulate databases and on software that's designed to search for information in databases.

WHAT KIND OF DATABASES AM I LIKELY TO RUN INTO?

In a typical day, you're likely to encounter many types of databases such as a library card catalog, your bank's database of checking and savings account balances, CD-ROM encyclopedias, the computer's directory of files, and your e-mail address book.

WHAT'S THE DIFFERENCE BETWEEN A STRUCTURED DATABASE AND A FREE FORM DATABASE?

Databases come in two flavors: structured databases and free-form databases. A **structured database** contains information about various types of entities (people, places, objects, events, or ideas) and about the relationships among the entities. Figure 1 shows an example of records from a structured database for a computerized library card catalog.

Figure 1 A structured database

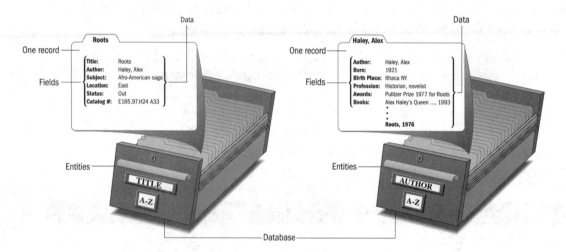

Structured databases typically store data that describes collections of related entities. A medical database stores data for collections of patients, physicians, symptoms, treatments, and so on. An inventory database stores data for a collection of items stocked on store and warehouse shelves. Examples of structured databases are plentiful; here are a few examples:

Career/User/Industry	Maintains a Database of:
Research scientist	Results for each successive run of an experiment
Department of Motor Vehicles	Licensed cars and drivers
Credit card company	Customer purchases, payments, and balances
Video store	Information about the videos it rents, its members, and its suppliers
Sierra Club	Members
U.S. Weather Service	High and low temperatures collected from cities around the country
The FBI	Criminals
Hospital pharmacy	Medicines, drugs, and patients
Sociologist	The results of a survey

A **free-form database** is a loosely structured collection of information, usually stored as documents rather than as records. You might consider the collection of word processing documents stored on your computer to be a free-form database of your own writing. A CD-ROM containing documents and videos of the Civil War would be another example. You might also identify as free-form databases some Internet services such as Gopherspace and the World Wide Web. Gopherspace is a list of documents stored on a collection of computers from all over the world. The World Wide Web (or Web for short) is a collection of millions of linked documents, again, stored on computers the world over. Whether stored on your hard disk, a CD-ROM, or the Internet, free-form databases have the potential to contain varied and useful information for you as a student or as a career professional.

WHAT BASIC DATABASE TERMINOLOGY DO I NEED TO KNOW?

The basic terminology that you need to know and understand in order to work with databases includes field, record, relationship, table, common field, primary key, foreign key, and one-to-many relationships. For examples of these terms, we'll be looking at a fictional employee database from Midtown General Hospital:

A **field** is a single characteristic of a person, place, object, event, or idea. (When working with databases, for simplicity a person, place, object, event, or idea is often referred to as an entity.) A field is the basic building block of data.

In Figure 2 on the next page, you can see that a field contains the smallest unit of meaningful data. A field can be either variable-length or fixed-length (compare the address field with the SocNum field). Every field in a file is assigned a data type. Two common data types are character (LastName field) and numeric (HoursWorked field). The data you can enter into a field depends on the field's data type.

A **field name** describes the contents of each field. In Figure 2, the field name SocNum describes a field containing an employee's social security number.

A **field value** is the specific content of a field. For example the LastName value of the first employee is Ang.

A **table** is a collection of fields that describes an entity. For example, in Figure 2 the Employee table collects together all of the fields that describe an employee— LastName, FirstName, Address, SocNum.

A **record** is a specific set of field values. It is also the set of field values that span a row in a table. For example, one of the records in the Employee table in Figure 2 contains fields of data about the entity Ang, Susan.

overview

Figure 2 *Database terminology   In Midtown General Hospital's Employee database, the data for each record are stored in tables. The record for Margaret Houlihan in the Employee table has four fields. The arrow highlights the relationship between the Employee table and the Timecard table. SocNum is a common field in these two tables. In the Employee table, SocNum is a primary key. In the Timecard table, SocNum is a foreign key, and it establishes a relationship between the two tables. In the Timecard table, you can see how the field SocNum sets up a one-to-many relationship between timecards and employees.*

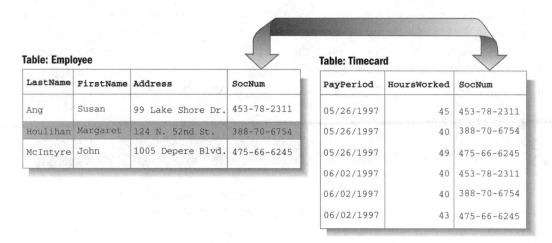

Relationships are the associations among tables in a database that organize the many records and the data in them. For example, in Figure 2 there is a relationship between an employee entity and a timecard entity. You could describe this relationship by saying "an employee has a time card."

A **primary key** is a field or collection of fields whose value uniquely identifies each record in a table. SocNum in the Employee table is a primary key, and the combination of PayPeriod and SocNum in the Timecard table is a primary key.

A **foreign key** is a primary key from one table that is included in a second table in order to establish a relationship between the two tables; the primary key that is included in the second table is called the foreign key. For example, the primary key SocNum from the Employee table is included in the Timecard table in order to establish a relationship between timecard entities and employee entities. SocNum is common to both tables, and in the Timecard table SocNum is a foreign key.

A **one-to-many relationship** means that one record in a particular table may be related to more than one record in another table. For example, one employee record can have many timecard records. However, each timecard record is related to a single employee record.

The Employee and Timecard tables:

Table: Employee

LastName	FirstName	Address	SocNum
Ang	Susan	99 Lake Shore Dr.	453-78-2311
Houlihan	Margaret	124 N. 52nd St.	388-70-6754
McIntyre	John	1005 Depere Blvd.	475-66-6245

Table: Timecard

PayPeriod	HoursWorked	SocNum
05/26/1997	45	453-78-2311
05/26/1997	40	388-70-6754
05/26/1997	49	475-66-6245
06/02/1997	40	453-78-2311
06/02/1997	40	388-70-6754
06/02/1997	43	475-66-6245

overview

HOW DO I DESIGN AND BUILD A DATABASE?

To create and manage your own databases, you need software called a database management system. A **database management system** (DBMS) lets you create and manage interrelated data.

A database management system can be a useful tool, but only if you first carefully design the database so that it meets the needs of those who will use it. The key to an effective file or database is the initial design of its structure. With a good structure, you can flexibly manipulate the data to provide meaningful, accurate, and timely information for decision making.

In database design, you determine the fields, tables, and relationships needed to satisfy the data and processing requirements. When you design a database, you should follow these guidelines:

- Identify all the fields needed to produce the required information.

- Determine the entities involved in the data requirements. The type of entity in a table usually suggests the name for the table in a database.

- Group related fields by entity into tables.

- Designate a primary key for each table. A primary key in each table will help ensure that records are selected accurately once the database is functioning.

- Include a common field in related tables.

- Avoid data redundancy. **Data redundancy** occurs when you store the same data in more than one place, which can cause inaccuracies.

- Determine the properties or characteristics of each field, for example the field name, maximum field length, field description, and the field's valid values and data type.

overview

HOW DO I ENTER DATA INTO MY DATABASE?

When you design the database or specify the database structure, you design a blank form that will hold data. After the form is complete, you can begin to enter data. You can see a blank form in Figure 3.

Employee	
LastName	
FirstName	
Address	
ZipCode	
Phone	
Gender	
SocNum	
StartDate	
JobCode	
DeptCode	
HourlyWage	
Exemptions	
BirthDate	

Employee	
LastName	Houlihan
FirstName	Margaret
Address	124 N. 52nd St.
ZipCode	48236
Phone	885-7860
Gender	F
SocNum	388-70-6754
StartDate	10/05/1985
JobCode	RN
DeptCode	IC
HourlyWage	14.80
Exemptions	1
BirthDate	02/14/1951

Figure 3 *A database entry form   This database entry form for the Midtown General Hospital Employee database shows all of the fields in the database.*

As you enter each record, it is assigned a record number. The first record you enter becomes record #1. The second record you enter becomes record #2, and so forth.

Consistency is important for data entry because it affects the efficiency of your searches. Suppose you're entering employee data for registered nurses and you enter "RN" as the job code for some employees, but you enter "NURS" for other who hold the same position. If you later want the database software to print a list of all nurses, and you ask for all the RNs, the employees you identified as NURS will not be included on the list.

Another issue related to entering consistent data is case sensitivity. Case sensitivity means that uppercase letters are not equivalent to their lowercase counterparts. In a case-sensitive database, the state abbreviation MI is not the same as the abbreviation Mi. Not all data management environments are case sensitive. You must read the documentation to determine whether a particular data management environment is case sensitive.

HOW DO I UPDATE OR CHANGE DATA IN MY DATABASE?

Updating a database is the process of adding, changing, and deleting records to keep it current and accurate. To update data in a database, you first need to find the record you want to update. Next, you make the changes and, if necessary, indicate that you want to save the record in its changed format.

Different database management environments have different ways of saving updated records. With many environments, changes are automatically saved as soon as you move to the next record. With other environments, you must issue a command to save the changes you make. To learn the specific procedures for the database management environment you use, you should refer to the software documentation or online Help.

In addition to individual changes, computers make it easy to perform global updates to change the data in more than one record at a time. Consider the Employee file in the Midtown General Hospital database. A number of employees are working at $4.75 per hour, the minimum wage set by the government. Suppose that the minimum wage increases to $5.65 per hour. Instead of searching for each employee with an hourly wage of $4.75 and manually changing the numbers to $5.65, you could enter a command such as:

UPDATE Employee SET HourlyWage = 5.65 WHERE HourlyWage <5.65.

Let's see how this command performs a global update. The UPDATE command means you want to change the data in some or all of the records. Employee is the name of the table that contains the data you want to change. SET HourlyWage = 5.65 tells the system to change the data in the HourlyWage field to 5.65. WHERE HourlyWage <5.65 tells the DBMS to change only those records in which the current hourly wage is less than $5.65.

CAN I FIND INFORMATION IN A DATABASE JUST BY TYPING IN A QUESTION?

A realistic file or database contains hundreds or thousands of records. If you want to find a particular record or a particular group of records, scrolling through every record is too cumbersome. Instead, you enter search specifications called a query, and the computer will quickly locate the records you seek. For example, if you want a list of everyone who has "Jones" as a last name, you would use a query to tell the computer to look for all the records with "Jones" in the LastName field.

A **query language** is a set of command words that you can use to direct the computer to locate information, sort records, and change the data in those records. In situations where fairly sophisticated users want to access a structured database, a query language provides good flexibility for pinpointing information. A popular query language for both mainframes and microcomputers is Structured Query Language, more commonly called SQL.

Because of its structure, a computer can generally locate data in a structured database faster than it can locate information in a free-form database. For example, in a library catalog—a structured database—the book titles are stored in a particular field, so the computer can quickly find the record for the popular novel *Waiting to Exhale*. You use SQL to search for information in a structured database.

overview

To locate all the Byzantine statues in an art museum database you would enter an SQL query something like this:

*Select * from artworks where style = 'Byzantine' and media = 'statue'*

Before you can compose such a query, you must have a fairly extensive knowledge of the database and its structure. You must know that the name of the database is "artworks." You must also know that the artistic style of each work is stored in a field called "Style" and that works are categorized as painting, statue, pottery, and so on, in a field called "Media." You can see that this interface is not suitable for casual users. Imagine if you had to compose SQL queries to use your library card catalog! Many people would find it easier to just wander around the stacks.

WHAT IS QUERY BY EXAMPLE AND HOW DOES IT WORK?

Although computers can more easily find information in structured databases, the structure can cause a problem for humans. The problem is that users might not know the format for the records in a database. For example, how would you know whether an online library card catalog stores book titles in a field called Title, BookTitle, or T? Is the title the first field? Or does the first field contain the name of the author? One way to help users search structured databases is by providing a **query by example** (**QBE** for short) user interface like the one shown in Figure 4.

Books

Granville State University Library
Books On-Line
Public Access Card Catalog

Instructions: Fill in one or more of the blanks below to describe the materials you are trying to find. If you need more help, click [?]

Author: _____

Title: *Economics*

Date: 1993-

Publisher: _____

ISBN: _____

Figure 4 *Query by example user interface*

When you use a QBE interface, you see a blank record on the screen. Into this record you enter examples of what you want the computer to find. In Figure 4 the user has entered *Economics* in the title field to indicate the word economics should appear somewhere in the title of the book. The user did not enter Economics (without the asterisks) because that would tell the computer to find books titled only "Economics," thereby eliminating multiword titles. Just entering "Economics" would also omit multiword titles such as "Economics of Peace" from the search. The user also entered "1993 -" in the Publication Date field to indicate that the computer should look only for books published in 1993 or later.

As you might guess from this example, using QBE requires you to learn a few "tricks" such as the use of the asterisk and dash. Different QBE software might use different symbols. Your best bet when using a new QBE is to read the help instructions carefully before you set up your query.

CAN I FIND INFORMATION BY ASKING A QUESTION IN PLAIN ENGLISH?

Advances in artificial intelligence have made some progress in the ability of computers to understand queries formulated in **natural languages** such as English, French, or Japanese. To make such natural language queries you don't need to learn an esoteric query language. Instead, you can enter questions using everyday words.

Computers still have some interpretation difficulties arising from ambiguities in human languages, so the use of natural language query software is not widespread. However, you are likely to encounter it in the online Help for applications software. Microsoft Excel, for example, has a natural-language query facility, shown in Figure 5.

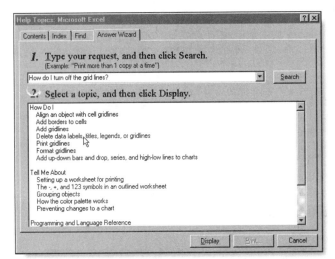

Figure 5 Excel's natural-language query facility

WHAT ARE BOOLEAN OPERATORS, AND HOW DO I USE THEM?

Most popular structured query languages use command words, expressions, relational operators, and Boolean operators to formulate a query. Earlier, you saw examples of command words, expressions, and relational operators. What are Boolean operators?

The mathematician George Boole defined a system of logic now called Boolean logic or Boolean algebra. Boolean algebra uses three main operations: NOT, AND, and OR. Sometimes Boolean operators are simply called logical operators. Boolean operators or logical operators allow you to set up complex queries. They allow you to select records from a database based on multiple selection criteria—brown and blond hair, green or brown eyes, not male.

The Boolean definitions of AND, OR, and NOT are very specific compared to our casual use of these words. AND means that a thing must meet both selection criteria. It is restrictive. OR means that a thing must fit either criterion. It is more inclusive. NOT means "everything that does not match the criterion." Let's look at some examples, using the Midtown General Hospital Employee database. We can use Venn diagrams to represent the queries and tables from the database. We'll use a rectangle to represent a table and circles to represent records and field values. We'll use shading to represent the meaning of AND, OR, and NOT.

A complex query, such as one to find only those employees who are registered nurses and have Houlihan for their last name and are female, requires the use of Boolean operators. Let's use the employees, shown in Figure 6, to visualize the results from queries of the Midtown General Hospital Employee database.

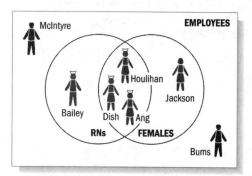

Figure 6 *Midtown Employees   In Venn diagrams that describe Midtown's employees, a rectangle represents all of the employees at the hospital. The left circle represents all of the RNs, and the right circle represents all of the Females. The overlapping area in the middle represents RNs who are females.*

For example, the search criteria JobCode = 'RN' AND Gender = 'F' requests only those records for female registered nurses. If Margaret Houlihan is a female and a registered nurse, her record would match the search criteria. Figure 7 shows the results of such a search.

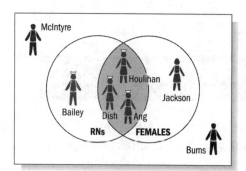

Figure 7 *JobCode = 'RN' AND Gender = 'F'   The shaded area in the overlapping circles shows the employees who are RNs and females.*

The logical operator OR connects two expressions, but only one of them must be true to match the search criteria. The search criteria JobCode = 'RN' OR Gender = 'F' would produce all the records for females, regardless of their job code. The search would also produce all the records for registered nurses of either gender.

The logical operator NOT precedes a simple or complex expression and, in a search specification, produces the records that do not match the expression. For example, the expression NOT JobCode = 'RN' would produce records for any employee who is not a registered nurse. What about the search criteria NOT(JobCode = 'RN' AND Gender = 'F')? Think of it this way: The computer will locate the records for all employees who are registered nurses and female (like Margaret Houlihan, who is a female registered nurse), but it will not produce these records. Instead it will produce all the other records. So, will the search NOT(JobCode = 'RN' AND Gender = 'F') produce Rick Bailey? Yes, it will and Figure 8 shows why.

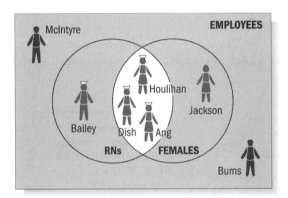

Figure 8 NOT(JobCode = 'RN' AND Gender = 'F')   The shaded area (everything *except the area of overlapping circles*) shows all the employees who are not RNs and not females.

HOW CAN I GENERATE DIFFERENT VIEWS OF MY DATA FOR QUERIES, FORMS, AND REPORTS?

It is easier to use information if it is presented in a sequence related to how the information is going to be used. For example, if you want to view a list of employees and you are looking for a specific employee by name, it is handy to have the employee records alphabetized by last name. If, on the other hand, you want to view a list of employees to compare hourly wages, it is useful to have the records in numeric order according to the number in the HourlyWage field.

A sort key is the field used to arrange records in order. Suppose Midtown managers want employee records arranged alphabetically by last name. The sort key would be LastName. Alternatively, if they want the records arranged by hourly wage, the sort key would be HourlyWage.

There are two ways to organize records in a table; you can sort them or you can index them. If you change the order of the table itself by essentially rearranging the sequence of the records on the disk, you are sorting. Because the records are rearranged, each record receives a new record number to indicate its new position in the table. For example, in a table sorted by last name, the record with the last name that appears first in the alphabet would become record #1. Sorting is an acceptable

procedure for smaller tables in which the time to sort the records is minimal. Sorting is also acceptable for tables that you don't want sorted multiple ways. However, if you sometimes need to view a table in alphabetical order by last name, but at other times you need to view the table in order by price, sorting is not very efficient.

An alternative way to organize records is indexing. **Indexing** leaves the records in their original order and retains the original record numbers but creates additional tables, called index tables. An **index table** allows you to display information in order. Think of an index table as being similar to the index of a book. The index of a book contains topics in alphabetical order, which allows you to find a topic in the index list easily. Next to the topic is a page number that points to the location of the actual information about the topic.

Figure 9 shows how an index table lists the contents of the LastName field in alphabetical order, then uses the record number as a pointer to the corresponding record number in the original table.

Record #	LastName	FirstName	Gender	StartDate	JobCode
1	Houlihan	Margaret	F	10/05/1985	RN
2	McIntyre	John	M	04/14/1986	SMD
3	Ang	Susan	F	08/10/1988	RN
4	Jackson	Tony	F	12/04/1989	SMD
5	Burns	Frank	M	05/04/1990	SMD
6	Dish	Betty	F	01/16/1992	RN
7	Bailey	Rick	M	02/03/1992	RN

Database table

LastName	Record #
Ang	3
Bailey	7
Burns	5
Dish	6
Houlihan	1
Jackson	4
Bailey	2

Index file

Figure 9 *Indexing Records are numbered in the order in which they are entered; the employee with the earliest start date is record 1. To index the records by last name, the computer creates an index table containing the data in the LastName field and the original record numbers. Notice that in the original table, Susan Ang is record #3. In the index table, Susan's record is listed first because her name is first in the alphabet. Her record number is 3, as it was in the original table. The computer uses the index table to look up information from the original database table.*

What makes indexing so flexible is that you can have multiple index tables for each of your data tables. For example, Midtown could have three index tables for the employee data table—one index table to arrange employees by last name, one to arrange employees by hourly wage, and one to arrange employees by job category.

In some database management systems, the distinction between sorting and indexing will help you more effectively use the DBMS to organize your data. However, you should be aware that not all data management environments differentiate between the terms "sort" and "index." For example, Microsoft Access uses the term "sort" for procedures that organize data without rearranging records.

WHAT ARE SOME DIFFERENT WAYS THAT I CAN USE THE INFORMATION THAT I FIND?

The power of information comes not only from finding it, but from using it. In an information-rich society, finding information that is astonishing, amusing, and informative is not difficult. Finding information that is bizarre, offensive, destructive, and confidential is not difficult either. Keep in mind that the information you seek, collect, and disperse is a reflection of your values and ethics. It seems that laws and regulations on the publication and use of information in electronic form have not kept up with the technology. Therefore, it is up to you to "use it, but don't abuse it." Once you find information in a database, you can use it in a number of ways.

Print it. When you find information in a structured database, you can generally print out a single record or a list of selected records. You might want to print a particular record, for example, if you're looking through a real estate database and find your dream house. In another scenario, suppose you were looking in the ERIC database to find some academic articles for a paper you're writing about male role models in elementary schools. You could print out a list of article titles and the journals in which they appeared. If call numbers for the journals are available, including that information on the printout would make it much easier to locate the articles in your library.

Export it. You might find some data that you want to analyze or graph using spreadsheet software. Many databases automatically **export data** by transforming it into a format that's acceptable to your spreadsheet software. If your database does not have this capability, your spreadsheet software might be able to **import data** by reading the database data and translating it into a worksheet. As another option, your spreadsheet software might include a wizard to help you transport data between databases and worksheets.

Copy and Paste. Most of today's graphical user interfaces provide a way to highlight database information you see on the screen and copy it to a worksheet or document. This technique is especially useful with the information you find in

free-form databases because often you want just the information from one section of one document. For example, suppose you've been surfing the Internet for information on the forest canopies for your botany seminar. You locate a Green Peace document that contains relevant information. Figure 10 shows you how to copy this information from the Web to one of your own word processing documents.

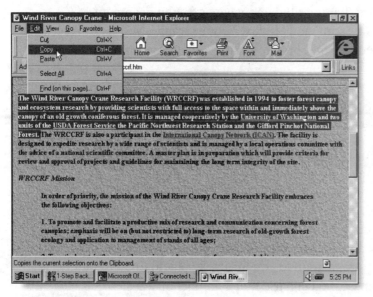

Figure 10 Copying information

Save it. When you find a group of records in a structured database that you want to work with later, your database software might provide you with an option to save the records as a file on a hard or floppy disk. If you opt for this route, you should be aware that in order to manipulate the records you are likely to need the same database software that was originally used to enter and create the records. This is not always practical, so you might have to use export or copy options instead.

If you find data on the Web, the software you're using to access the information usually provides you with a way to save it on your own computer. This is particularly useful if you find a long document that you want to read at your leisure.

Transmit it. Developments in computerization would have had much less impact on the way we live were it not for parallel developments in communications technology. Today, we're plugged into a "global village" where e-mail arrives just minutes after it was sent and where you can simultaneously "chat" online with people from countries all over the world. You can electronically distribute the information you collect; an easy way is to insert information into e-mail messages. You can also post information on one of the many bulletin boards or Internet news groups. A more ambitious project would be to develop your own World Wide Web site from which people could view your Web pages and download databases.

Whether you print, import, copy, save, or transmit the data you find in databases, it is your responsibility to use it appropriately. Respect copyrights by giving credit to the original author in a footnote or end note. The information in corporate and government databases is often confidential. When you have access to such data, respect the privacy of the individuals who are the subject of the data. Don't divulge the information you find or introduce inaccuracies into the database.

WHAT COMMERCIAL DATABASE SOFTWARE IS AVAILABLE?

The amount of data in many of today's databases would be impossible to manage without computers. Banking systems must process hundreds of millions of checks each year. The United States Internal Revenue Service keeps records for over $500 billion collected each year from 100 million taxpayers. Credit records on more than 86 million Americans are maintained by credit-reporting companies. Phone companies must maintain records for more than 500 million telephone calls placed each day. How would our lives be different without the ability to process this amount of information? Would we return to the days of the neighborhood tax collector? Would we pay for everything in cash? Would we have to use pay phones for all our calls?

To create and manage databases, you need software such as a database management system or a file manager. Maintaining large commercial databases requires sophisticated data management software. Surprisingly, much of this software is available to the general public for use on microcomputers. In addition, microcomputer users can select from a variety of scaled-down, special-purpose, and easy-to-use data management software. Called **file managers**, this software helps you define the records and fields for the data you collect, then helps you add your data, sort it, search through it, and print it out. With a file manager you can create what is essentially a computerized card file.

Microsoft Works and ClarisWorks contain low-cost, all-purpose file managers that you can use to maintain your own computerized card files. A number of special-purpose file managers might also interest you. If you want to keep a database for appointments and due dates, consider Lotus Organizer or Outlook's Schedule It! Sales representatives who want to keep track of potential customers might consider Symantec's Act! or Janna's Contact.

Best-selling microcomputer database management software includes Microsoft Access, ACI's 4th Dimension, Claris's FileMaker Pro, Lotus Approach, Borland's Visual dBase, and Borland's Paradox. Depending on the package you select, you'll spend between $200 and $1,200. Figure 11 on the next page shows some popular microcomputer database management software.

Figure 11 *Microcomputer database management software*

CheckPoint _____

1   In popular terminology, a(n) _____ is a collection of information stored on one or more computers.

2   A(n) _____ database is a file of information organized in a uniform format of records and fields, whereas a(n) _____ database is a loosely structured collection of information.

3   The basic building block of data in a database is a(n) _____.

4   True or False? One record in a table can be related only to one record in another table.

5   True or False? Consistency is important for data entry because they affect the efficiency of searches.

6   Query by example, a query language, and a natural language are all methods used to _____ information in a database.

7   When using a(n) _____ user interface to search a database, you use a blank record to enter examples of the data you want the computer to find.

8   A(n) _____ such as SQL consists of a set of command words that you can use to direct the computer to create databases, locate information, sort records, and change the data in those records.

9   True or false? Once you locate information in a database, you can print it, export it to other software packages, copy and paste it into other software, save it for future reference, or transmit it.

10   You can use a file manager or _____ to create and manage data.

Microsoft Access

Tutorial 1: Access Basics

Tutorial 1

Access Basics

Entertainment

The entertainment world has certainly come a long way. Today most major cities have a large building that hosts events from a Willie Nelson concert to a Montreal Canadians game! The building usually contains or can be easily converted into one or more arenas, basketball courts, ice rinks, performing arts halls, theaters, and recreation facilities. Cities that have such buildings provide the public with a full spectrum of exciting events: concerts, plays, sporting events, conventions, food fairs, crafts exhibitions, boat shows, dog shows, home shows, and much much more. For a typical event, such as a large concert, building owners, managers, and city officials want to know how many tickets each performer sold. What were their gross sales? Which promoters were most effective? You'll find out here how database management software helps provide answers to these questions and many more.

Doing the e-Thing

You'll find out how to get started with the e-Course software tutorials. This is an easy way to learn how to use computer software.

Projects

Tutorial 1 Projects include planning your route to the top with the Highpointers Club, finding your best day of the year, and playing music with Elvis or an Elvis impersonator.

If you're not assigned Project 20, you should read the Project or, better yet, work through it. Project 20 deals with compacting a database, which is a process you'll want to periodically perform on a database so that it doesn't grow excessively large as you use it.

WHAT'S ONLINE

Disks

You'll need two blank formatted disks for Tutorial 1. You'll need one disk for completing the online Steps and practice activities and the other disk to use as a **Project Disk**. You'll find out how to make and use your Project Disk when you get to the Projects section of the WorkText.

If you'd like to keep track of your progress, you'll also need a third blank formatted disk ready when you begin the online Steps for Tutorial 1. As you log in, the e-Course software will create a **Tracking Disk** for you. The Tracking Disk will keep a record of the length of time you spend on each e-Course session and your scores on the CheckPoint questions you answer online. If your instructor will collect your Tracking Disk for grading, make sure you have a backup copy!

Entertainment

Entertainment is big business, and a modern, well-equipped events center can be instrumental in the success of this business. The right building in the right location with the right amenities can attract top performers and high-profile events, and will entice local residents and out-of-town visitors to spend their money. And the financial success of an events center ripples through a city's economy. People buy tickets, luxury boxes, refreshments, and souvenirs. Parking lots and garages fill up. Business increases at nearby restaurants, retail stores, and museums. Occupancy rates at nearby hotels and motels go up. Use of the local airport and public transportation increases. Tax revenues grow. And besides the money, the city benefits from the enhanced image that cultural events and sports' franchises provide.

Hundreds of millions of dollars from both the public and private sectors are needed to construct and maintain such an events center. A major part of managing an events center is tracking and monitoring enormous amounts of data about, for example:

- event management
- marketing
- catering
- food/beverage point-of-sale
- recipe/menu management

- inventory management
- purchasing and receiving
- TV and radio contracts
- commissions
- general ledger

All this data must be tracked accurately and productively for an events center to be successful. The data must help managers, staff, investors, government, or the public answer many general questions such as: Which part of the operations have increasing costs? Where are revenues increasing? Which contracts are up for renewal in the next month? What's the home schedule next season for the city's hockey team? How much does the center owe this month for taxes?

Or it might help to answer specific questions such as: Which concerts had the highest gross sales? How many tickets were sold for each concert? What was the average price per ticket sold? Which concert promoters have been most effective?

So how can an event center's management track its data quickly and accurately? By creating a database and using database management software. For example, if you wanted to know the year's top concerts in gross sales, you could learn the answer in a matter of seconds (Figure 1.1).

Figure 1.1 *The year's top grossing concerts*

Gross Sales	Performer	Tickets Sold	Promoter Name	Per Ticket
$274,720	Gloria Estefan	11,324	Creative Artists	24.26
$263,410	Reba McEntire	10,800	Myridian Limited	24.39
$259,280	Kiss	11,278	Creative Artists	22.99
$259,115	Hootie & the Blowfish	11,222	Myridian Limited	23.09
$256,805	Smashing Pumpkins	11,348	Myridian Limited	22.63
$255,940	Brooks & Dunn	11,128	Creative Artists	23.00
$255,050	Bonnie Raitt	10,937	Myridian Limited	23.32
$252,595	Shania Twain	10,949	Myridian Limited	23.07
$252,030	Alabama	10,436	Myridian Limited	24.15
$247,355	Bush	11,179	Bookings Institute	22.13
$246,375	Stone Temple Pilots	10,950	Jackson Enterprises	22.50

So let's get started with the e-Course online Steps to see how database management software works.

GET STARTED ONLINE WITH e-COURSE

The e-Course software is designed to teach you how to use the Microsoft Access database management software. The first time you use the e-Course software, you'll probably want to set up a Tracking Disk, which keeps track of your progress and your CheckPoint scores. Now, it's time to use your computer.

To start the e-Course software and set up a Tracking Disk:

1: Label a formatted disk "Tracking Disk" and place it in the disk drive. (This step is optional, but if you do not insert a disk, you will not have an electronic record of your progress.)

2: Start your computer, and then click the **Start** button.

3: Point to **Programs**.

4: Point to **e-Course**.

scenario

5: Click **e-Course Access**.

6: If you see a message saying "The tracking file was not found on drive A" click the button labeled "Copy the tracking database to a disk in drive A." This will copy some files onto your disk, and then display the Login window.

→ If you're in a computer lab and e-Course is not on the Programs menu, ask your technical support person how to start the e-Course software. If you're using your own computer, you must install the e-Course software before you use it. Refer to the TechTalk section of this WorkText.

The first time you log in, e-Course asks you to enter your name and other information that automatically appears on your CheckPoint Reports. This information is stored on your Tracking Disk, so you won't have to enter it the next time you log in.

To log in the first time:

1: On the Login screen, fill in the blanks with your **first name**, **last name**, **course section**, and **student number**. If you don't know your course section or student number, just type anything—you can change it later.

2: Click the **OK** button. In a few seconds, you should see the e-Course Welcome screen.

At the e-Course Welcome screen, you can print your Task Reference. The Task Reference will help refresh your memory about how to do the tasks you learn in the tutorials.

To print the Task Reference:

1: Click **Task Reference** on the Welcome screen menu bar.

2: Click **View/Print Task Reference**.

3: After the Task Reference appears, click **File** on the menu bar, and then click **Print**.

4: When the printout is complete, click **File** again, and then click **Exit**.

e-Course is easy to use. After the short e-Course Introductory Tour, you'll be ready to use all the e-Course features.

To start the e-Course Introductory Tour:

1: Click the **Introductory Tour** button on the Welcome screen.

2: Follow the instructions on the screen to navigate through the tour.

When you've finished the Introductory Tour, it's time to get started on Tutorial 1!

To start Tutorial 1:

1: Click **Tutorials** on the menu bar at the top of the Welcome screen.

2: Point to **Tutorial 1**.

3: Click a topic—you should begin with Topic 1.

Review Questions

Fill in the blank with the correct word or phrase.

1   Access is a relational _____ management system used to manage data.

2   A(n) _____ box is a special window in which you make choices for a task you need to complete.

3   You first need to _____ an existing database before you can work with it.

4   Data in a database is stored in _____.

5   A(n) _____ appears when you right-click a table name.

6   A(n) _____ contains data about one person, place, object, event, or idea.

7   Columns of data in a database are referred to as _____.

8   A(n) _____ presents a customized view of data from a database.

9   You use _____ buttons to change the current record to look at a different record on a form.

10 When you update a database, you _____, change, and delete the data.

11 A pencil symbol in a record selector shows a record being edited but not yet _____ to the database.

12 Access _____ an open database to your disk automatically.

13 You can use the Print _____ feature of Access to review what will print before you print it.

review questions

MULTIPLE CHOICE

*Select the letter of the **one** best answer.*

---

14 Microsoft Access is a:

  a database

  b database management system

  c table

  d window

---

15 A copy of the database file on disk is transferred into RAM when you _____ a database.

  a close

  b copy

  c open

  d save

---

16 Access databases have the file extension:

  a .doc

  b .exc

  c .mdb

  d .xls

---

17 The _____ window contains tabs for each of the six types of objects in an Access database.

  a Access

  b Database

  c Dialog

  d Table

---

18 Access data is stored in:

  a fields

  b forms

  c records

  d tables

---

19 A row in an Access table is called a(n):

  a event

  b field

  c record

  d selector

---

20 The _____ appear to the left of each record in an Access table.

  a current records

  b fields

  c record selectors

  d shortcuts

---

21 A column in an Access table is called a:

  a characteristic

  b field

  c record

  d selector

review questions

22 You can customize your view of data from an Access database with a:

a form

b navigator

c table

d window

23 Access has a navigation button to change to the _____ record.

a current

b minimum

c previous

d selector

24 Suppose a field has a value of $1,874. Using the fewest keystrokes, you'd enter the value as:

a $1,874

b $1,874

c 1,874

d 1874

25 To move from record to record on a form, you use the:

a dialog boxes

b field names

c navigation buttons

d record selectors

26 Updating a database involves all the following except:

a adding records

b changing records

c deleting records

d opening records

27 The next record available for a new record is identified by a _____ symbol in its record selector.

a caret

c solid, right-pointing-triangle

b pencil

d star

28 **The current record is identified by a _____ symbol in its record selector.**

   a caret

   b pencil

   c solid, right-pointing-triangle

   d star

MATCHING

Select a letter from the right column that correctly matches each item in the left column.

29   **a** a collection of data

30   **b** a column in a table

31   **c** a screen object you can use to work with one record at a time

32   **d** a menu of options that appears when you right-click an object

33   **e** another name for an open table

34   **f** a row in a table

35 **database**   **g** copy a database into RAM

36 **datasheet**   **h** data appears in a row-and-column format

37 **field**   **i** the current record symbol

38 **form**   **j** the first record button

39 **open**   **k** the next new record button

40 **record**   **l** Open Database button

41 **shortcut**   **m** the previous record button

42 **table**   **n** the record edited but not yet saved symbol

review questions

Use a separate sheet of paper to write out your answers to the following questions.

43 Describe how you move a dialog box.

44 Explain what happens when you open a database.

45 Explain the difference between a field and a record in a database table.

46 What's the purpose of the navigation buttons? What information is provided by the two numbers that are associated with the navigation buttons?

47 Which three actions can you take when you update the data in a database to keep it current and accurate?

48 What purposes are served by the record selectors?

49 When is an Access database saved?

50 Describe the process used to delete a record from a table.

Projects

These Projects are designed to help you review and develop the skills you learned in the online Steps of Tutorial 1. Complete each Project using Microsoft Access. *If you have not yet made the Project Disk for Tutorial 1, start the e-Course software, click the Project Disk menu, and follow the instructions on the screen.*

If you've forgotten some of the skills you need to complete the Projects, refer to the Task Reference.

REVIEW SKILLS

1   Inside Concerts   File: Arena.mdb

In the online Steps, you used the Concerts database to learn how to open and close a database and how to open, navigate, update, print, and close a table. In this Project, you'll review these skills using the Arena database, which is similar to the Concerts database.

Open the Arena database from your Project Disk.

Add a new record to the Arena Concert table with the following values:

Concert	Performer	Gross Sales	Promoter	Tickets Sold
72	Wilco	$210,250	1	9,870

Delete the Phil Collins concert.

Write down the number of records in the Arena Concert table and the record number for the R.E.M. concert.

Print the entire Arena Concert table. At the top of your printout, write your name, the number of records in the Arena Concert table, and the record number for the R.E.M. concert.

projects

2 Promote That Concert   File: Arena.mdb

In the online Steps, you used the Concerts database to learn how to open and close a database and how to open, navigate, update, print, and close a table. In this Project, you'll review these skills using the Arena database, which is similar to the Concerts database.

Open the Arena database from your Project Disk.

Add a new record to the Promoter table with the following values:

Promoter	Promoter Name	Artist Holds
8	Count Your Stars	50

For Promoter 4, change the Promoter Name to Book Kings Institute and the Artist Holds to 60.

Write down the number of records in the Promoter table and the record number for Count Your Stars.

Print the entire Promoter table. At the top of your printout, write your name, the number of records in the Promoter table, and the record number for Count Your Stars.

3 Form an Opinion   File: Arena.mdb

In the online Steps, you used the Concerts database to learn how to open and close a database and how to open, navigate, and close a form. In this Project, you'll review these skills using the Arena database, which is similar to the Concerts database.

Open the Arena database from your Project Disk.

Open the Arena Concert Data form and use the information you find in this form to answer the following questions:

a   What's the record number for the last record?

b   What's the name of the performer in the third record?

c   What's the record number for Nine Inch Nails?

d   How many tickets were sold for the second concert?

4 According to Form   File: Arena.mdb

In the online Steps, you used the Concerts database to learn how to open and close a database and how to open, navigate, and close a form. In this Project, you'll review these skills using the Arena database, which is similar to the Concerts database.

Open the Arena database from your Project Disk.

Open the Promoter Data form and use the information you find in this form to answer the following questions.

a What's the record number for the last record?

b What's the name of the promoter in the third record?

c What's the record number for Myridian Limited?

d What's the number of the promoter with the highest value for the Artist Holds field?

5 Promoters and their Concerts   File: Arena.mdb

In the online Steps, you used the Concerts database to learn how to open and close a database and how to open, navigate, and close a form. In this Project, you'll review these skills using the Arena database, which is similar to the Concerts database.

Open the Arena database from your Project Disk.

Open the form named Promoters and their Concerts. The form contains two sets of navigation buttons. Experiment with the buttons.

a Write a description of the purpose of each set.

b For the promoter named Myridian Limited, how many concerts did it promote and who's the performer for its last concert record?

APPLY SKILLS

6 It's Your Witness   File: Experts.mdb

Trials in the news the past few years have made household names out of many defendants, lawyers, and witnesses. Did you ever wonder how the prosecution and defense find the expert witnesses they use for testimony about subjects such as DNA, mental disorders, and fingerprinting? Each law firm keeps a database about expert witnesses. The Experts database is an example of such a database.

projects

Open the Experts database from your Project Disk and then answer the following questions:

   a   How many tables are in the Experts database?

   b   How many records are in the Witnesses table?

   c   How many fields are there in the Witnesses table?

   d   What's the value of the Expertise field for the 17th record?

   e   How many of witnesses are doctors?

7   Getting High   File: Hipoints.mdb

The Highpointers Club supports its members' interest in getting to the highest point in each of the U.S. states. Fifty-one individuals have achieved the goal of standing atop the highest point in each of the 50 states. The Hipoints database keeps track of the progress of each Highpointers Club member.

Open the Hipoints database from your Project Disk. Add yourself to the Climber table as Climber 1. Then add yourself to the Climbs table, using any state and today's date for the other field values. Print the Climber table, and then close the Hipoints database.

8   House Keeping   File: Homes.mdb

Real estate agencies in the same area usually share listings of homes for sale. This increases the pool of agents who can find a buyer for your home. The Homes database contains listings of homes for sale.

Open the Homes database from your Project Disk. Add your home to the Listed Homes table, using a value of AW3375 for the Listing field and $150,000 for the Asking Price field. Delete the record for the city of Borculo, and then print the table.

9   String Along   File: Guitars.mdb

Are you interested in buying a vintage guitar? Then the Guitars database is the place to find your dream guitar.

Open the Guitars database from your Project Disk. For record 11 in the Vintage Guitars table, change the model to Stratocaster, the year to 1973, and the price to Ask.

In the last record, type your name in the Model field.

When you've finished updating, print the Vintage Guitars table, and then close the Guitars database.

projects

10 Filling a Table   File: Books.mdb

So far, when you've opened tables in databases, they've already had one or more records. Now is your chance to enter records in a table that contains no records.

Open the Books database from your Project Disk, and then open the Books Read table. Study the table names so that you understand what values you'll need to enter. Add five books you've read to the Books Read table, and then print the table.

BUILD SKILLS

11 Taped Reminders   File: Tapes.mdb

Do you use your VCR to tape TV programs? Do you have dozens of tapes and have trouble finding which tape has the program you'd like to watch again? If so, then the Tapes database is an example of a simple way for you to keep track of your collection.

Open the Tapes database from your Project Disk.

Add a new tape to the Taped Programs table. The tape should have a Tape# value between 10 and 19 and should contain three taped shows, one show per new record.

Print the Taped Programs table, close the table, reopen the table, and then print the table a second time.

Notice that the records for your tape are located in different positions on the two printouts.

a Describe where your three records appear in the second printout compared to the other records in the table.

b If you can, explain why the records appear where they do.

12 More Ways to Fix Mistakes   File: Celebs.mdb

In the online Steps, you learned how to correct simple mistakes when entering or correcting field values. Now you'll work with other Access features for correcting mistakes.

Open the Celebs database from your Project Disk, and then open the Celebrity table. Look at the fields and records in the table.

a Notice the ⟲ Undo button on the toolbar, and then write down the first option on the Edit menu. What do you notice about the button and the option?

projects

b For the Celebrity field value in the second record, click between the letters "l" and "t," and then press the Delete key. What's the first option on the Edit menu? What's different about the appearance of both this option and the Undo button?

c Click the Undo button. What happened to the Celebrity field value?

d Click the Undo button. What's the first option on the Edit menu? Describe the appearance of this option, the Undo button, and the Celebrity field value.

e Press the Delete key. What's the first option on the Edit menu? Describe the appearance of this option, the Undo button, and the Celebrity field value.

f Press the Enter key. What's the first option on the Edit menu? Describe the appearance of this option, the Undo button, and the Impersonator ID field value.

g Click the Undo button. What's the first option on the Edit menu? Describe the appearance of this option and the Undo button. What has happened to the field values for the second record?

13 Using a Form for Updating   File: Events.mdb

In the online Steps, you learned how to update a database using a table. Now you'll use a form for updating.

Open the Events database from your Project Disk, and then open the Event Calendar Data form. Look at the fields and records in the table.

To use a form to update a database:

1: Click the 🗗 **Restore** button on the menu bar, so that the form is restored but the Access window is maximized.

2: Add a record with the following values for the first three fields:

Celebration:	National Honesty Day
Month When:	April
Day When:	30

a When the insertion point is in the Event field and you press the Enter key, what happens? Make sure you change back to the new record before completing your answer.

3: Add a second record with the following values for the first three fields:

Celebration: National [insert your name here] Month

Month When: [use the current month]

Day When: [leave blank]

4: Delete the record for National Puzzle Day, record 3. (Hint: Where is the current record symbol located?)

5: Use the Event Calendar table to print the data.

14 Orienting Your Printing   File: Contents.mdb

Some paintings and pictures are taller than they are wide, and others are wider than they are tall. Because people often appear in the former and outdoor scenes in the latter, they are called portrait and landscape, respectively. The Page Setup option on the File menu offers these two orientations for printing your data. In this Project, you'll learn how to select these orientations.

Open the Contents database from your Project Disk, and then open the Household Inventory Items table. Use Print Preview to review the table; be sure you notice the number of pages. Select the Page Setup option on the File menu. Look at the default orientation for the page, change to the other page orientation choice, and then print the table on one page.

15 Sizing Table Columns   File: Property.mdb

You need to change the width of a column for a field in a table whenever you can't see the entire field name or value. You can change the width of a single column or multiple columns at a time. In this Project, you'll learn how to change the width of table columns.

Open the Property database from your Project Disk, and then open the Property table. Look at the fields and records in the table.

Similar to the record selectors to the left of each record, there are field (column) selectors at the top of each field. The field selectors contain the field names. Position the pointer at the right edge of the field selector for the second field. When the pointer changes to ✛, double-click.

   a Write down what happened.

Position the pointer at the right edge of the field selector for the first field. When the pointer changes to ✛, drag to the right until the column is sized to your liking.

Position the pointer in the field selector for the third field. When the pointer changes to ⬇, drag to the right until the pointer is in the field selector for the fourth field.

b Write down what happened.

Position the pointer at the right edge of the field selector for the fourth field. When the pointer changes to ✛, double-click.

c Write down what happened.

Select all six columns, and then resize them all at once by double-clicking the right edge of the field selector for the sixth field. Then print the table.

Write a one-page report that describes the different ways to change the width of table columns.

EXPLORE

16 Sample Database File: Northwind.mdb or Nwind.mdb

Microsoft Access comes with sample databases you can use to explore many of Access's features. In this Project, you'll explore one of these sample databases.

Open the Northwind (or Nwind) database; your instructor will tell you where you can find it. If a splash screen appears, click the OK button.

a Open the Orders table, and write down the number of records and fields in this table.

b After closing the Orders table, change the Database window to its restored size, if necessary. You can best appreciate the forms you'll view if they're restored size. Then open the Categories form. Use the scroll bars and navigation buttons to view all the records. Record a short description of all the new features you see on this form.

c Open the Customer Phone List form. Record a short description of all the new features you see on this form.

d In a similar fashion, carefully study the Customers, Employees, and Products forms.

e Write a one-page paper describing the results from your work with the Northwind (or Nwind) database.

17 Access Help Topics

Access has a standard Windows online Help facility. In this Project, you'll explore the Help facility's Contents feature.

a Click Help on the menu bar, and then click Contents and Index. Click the Contents tab, double-click "Getting Help," and then double-click "Ways to get assistance while you work." Study the screen, click each of the five labels, and read the displayed information. Write out the names on each of the five labels and a short description of what you learned from reading the displayed information. Then close the Help window.

b Click Help on the menu bar, click Contents and Index, and then double click "Introduction to Microsoft Access 97." Double-click the topic "Databases: What they are and how they work," and review the material. Click the numbers beneath the title bar to navigate through all the screens for the topic, and then click the Help Topics button to return to the Contents tab to make another selection. Double-click "Tables," and then repeat the above process to review the topics "Tables: What they are and how they work" and "Ways to work with data in a table's datasheet." Double-click "Forms" and repeat the above process to review the topic "Forms: What they are and how they work." Write a short description of what you learned about each of the four choices.

18 Help: Office Assistant

Access's online Help facility provides how-to information about Access features and procedures. One of the most popular ways to access the Help facility is to use an "agent," such as the Office Assistant. To use one of these help agents, you simply type a question. The agent looks through the Help facility, and then shows you a list of topics likely to contain relevant information. You can look at one or more of these topics until you find the information you need. In this Project, you'll use a help agent to learn how to print a form.

To use Access's Help agent:

1: Click **Help** on the menu bar.

2: Click **Microsoft Access Help**.

3: Type **How do I print?**, and then click the **Search** button.

4: Click **Print a form**.

projects

5: In turn, click each of the first five buttons, read each explanation, and then click the **Back** button to return to the selection screen.

Write a one-page paper describing the options available for printing a form.

19 What's This? Tips   File: Arena.mdb

If you have a question about a particular window component or menu option, Access can provide context-sensitive help, which is help about the specific component or option you click. In this Project, you'll explore the What's This? feature.

Open the Arena database from your Project Disk.

To display a What's This? Tip:

1: Click **Help** on the menu bar and then click **What's This?**.

2: Position the pointer on a button, option, or other screen component, and then click.

3: Read the displayed information, and then click anywhere on the screen to remove the information box.

Now that you know how to display a What's This? Tip, use that technique to answer the following questions:

    a   What is the description that appears for the Open Database button?

    b   What is the description that appears for the Print Preview button?

    c   What is the description that appears for the Tables tab?

    d   What is the description that appears for the Print Preview option on the File menu?

20 Compact a Database   File: Records.mdb

Whenever you delete a record or an object, such as a form or report, in an Access database, the space occupied by the deleted material is not automatically made available. Thus, over time your database will grow in size as you use it. In fact, the act of opening a database can cause the database to grow.

You compact a database to make it smaller, thereby making more space available on your disk. When you compact a database, it must not be open.

To compact a database:

1: If you're not already in Access, start Access, and then click the **Cancel** button on the initial dialog box.

2: Click **Tools** on the menu bar, point to **Database Utilities**, and then click **Compact Database**. The Database to Compact From dialog box appears.

3: Click ▼ on the *Look in* box, click the drive that contains your Project Disk and, if necessary, double-click the folder name. Click **Records.mdb**, and then click the **Compact** button.

4: Although you can compact a database upon itself, it is safer to compact to a new database. You specify a name for the new database in the Compact Database Into dialog box. Type **NewRecords.mdb** in the *File name* box, and then click the **Save** button.

5: The database is now compacted. Exit Access.

Now you'll delete the original (uncompacted) version of the database and then rename the compacted version. You'll do this in Windows Explorer.

To delete the old database and rename the new database:

1: Click the **Start** button on the taskbar, point to **Programs**, and then click **Windows Explorer** on the menu that appears.

2: Scrolling as needed, click the drive or folder containing your Project Disk in the All Folders pane in the left portion of the screen. The contents of the highlighted drive or folder are displayed in the Contents pane in the right portion of the screen. Both the Records and the NewRecords databases appear in the Contents pane file list. Make a note of the size of both databases (size is listed in the Size column of the Contents pane). Right-click **Records** in the file list, and then click **Delete** on the shortcut menu that appears. Answer **Yes** when asked to confirm the delete operation.

3: Right-click **NewRecords** in the file list, and then click **Rename** on the shortcut menu.

4: Click **NewRecords** to remove the highlight and position the insertion point, edit the name to delete the letters "New", and then press the **Enter** key. The name of the compacted version of the database is now changed to Records.

5: Exit Windows Explorer.

   a What was the size of the original (uncompacted) database?

   b What is the size of the compacted version of the database?

projects

21 Tracking Databases

You often find databases mentioned in newspapers, magazines, and books. In this Project, you'll look for discussions, descriptions, or illustrations of databases in current books and issues of newspapers and magazines. (You might find that terms such as data banks, warehouses, and records are used synonymously with database.) Find seven references to databases, and then write a paper that includes the following information. Your instructor will provide you with the length and format requirements.

    a Describe each mention of database you found.

    b Evaluate the material you found about databases. Some issues you might want to consider: Do databases get mentioned more often in favorable or unfavorable situations? Did you find that databases are mentioned in one circumstance more than others? How prominent a role did databases play in the material you found?

22 Database Management System Models

In the online Steps, you learned that Access is a relational database management system that helps you manage data. The word "relational" applies to one of the models, or classifications, associated with database management systems. In this Project, you'll investigate the relational model and compare it to the other models.

Using the resources in your library and/or on the Internet, determine the characteristics of the relational, object-oriented, network or CODASYL, and hierarchical models. How do they differ? What are their advantages and disadvantages? Which ones are widely used today, and which have more of an historical significance?

After you have completed your research, write a paper that presents your information. Your instructor will provide you with specifications for length and format.

23 The Beginnings of Database Management Systems

The first commercial database management system (DBMS), the Generalized Update Access Method (GUAM), was developed by IBM in 1964 to help support the U.S. space program. In the late 1960s, businesses began to use DBMSs for the first time. In this Project, you'll investigate the early days of DBMS development.

projects

Using the resources in your library and/or on the Internet, trace the history of DBMS software from the early 1960s to the early 1970s. Find out which companies and individuals were the major DBMS software developers. What were the names of their products? How were the products classified (for example, hierarchical and network)? What features did the products have? What problems did the products have?

After you have completed your research, write a paper that presents your information. Your instructor will provide you with specifications for length and format.

24 Interview Database Management System Users

Businesses and individuals use database management systems (DBMSs) in a wide variety of applications. In this Project, you'll investigate the databases people use at home or for business.

a Prepare a short list of questions (five to seven questions) to ask about the databases and specific DBMS your interviewee uses. The questions should help you to determine the specific DBMS used, why it was chosen, which features the individual likes best or uses most often, and how well it satisfies the individual's needs. The questions should also help you to find out which databases the individual uses and how important they are to the individual.

b Use your list of questions to interview two people who own or use computer databases.

c Write a report describing your results and conclusions. Include a list of the questions you used and your notes from the interviews. Your instructor will provide you with length and format specifications.

projects

25 Other Database Management Systems

Access is not the only database management system (DBMS) you can use to help manage your data. In this Project, you'll investigate other available DBMSs.

a Look through computer magazine ads, visit computer stores, and/or search the Internet to locate sales and comparison information about Access and four other DBMSs.

b Write a report that compares the prices, claims, and features for these five DBMS products. Your instructor will provide you with the length and format specifications for this report.

Microsoft Access

Tutorial 2: Finding Information in a Database

Finding Information in a Database

WHAT'S INSIDE

Traveler's Check

Check out everything you can about another country before you travel to it. It will certainly make your trip more enjoyable and might help prevent you having stories to later tell friends about your "travel nightmares." You can check out all the different ways you can get the travel information you need by using an Access database. In this tutorial, you'll learn how to use queries to find information from an Access database.

Projects

Tutorial 2 Projects include planning your X-Files purchases, joining a group of impersonators, learning about North America, and taxing your brain cells.

If you're not assigned Projects 11, 14, 16, 17, and 20, you might want to at least read these Projects or, better yet, work through them. In Project 11, you'll learn how to sort query results using multiple fields. Project 14 deals with finding data in a table. In Project 16, you'll learn how to use multiple conditions in a query. Project 17 shows you how to update data using a query. And Project 20 shows you how to perform record calculations.

WHAT'S ONLINE

1 Query by Example
- Select the Table for a Query
- The Query Window
- Add All Fields to a Query
- Run a Query
- Remove Fields From a Query
- Specify a Condition in a Query
- Save a Query
- Close a Query

2 Sort Query Results
- Run a Saved Query
- Sort Data
- Save a Query With a New Name

3 Omit Duplicates
- Use the Simple Query Wizard
- Omit Duplicates
- Save Changes to a Query

4 Query on Calculated Fields
- Calculated Fields
- Create a Calculated Field
- Resize a Column
- Change a Field's Properties

5 Join Tables
- Databases and Relationships
- Join Tables
- Create a Two-Table Query

Traveler's Check

Traveling to another country can be exciting and can improve your understanding of other cultures. But you want to be sure to do a "traveler's check"—plan carefully for your trip to get the most out of it. As part of your planning, you need to find answers to many questions. How far away is the country? How big is the country? What's its population? What continent or region is it part of? What currency is used there? Are the exchange rates favorable for a trip at this time? Do you need special visas to enter the country? Do you need specific shots to protect yourself against local diseases? Getting the right answers to some of these questions could save you a lot of time and money, not to mention aggravation. For example, it would be a major inconvenience to travel to New Zealand in December not knowing that December is a summer month "down under." Having this information would make a major impact on the seasonal pricing and occupancy rates for hotels, the particular towns and cities you visit, the activities you plan, and even the clothes you pack!

You could buy the usual guide books and spend time reading and researching your destination. But this would take a lot of time and flipping from here to there to find the answers to your specific questions. If, however, data about your destination country is stored in a database, you could save a lot of time and money by *querying* this database—in other words "asking" this database questions and having it retrieve the information you need. To do this you'd use what's called the database's **query feature** to ask a question. Then, with a click of a button, you'd have the answer. In Tutorial 2, you'll learn how use the query feature of Access. So let's get "checking."

Review Questions

Fill in the blank with the correct word or phrase.

1   A(n) _____ is a question you ask about data stored in a database.

2   To start a new query, you can hold down the _____ key while pressing the letter N.

3   You use the Query window in _____ view to create a query.

4   The _____ is a window that lists all the fields in a table.

5   To display the answer to a query, you _____ the query.

6   Uncheck a field's _____ box to keep it in the query but stop it from appearing in the query results.

7   To indicate in a query which records you want to select, you specify a(n) _____.

8   _____ is the process of rearranging records in a specified order.

9   Records are sorted by decreasing field value when you choose _____ sort sequence for a field.

10 The Simple Query _____ prompts you through the steps to create a query.

11 The Query Properties dialog box is also called the _____.

12 When setting the Unique Values property for a query, you choose one value from a list of _____ possible values.

review questions

13 A calculated field appears in a(n) _____ datasheet but does not exist in a database.

14 A(n) _____ is a characteristic of an object that you can set.

15 Format and Decimal Places are examples of _____ that you can set for a field.

16 A common field establishes a(n) _____ between two tables.

17 In a one-to-many relationship, one table is called the _____ table and the other table is called the related table.

18 The process of relating tables is called performing a(n) _____.

MULTIPLE CHOICE

*Select the letter of the **one** best answer.*

---

19 **A query is a(n):**

  a answer

  b condition

  c question

  d window

---

20 **To start a new query, you can hold down the _____ key while pressing the letter N.**

  a Alt

  b Ctrl

  c Esc

  d Tab

---

21 **To create a query, you use the Query window in _____ view.**

  a datasheet

  b design

  c example

  d field

22 To select a column in the query results, you click the field _____ for the field.

   a button

   b grid

   c property

   d selector

23 _____ is an example of a condition.

   a >864

   b 86>4

   c 864>

   d none of the above

24 Unique Values is a property for a:

   a field

   b query

   c relationship

   d sort

25 _____ is an example of a calculation, where Length and Width are two fields from a database.

   a Length*Width

   b (Length)*(Width)

   c [Length]*[Width]

   d {Length}*{Width}

26 You use a(n) _____ to separate the field name from the calculation for a calculated field.

   a bracket

   b equal sign

   c colon

   d slash

27 To resize a column, you position the pointer on the _____ edge of the field selector.

  a bottom

  b left

  c right

  d top

28 Standard is one of the settings you can choose for a field's _____ property.

  a Decimal Places

  b Format

  c Join

  d Unique Values

29 You can resize a _____ to its best fit.

  a calculation

  b column

  c condition

  d criterion

30 Yes and No are the settings you can choose for a field's _____ property.

  a Decimal Places

  b Format

  c Join

  d Unique Values

31 A _____ field establishes a relationship between two tables.

  a common

  b primary

  c query

  d related

32 In a one-to-many relationship, one record in the _____ table matches many records in the other table.

   a common

   b primary

   c query

   d related

33 In a one-to-many relationship, one record in the _____ table matches one record in the other table.

   a common

   b primary

   c query

   d related

MATCHING

Select the letter from the right column that correctly matches each item in the left column.

34	**Ascending**	**a**	a characteristic
35	**Condition**	**b**	answer a query
36	**Design grid**	**c**	a question
37	**Field list**	**d**	a relationship type
38	**One-to-many**	**e**	a rule
39	**Property**	**f**	a sequence type
40	**Query**	**g**	a window
41	**Run**	**h**	option for displaying a field
42	**Show box**	**i**	where selected fields for a query are placed

review questions

Use a separate sheet of paper to write out your answers to the following questions.

43 Describe the relationship between the field list and design grid In the Query window in Design view.

44 How do the query and table datasheets differ?

45 What two methods can you use to remove fields from a query?

46 When would you want to omit duplicate records from the query results?

47 Describe a one-to-many relationship between two tables.

Projects

hese Projects are designed to help you review and develop the skills you learned in Tutorial 2. Complete each Project using Microsoft Access. *If you have not yet made the Project Disk for Tutorial 2, start the e-Course software, click the Project Disk menu, and follow the instructions on the screen.*

If you've forgotten some of the skills you need to complete the Projects, refer to the Task Reference.

REVIEW SKILLS

1   Travel On   File: Vacation.mdb

In the online Steps, you used the Travel database to learn how to create queries. In this Project, you'll review some of these skills using the Vacation database, which is similar to the Travel database.

Open the Vacation database from your Project Disk. Create a query that includes the Country, Capital, and Currency fields from the Country table. Sort the query in ascending order by the Capital field, run the query, and then print the query. Save the query with the name World Capitals, and then close the Vacation database.

2   Location, Location, Location   File: Vacation.mdb

In the online Steps, you used the Travel database to learn how to create queries and to sort and omit duplicate records in your query results. In this Project, you'll review these skills using the Vacation database, which is similar to the Travel database.

Open the Vacation database from your Project Disk.

   a Create a query that includes the Location field from the Country table; and then run the query. How many records appear in the query results?

   b Modify the design of the query to omit duplicates, and then run the query. How many records appear in this query's results?

Save the query with the name Unique Locations, print the query, and then close the Vacation database.

projects

3   It's a Small World   File: Vacation.mdb

In the online Steps, you used the Travel database to learn how to create queries and
to sort your query results. In this Project, you'll review these skills using the
Vacation database, which is similar to the Travel database.

Open the Vacation database from your Project Disk. Create a query that includes
the Country, Land Area, and Timezone fields from the Country table. Sort the
query in descending order by the Land Area field, and select those records whose
land area is less than 100,000. Run the query, save the query with the name Smaller
Countries, and then print the query. Close the query and then close the Vacation
database.

4   Together Again   File: Vacation.mdb

In the online Steps, you used the Travel database to learn how to create queries,
join together two tables, and sort your query results. In this Project, you'll review
these skills using the Vacation database, which is similar to the Travel database.

Open the Vacation database from your Project Disk. Create a join between the
Location table (the primary table) and the Country table (the related table) using the
Location field as the common field.

Create a query that includes, in order, the Location Name field from the
Location table, and the Country and Timezone fields from the Country table. Sort
the query in descending order by the Timezone field, and then run the query.

Save the query with the name Countries by Timezone, and then print the query.
Close the query, and then close the Vacation database.

5   Foreign Exchange   File: Vacation.mdb

In the online Steps, you used the Travel database to learn how to create queries,
join together two tables, use a calculated field, and sort your query results. In this
Project, you'll review these skills using the Vacation database, which is similar to
the Travel database.

Open the Vacation database from your Project Disk. Create a join between the
Exchange Rate table (the primary table) and the Country table (the related table),
using the Currency field as the common field.

Create a query that includes, in order, the Country field from the Country table
and the US Dollar Equivalent field from the Exchange Rate table.

Add a calculated field named Dollars for 1000 Units, which is the result of multiplying 1000 by the US Dollar Equivalent field. Keep the US Dollar Equivalent field in the query, but remove it from the query results.

Sort the query in ascending order by the calculated field, run the query, and then resize the column for the calculated field.

Save the query with the name Cost for 1000 Foreign Units, and then print the query. Close the query, and then close the Vacation database.

APPLY SKILLS

6   Trust No One   File: Xfiles.mdb

Watch your favorite TV show wearing an X-Files T-shirt and cap and drinking from an X-Files mug. You can buy X-Files merchandise that includes posters, autographs, trading cards, pins, caps, mugs, and T-shirts. A mail-order firm uses the Xfiles database to keep track of all the X-Files merchandise it sells.

Open the Xfiles database from your Project Disk. Create a query that includes all the fields from the X-Files Merchandise table. Sort the query in ascending order by the Type field, and then run the query. Save the query with the name X-Files by Type, and then print the query. Close the query, and then close the Xfiles database.

7   Divide and Conquer   File: Arena.mdb

You have a choice of the price you can pay for most concert tickets, depending on where you'd like to sit and how much money you want to spend. The gross ticket sales and the number of tickets sold determine the average price per ticket. In this Project, you'll display a calculated average price per ticket.

Open the Arena database from your Project Disk. Create a query that includes all the fields from the Arena Concert table. Add a calculated field named Price Per Ticket, which is the result of dividing the Gross Sales field by the Tickets Sold field. Change the calculated field's Format property to Standard and its Decimal Places property to 2.

Sort the query in descending order by the calculated field, and then run the query.

Save the query with the name Concerts by Average Price per Ticket, and then print the query. Close the query, and then close the Arena database.

projects

8 Show Off   File: Reading.mdb

In the online Steps, you learned how to create queries, remove a field from the query results, and select records based on a condition. In this Project, you'll review these skills.

Open the Reading database from your Project Disk. Create a query that includes all the fields from the Books Read table. Keep the first field, which has a name of Type-F(iction) or N(on Fiction), in the query but remove it from the query results. Select only those records having "F" as a value for the Type-F(iction) or N(on Fiction) field.

Sort the query in ascending order by the Author field, and then run the query.

Save the query with the name Books Read by Author, and then print the query. Close the query, and then close the Reading database.

9 A Little Bit of Country   File: Namerica.mdb

In the online Steps you learned how to create queries and to omit duplicate records in your query results. In this Project, you'll review these skills.

Open the Namerica database from your Project Disk.

a Create a query that includes the Country field from the State/Province table, and then run the query. How many records appear in the query results?

b Modify the design of the query to omit duplicates, and then run the query. How many records appear in the query results?

Save the query with the name Unique Countries, and then print the query. Close the query, and then close the Namerica database.

10 Star Gazing   File: Celebs.mdb

Can you impersonate a famous celebrity? If so, you can "join" the Celebs database, which contains people who have similar talents. In this Project, you'll join together three tables and create a query using fields from all three tables.

Open the Celebs database from your Project Disk. Create a join between the Availability table (the primary table) and the Impersonator table (the related table), using the Avail Code field as the common field. Then create a join between the Impersonator table (the primary table) and the Celebrity table (the related table), using the ID field from the Impersonator table and the Impersonator ID field from the Celebrity table as the common field.

Create a query that includes, in order, the Celebrity and Type fields from the Celebrity table, the Name field from the Impersonator table, and the Availability field from the Availability table. Sort the query in descending order by the Celebrity field, and then run the query.

Save the query with the name Celebrity Impersonators, and then print the query. Close the query, and then close the Celebs database.

BUILD SKILLS

11 Sort Multiple Fields   File: Events.mdb

At times you'd like to be able to sort on two or more fields. For example, the Event Calendar table in the Events database has a month column and a separate day column. To display events by date, you have to sort first on the month column and then on the day column. In this Project, you'll create a query and perform this multiple-field sort.

Open the Events database from your Project Disk. Create a query that includes, in order, the Celebration, Month When, and Day When fields from the Event Calendar table.

To specify a multiple-field sort:

1: Sort the query in ascending order by the Month When field and then by the Day When field.

Run the query, save the query with the name Celebrations by Date, and then print the query. Close the query, and then close the Events database.

a   Write a brief description and explanation of the order of the sorted records.

12 Sort a Table   File: Tapes.mdb

In the online Steps, you learned how to sort a query datasheet. You can also sort a table datasheet and, in this Project, you'll learn how to do this.

Open the Tapes database from your Project Disk, open the Taped Programs table, and then print the Taped Programs table.

To sort a table datasheet:

1: Sort the table in ascending order by the Program field. (Hint: Position the insertion point in one of the values for the Program field, and then click the Sort Ascending button on the toolbar.)

projects

Print the table a second time. Close the table, but do not save your table changes when prompted. Then close the Tapes database.

a On the sorted print of the table, explain when you would choose to sort a table instead of creating a query that includes a sort.

13 Use Filters   File: Contents.mdb

Queries allow you to display selected fields and selected records. If you want to look at all the fields in a table but only selected records, you can use a filter instead of a query. In this Project, you'll learn how to use filters.

Open the Contents database from your Project Disk, and then open the Household Inventory Items table. Use landscape orientation to print the Household Inventory Items table. (Hint: Use the Page Setup option on the File menu.) Now you are ready to use filters.

To use a filter:

1: Highlight **1996** for any appropriate Purchase Date field value, click the [icon] **Filter By Selection** button on the toolbar, and then print the results.

2: Click the [icon] **Remove Filter** button on the toolbar.

3: Highlight any **Garage** field value in the Room column, click the [icon] **Filter By Selection** button on the toolbar, and then print the results.

4: Click the [icon] **Remove Filter** button on the toolbar.

5: Click the [icon] **Filter By Form** button on the toolbar to display a blank datasheet in which you specify conditions for selecting records.

6: Click the white box in the Value column, type **>=40**, press the **Tab** key, click [icon] in the Room column, click **Kitchen**, click the [icon] **Apply Filter** button on the toolbar, and then print the results.

a Which records appear?

7: Click the [icon] **Filter By Form** button, select **"Kitchen"** in the Room column, and then press the **Delete** key.

8: Click the **Or** tab near the bottom of the window, click [icon] in the Room column, click **Kitchen**, click the [icon] **Apply Filter** button on the toolbar, and then print the results.

b Which records appear?

Close the table, but do not save your table changes when prompted. Then close the Contents database.

14 Find Specific Values for Specific Fields

File: Homes.mdb

If you're interested in finding table records that have a specific value for a specific field, you can do so while the table is open. In this Project, you'll learn how to find data in a table datasheet. Open the Homes database from your Project Disk, and then open the Listed Homes table.

To find data in a table datasheet:

1: Click the first field value in the City column, and then click the **Find** button on the toolbar.

2: Type **Chester** in the *Find What* box, and then click the **Find First** button.

   a What is the record number of the current record?

3: Click the **Find Next** button.

   b What is the record number of the current record?

4: Click the **Close** button. Close the table, and then close the Homes database.

15 Sort Nonadjacent Fields   File: Experts.mdb

In the online Steps, you rearranged the order of records in a query datasheet based on a single field. In this Project, you'll create a query and perform a multiple-field sort, where the fields used for the sort are not adjacent and are in the wrong order.

Open the Experts database from your Project Disk.

To sort nonadjacent and/or out of order fields:

1: Create a query that includes, in order, the Expertise, Name, Street, State, City, and State (for the second time) fields from the Witnesses table.

2: Uncheck the *Show* box for the first State field.

3: Sort the query in ascending order by the first State field and then by the City field.

Run the query, save the query with the name Witnesses by Location, and then print the query. Close the query and then close the Experts database.

projects

16 Use Multiple Conditions   File: Property.mdb

In the online Steps, you selected records using a condition in a query. Often you need to select records based on multiple conditions. Sometimes you want records selected if they satisfy either condition, while at other times you want records selected if they satisfy both conditions. In this Project, you'll create a query and use multiple conditions to select records.

Open the Property database from your Project Disk.

To select records based on multiple conditions:

1: Create a query that includes all fields from the Property table.

2: Enter a value of **GE** in the *Criteria* box for the Township field.

3: Enter in the *or* box, just below the *Criteria* box, a value of **1** for the Property Type field.

4: Run the query.

5: Resize to their best fit all fields in the query datasheet.

   a Which records appear?

6: Save the query with the name Multiple Conditions, and then print the query.

7: Switch back to Design view, delete the condition for the Property Type field, and then enter a value of **1** in the *Criteria* box for the Property Type field.

8: Run the query.

   b Which records appear?

9: Print the query, and save it. Close the query, and then close the Property database.

17 Update Data Using a Query   File: Guitars.mdb

Just as you can update data using a table or form, you can update data using a query. In this Project, you'll create a query and use it to update data in a database.

Open the Guitars database from your Project Disk. Create a query that includes, in order, the Brand, Model, Year, and Guitar Id fields from the Vintage Guitars table. Sort the query in ascending order by the Year field, and then run the query.

To update data in a query:

1: Change the Year field value for the Fender Telecaster from 1952 to **1953**.

2: Delete the record for the Gibson J200.

Save the query with the name Vintage Guitars by Year, and then print the query. Close the query, and then close the Guitars database.

18 Compare QBE and SQL   File: Localtax.mdb

In the online Steps, you did your work with queries using query by example (QBE). Another, more standard way to work with queries is Structured Query Language (SQL). In this Project, you'll compare QBE and SQL.

Open the Localtax database from your Project Disk, and then open the query named Tax Roll. Print this query. On the query printout write down the names of the fields involved in the query and the names of the tables the fields come from.

To view the SQL statement:

1: Switch to Design view, click ⏷ on the ▦⏷ **Query View** button, which is the leftmost button on the toolbar, and then click **SQL View**.

2: Deselect the highlighted text.

On that same query printout, write down the SQL statement, which begins with the word "SELECT." Close the query, and then close the Localtax database.

Study the SQL statement, and then write an explanation of how to relate the SQL statement to the QBE form of the query.

19 Group Records and Modify a Query
File: Hipoints.mdb

The officers of the Highpointers Club want to display all climbers and the dates of their first and last climbs to the highest point in each of the U.S. states. They also want to display all climbers in alphabetical order. In this Project, you'll learn how to group data and display minimum and maximum values and how to remove fields from a query.

Open the Hipoints database from your Project Disk. Create a join between the Climber table (the primary table) and the Climbs table (the related table) using the Climber field as the common field.

projects

To group records and display minimum and maximum values:

1: Create a query that includes, in order, the Climber Last Name and Climber First Name fields from the Climber table, the Climb Date field from the Climbs table, and then a second copy of the Climb Date field.

2: Click the Σ **Totals** button on the toolbar.

3: For the first Climb Date field, click the *Total* box, click ▼, and then click **Min**. Repeat for the second Climb Date field, but select **Max** instead.

4: Sort the query in ascending order by the second Climb Date field.

5: Run the query. If any columns need resizing, resize them.

6: Save the query with the name **Climber Start and End Dates**, and then print the query.

Now you'll modify the query to display all climbers in alphabetical order.

To modify a query by removing fields and removing a table:

1: Switch to Design view, delete the two Climb Date fields from the design grid, and then click the Σ **Totals** button on the toolbar.

2: Click the Climbs field list title bar, click **Query** on the menu bar, and then click **Remove Table**.

3: Sort the query in ascending order by the Climber Last Name field and then by the Climber First Name field.

4: Run the query, save the query with the new name of **Climbers in Alphabetical Order**, and then print the query.

5: Close the query, and then close the Hipoints database.

20 Perform Record Calculations and Create a Crosstab Query   File: Funds.mdb

In the online Steps, you learned how to use the fields from a database in an expression for a calculated field, which you then displayed in a query. Often you need to perform calculations, such as sums and averages, on groups of records, or all records, in a query. At other times, you might need to perform calculations in a query on groups of records, or all records, and display the results in a spreadsheet format with row and column headings; such a query is called a *crosstab query*. In this Project, you'll learn how to use both these types of calculations in queries.

projects

Open the Funds database from your Project Disk. Create a query that includes, in order, the Company and One Year fields from the Mutual Fund table, and then the One Year field three additional times.

To use record calculations:

1: Click the Σ **Totals** button on the toolbar.

2: Click the *Total* box for the first One Year field, click ⏷, and then click **Sum**. Repeat for the next three One Year fields; but instead of Sum select, in order, **Avg**, **Min**, and **Max**.

3: Run the query. If any columns need resizing, resize them.

4: Save the query with the name **Company Statistics**, and then print the query.

5: Switch back to Design view, and then delete the Company column from the design grid.

6: Run the query.

7: Save the query with the new name **Overall Statistics**, print the query, and then close the query.

Now you'll create a crosstab query using the Mutual Fund table.

To create a crosstab query:

1: Click the **New** button, click **Crosstab Query Wizard**, and then click the **OK** button.

2: Make sure the Tables option is selected and the Mutual Fund table is highlighted, and then click the **Next** button to move to the next Crosstab Query Wizard dialog box.

3: Click **Category**, click the ▣ button to add the field to the *Selected Fields* box, and then click the **Next** button.

4: Make sure Company is highlighted, and then click the **Next** button.

5: Click **Five Years** in the *Fields* box, click **Max** in the *Functions* box, make sure the "Yes, include row sums" check box is unchecked, click the **Next** button, and then click the **Finish** button.

6: Print the query, close the query, and then close the Funds database.

projects

21 Standard Languages

Structured Query Language (SQL) is a programming language used in relational database management systems. Professional organizations, such as the International Organization for Standardization (IOS), the American National Standards Institute (ANSI), and the Federal Information Processing Standard (FIPS), have adopted SQL as an international and national standard language. The current standard is called SQL2 or SQL/92. Revisions to this standard are underway and, when adopted as the next standard, the new language will be called SQL3. In this Project, you'll investigate standard programming languages and standard human spoken languages.

Using the resources in your library and on the Internet, find two or more other standard programming languages. What programming situations are these programming languages best suited for? What are the advantages and disadvantages of standard programming languages, including SQL? Are most programming languages considered to be standard or non-standard? Are there human spoken languages that are considered to be standard languages? (For example, consider the United Nations and the International Court of Justice, or World Court.) If so, which languages are standard languages, and what are their advantages and disadvantages? Highlight any differences in the advantages and disadvantages between standard programming languages and standard human spoken languages.

After you have completed your research, write a paper that presents your information. Your instructor will provide you with specifications for length and format.

22 SQL

Structured Query Language (SQL) is a programming language used in relational database management systems. Professional organizations, such as the International Organization for Standardization (ISO), the American National Standards Institute (ANSI), and the Federal Information Processing Standard (FIPS), have adopted SQL as an international and national standard language. The current standard is called SQL2 or SQL/92. Revisions to this standard are underway and, when adopted as the next standard, the new language will be called SQL3. In this Project, you'll investigate SQL.

Using the resources in your library and on the Internet, determine the general features and capabilities of the current SQL2 standard. Which are considered to be data definition features, and which are considered to be data manipulation features? Then determine the major new features proposed for SQL3.

After you have completed your research, write a paper that presents your information. Your instructor will provide you with specifications for length and format.

23 Business Interactions on the Web

The World Wide Web (also called the "Web" or "WWW") is being used more and more for business interactions. For example, you can order merchandise and complete surveys over the Web for a growing number of businesses and organizations. Many of these business interactions use databases to retain the data that constitutes the Web transaction. In this Project, you'll investigate the use of databases in these situations.

Using the resources in your library and on the Internet, find at least five examples of Web sites that conduct business on the Web. What are these sites and what are the specifics of their business interactions? Also, determine if there are special precautions, such as security, that these sites must take and if there are specific database management systems that are better suited for handling business on the Web.

After you have completed your research, write a paper that presents your information. Your instructor will provide you with specifications for length and format.

24 Databases on the Web

The World Wide Web (also called the "Web" or "WWW") contains a growing number of databases, data repositories, or information banks. You can find them for movies, music, products such as books and clothing, organizations, and so on. It's usually not possible to determine if a "true" database, which is under the control of a database management system, is involved with the data dispensed from those Web sites. Regardless, many of these Web sites are vast sources of data. In this Project you'll investigate examples of these "databases."

Using the resources in your library and on the Internet, find at least eight Web sites that dispense large quantities of data (including visual data). You might focus on topics that you're familiar with, so that you can better judge their completeness. What are these sites? What types of data do they provide? How complete is the data? How accurate is the data? How easy is it to find specific data? What are your overall impressions about the database and your interaction with it; include both positive and negative impressions.

projects

After you have completed your research, write a paper that presents your information. Your instructor will provide you with specifications for length and format.

25 Secure and Private Databases

You don't want your credit card number getting into the wrong hands when you use it at a business establishment, over the phone, or on the Web. You also don't want your social security number, driver's license number, salary, and other forms of identification and personal data, used for the wrong purposes. In this Project, you'll investigate the types of security companies and organizations use to protect the privacy of the data they store about you in their databases.

Using the resources in your library and on the Internet, investigate the security features provided by database management systems to protect the privacy of your data. Do companies and organizations supplement these security features with additional measures to further protect your data?

After you have completed your research, write a paper that presents your information. Your instructor will provide you with specifications for length and format.

Microsoft Access

Tutorial 3: Database Reports and Graphs

Tutorial 3

Database Reports and Graphs

Keep Fit USA

How do you keep in shape? Jogging? Hiking? Playing team sports? Yoga? Lifting weights? Whatever you do for exercise, you've likely had no problem finding a store willing to sell you the necessary equipment. *Keep Fit USA* is a chain of stores in Indiana, Michigan, and Ohio specializing in sports, recreation and exercise equipment, athletic clothing and footwear, and sports memorabilia. In this tutorial you'll learn how *Keep Fit USA* uses reports and graphs from an Access database to help managers make decisions.

Projects

In the Tutorial 3 Projects you'll create a report listing expert witnesses by their areas of expertise, create a report on climbers and the dates and locations of their climbs, create mailing labels for an environmental magazine, chart the one-year and five-year yield averages for a series of mutual funds, and more.

   If you're not assigned Projects 12, 13, 14, 18, and 19, you might want to at least read these Projects or, better yet, work through them. Project 12 shows you how to change the chart type for an existing chart, and Project 13 shows you how to change the style for an existing report. Project 14 demonstrates how to create a sorted report with group levels that uses data from two tables. Project 18 deals with adding a field to an existing report. In Project 19 you'll see how to add subtotals and totals to a report.

WHAT'S ONLINE

1 Preview and Print a Report
- Preview a Saved Report
- Change Preview Pages
- Print Selected Pages

2 Use the Report Wizard
- Use the Report Wizard
- Group and Sort Data Using Report Wizard
- Select Report Layout Options
- Print an Entire Report

3 Modify a Report Layout
- The Design View Window
- Check Design View Settings
- Report Sections
- Controls
- Move the Report Title
- Change the Height of a Section
- Select and Delete Multiple Controls
- Resize Controls
- Preview Design Changes
- Move Controls
- Save Design Changes

4 Sort and Group Report Data
- Change the Sort Field and Sort Order
- Preview and Save Design Changes
- Add a Group Footer

5 Add a Graphic to a Report
- The Toolbox
- Add a Graphic to the Report Header Section
- Change a Property of a Graphic
- Resize a Graphic

6 Graph Data from a Database
- Use the Chart Wizard
- Select a Chart Type
- Print and Save a Chart

Keep Fit USA

If you were running a business, you'd be well-advised to ask many questions. What's the average monthly sales figure for each store? Which store is the most profitable? Which merchandise category accounts for the greatest percentage of sales? What were the total gross sales figures in each store last month? Answers to these questions and others would tell you quickly how healthy your business is. The answers would also help you make better business decisions.

If your business, like the *Keep Fit USA* chain, stores its data in a database, then you could easily find the answers to the questions you would ask. Even better, you could present the information in an attractively formatted report, which would help your presentation to potential investors; or you could create a graph to present the information pictorially, a presentation method that makes immediate impact. In Tutorial 3, you'll learn how Access allows you to create reports and graphs.

Review Questions

Fill in the blank with the correct word or phrase.

1   A(n) _____ is a formatted printout of the contents of one or more tables or queries in a database.

2   When previewing a report, to see the entire first page in miniature you would click _____ in the Zoom Control list box.

3   The simplest way to create a new report is to use the _____.

4   When you use a(n) _____, you collect together records that share a common value.

5   With a(n) _____ report layout, one column appears for each field.

6   With the _____ page orientation, the paper is positioned so it's taller than wide.

7   With the _____ page orientation, the paper is positioned so it's wider than tall.

8   The easiest way to print an entire report is to use the _____.

9   You must be in _____ view to modify a report layout.

10 To preview a multipage report, you must use the _____ buttons in the lower-left corner of the preview window.

11 The Report Wizard places the report's title in the _____ section of the report.

12 The _____ section appears at the bottom of each page of a report.

13 Each box, line, or other object you see in the dotted design grid is called a(n) _____.

review questions

14 To select multiple controls, you hold down the _____ key as you click each control in turn.

15 A(n) _____ prints after all the records that have the same value for the group field.

16 To create a graph, you can use the _____, which prompts you through the necessary steps.

MULTIPLE CHOICE

*Select the letter of the **one** best answer.*

17 **The source of data for a report can be:**

    a a table only

    b a query only

    c either a table or a query

    d a table, a query, or a form

18 **Which of the following is a report layout option?**

    a standard

    b horizontal

    c tabular

    d all of the above

19 **Which of the following is not a choice you need to make when creating a report using the Report Wizard?**

    a report layout

    b page orientation

    c number of copies

    d style

20 **When you select a control such as a report title, which of the eight handles that appears on the control's border is the move handle?**

    a top left

    b top center

    c bottom center

    d bottom right

21 **Which key do you use when selecting multiple controls?**

    a Tab

    b Ctrl

    c Shift

    d Alt

22 **To change the sort field in an existing report, you click the _____ button.**

    a Sort

    b Properties

    c Toolbox

    d Sorting and Grouping

23 **You can resize a graphic without distorting its proportions if the SizeMode property of the graphic is:**

    a Standard   **c** Proportional

    b Zoom   **d** Fixed

MATCHING

Select the letter from the right column that correctly matches each item in the left column.

24 **page is taller than wide**   **a** last page button

25 ◄   **b** an object on a report

26 **page is wider than tall**   **c** Previous page button

27 ►| **d** landscape orientation

                                         e bar chart

28

29 **control**   **f** portrait orientation

                                         g Next page button

30

31 ►   **h** a special toolbar

                                         i graphic

32

33 |◄   **j** column chart

34 **toolbox**   **k** First page button

                                         l pie chart

35

SHORT ANSWER

Use a separate sheet of paper to write out your answers to the following questions.

36 The Report Wizard places the report title near the left margin of the report header section. Assume you're in Design view. Explain all the steps you would perform to center the title.

37 Why would you need to or want to select multiple controls? How do you select multiple controls?

38 What does it mean to use a grouping level? Must a group field also be a sort field?

39 Assume you've just inserted a graphic in a report and now want to resize the graphic. What must you do first? Why?

40 What is the toolbox? How do you display it?

Projects

These Projects are designed to help you review and develop the skills you learned in Tutorial 3. Complete each Project using Microsoft Access. *If you have not yet made the Project Disks for Tutorial 3, start the e-Course software, click the Project Disk menu, and follow the instructions on the screen.*

If you've forgotten some of the skills you need to complete the Projects, refer to the Task Reference.

REVIEW SKILLS

1   Warming Up   File: Workout.mdb

In the online Steps, you used the Keepfit database to learn how to preview a report and change preview pages. In this Project, you'll review these skills using the Workout database, which is similar to the Keepfit database.

Open the Workout database from your Project Disk. Preview the report Store Sales by Month. Page through the report until you locate the page that shows a zip code of 49008, and then print only that page of the report.

Close the report, and then close the Workout database.

2   Tell Me the Big Numbers   File: Workout.mdb

In the online Steps, you used the Keepfit database to learn how to create a report using the Report Wizard. In this Project, you'll review some of these skills using the Workout database, which is similar to the Keepfit database.

Open the Workout database from your Project Disk. Use the Report Wizard to create a report based on the Sales by Store query. Add to the Selected Fields box, in order, the fields Store and Total Sales. Use no grouping levels or sort fields. Select a landscape orientation, and use the Corporate style for the report. Title the report "Total Sales by Store."

Print the entire report, close the report, and then close the Workout database.

projects

3 Watch that Fine Print   File: Workout.mdb

In the online Steps, you used the Keepfit database to learn how to modify a report layout. In this Project, you'll review these skills using the Workout database, which is similar to the Keepfit database.

Open the Workout database from your Project Disk. Then open the Categories report in Design view. Preview the report, notice the small font size used for the various category codes and descriptions, and then click the Close button on the Preview toolbar.

Select the multiple controls Cat Code and Category Description in the detail section, and then change the font size to 10.

Select the multiple controls Category description in the detail section and the thick line in the page header section, and then resize the selected controls from their right ends so that they line up with the right edge of the graphic.

Select the Cat Code control in the detail section and resize the selected control from its left so that the left edge is approximately aligned with the left edge of the "t" in the Cat Code control in the page header section.

Save the modified design, print the entire report, close the report, and then close the Workout database.

4 The Name Game
Files: Workout.mdb and Keepfit.bmp

In the online Steps, you used the Keepfit database to learn how to add a graphic to a report. In this Project, you'll review these skills using the Workout database, which is similar to the Keepfit database.

Open the Workout database from your Project Disk. Then open the Store Sales by Month report in Design view.

Move the Store Sales by Month control in the page header section so that its right edge is at 5.75" on the horizontal ruler. Add the graphic named "Keepfit.bmp," which is located on your Project Disk, at the top of the page header section, aligning its left edge at .75" on the horizontal ruler. If necessary, resize the height of the page header section so that its bottom is about two grid dots below the thick line. Save the modified design.

Print page 3 of the report, close the report, and then close the Workout database.

5   A Piece of Pie   File: Workout.mdb

In the online Steps, you used the Keepfit database to learn how to create charts. In this Project, you'll review these skills using the Workout database, which is similar to the Keepfit database.

Open the Workout database from your Project Disk. Use the Chart Wizard to create a chart using the Sales Detail query. Include the Sales and Month fields in the chart. Select the 3-D pie chart, use the default data layout, and use a chart title of "Sales by Month." Print the chart.

Close the report but do not save it, and then close the Workout database.

APPLY SKILLS

6   Get Me an Elvis Presley   File: Notables.mdb

In the online Steps, you learned how to preview a report and change preview pages. In this Project, you'll review these skills with a report of celebrities and their vocal (sound-alike) and visual (look-alike) impersonators.

Open the Notables database from your Project Disk, click the Reports tab, and then preview the *Celebrities and Their Impersonators* report. Notice that this report uses a vertical, or columnar, layout rather than a tabular layout. In a vertical layout report, fields are printed one above another, with field labels printed to the left of the fields.

Notice also that the report is a multiple-column report. In a multiple-column report, the report header and footer and page header and footer span the full width of the page; the group header and footer and detail section span the width of one column. This particular report has a report header, a detail section with two columns, and a page footer.

Page through the report to answer the following questions, and then close the report and close the Notables database when you're finished.

    a   How many impersonators do visual impersonations of Elvis Presley? What are their names?

    b   What celebrity or celebrities does Jeri Lewis impersonate?

    c   Which impersonator does a vocal impression of Queen Elizabeth?

projects

7   Where's *Casablanca?*   File: Tapes.mdb

In the online Steps, you learned how to create a report using the Report Wizard. In this Project, you'll review these skills as you create a report of programs recorded on videotape.

Open the Tapes database from your Project Disk, click the Reports tab, and then use the Report Wizard to create a new report based on the Taped Programs table. Add to the Selected Fields box, in order, the fields Program, Length, Tape#, and Position. Use no grouping levels. In the third Report Wizard dialog box you do want to specify a sort field. Click the ▼ for the first sort field, and then click Program.

In the next Report Wizard dialog box, select a tabular layout and a portrait orientation. Then specify the Bold style for the report, and title the report "Programs on Tape."

Page through the preview to verify that the report looks as it should. Then print the entire report, close the report, and close the Tapes database.

8   Small Countries   File: Namerica.mdb

In the online Steps, you learned how to modify a report. In this Project, you'll review these skills as you modify a report of states and provinces by country within North America.

Open the Namerica database from your Project Disk, click the Reports tab, and then preview the State/Provinces by Country report. Locate each of the following report features in the previewed report:

- a report header with the report title
- a State/Province header with a flag graphic, the country name, and the four column headings for the detail
- a detail section that includes the state/province name, the capital, the population, and the area
- a blank State/Province footer for spacing purposes
- a page footer showing the date and page number

The only problem with the report is that the values for the four detail fields are printed in a small font that is difficult to read. You'll modify the report to increase the font size of the detail section controls. Because the font size change might produce layout problems, you'll then resize and/or move controls as needed.

Open the State/Provinces by Country report in Design view. Select the multiple controls State/Province, Capital, Population, and Area in the detail section, click the Font Size [▼], and then click 10. Click the [🔍] Print Preview button on the toolbar, and then scroll the report to view the Canada entries. Notice that the names of two provinces (Northwest Territories and Prince Edward Island), the name of one capital (Charlottetown), and the area of one province (Northwest Territories) do not print completely.

Close the Print Preview window to return to Design view. Select the multiple controls State/Province, Capital, and Population in *both* the group header and the detail sections, and then move them one dot to the left. Then select and resize the Area control in the detail section, dragging its left edge to make it one dot wider. Now the largest area value will print in full.

Select the multiple controls State/Province in the group header and State/Province in the detail section, and then move them four dots to the left. With both controls still selected, resize both controls by dragging the left edge of one of the two selected controls to the left to make it six dots wider. Now the largest State/Province name will print in full.

Then select the multiple controls Capital in the group header and Capital in the detail section and resize them, making them four dots wider, so that the largest Capital name will print in full.

Print the entire report, close the report (saving changes), and then close the Namerica database.

9   Who Knows What?   File: Experts.mdb

In the online Steps, you learned how to create a report using the Report Wizard. In this Project, you'll review these skills as you create a report of expert witnesses grouped by their expertise.

Open the Experts database from your Project Disk. Click the Reports tab, and then use the Report Wizard to create a new report based on the Witnesses table. Add to the Selected Fields box, in order, the fields Expertise, Name, Street, City, State, Zip, and Phone. In the second Report Wizard dialog box, add Expertise as a grouping level. Use no sort fields. Select the Stepped layout and a landscape orientation in the fourth dialog box. Use the Soft Gray style for the report, and then title the report "Expertise and Witnesses."

The report needs to be modified, so open the report in Design view. Resize the title control in the report header to extend it to the right to the 4½" mark on the horizontal ruler, so that the entire report title is printed.

projects

Click the Expertise control in the Expertise header, change the font to 12 pt bold Arial, and resize it to extend to the right to the 2½" mark on the horizontal ruler. To remove the border from that control, click the [icon] Properties button on the toolbar, click the Border Style box, click its [icon], click Transparent, and then close the property sheet.

Select the multiple controls State in the page header section and State in the detail section (scrolling as needed), and then move them left two dots. Repeat for the two Zip controls, moving them left one dot.

The controls for the Zip and Phone fields in the detail section are too small for their fields. Resize the Zip control to make it two dots wider on the right. Then resize the Phone control to make it extend to the edge of the grid on the right.

For each particular expertise, the report will print a header line followed by detail lines for all the witnesses with that expertise. You want to ensure that an Expertise header and all its detail appear together on a page. Click the [icon] Sorting and Grouping button on the toolbar to display the Sorting and Grouping dialog box, click the Keep Together box, click its [icon], click Whole group, and then close the Sorting and Grouping dialog box.

Print the entire report, close the report (saving changes), and then close the Experts database.

10 Try a Doughnut!   File: Reading.mdb

If you're a book lover, then you might want to keep track of the books you've read in a database, much like the Reading database. Suppose you want to create a chart to visually illustrate the proportion of fiction books to nonfiction books you have read.

Open the Reading database from your Project Disk. Use the Chart Wizard to create a chart using the Fiction/Nonfiction Counts query. Include all fields in the chart. Select the doughnut chart, use the default data layout, and title the chart "Books Read: Fiction vs. Nonfiction." Print the chart.

Close the report, saving it as "Books Read by Type Chart," and then close the Reading database.

BUILD SKILLS

11 Add a Group Header   File: Xfiles.mdb

Suppose you created a report of X-Files merchandise and you didn't define any grouping levels for the report, but you did specify that the detail should be sorted in Type order. Now you decide that you do want to include a group header for the Type field. In this Project you'll modify an existing report to add a group header.

Open the Xfiles database from your Project Disk, click the Reports tab, and then preview the X-Files Merchandise report. Notice that the detail is printed in Type order, and that the value of the Type field appears on each detail line. Close the report and then open the report in Design view.

Click the ⬚ Sorting and Grouping button on the toolbar to display the Sorting and Grouping dialog box. Notice that Type and Description are listed as sorting fields. You can create a grouping level for a sorting field. Click Group Header, click its ▼, click Yes, and then close the Sorting and Grouping dialog box. A Type header section is added to the design grid.

You want to print the Type field in the Type header, so you need to move the control for that field. Click and drag the Type control from the detail section straight up to the Type header, positioning the top of the control box at the very top of the Type header.

Preview the report and check the effects of the changes you made, and then print the report. Close the report (saving changes), and then close the Experts database.

12 Change Chart Type   File: Contents.mdb

Suppose you've created a chart, and then decide that you want to change the chart to another type. In this Project, you'll change a column chart showing the total of the item values for each room into a 3-D pie chart that illustrates the proportion of the total inventory value contained in each room.

To change the chart type:

1: Open the **Contents** database, click the **Reports** tab, and then open **Inventory Values by Room Chart** in Design view.

2: Double-click the chart control to edit it. A Microsoft Graph window opens, with its own toolbar and a datasheet of the values in the chart. A chart window appears on top of the datasheet.

3: Click **Chart** on the Microsoft Graph menu bar.

4: Click **Pie** in the *Chart Type* box, and then click the upper-middle **Chart sub-type** icon.

5: Click the **OK** button to change the chart to a 3-D pie chart, and then close the Microsoft Graph window.

Print the chart. Close the chart, saving changes, and then close the Contents database.

13 Change an AutoFormat and Label a Report

File: Arena.mdb

When you create a report using Report Wizard, you must specify a style. If you decide when you see the completed report that you'd prefer a different style, can you change the style?

In this Project you'll change the style for the Promoter/Performer report in the Arena database from Casual to Corporate and add a label to the report.

Open the Arena database from your Project Disk, click the Reports tab, preview the Promoter/Performer report, and then print the report. Write "Casual style" at the top of the printed report. Close the report and then open it in Design view.

To change the style of a report:

1: Click the 🗒️ **AutoFormat** button on the toolbar to open the AutoFormat dialog box.

2: Click **Corporate**, and then click the **OK** button. After a few moments, the report design is redisplayed using the new style.

Next you'll add your name as a label to the report.

To add a label to a report:

1: If necessary, click the 🛠️ **Toolbox** button to display the toolbox.

2: Click the ⏹️ **Label** button on the toolbox, move the pointer to the report header section on the report, and then click the mouse button when the ＋ on the ⁺A pointer is at the top of the report header section and at the 4.5" mark on the horizontal ruler.

3: Type your name, and then click the 💾 **Save** button on the toolbar.

Print the complete report, and then write "Corporate style" at the top of the printed report.

Close the report, and then close the Arena database.

14 Grouping and Sorting In a Report Using Data From Two Tables   File: Heights.mdb

In the online Steps, you learned how to use a single table or query with the Report Wizard. In this Project you'll create a report with the Report Wizard, using data from two tables, and grouping and sorting the detail.

To create a report with grouping and sorting using two tables:

1: Open the **Heights** database, click the **Reports** tab on the Database window, click the **New** button, click **Report Wizard**, select the **Climber** table, and then click the **OK** button.

2: In the first Report Wizard dialog box, add **Climber Last Name** and **Climber First Name** (in that order) to the selected fields list. Then select the **Climbs** table in the Tables/Queries list box, and add **Climb Date** and **State** (in that order) to the selected fields list.

3: The second Report Wizard dialog box indicates that the report will be viewed by climber, which is what you want, so move to the third Report Wizard dialog box.

4: You want to group last name above first name, so click **Climber Last Name**, click the ▷ button, and then move to the fourth Report Wizard dialog box.

5: You want the detail records in date order, so select **Climb Date** as the first sort field, and then move to the next Report Wizard dialog box.

6: Select the **Stepped** layout and the **Formal** style in the next two Report Wizard dialog boxes, type **Climbers and Climbs** as the report title, and then finish the report.

7: Close the Preview window, and then open the Climbers and Climbs report in Design view.

8: Click and drag the **Climber Last Name** control in the Climber Last Name header straight down into the detail section of the dotted grid. Repeat for the **Climber First Name** control in the Climber header.

9: Click the **Climber Last Name** control in the detail, change the font size to 10 and remove the italic formatting, and then resize that control from the bottom so it's only as tall as the Climber First Name control. Click the ▦ **Properties** button on the toolbar, click **Hide Duplicates**, click its ▾, click **Yes**, and then close the property

sheet. Repeat the last operation (hiding duplicates) for the Climber First Name control in the detail section.

10: Change the height of the report header section so it's only as tall as the control it contains. Then change the heights of both the Climber Last Name header section and the Climber Header section to zero.

11: Print the report. Close the report, saving your changes, and then close the Heights database.

15 Create and Resize a Chart with Two Data Series
File: Funds.mdb

Suppose you want to plot two sets of data—the average one-year yield and the average five-year yield of the mutual funds offered by various companies—on the same chart so that you can compare the yields. In this Project, you'll create a chart using two data series, and then edit the chart to resize it.

To create and edit a chart using two data series:

1: Open the **Funds** database, and then click the **Reports** tab.

2: Use the Chart Wizard to create a chart based on the **Mutual Fund** table. Include the **Company**, **One Year**, and **Five Years** fields in the chart, and select the **3-D Bar Chart**.

3: In the third Chart Wizard dialog box, drag the **Five Years** button over to the chart in the left portion of the dialog box, and then drop it on top of the button labeled "Sum Of One Year." Now both data series will be charted.

4: You want to chart average yields rather than the sum of yields, so double-click the **Sum Of One Year** button, click **Average** in the Summarize dialog box, and then click the **OK** button. Repeat for the Sum Of Five Years button.

5: Type **Mutual Fund Yield Comparison** as the chart title.

6: Look at the finished chart in the preview window and notice that only two of the five companies are listed along the y-axis; this is because the chart area is too small to display all five company names. Close the preview window, and then save the chart as "Yield Comparison Chart."

7: Open the chart in Design view, and then double-click the chart to edit it. A Microsoft Graph window opens, with its own toolbar and a datasheet of the values in the chart. A chart window appears on top of the datasheet. To increase the size of the chart window, first drag its left edge as far to the left as possible, and then drag its right edge to the right as far as possible. (Note: Your chart might show North, West, and East along the y-axis instead of the company names. The company names will

projects

appear, however, when you preview or print the report.) Then click the ☒ **Close** button in the Microsoft Graph window.

8: Resize the chart control by dragging its right edge to the 5.5" mark on the horizontal ruler.

9: Print the chart. Then close the chart, saving your changes, and close the Funds database.

EXPLORE

16 Label Wizard   Files: Habitat.mdb and Habitat.bmp

Habitat, a magazine dealing with environmental issues, is published bimonthly in January, March, May, and so on. The publisher plans to do a mass mailing to subscribers offering a special rate on a new magazine called *Habitat Extra*, to be issued in the alternate months. In this Project, you'll create mailing labels using the Label Wizard, and then add a graphic and a border to the labels.

To create the mass mailing labels:

1: Open the **Habitat** database, click the **Reports** tab, click the **New** button, click the **Label Wizard**, and select the **Subscribers** table.

2: Make sure both the English and Sheet Feed options are selected, and then select **5199-F 1 5/6" x 3 1/16"** as the label size.

3: Change the font name to **Arial**, the font size to **12**, and the font weight to **Normal**, and then make sure the text color is black and that neither the Italic nor the Underline options are selected.

4: Now you'll specify the four-line label text. Click **Full Name** in the *Available Fields* box, click the ⊳ button, and then press the **Enter** key.

Click **Address** in the *Available Fields* box, click the ⊳ button, and then press the **Enter** key.

Click **City**, click the ⊳ button, press the spacebar, click **Prov/St**, click the ⊳ button, press the spacebar twice, click **Zip Code**, click the ⊳ button, and then press the **Enter** key.

Click **Country** in the *Available Fields* box, and then click the ⊳ button. The four lines of label text are now defined.

5: Specify **Zip Code** as the field to sort by. Then type **Subscriber Labels** as the report title.

6: When Access attempts to preview the finished labels, you may see a message box saying that some data may not be displayed. If so, click the **OK** button to close the

message box, click **File** on the menu bar, click **Page Setup**, change the Left Margin value to **0.9"**, and then click the **OK** button.

7: Close the Preview window, and then open **Subscriber Labels** in Design view. The dotted grid is the exact size of one label, and there is one control for each address line. Select the multiple controls for all four address lines, and position the pointer in the blank area of the first address line. When the pointer changes to a hand, drag the controls straight down so the bottom of the fourth control is aligned with the 1.5" mark.

8: Add the graphic named "Habitat.bmp," which is located on your Project Disk, in the dotted grid above the controls. With the graphic control still selected, click the **Properties** button on the toolbar, click **SizeMode**, click its ▼, click **Zoom**, and then close the property sheet. Resize the graphic so it is 1" wide and 3/8" tall, and then move it so its right edge aligns with the right edge of the address controls and its bottom edge is on the top edge of the first address control.

9: Now you'll add a border to the label, just inside the label edges. Click the **Rectangle** button on the toolbox, click on the first dot in from the upper-left corner of the dotted grid, and then drag to the last dot in from the lower-right corner of the grid. With the rectangle still selected, click **Format** on the menu bar, and then click **Send to Back**.

10: Save the modified design, preview the labels, print only page 21 of the labels (using regular 8½ x 11-inch paper), and then close the database.

17 Explore the SizeMode Property
File: Homes.mdb and Houses.wmf

In the online Steps, you changed the SizeMode property of the graphics you added so you could resize the graphic without distorting its proportions. In this Project you'll explore what happens when you resize three graphics, each with a different setting for the SizeMode property.

To explore the SizeMode property:

1: Open the **Homes** database, and then open the **Listed Homes by City** report in Design view.

2: Add the graphic named **Houses.wmf** from your Project Disk, positioning it in the far upper-left corner of the report header section.

3: With the graphic still selected, click the **Properties** button on the toolbar, click **Border Style** (make sure the All tab is selected), click its ▼, click **Solid**, click **Border Width**, click its ▼, click **1 pt**, and then close the property sheet.

4: Click the **Copy** button on the toolbar, and then click the **Paste** button twice. Drag one of the copies so that it's at the top edge of the report and its left edge is at

projects

the 1.5" mark on the horizontal ruler. Drag the other copy so that it's at the top edge of the report and its left edge is at the 3" mark on the horizontal ruler. Then change the height of the report header section so that its lower edge coincides with the lower edge of the Listed Homes by City control.

5: Now you'll define a different setting of the SizeMode property for each graphic. Change the SizeMode property for the first graphic to **Clip**. Change the SizeMode property for the second graphic to **Stretch**. Finally, change the SizeMode property for the third graphic to **Zoom**.

6: Without changing its upper-left position, change the graphic size of the first graphic so that it is 1" tall and ¾" wide. Repeat for the second and the third graphics.

7: Print the report. Close the report, saving changes, and then close the Homes database.

8: Look at the printed report, compare the three graphics, and then write an explanation of what happens when resizing a graphic for each of the three SizeMode settings.

18 Add a Field to a Report   File: Guitars.mdb

Suppose you created a report and now realize you need another field in the report. Do you have to start from scratch? No, you can add one or more fields to a report in Design view. In this Project, you'll add the Year field to an existing report on vintage guitars.

To add a field to the vintage guitars report:

1: Open the Guitars database, and then open the **Vintage Guitars** report in Design view.

2: You want to add the Year field between Model and Price, so first you need to make room. Select the multiple controls: the **Price** and **Comments** boxes in the page header section and the Price and Comments boxes in the detail section. Move the controls to the right so the right edges of the Comments boxes align with the 5¾" mark on the horizontal ruler.

3: Click the **Field List** button in the Access toolbar, click **Year** in the displayed list, and then drag that highlighted field name down into the detail section, in the area between Model and Price. Close the **field** list box. Then move the **Year** box (but not its label box) to align its top with the tops of the other boxes in the detail section and so there are three dots between the end of the Model box and the beginning of the Year box. Close the toolbox.

4: Now you'll move the label into the page header with the other labels. Click the **Year** label box in the detail section, and then click the **Cut** button on the toolbar. Click in the page header section to select that section, and then click the **Paste** button on the toolbar. By default, Access pastes the label in the upper-left corner of the

section. Move that label into an appropriate position, left-aligned above the *Year* box in the detail section.

5: Click the **Year** label again so you can edit its text, and then delete the **:** (colon).

6: Resize the Year control in the detail section so it is as tall as the other controls in that section and so that its right edge is at the 2¾" mark on the horizontal ruler. The *Year* box is now the same size as the *Year* label box

7: Select the thick line at the bottom of the page header section, hold down the Shift key, and then resize the selected control so it's right edge is at the 5¾" mark on the horizontal ruler.

8: Print the report.

9: Close the report, saving your changes, and then close the Guitars database.

19   Add Subtotals and Grand Totals to a Report
File: Localtax.mdb

Suppose you want to add subtotals and totals to a report such as the Tax Roll report. Totals for a group of records, often called subtotals, are typically printed in a group header or footer; grand totals are usually printed in the report header or footer. In this Project, you'll edit a tax roll report to add a group footer section to the report and then add a calculated total to the group footer and the report footer.

To add subtotals and grand totals to the tax roll report:

1: Open the **Localtax** database, and then open the **Tax Roll** report in Design view.

2: First you'll add a group footer section. Click the ☷ **Sorting and Grouping** button on the toolbar, click **Group Footer** in the Sorting and Grouping dialog box, click its ▾, click **Yes**, and then close the Sorting and Grouping dialog box. A Township Name footer section is added to the report design.

3: Now you'll add a text box to the group footer. Click the 🔲 **Text Box** button on the toolbox, and then click in the Township Name footer at the top of that section immediately below the left edge of the Tax box above it. Click the label box (which contains "Text:" followed by a number), and then press the **Delete** key.

4: Next you'll specify a formula to calculate a subtotal of the tax amounts for the group. Right-click the new text box, click **Properties**, click the *Control Source* box, and then type **=Sum([Tax])**

5: To format the subtotal, click the **=Sum([Tax])** control to select it, click **Format** in the property sheet, click its ▾, click **Currency**, and then close the property sheet.

6: Now you'll copy the =Sum([Tax]) control into the report footer. Click the 🖹 **Copy** button on the toolbar, click the report footer section to select that section, and then click the 📋 **Paste** button on the toolbar. The height of the report footer is increased and the =Sum([Tax]) control is pasted in the report footer section.

7: By default, Access pastes into the upper-left corner of the section, so you need to move the control. First change the height of the report footer section to make it three dots taller. Then move the new *Sum([Tax])* box into an appropriate position, aligned under the *=Sum([Tax])* box in the Township Name footer and with its lower edge at the bottom of the report footer section.

8: To identify the subtotal and total for users of the report, you can label them as such; alternatively, you can draw lines above them to visually indicate that the values above the line are summed. You'll use the line technique. Click the ◻ **Line** button on the toolbox, and then hold down the Shift key and click and drag along the top of the =Sum([Tax]) box in the Township Name footer. Repeat to draw a line along the top of the =Sum([Tax]) box in the report footer, and then draw a second line the same length immediately above the other line.

9: Print the report. Then close the report, saving your changes, and close the Localtax database.

20 Inserting an Access Query into Word
File: Letter.doc and Events.mdb

Did you know that you can include Access information in another type of file, such as a Word document, an Excel spreadsheet, or a PowerPoint presentation? In this Project you'll insert an Access query into a Word document.

To insert an Access query into an existing letter:

1: Exit Access (if necessary), start Microsoft Word, and then open the **Letter.doc** file on your Project Disk. Scroll the letter until you can see one paragraph mark (¶) below another on the left side of the document. Click immediately to the left of the second paragraph mark to position the insertion point at that location.

2: Click **View** on the menu bar, point to **Toolbars**, click **Database**, and then click the 🗄 **Insert Database** button to open the Database dialog box.

3: Next, click the **Get Data** button. The Open Data Source window appears. Change the *Look In* list box to the location of your Project Disk, click the *Files of type* ▼, and then click **MS Access Databases (*.mdb)**. Click **Events** (or Events.mdb) in the center list box, and then click the **Open** button. At this point, Access starts, as you can tell by the Access button that appears on the taskbar. After a few moments the Microsoft Access dialog box opens.

projects

4: Click the **Queries** tab, make sure **February Events** is highlighted, click the *Link to Query* check box to uncheck it, and then click the **OK** button.

5: Click the **Insert Data** button in the Database dialog box. Make sure the **All** option is selected in the Insert Data dialog box that appears, and then click the **OK** button. The February Events query is then inserted into the Word document as a Word table. Click **View** on the menu bar, point to **Toolbars**, and then click **Database** to hide the Database toolbar.

6: Next you'll format the table to improve its appearance. Click anywhere inside the table, click **Table** on the menu bar, and then click **Select Table**. Use the buttons on Word's Formatting toolbar to change the font of the selected table to **12 pt Century Schoolbook**.

7: With the table still selected, click **Table** on the menu bar, and then click **Table AutoFormat**. In the Table AutoFormat dialog box, click the **Simple 3** option in the *Formats* list box, and then click the **OK** button.

8: Next you'll center the table. With the table still selected, click **Table** on the menu bar, and then click **Cell Height and Width**. Click the **Row** tab (if necessary) in the dialog box, click the **Center** option, and then click the **OK** button.

9: Click the ⬛ **Print** button on the toolbar to print the letter, and then click the ☒ **Close** button on the Word title bar to exit Word (don't save changes). Sign your name at the bottom of the printed letter.

INVESTIGATE

21 Report Design

You want the reports that you design to be easy to read and interpret, and attractive. After all, the purpose of a report is to furnish information, so the information should be clearly presented. The entire subject of report design, including identifying information (report titles, field labels, dates, page numbers, and so on), report styles (font, font sizes), and report layout (spacing, field order and placement, grouping levels, and so on) is part of the larger topic of document design.

Using the resources in your library and on the Internet, research document design, especially as it relates to reports such as those you've created in Access. What are the characteristics of a good report? What should you look out for and try to avoid when designing a report?

After you have completed your research, write a paper that presents your findings. Your instructor will provide you with specifications for length and format.

22 Shopping for Graphing Software

Although you might not have been aware of it, when you created charts in this tutorial you were using Microsoft Graph, which is a program designed to work within other Microsoft applications such as Access, Word, and Excel.

Many graphics software packages are available today that make it easy to quickly create a wide variety of eye-catching charts. Look through computer magazine ads, visit computer stores, and/or search the Internet to locate four graphics software packages.

Compare the four packages you selected. Consider questions such as: What types of charts can they create? What are the computer system requirements (memory, disk space, and so on) for each? Do they require a CD-ROM? With what application systems can they interface? Is there an easy way to import Access data into the package? How much does each package cost?

Write a paper that presents the results of your comparisons. Your instructor will provide you with specifications for length and format.

23 Pie, Bar, Column, or What?

Suppose you have some information that you wish to chart. What's the best choice for the chart type—a pie chart? A column chart? A bar chart? An XY (scatter) chart? Or some other type of chart? Or doesn't it matter?

Using the resources in your library and/or on the Internet, research graphical data presentation to learn how to determine which type of chart is appropriate in a given situation or what kinds of information each of the different types of charts can convey. (Note: You can also get information on this topic from Microsoft Graph's Help system. To start Microsoft Graph, first start Word or Excel, click Insert on the menu bar, click Object, and then select Microsoft Graph.)

After you have completed your research, write a paper that presents your findings. Your instructor will provide you with specifications for length and format.

24 Catastrophe!

One problem with catastrophes is that they occur with little or no warning. How do companies protect their data from loss in the event of equipment failure, natural disaster, sabotage, or software failure?

Using the resources in your library and/or on the Internet, research measures that companies use to protect their databases, and find out what kind of disaster recovery procedures are typically available with a database management system.

projects

After you have completed your research, write a paper that presents your information. Your instructor will provide you with specifications for length and format.

25 Distributed DBMSs

A **distributed database** is a database that is stored on computers at several sites of a computer network and that users can access from any site in the network. A distributed **DBMS** is a database management system that is capable of supporting and manipulating a distributed database.

Using the resources in your library and/or on the Internet, investigate distributed databases and DBMSs. What are the advantages of distributed databases? What are some of the problems specific to distributed databases? What special capabilities must a database management system have to be able to manage a distributed database? What are some of the DBMSs currently on the market that manage distributed databases?

After you have completed your research, write a paper that presents your information. Your instructor will provide you with specifications for length and format.

Microsoft Access

Tutorial 4: Creating a Database

Tutorial 4

Creating a Database

WHAT'S INSIDE

Made in the Shade

Maybe you don't remember the '84 pop hit "Sunglasses at Night" by Corey Hart, but you've probably worn sunglasses at least once in your life. In this Tutorial you'll create a database for Made in the Shade, a designer sunglasses store.

Projects

In the Tutorial 4 Projects you'll create several databases, including one to catalog your family photos, one for a shirt-of-the-month club, and one you can use as your personal address book. You'll also import data into a database from a Word text file and an Excel spreadsheet, and copy an object from another Access database.

Two three-part Projects can provide experience in creating an actual database with several tables. In the Newspaper Work Projects, you'll create the database and tables for keeping track of the articles printed in your local newspaper. In the Gift Baskets Projects, you'll define the tables for a gift basket business and actually "design" one complete gift basket.

If you're not assigned Projects 6, 11, 12, 13, 17, 18, and 9, 14, and 19, you might want to at least read these Projects or, better yet, work through them. In Project 6 you'll work with Yes/No and Memo fields, and in Project 11 you'll use the Lookup Wizard to create a lookup field. The Database Wizard is used in Project 12. You'll create a form with two subforms in Project 13. Projects 17 and 18 deal with importing data from external sources into an Access database. Projects 9, 14, and 19 are the Newspaper Work Projects mentioned above, in which you'll create a table in datasheet view and create a join involving four tables.

1 Create a New Database

- Create a Database

2 Create a Table

- Start Creating a New Table
- Design View
- Define Fields
- Select the Primary Key
- Save the Table Structure

3 Modify the Structure of a Table

- Delete a Field from a Table
- Add a Field to a Table
- Move a Field
- View a Table Datasheet

4 Change Field Property Settings

- Change Settings for Displaying a Field
- Define Validation Rules
- Test Validation Rules

5 Create a Form

- Create a Form Using an AutoForm Wizard
- Save a New Form
- Create a Form Using the Form Wizard
- Modify a Form Design
- Change a Form's AutoFormat

Made in the Shade

Have you noticed the role that sunglasses play today? The right sunglasses can make a fashion statement or project an attitude. Some people even go so far as to say that wearing the right pair of shades helps them express themselves! Every major designer—from Armani to Ray Ban®—have their own line of sunglasses. They come in a variety of styles, shapes, and colors.

Beyond the fashion statement, sunglasses also provide health and performance benefits to wearers. For example, you can choose from a wide variety of lens types—some provide more or less UV protection, some have more or less distortion, some are so lightweight that you'll hardly know you're wearing them, some are more durable.

Today it's not uncommon for many sunglasses to have prices well over $150! Yes, sunglasses have become big business!

Made in the Shade is a small specialty shop, located in an upscale urban mall, that currently sells only designer sunglasses. The owner, Lindsay Aalto, is considering adding lines of fun and fashion eyewear—wire-framed glasses with lenses in a wide variety of colors, Benjamin Franklin glasses, and maybe even lorgnettes and monocles. But before she expands her inventory, Lindsay wants to do a thorough analysis of her current business. In this tutorial you'll work with Lindsay as she creates a new database to keep track of her current stock of designer sunglasses.

Review Questions

FILL-IN-THE-BLANKS

Fill in the blank with the correct word or phrase.

1   A new Access _____ requires 60 to 80KB of disk space.

2   When you name a field in a table, you cannot start the name with a(n) _____.

3   Use the _____ data type for numbers used in calculations not subject to round-off errors.

4   Use the _____ data type for names, addresses, and descriptions.

5   A(n) _____ uniquely identifies each record in a table.

6   The _____ property controls the display appearance of a field value.

7   For a field with its Format property set to _____, you can enter either .65 or 65%.

8   You can use a(n) _____ to work with one record at a time from a table.

9   The _____ Wizard places all the fields from a selected table or query on a form automatically.

10 An AutoForm Wizard creates a form but doesn't _____ it in the database.

11 The Form _____ prompts you through the steps to create a form.

12 A(n) _____ is a predefined style for a form or report.

review questions

*Select the letter of the **one** best answer.*

---

13 A new _____ **requires 60 to 80KB of disk space.**

   a database   **c** query

   b form   **d** table

---

14 When you create a new database, it contains:

   a one table

   b one table and one form

   c one table, query, form, and report

   d none of the above

---

15 The first objects you create in a database are its:

   a forms   **c** reports

   b queries   **d** tables

---

16 A field name can be up to _____ characters long.

   a 20   **c** 64

   b 50   **d** 255

---

17 A field _____ can contain letters, numbers, spaces, and special characters except a period, exclamation point, accent grave, and square brackets.

   a data type   **c** property

   b name   **d** value

---

18 Common field data types include all the following except:

   a currency   **c** number

   b letter   **d** text

---

19 A field's _____ property determines what field values you can enter for the field and what other properties the field will have.

   a data type   **c** format

   b description   **d** name

20 A(n) _____ key uniquely identifies each record in a table.

   a master   **c** record

   b primary   **d** unique

21 Fields appear in a table datasheet in:

   a alphabetical order

   b the order you arrange them in the datasheet

   c the same order you defined them in Design view

   d no specific order

22 A field's _____ property controls the display appearance of a field value.

   a Data Type   **c** Format

   b Display   **d** Style

23 You can set a field's _____ Rule property to accept only certain values.

   a Data

   b Format

   c Primary

   d Validation

24 The setting of a field's _____ Value property determines its field values when you fail to enter them in the table datasheet.

   a Automatic

   b Default

   c Defined

   d Initial

25 The _____ Wizard creates a form automatically without asking you any questions.

   a AutoForm

   b Design

   c Form

   d FreeForm

review questions

Select the letter from the right column that correctly matches each item in the left column.

26	**AutoForm**	**a**	a data type
27	**AutoFormat**	**b**	a table structure change
28	**Data type**	**c**	a wizard
29	**Date/Time**	**d**	can be up to 64 characters long
30	**Default Value**	**e**	controls the display appearance of a field value
31	**Design view**	**f**	determines the properties for a field
32	**Field name**	**g**	field value when no value is entered
33	**Format**	**h**	message displayed for incorrect field values
34	**Move a field**	**i**	predefined style
35	**Primary key**	**j**	uniquely identifies records in a table
36	**Validation Text**	**k**	where fields are defined

SHORT ANSWER

Use a separate sheet of paper to write out your answers to the following questions.

37 Describe the rules for naming fields.

38 Explain when you would use each of the common data types—text, number, date/time, and currency.

39 Why should you select a primary key for each table?

40 When you define a new field, which field properties are you required to set?

41 Explain the difference between an AutoForm Wizard and the Form Wizard.

Projects

These Projects are designed to help you review and develop the skills you learned in Tutorial 4. Complete each Project using Microsoft Access. *If you have not yet made the Project Disks for Tutorial 4, start the e-Course software, click the Project Disk menu, and follow the instructions on the screen.*

If you've forgotten some of the skills you need to complete the Projects, refer to the Task Reference.

REVIEW SKILLS

1   Start From Scratch

In the online Steps, you created the Shades database. In this Project, you'll review these skills by creating the Sunspecs database, which will be similar to the Shades database.

Create a database, save it as Sunspecs on your Project Disk, and then close the Sunspecs database without closing Access.

Click File and then click Sunspecs.mdb at the top of the list near the bottom of the File menu to reopen the database. Click File, click Database Properties, and then click the General tab (if necessary).

    a   What is the size of the Sunspecs database?

Click the OK button, and then close the Sunspecs database.

2   Set the Table   File: Sunspec1.mdb

In the online Steps, you created a table called Designer Sunglass as the first table in the Shades database. In this Project, you'll review these skills as you add a table to the new Sunspec1 database.

Open the Sunspec1 database from your Project Disk. Start a new table, and then define a field for each of the following:

1. Brand Name (Text)
2. Series (Text)
3. Model (Text)
4. Frame (Text)
5. Lens (Text)
6. Lens Material (Text)
7. List Price (Currency)

projects

Select as the primary key the field Model, and then save the table with the name Inventory.

Switch to datasheet view, and then add the following two records to the table:

Brand Name	Series	Model	Frame	Lens	Lens Material	List Price
Ray-Ban	Classic	RC-1661	Arista	Brown	Polycarbonate	$200
Revo	Oval	VO-1108	Pewter	Blue	Glass	$170

Resize to its best fit each column in the table. Print the table, close the table saving your changes, and then close the Sunspec1 database.

3   Just In Case   File: Sunspec2.mdb

In the online Steps, you used the Shades database to learn how to modify the structure of a table. In this Project, you'll review these skills, using the Sunspec2 database, which is similar to the Shades database.

Open the Sunspec2 database from your Project Disk. Then open the Designer Inventory table. Notice the Polaroid field, which is a Yes/No field. A check mark in the check box represents the value "Yes," meaning that the lens is Polaroid.

Change to Design view, move the Model field so that it is the first field in the table, and then add a field named Case with a Yes/No data type between the Frame and List Price fields. Save the table, and then view the table datasheet.

Resize to its best fit the Case column. The Revo brand sunglasses are the only ones that come with a case. Click the Case check box for the eight table entries for Revo to change those values to "Yes".

Click File, click Page Setup, and then change the left and right margin values to 0.8". Print the table, close the table saving your changes, and then close the Sunspec2 database.

4   Did You Say Plastic?   Files: Sunspec3.mdb

In the online Steps, you used the Shades database to learn how to change field property settings. In this Project, you'll review these skills, using the Sunspec3 database, which is similar to the Shades database.

Open the Sunspec3 database from your Project Disk. Then open the Designer Sunglasses table in Design view. The Lens Material field has only three valid values: "Plastic," "Glass" or "Polycarbonate." Make these property setting changes for the Lens Material field:

- Field Size—13

- Validation Rule—must be "Plastic" or "Glass" or "Polycarbonate"

- Validation Text—use an appropriate message

Make these property setting changes for the Price field:

- Format—General Number

- Decimal Places—0

Save the table, clicking the Yes button in any message box that's displayed. View the table datasheet, and then test the validation rule for the Lens Material field by trying values such as "Glastic" or "Polycarnate" for the first record; be sure to restore the value to "Plastic" when you're done.

Print the table, and then close the SunSpec3 database.

5   International Shades   File: Sunspec4.mdb

In the online Steps, you used the Shades database to learn how to create a form. In this Project, you'll review these skills, using the Sunspec4 database, which is similar to the Shades database.

Open the Sunspec4 database from your Project Disk, and then click the Forms tab. Use the Form Wizard to create a form as follows:

- Use the Designer Shades table.

- Include all fields from that table, in the same order as listed. Also include the Discount % field from the Discount table.

- View the data by Designer Shades.

- Use the Columnar layout.

- Use the International style.

- Use "Designer Shades" as the form title.

Print the 18th record, close the form, and then close the Sunspec4 database.

projects

6 Old Family Photos

Suppose you've decided to catalog all your old family photos. In this Project you'll create a new database, define a table, and then add records to the table.

Create a database named Photos on your Project Disk. Start a new table, and then define a field for each of the following:

1. ID (Text)
2. Subject (Text)
3. When Taken (Text)
4. Color (Yes/No)
5. Description (Memo)

A Yes/No field is a field that can contain one of two values, represented by yes or no, true or false, or off or on. A Memo field is similar to a Text field, except that a Text field is at most 255 characters, but a Memo field can contain up to 64,000 characters.

Select as the primary key the field ID, and then save the table with the name Photographs.

View the table datasheet, and then add the following two records to the table:

ID	Subject	When Taken	Color	Description
A1-1	Great-Grandma Hollis	around 1913	No	Great-Grandma Elizabeth Marie Hollis all dressed up and wearing a big, fancy hat
A1-2	Hollis family	July 4, 1915?	No	Family picnic. Bunting decorates the tables, and flags are visible in the background

Hint: To specify a "no" value for a yes/no field, simply tab over the field; to specify a "yes" value, either click the check box or press the spacebar.

Add three additional records to the table, at least one of which should be a color photo. For the table to print on a single page in landscape orientation, your descriptions should be no more than six characters longer than the descriptions in the first two table records.

Resize each column in the table to its best fit. To change to landscape orientation, click File, click Page Setup, click the Page tab, click Landscape, and then click the OK button.

Preview the table; if the last several characters of the longest Description don't appear, make the column slightly wider.

Print the table, close the table (saving changes), and then close the Photos database.

7 It's a Gift   File: Contents.mdb

In the online Steps, you learned how to modify the structure of a table. In this Project, you'll modify a table's structure by moving a field and adding a field to an existing table.

Open the Contents database from your Project Disk, and then open the Household Inventory Items table in Design view.

Move the Room field so that it is located between the Model# and Purchase Date fields. Then add a field named "Gift" with a yes/no data type after the Purchase Date field. Save the table, and then view the table datasheet.

Resize the Gift column to its best fit. Click the Gift check box for the six table entries with a 12/25 Purchase Date to change those values to "Yes".

Click File, click Page Setup, click the Page tab, click Landscape, and then click the OK button. Print the table, close the table, and then close the Contents database.

8 National Celebrate Databases Month?
File: Events.mdb

In the online Steps, you learned how to create a form. In this Project you'll use an AutoForm Wizard to create a tabular form, modify the form, change the form's AutoFormat, and then use the form to add records to a table.

Open the Events database from your Project Disk, and then click the Forms tab. Create a form using the AutoForm: Tabular Wizard for the Event Calendar table.

By default, the AutoForm Wizard uses whatever AutoFormat was most recently selected. Change to Design view, click the AutoFormat button on the toolbar, click Evergreen, and then click the OK button.

Drag the right edge of the design grid to the 5.5" mark to widen the form. Select the multiple controls Month When, Day When, and Event in both the form header and detail sections, and then move the six selected controls to the right so that the right edge of the detail section Event control is one row of dots from the right edge of the design grid. Resize the Celebration control in the detail section, dragging its right edge to the left edge of the Month When control.

Save the form with the name Tabular Event Calendar. Switch to Form view. Scroll to the bottom of the form, and then add four events of your own choosing; for each specify either the current month or a day or week in the current month.

Click File, click Page Setup, change the top and bottom margins to 0.8", and then click the OK button. Print the form, close the form, and then close the Events database.

9 Newspaper Work, Part 1

Note: This Project is the first of a series of Projects that use the same database. The Newspaper Work Projects are 9, 14, and 19.

Suppose the publisher of your local newspaper has decided she wants a database to track articles printed in the newspaper starting with today's edition, and that she's asked you to create the database. You'll complete that task in this Project and in Projects 14 and 19. In this Project you'll create the Paper database and then create one of its tables by entering data in a datasheet. *To complete this Project you'll need a copy of the current edition of your local newspaper.*

Create a database named Paper on your Project Disk. To create a table by entering data in a datasheet, click the New button on the Database window, and then double-click Datasheet View. A blank datasheet is displayed with column names of Field1, Field2, and so on. First you'll rename the columns you will use. Double-click "Field1," and then type "Section Code." Repeat to rename "Field2" as "Section."

Now you'll enter data in the datasheet. In the first record, type "FP" in the first column and "Front page" in the second column. Type "SP" and "Sports" for the second record, "ED" and "Editorial page" for the third record, and "OP" and "Op-Ed page" for the fourth record. Continue to add records for every section in your newspaper, using a unique two-character Section Code for each.

Click the Save button on the toolbar, and then name the table Section. Click the No button when asked if you want to create a primary key.

Resize each of the two columns to its best fit. Change to Design view, select as the primary key the field Section Code, and then change its Field Size property setting to 2. Save the table (answer Yes when asked if you want to continue), view the table datasheet, print the table, close the table, and then close the Paper database.

10 Gift Baskets, Part 1   File: Basket.mdb

Note: This Project is the first of a series of Projects that use the same database. The Gift Baskets Projects are 10, 15, and 20.

Suppose you and a friend are starting a gift basket business, and you've decided to use a database to keep track of the types of baskets you'll sell, the items you'll include in the baskets, and the sources from which you'll purchase various items. You'll complete that database in this Project and in Projects 15 and 20.

The Basket database has already been created, and includes two tables. In this Project you'll enter additional records in each of those two tables, and then you'll create a third table.

Open the Basket database from your Project Disk, and then open the Sources table. Add three records for sources from which you could purchase candy, fruit, and other grocery items (you may make up the data). Print the table, and then close the table.

Open the Baskets table, and then add records for two baskets you think your company should offer, leaving the Price value as $0.00. (Hint: You can look at the printout of the Sources table for basket ideas.) Print the table, and then close the table.

Start a new table, and then define the following fields:

1. Item Number (Number)
2. Item (Text)
3. Cost (Currency)
4. Source Code (Text)

Select as the primary key the field Item Number. Change the Decimal Places property for the Cost field to 2, and then change the Field Size property for the Source Code field to 3. Save the table with the name Items, and then close the Basket database.

BUILD SKILLS

11 Create a Database and Use the Lookup Wizard

Suppose a friend is starting a new Shirt-Of-The-Month Club mail-order business. She has designed 14 motifs to be applied to T-shirts or sweatshirts: one motif for each of the 12 months of the year (hearts for February, shamrocks for March, and so on), an alternate motif for July, and a special birthday motif. The October through March motifs are applied to sweatshirts; T-shirts are used for the other eight motifs. The two July choices are a Canadian maple leaf motif or a US flag motif.

projects

Customers may order one, three, six, or twelve shirts. Orders are filled starting with the month following the receipt of the order, with orders of three or more shirts filled in consecutive months. If a customer orders 12 shirts, then a thirteenth free birthday T-shirt is also sent in the birthday month indicated on the order. Orders that will include a July T-shirt must specify a motif choice for that month.

In this Project, you'll create the Shirts database and the Orders table. (For simplicity, you'll assume that the shirts are to be sent to the person who placed the order.)

Create a database named Shirts on your Project Disk. Start a new table, and then define a field for each of the following:

1. Order# (AutoNumber)

2. Name (Text)

3. Address (Text)

4. City (Text)

5. State/Province (Text)

6. Zip (Text)

7. #Months (Number)

8. Start Month (Number)

9. Start Year (Number)

10. Birthday Month (Number)

11. July Choice (Text)

Select as the primary key the field Order#. Define a Validation Rule for the #Months field specifying valid field values as 1 or 3 or 6 or 12, and then create an appropriate message for the Validation Text property. Similarly, define a Validation Rule and Validation Text for the Start Month field (must be between 1 and 12) and the Birthday Month field (must be between 0 and 12).

Now you'll change the July Choice field to a Lookup field, which is a field that displays a list of valid choices for the field value.

To define a Lookup field using the Lookup Wizard:

1: Click **Text** in the Data Type column for July Choice field, click ▼, and then click **Lookup Wizard**.

2: You can use an existing table or query to supply the values for the lookup list, or you can type the values yourself. You decide to do the latter, so click **I will type in the values that I want.**, and then move to the next Lookup Wizard dialog box.

3: You need only one lookup column, so you needn't change the default number of columns. Click in the cell beneath the Col1 heading, type **NA** (for "not applicable") in that cell, press the down arrow key, type **US Flag** in the second cell, press the down arrow key, and then type **Maple Leaf** in the third cell. Double-click the right edges of the Col1 heading to get the best fit for the column, and then move to the next Lookup Wizard dialog box.

4: The default name "July Choice" is an acceptable label for the lookup column, so click the **Finish** button.

Save the table with the name Orders.

View the table datasheet, and then add the records shown below to the table, making up values for Name, Address, City, State/Province, and Zip. When you get to the July Choice column, click ▾, and then click the appropriate choice.

Order#	#Months	Start Month	Start Year	Birthday Month	July Choice
1	3	2	1998	0	NA
2	12	2	1998	4	US Flag
3	6	2	1998	0	Maple Leaf
4	1	2	1998	0	NA

Resize all the columns in the Orders table to their best fit. Print the table, close the table (saving changes), and then close the Shirts database.

12 Use the Database Wizard

Microsoft Access provides two methods to create a database. You can create a blank database and then add the tables, forms, reports, and other objects later. This is the most flexible method, but it requires you to define each database element separately. Alternately, you can use the Database Wizard to create in one operation the required tables, forms, and reports for the type of database you choose. This is the easiest way to start creating your database; it's also a way to ensure that all the queries, forms, and reports are accurate and are consistent with one another. But no matter which method you use, you can modify your database at any time after you've created it.

In this Project, you'll use the Database Wizard to create an address book database.

To use the Database Wizard:

1: Click the New button on the toolbar, click the **Databases** tab, click the **Address Book** icon, and then click the **OK** button. The File New Database dialog box appears.

2: Click on the *Save in* box, click the drive containing your Project Disk, and then (if necessary) double-click the folder name. Make sure the name in *File name* box is "Address Book," and then click the **Create** button.

3: After a few moments, the first Database Wizard dialog box appears. Click the **Next** button to move to the second Database Wizard dialog box.

4: You won't need to select any additional fields, and you don't want sample data, so click the **Next** button to move to the third Database Wizard dialog box.

5: Click **Dusk** to select that style for screen displays, and then click the **Next** button to move to the fourth Database Wizard dialog box.

6: Click **Formal** to select that style for printed reports, and then click the **Next** button to move to the fifth Database Wizard dialog box.

7: "Address Book" is an acceptable name for the database, and you won't include a picture, so click the **Next** button to move to the sixth Database Wizard dialog box.

8: Click the **Finish** button to create the database.

The interface that appears is called a "switchboard," which is a form that will appear whenever you open the Address Book database and which provides controlled access to the database's tables, forms, queries, and reports. The switchboard form heading, "Address Book," uses a font different from the font used for the four options. You'll change the font used for the four options to make the database presentation more readable and colorful.

To modify the switchboard:

1: Switch to Design view, click **Address Book**, double-click the Format Painter button, click each of the top four boxes (which are to the right of the top four buttons), and then click the Format Painter button.

2: Select the top four boxes, click the *Font Size* box, and then click **11**.

3: Right-click one of the selected boxes, point to **Font/Fore Color**, and then click the blue color in the second row (third box from the right).

4: Click the View button, and then click the Save button.

The address book adds, by default, an input mask that will not let you enter a text postal code, such as those for a Canadian address. You'll remove that mask so you can add addresses for people outside the U.S.

To allow for entry of non-numeric postal codes:

1: Click the ⬚ **Restore** button in the lower-left corner of the screen, click the **Tables** tab, and then open the Addresses table in Design view.

2: Click **PostalCode** and then delete the **Input Mask**. Save your changes and close the Addresses table.

3: Click the **Forms** tab, open the Addresses form in Design view, right-click the unboxed **PostalCode**, and then click **Properties**.

4: Locate and delete the **Input Mask**, close the property sheet, save your changes, close the **Addresses** form, and then click the ⬚ **Minimize** button on the Database window.

Now you'll use a switchboard command button and add address records to the database.

To add address records:

1: Click the **Enter/View Addresses** button on the main switchboard. The Addresses form appears. This is a two-page form. To switch pages, click one of the page number buttons at the bottom of the form.

2: Enter at least five address records, either real or imaginary. To skip a field, simply press the **Enter** key. Don't forget to fill in the page 2 information for your five address records. Add at least one address record with the current month as the month in a Birthdate field, and make sure the Send Card field for that record contains a check mark. When you've completed an address record, use the onscreen navigation buttons to move to a new record. When you've finished entering address records, click the ⬚ **Close** button to return to the main switchboard.

Hint: You must enter a numeric value for the year in the Birthdate field, even if you know only the birth month and day. You might use 00 in that case.

Next, you'll preview and print two reports.

To preview and print reports:

1: Click the **Preview Reports** button on the main switchboard. The Reports switchboard appears.

2: Click **Preview the Address by Last Name Report** button. Click the ⬚ **Print** button on the toolbar to print the report, and then close the preview window. Repeat for the **Birthdays This Month Report**.

projects

3: Click the **Return to Main Switchboard** button.

To close the database, click the Exit This Database button on the main switchboard.

13 Create a Form with Two Subforms and Change a Control Type   File: Notables.mdb

Suppose the manager of the celebrity look-alikes and sound-alikes needs a form he can use to learn who is available during specific time periods, who they can impersonate, and what type of impersonation (vocal or visual) they do. In this Project you'll create and modify a form with two subforms.

A **subform** is a form within a form. You use a subform when you want to display data from two related tables. For example, each record in the Impersonator table has one or more records in the Celebrity table-- one record for each celebrity the impersonator impersonates. In this instance, you'd use a subform to display all the celebrities for a given impersonator at the same time you're displaying the impersonator in the main form.

Open the Notables database from your Project Disk, and then click the Forms tab.

To create a form with two subforms:

1: Use the Form Wizard for the Availability table. Select, in this order, the fields Availability from the Availability table, Name from the Impersonator table, and Celebrity and Type from the Celebrity table.

2: On the second Form Wizard dialog box, make sure Form with subform(s) is selected.

3: On the third Form Wizard dialog box, click **Tabular** for both subforms.

4: Select the **Standard** style on the fourth Form Wizard dialog box, and then click the **Finish** button.

Practice moving through the form and the two subforms to see how they work. Locate the seventh Availability record, then locate the second Impersonator record for that availability, and then look through the Celebrity records. Notice that Jackie Mannerly is available at all times (availability = Open) and that she does five vocal impressions.

You'll next add your name as a title to the main form.

To title a form:

1: Change to Design view. If necessary, click the ⚒ **Toolbox** button to display the toolbox.

2: Click the *Aa* **Label** button on the toolbox, move the pointer to the detail section on the main form, and then click the mouse button when the ✛ on the $\overset{+}{\text{A}}$ pointer is at the top of the detail section and at the 3" mark on the horizontal ruler.

3: Type your name, and then click the 💾 **Save** button on the toolbar.

The ▾ that appears on the Type box in the Celebrity subform is distracting, so you'll remove it by changing that control from a combo box to a text box.

To change a control type:

1: On the Availability form design grid, the two subforms appear as white blocks. Double-click the **Celebrity** subform to open that subform.

2: Right-click the **Type** control in the detail section, point to **Change to**, and then click **Text Box**.

3: Resize the Type control in the detail section by dragging its right edge to the 1.75" mark on the Ruler.

4: Close the Celebrity subform (saving changes), and then switch to Form view.

Locate the seventh Availability record, the second impersonator record for that availability, and the fourth celebrity record for that impersonator, and then print the selected record. (Don't worry if the records shown on the printout don't match those shown on the screen—just verify that the form appears on the printout.)

Close the Availability form (saving changes, if a prompt appears), and then close the Notables database.

14 Newspaper Work, Part 2 - Create a Table with a Lookup Field   File: Paper.mdb

Note: You must have completed Project 9 before doing this Project.

In Project 9 you created the Paper database, with a Section table, for the publisher of your local newspaper, who wants a database to track articles printed in the newspaper. You'll continue to develop the database in this Project and in Project 19. In this Project you'll create two more tables for the database and enter data in each.

projects

To complete this Project you'll need the same copy of your local newspaper that you used in Project 9.

Open the Paper database from your Project Disk. First you'll create the Article table. That table will include Section as a lookup field, which means that you'll select a newspaper section from the Section table when you enter a value for that field.

To create the Article table with a lookup field:

1: Start a new table. Define the following fields:

- Article# (AutoNumber): select as the primary key

- Title (Text)

- Page (Text): change the Field Size property setting to 3

- Date (Date/Time): change the Format property to Short Date

2: Define Section as the fifth field, tab to the *Data Type* box, click ▼, and then click **Lookup Wizard**. The option to look up values in a table or query is selected on the first Lookup Wizard dialog box, so click the **Next** button.

3: The Section table is already selected on the second Lookup Wizard dialog box, so click the **Next** button.

4: Click the ⟩⟩ button to add both fields to the selected field list, and then click the **Next** button.

5: The settings on the remaining Lookup Wizard dialog boxes need not be changed, so click the **Finish** button. Click the **Yes** button on the message box that appears. Type **Article** for the table name, press the **Enter** key, and then click the **OK** button in the message box that appears.

View the table datasheet, and then add to the table at least ten records, each record representing an article in the current edition of your local newspaper. If your newspaper prefixes page numbers with letters, you can enter a page number as "A12" or "C3", for example. When you're entering the Section field, click the ▼, and then click the appropriate section in the displayed list.

Note: Be sure to keep the articles you've entered; you'll need the name of the reporter for each of the articles in the next part of this Project as well as in Project 19.

Resize each column in the Article table to its best fit, save the table, print the table, and then close the table.

Next you'll create the Reporter table. Start a new table, and then define the following fields:

- Reporter ID (Text): select as the primary key, and change the Field Size property setting to 3

- Reporter (Text)

Save the table as Reporter, and then view the table datasheet.

Add records for the reporters of all of the articles you entered in the Article table. For the Reporter ID, enter a unique code up to three characters in length. You can use the reporter's initials, and then append a number if more than one reporter has the same initials. If an article had more than one reporter, enter a record for each. Create an additional record with a Reporter ID of "---" and with "(none)" as the Reporter.

Resize each column in the Reporter table to its best fit, save the table, print the table, close the table, and then close the database.

15 Gift Baskets, Part 2 - Import a Text File
Files: Basket.mdb and Items.txt

Note: You must have completed Project 10 before doing this Project.

In Project 10, you began work on the Basket database, which you'll use in your new business to keep track of the types of baskets you'll sell, the items you'll include in the baskets, and the sources from which you'll purchase various items. In this Project you'll add several records to the Items table, which you created in Project 10. Then you'll import additional records for the Items table from an existing text file.

Open the Basket database from your Project Disk, and then open the Items table. Using Item Number field values starting with 1 and increasing by 1 for each record, add at least 8 but no more than 15 records to the table for various fruit and candy items that could be included in a basket, such as an apple, a grape bunch, a banana, or a peppermint candy. Try to use reasonably realistic prices, such as $0.25 for a banana or $0.05 for a peppermint. For the Source Code, select one of the sources for candy, fruit, and other grocery items that you added to the Sources table in Project 10.

Save the table, and then close the table. Now you'll import additional records for the Items table from a text file.

To import a text file:

1: Click **File** on the menu bar, point to **Get External Data**, and then click **Import**. The Import dialog box appears.

2: Click [▼] on the *Files of type* box, and then click **Text Files**.

3: Click [▼] on the *Look in* box, click the drive containing your Project Disk, and then (if necessary) double-click the folder name. Click **Items** in the file list, and then click the **Import** button. The first Text Import Wizard dialog box appears.

4: Make sure the Delimited option is selected, and then click the **Next** button.

5: Make sure the Comma option is selected, and then click the **Next** button.

6: Click **In an Existing Table**, click [▼], click **Items**, and then click the **Next** button.

7: Click the **Finish** button. Click the **OK** button when the import process is complete.

Open the Items table, and then verify that it now contains additional items (Item Numbers of 20 through 56). Resize each table column to its best fit, save your table changes, print the table, close the table, and then close the Basket database.

EXPLORE

16 Create an Index   File: Namerica.mdb

An index helps Microsoft Access find and sort records faster. Access uses indexes in a table as you use an index in a book: to find data, it looks up the location of the data in the index. You can create indexes based on a single field or on multiple fields.

The primary key of a table is automatically indexed, and you can't index a field whose data type is Memo or OLE Object. For other fields, you should consider indexing a field if all the following apply:

- The field's data type is Text, Number, Currency, or Date/Time.

- You anticipate searching for values stored in the field.

- You anticipate sorting values in the field.

- You anticipate storing many different values in the field.

You have two choices when creating an index. If you create a unique index, Access won't allow two records in the table to have the same value for that indexed field. Or, you can create an index that allows duplicate values.

In this Project, you'll create an index for the Capital field in the State/Province table of the Namerica database. First you'll create an index that allows duplicate values, and then you'll change it to a unique index.

Open the Namerica database from your Project Disk, and then open the State/Province table in Design view.

To create an index:

1: Click **Capital**, click **Indexed**, click 🔽, and then click **Yes (Duplicates OK)**.

2: Save the table changes, and then view the table datasheet.

3: Select **Juneau** in the third record, type **Denver**, and then click the Capital field value for another record. Notice that "Denver" duplicates the value of the Capital field in the Colorado record and that you're allowed to have duplicate field values.

4: Click the 🔙 **Undo** button to change back to "Juneau" as the capital, click the 💾 **Save** button to save the change, and then close the State/Province table.

5: Open the State/Province table in Design view, click **Capital**, click **Indexed**, click 🔽, and then click **Yes (No Duplicates)**.

6: Save the table changes, and then view the table datasheet.

7: Select **Juneau** in the third record, type **Denver**, and then click the Capital field value for another record.

  a What message appears?

8: Click the **OK** button, click the 🔙 **Undo** button, click the 💾 **Save** button to save the change, close the State/Province table, and then close the Namerica database.

17 Copy an Access Form
Files: Funds.mdb and Mtlfunds.mdb

Suppose you need a form for the Funds database so you can view and update records to the Mutual Funds and Objectives tables; suppose also that an earlier version of the Funds database, Mtlfunds, already has a form you'd like to use. You can get that form into the Funds database in one of three ways:

- import the form from the Mtlfunds database

- copy the form in the Mtlfunds database and then paste it in the Funds database

- use a drag-and-drop technique to copy the form to the Funds database

projects

In all three cases, once the form is copied or imported into the Funds database, you can modify it as needed. In this Project, you'll use the drag-and-drop technique to copy the form.

To copy a form from one database into another:

1: Start Access and open the **Funds** database from your Project Disk.

2: Start another instance of Access, open the Mtlfunds database from your Project Disk, and then click the **Forms** tab. There are now two Access buttons on the taskbar, once for each instance of Access that is running.

3: Right-click a blank area of the taskbar, and then click **Tile Vertically**. The two Access windows now appear side by side.

4: Click and drag **Mutual Funds** in the Mtlfunds database window over into the Funds window (notice that the Forms tab is then automatically selected in the Funds window), and then release the mouse button. The form is now copied into the Funds database.

5: Right-click a blank area of the taskbar, and then click **Undo Tile**.

6: Click the second (rightmost) **Microsoft Access** button on the taskbar, close the Mtlfunds database and then close it's version of Access. The Funds database is now the active window.

Open the Mutual Funds form, and then (if necessary) maximize the form window (you may have to drag the title bar to the left to see the ▢ Maximize button). Note: This form is designed to fill the screen for a screen resolution of 800 x 600 pixels; if you're using a lower resolution, you'll have to use the scroll bars to view the entire form.

View the 43rd record. Click File, click Page Setup, click the Page tab, and then click the Landscape option. Then print the current (selected) record.

Close the form, and then close the Funds database.

18 Import a Spreadsheet and Create an Append Query
Files: Reading.mdb and Justread.xls

You can import or link data from a Microsoft Excel spreadsheet into an Access database. When you import data, you add the contents of the originating file to the database. When you link data, you do not add the contents of the originating file to the database; rather, you create a connection to the data and can use it as if it were part of the database. You use a similar procedure for importing and for linking data.

In this Project, you'll import an Excel spreadsheet containing the books you most recently read and add the records to the Books Read table in the Reading database.

Open the Reading database from your Project disk.

To import a spreadsheet:

1: Click **File** on the menu bar, point to **Get External Data**, and then click **Import**. The Import dialog box appears.

2: Click ▼ on the *Files of type* box, and then click **Microsoft Excel**.

3: Click ▼ on the *Look in* box, click the drive containing your Project Disk, and then (if necessary) double-click the folder name. Click **Justread** in the file list, and then click the **Import** button.

4: In the first Import Spreadsheet Wizard dialog box, click **First Row Contains Column Headings** to put a check mark in the checkbox, and then click the **Next** button.

5: Click the **Next** button to move to the third Spreadsheet Wizard dialog box.

6: Click the **Next** button, click **Choose my Own Primary Key**, click ▼, click **Title**, and then click the **Next** button.

7: In the next Import Spreadsheet Wizard dialog box, type **New Books Read**, and then click the **Finish** button. Click the **OK** button when the import process is complete.

You now have two tables containing information about the books you've read: Books Read and New Books Read. To add the records from the New Books Read table to the Books Read table, you need to create an append query.

To create an append query:

1: Start a new query using the New Books Read table.

2: Click the ▼ next to the 🗔 ▼ **Query Type** button on the toolbar, and then click **Append Query**. In the Append dialog box, type **Books Read**, and then click the **OK** button.

3: Add all fields in the New Books table to the query. Because the Author and Title field names match field names in the Books Read database, the Append To information is automatically filled in for those two fields. You'll have to supply that information for the Type field. Click the *Append To* box for the Type field, click ▼, and then click **Type-F(iction) or N(on Fiction)**.

4: Click the ⚠ **Run** button on the toolbar to run the append query. Click the **Yes** button in the message box advising you that you're about to append 13 rows to the Books Read table.

5: Close the query without saving changes.

Click the Tables tab, open the Books Read table, and then resize the Author column to its best fit. Verify that the Books Read table now contains 76 records (the original 63 records plus the 13 appended records).

Click File on the menu bar, click Page Setup, click the Page tab, click Landscape, and then click the OK button. Print the table, save your table changes, and then close the Books Read table.

You no longer need the New Books Read table, so right-click that table, and then click Delete. Then close the Reading Database.

19 Newspaper Work, Part 3 - Define Relationships and Create a Four-Table Query   File: Paper.mdb

Note: You must have completed Projects 9 and 14 before doing this Project.

In Project 9 you created the Paper database, with a Section table, for the publishers of your local newspaper, who want a database to track articles printed in their newspaper. In Project 14 you created the Article and Reporter tables. In this Project you'll create one more table for the database and enter data in the table. Then you'll define the relationships among the four tables, and then create a query using information from all four tables. To complete this Project you'll need the same copy of your local newspaper that you used in Projects 9 and 14.

First you'll create the Reporter/Article table. Start a new table, and then define the following fields:

- Reporter ID (Text): change the Field Size property setting to 3

- Article# (Number)

Select as the primary key the multiple fields Reporter ID and Article#. (Hint: Hold down the Ctrl key and then click each row selector. If the two fields do not remain selected when you right-click, and then use the 🔑 Primary Key button on the toolbar.) Save the table as Reporter/Article, and then view the table datasheet.

Add records for the reporters and their articles for all the articles in the Article table. If an article had more than one reporter, enter a record for each reporter. If no reporter is listed for an article, and then use the "---" Reporter ID for that article.

Resize each column in the Reporter/Article table to its best fit, save the table, print the table, and then close the table.

Next you'll create a join using all four tables in the Paper database.

To join the Paper tables:

1: Click the [▣] **Relationships** button on the toolbar. You need to create the relationship between the Section table and the Article table.

2: Double-click **Section**, and then double-click **Article** to add the tables to the Relationships window. Next double-click **Reporter/Article** and double-click **Reporter** to add the tables to the Relationships window, and then close the Show Table dialog box.

3: Create a join between the Article table (primary table) and the Article/Reporter table (related table), using the Article# field as the common field.

4: Create a join between the Reporter table (primary table) and the Article/Reporter table (related table), using the Reporter ID field as the common field.

5: Create a join between the Section table (primary table) and the Article table (related table), using the Section Code field as the common field.

Use the Simple Query Wizard to create a query that includes, in order, the Date, Title, and Page fields from the Article table, the Section field from the Section table, and the Reporter field from the Reporter table. Sort the query in ascending order by Date and then in ascending order by Page, run the query, and then print the query.

Save your query changes, close the query, and then close the Paper database.

20 Gift Baskets, Part 3 - Join Tables and Add Calculated Fields   File: Basket.mdb

Note: You must have completed Projects 10 and 15 before doing this Project.

In Projects 10 and 15, you worked with the Basket database, which you plan to use in your new business to keep track of the baskets you'll sell, the items you'll include in the baskets, and the sources from which you'll purchase various items. In this Project you'll create the Filled Basket table, and then join the tables in the Basket database. Then you'll create a report, add a calculated field to the report, and then use the report results to determine the price to charge for a basket.

Open the Basket database from your Project Disk. Start a new table, and then define the following fields:

- Basket Number (Number)
- Item Number (Number)
- #Items (Number)

Select as the primary key the multiple fields Basket Number and Item Number. (Hint: Hold down the Ctrl key and then click each row selector. If the two fields do not remain selected when you right-click, and then use the ![key] Primary Key button on the toolbar.) Save the table as Filled Baskets, and then view the table datasheet.

Next you'll "fill" one of the baskets (your choice) in the Baskets table by creating a series of records in the Filled Baskets table. A filled basket *must* include one each of the following items: a bow, shredded paper filler, a basket, and cellophane; therefore, you'll need four records in the Filled Baskets table for those four items. In addition, you'll need to create one record in the Filled Baskets table for each item you plan to include in the basket. For example, to include three baby bibs in a basket, you'd create a record with Item Number=22 and #Items=3.

When you've completed entering records for one complete basket, resize each column in the Filled Baskets table to its best fit, save your table changes, and then close the table.

Next you'll create a join using all four tables in the Basket database.

To join the Basket tables:

1: Click the ![relationships icon] **Relationships** button on the toolbar. Double-click each of the four tables to add the tables to the Relationships window. Then close the Show Table dialog box.

2: Create a join between the Sources table (primary table) and the Items table (related table), using the Source Code field as the common field.

3: Create a join between the Items table (primary table) and the Filled Baskets table (related table), using the Item Number field as the common field.

4: Create a join between the Baskets (primary table) and the Filled Baskets table (related table), using the Basket Number field as the common field.

Use the Report Wizard to create a report. Include, in order, the Basket Name and Price fields from the Baskets table, Source from the Sources table, Item and Cost from the Items table, and #Items from the Filled Baskets table. View the output by Baskets, sort the output by Source and then by Item, and use the Stepped layout and the Formal style. Save the report as Filled Baskets.

Change to Design view, and then delete the Basket Name and Price controls from the page header section. In the Basket Number header, resize the Price control from its right edge so that it is ten dots narrower. Resize the Cost control in the detail section from its right edge so that it is eight dots narrower.

Change the width of the design grid by dragging the right edge one inch to the right. Then select the multiple controls for the line at the top of the report header, for the line at the top of the page header, and for the line at the bottom of the page header. Then hold down the Shift key as you resize them to extend to right edge of the design grid. Finally move the Page control in the page footer to the right edge of the design grid.

Click File on the menu bar, click Page Setup, click the Page tab, click Landscape, and then click the OK button. Now you'll add the total cost calculations to the report.

To add a calculated field to the report:

1: First you'll add a group footer section. Click the [icon] **Sorting and Grouping** button on the Access toolbar, click **Group Footer** in the Sorting and Grouping dialog box, click its [icon] button, click **Yes**, and then close the Sorting and Grouping dialog box. A Basket Number footer section is added to the report design.

2: Now you'll add a text box to the detail section. Click the [abl icon] **Text Box** button on the toolbox, and then click in the detail section at the top of that section in the area to the right of the #Items control. Click the label box (which contains "Text:" followed by a number), and then press the **Delete** key.

3: Next you'll specify a formula to calculate a total cost for an item. Right-click the new text box, click **Properties**, click **Control Source**, type =[Cost]*[#Items], change the Format property to **Currency**, and then close the property sheet.

4: Right-click that new control again, and then click **Copy**. Right-click in the Basket Number footer section, and then click **Paste**. Move the pasted control to the far right to align it beneath the calculated control in the detail section.

5: Right-click the new control in the Basket Number footer section, click Properties, then edit the formula to add the word "Sum" and two parentheses to change the formula to **=Sum([Cost]*[#Items])**, and then close the property sheet.

6: Save the report, and then preview the report. Make a note of the total cost, and then close the report.

Now you need to determine a price for the basket that will cover the costs plus labor and other expenses, and that will provide a small profit. Open the Baskets table, change the Price field to the price you want to charge, and then close the Baskets table.

Print the Filled Baskets report. Then close the Basket database.

projects

21   Add Pictures to Records

Files: Flags.mdb and Bermuda.bmp

Access has ten data types, eight of which you used in the online Steps and/or the other Projects: AutoNumber, Currency, Date/Time, Lookup Wizard, Memo, Number, Text, and Yes/No. A ninth data type is OLE Object, where OLE stands for *Object Linking and Embedding*. You use the OLE Object data type for field values that are created in other programs as objects--such as pictures, drawings, sounds, and spreadsheets. When you insert such an object in a table field, you can view the object on a form or report. In this Project, you'll add a picture to a record.

Open the Flags database from your Project disk, click the Forms tab, and then open the State/Province form. View the first several records. Notice that a country flag appears for each record except the first record, which is the record for the country of Bermuda. You'll add Bermuda's flag to the Country table.

To add a picture to a record:

1: Close the State/Province form, click the **Tables** tab, and then open the Country table.

2: Right-click the Flag column for the first record, and then click **Insert Object**. The Insert Object dialog box appears.

3: Click **Create from File**, click the **Browse** button, click the drive containing your Project Disk, and then (if necessary) double-click the folder name. Click **Bermuda.bmp** in the file list, click the **Open** button, and then click the **OK** button. The picture named Bermuda.bmp is inserted as the value for the Flag field in the first record; "Bitmap Image" appears as the field value to indicate the picture has been added.

4: Close the Country table, click the **Forms** tab, and then open the State/Province form. The first record now displays the Bermuda flag.

Print the selected record (the first record), close the State/Province form, and then close the Flags database.

22   Create a Hyperlink

Files: Homes.mdb and Listings.doc

Access has ten data types, nine of which you used in the online Steps and/or the other Projects: AutoNumber, Currency, Date/Time, Lookup Wizard, Memo, Number, Text, and Yes/No, and OLE Object. A tenth data type is the hyperlink data type. You use the hyperlink data type to store the locations of other Office 97 documents or of sites on the World Wide Web, or simply the Web. When you click a hyperlink field value, Access starts the associated program and opens the document or Web page.

In this Project, you'll work with the Homes database to create and use hyperlinks to Listings.doc, a Word document.

To create hyperlinks:

1: Open the **Homes** database from your Project disk, and then open the **Listed Homes** table in Design view.

2: Add a new field to the end of the table. Type **Comments** as the field name, and select **Hyperlink** as the data type, save the table, and then switch to the table datasheet.

3: Right-click the Comments column for the first record, point to **Hyperlink**, and then click **Edit Hyperlink**. The Insert Hyperlink dialog box appears.

4: Click the top **Browse** button. If necessary, click ▼ on the *Look in* box, click the drive containing your Project Disk, and then (if necessary) double-click the folder name. Click **Listings.doc** in the file list, and then click the **OK** button.

5: Click the **Named location in file** box, type **Krasinski**, and then click the **OK** button. "Listings.doc" appears as the value for the Comments field in record 1 to indicate the hyperlink has been added.

6: Repeat Steps 3 through 5 for records 2 and 3, typing **Zychowicz** for record 2 and **Dowling** for record 3 in Step 5.

7: Use landscape orientation to print the Listed Homes table.

Next you'll use the hyperlinks you've created.

To use a hyperlink:

1: Click **Listings.doc** in record 1. Word starts and opens the Listings document to the bookmark named Krasinski. Close the Word document, and then exit Word.

2: Repeat Step 1 for records 2 and 3.

3: Close the table, and then close the Homes database.

23 Converting Objects to Web Pages

File: Orders.mdb

The World Wide Web, or simply the Web, is being used more and more for business interactions. For example, you can order merchandise over the Web or allow your customers to place orders over the Web. Access has a special tool to convert

projects

objects, such as a queries and forms, into documents for viewing on the Web; these documents are called **Web pages**. The Access tool adds special instructions, using the HyperText Markup Language (HTML), to the object. In this Project, you'll work with the Orders database to create and use Web pages.

To create Web pages:

1: Open the **Orders** database from your Project disk.

2: Click **File** on the menu bar, and then click **Save As HTML**. The Publish to the Web Wizard dialog box appears.

3: Click the **Next** button, click the **Queries** tab, click the **Receivables Aging Report Query** check box, click the **Forms** tab, and then click the **Orders by Customer** check box. Both the selected query and the selected form will be converted into Web pages.

4: Click the **Next** button, and then click the **Next** button in the following two dialog boxes. Make sure the text box displays the drive containing your Project Disk, and then click the **Next** button.

5: Click the **Yes, I want to create a home page** check box, press the **Tab** key, type your name in the box, and then click the **Finish** button. Access will create a home page, which will be your third Web page.

If you do not have a Web browser installed on your computer, close the Orders database, exit Access, and then skip the rest of this Project.

If you have a Web browser installed on your computer, you'll now use it to view the Web pages you've created.

To view Web pages:

1: Click **View** on the menu bar, point to **Toolbars**, and then click **Web**. The Web toolbar appears.

2: Click the **Go** button on the Web toolbar, and then click **Open**. The Open Internet Address dialog box appears.

3: Click the **Browse** button, make sure the *Look in* box contains the drive or folder containing your Project Disk, click the html file that has your name, click the **Open** button, and then click the **OK** button. Your Web browser starts and displays your home page.

4: Use your Web browser to print your home page.

5: Use your Web browser to view the other two Web pages you created.

6: Exit your Web browser.

7: If necessary, click **Microsoft Access** on the taskbar.

8: Click **View** on the menu bar, point to **Toolbars**, click **Web**, close the Orders database, and then exit Access.

INVESTIGATE

24 Relationships

In the Database e-SSentials chapter and in the "Join Tables" topic (Topic 5) in the Tutorial 2 online Steps you learned that in a one-to-many relationship, one record in the primary table matches many records in the related table, and one record in the related table matches one record in the primary table. In this Project you'll investigate the other types of relationships that can exist between tables.

Use the Access Help facility to learn about relationships. There are two types of relationships in addition to a one-to-many relationship—what are they? When you create a join in the Relationships window, how does Access determine what kind of relationship it is?

Recall that a table is a collection of fields related to a single entity (person, place, object, event, or idea). Think about the entities in an environment with which you're familiar (school, work, sports, recreation, and so on). Determine two entities in that environment that are related by a one-to-many relationship, and then do the same for the other two relationship types.

Write a paper of at least two pages discussing relationships, defining the different types of relationships, and explaining how Access determines the relationship type. Include your entity examples for each relationship type and clearly explain why the entities are so related.

25 Planning a Database

Access can be a useful tool, but only if you first carefully plan the database so it meets the needs of those who will use it. In planning a database, called database design, you first determine the fields, tables, and relationships needed to satisfy the data and processing requirements. When you design a database, you should follow these guidelines:

- Identify all the fields needed to produce the required information.
- Group related fields into tables.
- Determine each table's primary key. Recall that a primary key uniquely identifies each record in a table. For some tables, one of the fields, such as a Social Security number or credit card number, naturally serves the function

projects

of a primary key. For other tables, two or more fields might be needed to function as the primary key. In these cases, the primary key is referred to as a *concatenated key* or *composite key*. For example, a school grade table would use a combination of student number and course code to serve as the primary key. For a third category of tables, no single field or combination of fields can uniquely identify a record in a table. In these cases, you need to add a field whose sole purpose is to serve as the primary key.

- Include a common field in related tables. You use the common field to connect one table logically with another table, or to form a relationship between the tables.

- Avoid data redundancy. Data redundancy occurs when you store the same data in more than one place. With the exception of common fields to connect tables, you should avoid redundancy because it wastes storage space and can cause inconsistencies—for instance, you might type a field value one way in one table and a different way in the same table or in a second table.

- Determine the properties of each field. You need to identify the properties, or characteristics, of each field so that the database management system knows how to store, display, and process the field. These properties include the field name, the field's maximum number of characters or digits, the field's description, the field's valid values, and other field characteristics.

Demonstrate your understanding of database design by analyzing a particular set of data requirements for a library. Assume you have the following fields:

- Author Code
- Author Name
- Book Title
- Borrower Address
- Borrower Name
- Borrower Card Number
- Copies of Book

- ISBN (International Standard Book Number)
- Loan Date
- Publisher Code
- Publisher Name
- Publisher Address

A one-to-many relationship exists between publishers and books. Many-to-many relationships exist between authors and books and between borrowers and books.

Following the guidelines presented above, design the library database by determining the tables required, placing the fields into their appropriate tables, and identifying each table's primary key. Your instructor will provide you with specifications for the format of your database design.

projects

26 Normalization

If you're going to create new databases or add tables to existing databases, it's essential that you understand the process of normalization. A simple definition of **normalization** is that it is a process that enables you to analyze the design of a database to determine if it is good or bad and to improve it if it's bad. But before you can grasp normalization concepts, you need to know several key terms—some of which were introduced in the Database e-SSentials chapter and in the online Steps.

Using the resources in your library and/or on the Internet, find definitions from at least three different sources for each of the following database terms:

- entity
- primary key
- foreign key
- concatenated, or composite, key

- functional dependency
- partial dependency
- transitive dependency
- determinant

Also, find definitions for first normal form (1NF), second normal form (2NF), and third normal form (3NF). Describe the types of problems that can occur in a database that's not in 1NF, not in 2NF, and not in 3NF.

Demonstrate your understanding of normalization concepts by analyzing a particular database design. Assume you have the following three tables in a database:

a A table called Student, with fields Student Number, Student Name, Student Phone Number, Advisor Number, Advisor Name, and Total Credits Earned. Student Number is the primary key of the Student table.

b A table called Course, with fields Course Number and Course Description. Course Number is the primary key of the Course table.

c A table called Courses Completed, with fields Student Number, Course Number, and Grade. The primary key of this table is the combination of Student Number and Course Number.

For each of the three tables, determine if the table is in 1NF, in 2NF, or in 3NF, and explain why you decided as you did. State any assumptions you need to make about the data.

Write a paper that presents the results of your research and analysis. Be sure to document your sources. Your instructor will provide you with specifications for length and format of the paper.

projects

27 Macros and Modules

As you've learned, Microsoft Access provides a wealth of features through its wizards and through its options for creating and modifying tables, forms, reports, and queries. Yet Access also allows you to handle customized tasks using macros and using Visual Basic for Applications.

Use the Access Help facility to learn about Visual Basic for Applications and macros as they relate to event-driven applications, custom procedures, and modules. Find at least three types of tasks you can accomplish with macros, and three that you can accomplish with Visual Basic for Applications, that you couldn't do otherwise in Access.

Write a paper that presents the results of your research. Your instructor will provide you with specifications for length and format.

28 OLE!

Access 97 has ten data types, eight of which you used in the online Steps and/or the Projects: AutoNumber, Currency, Date/Time, Lookup Wizard, Memo, Number, Text, and Yes/No. A ninth data type is OLE Object, where OLE stands for Object Linking and Embedding.

Use the Access Help facility to learn about the OLE Object data type. What is it? What are some examples of fields that you might want to include in a database for which you would assign the OLE Object data type? Which Access objects (tables, queries, forms, reports) would display the actual field value for an OLE Object field? What are some of the possible data sources for the OLE Object data type?

Write a paper that presents the results of your research. Your instructor will provide you with specifications for length and format.

Answers to Database e-SSentials CheckPoint Questions

1   database

2   structured; free-form

3   field

4   False

5   True

6   find

7   Query by example

8   query language

9   True

10 database management software

Answers to Odd-Numbered Review Questions

Tutorial 1

1 Database	7 fields	13 Preview
3 open	9 navigation	
5 shortcut menu	11 saved	

MULTIPLE CHOICE

15 c	21 b	27 d
17 b	23 c	
19 c	25 c	

MATCHING

29 l	35 a	41 d
31 i	37 b	
33 k	39 g	

SHORT ANSWER

43 Drag the title bar of the dialog box to a new location.

45 A record contains data about one person, place, object, event, or idea, and is a single row in a table. A field represents a single characteristic of a record and is a single column in a table.

47 When you update a database, you add, change, and delete data.

49 An Access database is saved automatically by Access, both on a periodic basis and whenever you close the database.

Tutorial 2

FILL-IN-THE-BLANKS

1	query	11	property sheet
3	Design	13	query
5	run	15	properties
7	condition	17	primary
9	descending		

MULTIPLE CHOICE

19	c	27	c
21	b	29	b
23	a	31	a
25	c	33	d

MATCHING

35	e	39	a
37	g	41	b

SHORT ANSWER

43 The field list contains a list of the fields in a table. The design grid is where you place the fields and other criteria for the information you want to see in your query results. You drag the fields you want to see from the field list to the design grid. The order of the fields in the design grid is the order in which they will appear in the query results.

45 Two methods to remove fields from a query: a) You can delete a field from the design grid to remove it permanently from the query. b) You can uncheck the field's Show box in the design grid to keep the field in the query but remove it from the query datasheet.

47 For a one-to-many relationship, one record in the primary table matches many records in the related table, and one record in the related table matches one record in the primary table. The matching is established through the use of a common field stored in both tables.

answers

Tutorial 3

FILL-IN-THE-BLANKS

1   report

3   Report Wizard

5   tabular

7   landscape

9   Design

11   report header

13   control

15   group footer

MULTIPLE CHOICE

17   c

19   c

21   c

23   b

MATCHING

25   c

27   a

29   b

31   g

33   k

35   i

SHORT ANSWER

37   If you want to perform the same operation (moving, deleting, formatting, and so on) on a number of controls, you can save time by multiply selecting all the controls and then performing the operation on all of the selected controls at once. To select multiple controls, you click the first control, then hold down the Shift key as you click the remaining controls.

39   Before you resize a graphic, you must set the SizeMode property. For example, if you want to resize the graphic proportionately, without distortion, you need to set the SizeMode property to Zoom.

Tutorial 4

FILL-IN-THE-BLANKS

1 database

3 currency

5 primary key

7 Percent

9 AutoForm

11 Wizard

MULTIPLE CHOICE

13 a

15 d

17 b

19 a

21 c

23 d

25 a

MATCHING

27 i

29 a

31 k

33 e

35 j

answers

37 The rules for naming fields are: a name can be up to 64 characters long; a name can contain letters, numbers, spaces, and special characters except a period, exclamation point, accent grave, and square brackets; a name cannot start with a space.

39 You should select a primary key for each table so that you'll be able to distinguish one record from all the other records in the table.

41 An AutoForm Wizard places all the fields from a selected table or query on a form automatically, without asking you any questions. The Form Wizard prompts you through the steps to create a form. You can choose some or all of the fields in the selected table or query, choose fields from other tables and queries, and display the chosen fields in any order on the form. You can also choose a style for the form.

Presentation e-SSentials

> Most people, no matter how competent they are, break into a cold sweat when they have to speak in public. This is perfectly natural, like being afraid to touch eels. But once you learn a few of the "tricks of the trade" used by professionals, you find it's surprisingly easy, and can even be fun! I'm talking about eel-touching. Public speaking will always be awful.
>
> – Dave Barry in *Claw Your Way to the Top*

Some people are born performers and for them public speaking, speeches, and oral presentations are fun. For a large percentage of the population, however, public speaking is not high on the list of fun things to do.

Speeches and presentations aren't easy to avoid. You might have to present a new product idea to management, or maybe you've been chosen to explain a fund-raising project at your Rotary club chapter. Maybe you've been persuaded to give a 30-minute talk about your recent vacation, or perhaps you're trying to persuade the local city council not to put a freeway exit a block from your home. Public speaking is hard to avoid.

So what can you do to help become a better speaker? Numerous "self-help" books offer advice on public speaking. There's the practical advice: Use a clip-on microphone so you can step away from the lectern and still be heard. And then there's the whimsical advice: If you're intimidated by the people in your audience, imagine that they're all in their pajamas! One of the newest pieces of advice is to use presentation software to help you organize what you're going to say, not just to provide interesting visuals to keep your audience on track.

overview

WHAT IS PRESENTATION SOFTWARE?

Presentation software is a computer program that provides you with tools to create the outline or script for a presentation and to design a series of computer images that contain text, bullets, tables, charts, graphs, and graphics. The computer images you create with presentation software are typically referred to as **slides**. You can print these slides on paper or project them on a large screen or blank wall. Figure 1 shows an example of one slide for a presentation about Toronto nightlife.

Figure 1 *A slide for a presentation might contain text, bullets, and graphics.*

If you're shopping for presentation software, you'll find many packages to choose from. One of the most popular presentation software packages is **Microsoft PowerPoint**. Introduced in 1987, PowerPoint has been revised and updated with new features, including a command to convert your presentation slides into HTML format so you can post them on the Internet. Microsoft includes PowerPoint with its integrated software suite called Microsoft Office, which many computer buyers receive bundled with their new computers.

HOW DOES PRESENTATION SOFTWARE DIFFER FROM OTHER SOFTWARE SUCH AS WORD PROCESSING?

Presentation software is specifically designed to create visually appealing slides. When you work with presentation software, you are usually working with one slide at a time; whereas when you work with word-processing software, you are usually working with a document. Figure 2 shows you the screen display you'd see if you were using PowerPoint.

Figure 2 *In Slide View mode, PowerPoint displays one slide at a time, which you can modify. The buttons on the toolbars make it easy to change the font size and color. A Graph button on the toolbar made it easy to create the graph you see here.*

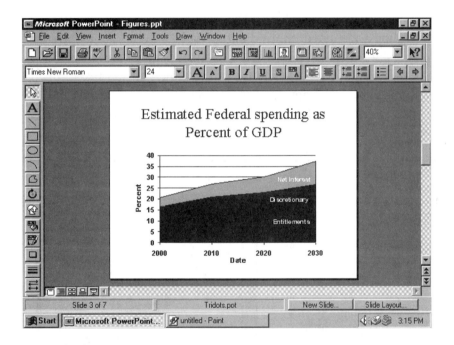

HOW DO I GET STARTED ON A PRESENTATION?

Suppose you have some presentation software and you need to give a speech. Where do you start? You start with substance. The greatest, most professional delivery, eye-popping graphics, and snazzy special effects amount to nothing if you don't have anything to say. Before you fire up your presentation software, take some time to think about the big picture. Ask yourself: Who? What? When? Where? Why?

- **Who** is your audience?
- **What** are the most important facts about your topic?

overview

- **When** will you be making your speech; who comes before and after? When's the event?
- **Where** will you be making your presentation? What's the environment?
- **Why** are you giving this speech? What's your goal or purpose? What do you want the audience to know, do, or feel when you're done with your speech?

HOW CAN I TAILOR MY PRESENTATIONS TO MY AUDIENCE?

You've probably heard the expression "in one ear and out the other." You don't want that to happen to the information you're presenting. To make your words and ideas "stick" with your audience you can tailor your presentation to the background, experience, emotions, and interests of your listeners.

As you're planning a presentation, find out as much as you can about your audience's age, gender, interests, politics, educational background, financial situation, ethnic background, and knowledge of the topic you're presenting. Then think about how you can use graphics, colors, sounds, facts, and anecdotes in ways that appeal to such an audience. Look at the slides in Figure 3. Which one is tailored to a younger audience?

Figure 3 *The "Bigger is Better" slide uses graphics, text treatment, and wording that would appeal to a younger crowd.*

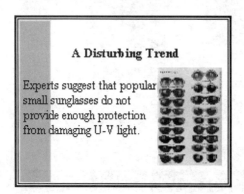

WHAT FACTORS IN THE ENVIRONMENT DO I NEED TO CONSIDER?

If possible, before you create your presentation, visit the room where you'll be speaking. The larger the room, the more distant your audience. Even with a large screen, you'll need to keep your slides readable by keeping them simple, using large text, and selecting a color scheme that provides good contrast.

Test the room lighting. What happens when you turn out all the lights? If the room is not dark, you'll need to use dark text on a light background so your slides are readable.

Where will you stand? Can you see the screen without turning your back to your audience? If not, how will you make sure the correct slide is displayed? Perhaps you will be able to see your slides in a computer monitor or maybe you'll want to position a small mirror to help you see your slides. Can all of the audience see the screen or will you or your computer equipment block their view? If so, you could rearrange the equipment or the seating.

HOW DO I CREATE THE SCRIPT FOR MY PRESENTATION?

First, think about the purpose of your presentation and the outcome you desire. Do you want to convince the board of directors to buy a pig farm? Do you want to explain the rules of good behavior so your summer campers will stay out of trouble? Do you want to assure the town council that the biker barbecue you're promoting will be just as tranquil as an ice cream social? Do you want to motivate your district democratic party volunteers to promote their candidate?

Once you have a clear idea about the purpose of your presentation, you can think about what you can say to achieve your purpose; and you can consider how to say it for maximum impact.

Your **presentation script** is the notes you'll follow when you speak. Your script might be in the form of an outline, key points, or a word-for-word narrative. Many experts suggest that you should not read a script word-for-word. It is better, they suggest, to speak conversationally and refer only occasionally to notes. Take this advice with a grain of salt. If you're an inexperienced speaker, have difficulty speaking standard English, are really nervous about speaking, don't feel entirely comfortable with your topic, or are giving a speech in which every word is legally or politically important, your presentation might be more successful if you carefully craft a word-for-word script and read it; but read it with feeling and in a way that your audience cannot tell you're reading.

You might want to compose the narrative for your presentation using word-processing software, but most presentation software provides you a way to enter your presentation script. For example, PowerPoint has an **Outline View** that helps you type in an outline for your presentation. PowerPoint also has a "notes" page that displays a small graphic of a slide and has room for you to enter what you want to say while that slide is displayed. You can print these notes pages, as shown in Figure 4, and use them during the presentation.

Figure 4 *You can easily use PowerPoint to generate a script that contains a "thumbnail" version of a slide and what you want to say about it.*

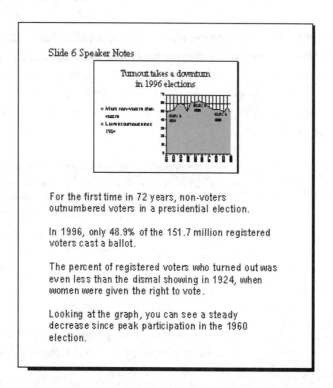

HOW DO I TURN MY SCRIPT INTO SLIDES?

Don't try to put everything you're going to say on the slides. Slides should provide just the highlights of your presentation and serve as cues for your narration. How do you know which parts of your presentation to put on slides? Here are some guidelines:

- the title of your presentation
- an overview of your presentation
- key facts
- lists
- quotes
- graphics such as bar graphs, photos, or cartoons
- recommendations or key conclusions

Your presentation software makes it easy to create each slide. First, you'll select the color scheme for the background and text of the slide. Then you'll select a slide layout. The **slide layout** refers to the position of elements on the slide. For example, a slide with a title layout would generally use a very large font and the space in which you'd type the title would be centered on the slide. In addition to a title layout, your presentation software will generally provide bullet, graph, graphic, organization chart, table, video, and blank layouts such as those in Figure 5.

Figure 5 *A wide variety of slide layouts let you incorporate titles, bulleted lists, tables, graphs, organization charts, and graphics.*

After you select the layout, you'll type in the text for the slide and add any additional elements such as graphs, tables, charts, or video clips. After you adjust the position of these elements, your slide is complete.

HOW DO I DESIGN MY SLIDES?

A design theme definitely helps to unify a presentation. The theme you choose should support your presentation topic and goals. If you're trying to excite your audience about the Humane Society building fund raiser, you might use bold, lively colors, cat and dog cartoons, and fun fonts. You can achieve a unifying visual theme for your presentation by using similar colors and fonts on all the slides.

Most presentation software provides pre-designed **templates**, such as those in Figure 6, that include professionally designed color schemes, graphics, and fonts selected to be the right size and color for good visibility. Although you can also create your own templates, it is easier to use those that have already been created for you.

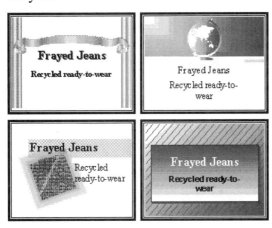

Figure 6 *Four professionally designed templates applied to the same title slide. Which one do you prefer?*

If you take the do-it-yourself route by designing your own slide template, you'll need to consider what color and type size to use for each of the elements on a slide—title, subtitles, bullet text, sub-bullets, and so on. In a corporate setting, you might have certain guidelines about color and use of your company's logo.

overview

Although you want a unified look for your slides, it would be boring if they were all exactly the same. You can introduce variations for some of your slides. For example, you could add a bright yellow color stripe or starburst to a slide to call attention to an important point.

HOW CAN I MAKE EFFECTIVE USE OF COLOR?

The four keys to presentation color are that color should:

- support the purpose of your presentation,
- reflect the topic of your presentation,
- enhance the readability of your slides, and
- appeal to your audience.

If you're planning to project your presentation, you should use a good level of contrast between background and text. Yellow text on a white background is virtually impossible to read when projected. A better selection would be navy blue text on a white background or yellow text on a dark green background.

Darker colors tend to recede, but hot colors jump out at you. Avoid using red text, except perhaps for a title. Remember that in many business situations red means "the red ink" and that's associated with losing money.

Blues and grays are conservative colors that are useful for reporting facts to which you want little reaction. Think of the stuffy old board members of the London bank in the film Mary Poppins. This is the audience that will appreciate blue and gray.

Did you know that about 8 percent of the male population is color blind so they can't distinguish well between red and green? For this reason, and because these colors don't go well together, you should avoid using combinations of red and green for slide text and backgrounds.

Although bright backgrounds with dark text might be suitable for a short, fun, exciting presentation, for a longer presentation, use more restful, cool, or subdued colors for backgrounds. Dark text on a bright background tends to produce a visual after-image. You should avoid too many slides with such a color scheme unless you really want to "burn in your point."

WHAT'S A BULLET?

Dinosaurs of the Gobi

- Velociraptor
- Oviraptor
- Protoceratops
- Ankylosaurus
- Troodontid

Figure 7 A slide with five bullets.

A **bullet** is a special character—usually a circle or square—that precedes each item in a list. For example the slide in Figure 7 has five bullets.

Slides with bullets are one of the most typical features of computerized presentations because the bullets provide a clear summary of each point you're trying to explain. Presentation software makes it easy to put bullets on slides and then animate them so the bullets and text "fly" onto the slide one at a time—with sound effects, if you like!

HOW DO I KNOW WHEN I'VE REACHED THE LAST BULLET ON A SLIDE?

When you've practiced your presentation, you should be familiar with the content of each slide. However, you might be reviving an old presentation or pinch hitting for a colleague. In this case, it helps to have a symbol that indicates the last bullet on a slide or in a series. An effective technique is to put a period at the end of the text on the last bullet, but omit the period on all the other bullets. When you see that period, you'll know its okay to say "and the last item in this sequence…".

WHAT IF I HAVE A TIME LIMIT?

Most presentations have a time limit, and you want to make sure to cover the most important information within that limit. You'll need a few rounds of practice to get the timing right.

Presentation software, such as PowerPoint, allows you to set up timing for each slide. There are two methods to set the slide timing. First, you can manually enter the number of seconds you would like a slide to appear. Second, you can start your presentation in practice mode and PowerPoint will remember how long you displayed each slide. You can then store this timing sequence and use it for your actual presentation. When timing your slides, remember that your audience does not want to look at the same slide for 10 minutes!

When you're giving your actual presentation, be sure you have a watch—but don't leave it on your wrist. You'll tend to check it too often and your audience will wonder whether you've got to rush off or are bored with your own presentation. Instead, put your watch somewhere that you can look at it without being too obvious.

WHERE CAN I FIND GRAPHICS TO ADD TO MY SLIDES?

You can find graphics by looking through any camera lens. Even if you don't have one of the new digital cameras, you can use a scanner to convert a photograph into a graphics file that you can store on your computer and use in a slide show. With a digital camera, you can skip the scanning step—your photos go from the camera directly into your computer. Or you can purchase a CD-ROM **clip-art collection** containing thousands of graphics. Another popular source of graphics is the Internet where you can browse around until you see an image you like and download it to your computer.

Graphics generally fall into one of two categories: vector graphics and bit-mapped graphics. A **vector graphic** is stored as line segments and color fills that can be easily enlarged or shrunk without distortion. Suppose you have a vector graphic of a diamond ring and you enlarge it. The enlarged ring will still appear round and smooth. Vector graphics tend to look a little like cartoons because they are formed by lines and fills. Most clip art is stored as vector graphics. You can identify vector graphics by their filename extensions: .wmf, .cgm, .wpg, and .mgx.

A **bit-mapped graphic** is stored as a series of colored dots. Look carefully at a color photograph in a newspaper and you can see that it is made up of dots—that's essentially how bit-mapped graphics work. Although they look more realistic than vector graphics, bit-mapped graphics do not re-size well. If you try to enlarge a small photo of a diamond ring that is a bit-mapped graphic, the ring will appear to have jagged edges. Bit-mapped graphics have filename extensions such as .bmp, .gif, .jpg, .pcx, and .tif.

So the rule of thumb is to use vector graphics when you need to change the size without distortion, but use bit-mapped graphics when you want a realistic-looking graphic whose size you won't have to change much. In Figure 8 compare the vector graphic on the left with the bit-mapped graphic on the right.

Figure 8 *The images on the left are bit-mapped, whereas the images on the right are vector graphics.*

ARE THERE COPYRIGHT RESTRICTIONS ON THE USE OF GRAPHICS?

Yes. Graphic images are protected under copyright law, so you should not use one without permission. Usually, when you purchase a clip-art collection, the license agreement gives you permission to use the graphics in your own, non-commercial presentations. You should read the license agreement before you buy, however, to make sure that the circumstances of your presentation are acceptable under the agreement.

If you find an interesting image on the Internet, you will often be able to discover its owner and get permission for its use via e-mail. After you obtain permission, it is courteous to give credit to the owner—just put a small by-line under the graphic when it appears on a slide.

HOW CAN I CREATE GRAPHS AND CHARTS FOR MY PRESENTATIONS?

Most presentation software provides an easy way to create organization charts as well as basic line, bar, and pie graphs.

An **organization chart**, typically used to show the "pecking order" of employees, depicts a hierarchy of boxes, connected by lines. A **graph**, sometimes called a **chart**, is a depiction of numeric data. Graphs and charts help people

overview

organize, summarize, and detect patterns in numbers—and they're certainly much easier to interpret than columns of numbers!

The graphs and charts you use for presentations and those you use for printed reports have essentially the same design rules:

- Match the format to your data; an organization chart shows a hierarchy; a line graph shows change over time; a bar graph shows comparisons; a pie chart show percentages.

- Include a descriptive title.

- Use labels to identify your data.

- Limit the amount of data so your chart or graph can be understood within the first three to five seconds.

- Make sure you accurately depict the data; don't distort data by stretching the graph; double-check names, labels, and numbers for accuracy.

WHAT ABOUT SOUND AND VIDEOS?

Multimedia elements includes graphics, sounds, and video. Careful use of multimedia elements emphasizes important points and helps keep your audience alert. Your presentation software probably has a collection of sounds that you can select to automatically play when you reach a certain slide or bullet. If you incorporate sound in your presentation, you'll need to make sure that your presentation equipment can amplify the sound for the entire audience. A computer speaker is just not sufficient for a large room or auditorium.

You can store short videos complete with sound track, usually called video clips, and view them using most presentation software. It's a neat effect—sort of like your slide suddenly comes alive. Presentation software is a suitable vehicle for short video clips—one minute or less. For long video segments, its probably better to pause your presentation and show a video tape.

Videos are neat, but they have a downside: Video files are huge and playback can be erratic on slower computers. Also the picture quality is not as good as on a TV set. Depending on your computer system, the video might play in a small window on the screen not easily seen by audience members in the back row. If you're considering video, try it in the room where you'll be presenting, using the equipment you'll have for your actual presentation. Sit in the back row and make sure your video is still effective.

overview

WHAT EQUIPMENT DO I NEED FOR A PRESENTATION?

If you're lucky, you'll be giving your presentation in a room already set up for computer presentations, and you'll have a professional operator to run the equipment. If you're not so lucky, you'll have to provide your own equipment, set it up, test it, and operate the presentation as you speak. Basic presentation equipment includes:

- **Computer**   Most presentation facilities use a desktop computer, but if you're carrying your own equipment, you'll probably use a notebook computer.

- **A projection device**   Three options are possible. First, an all-in-one projection device, often mounted on the ceiling, connects to a computer and projects the image from the computer monitor onto the large wall screen. Second, a computer projector works without a computer—you simply insert the disk containing your presentation into the projector's disk drive and away you go! The third and least expensive option is to connect the computer to an LCD panel, which you then put on an overhead projector.

- **Screen or blank wall**   You'll want to make sure your screen is large enough to project an image that your audience can see from the back of the room.

- **Power outlet** and possibly an **extension cord**   The extension cord is easy to forget. Don't leave home without it!

- **Sound system**   In a large room, you'll need a microphone and some way to amplify your computer's speaker if you've included sound and video in your presentation.

Figure 9 Basic equipment for a presentation includes a computer, a computer projection device, and a screen. It's also handy to have an extension cord.

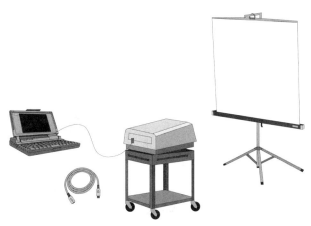

overview

HOW DO I PUT MY SLIDES ONTO THE COMPUTER IN THE PRESENTATION HALL?

Your presentation software stores the slides for a presentation in a file. PowerPoint, for example, stores presentations in a file with a .ppt extension, sometimes referred to as "a ppt file." Suppose you've created a series of slides for your presentation. Only problem is that the slide file is stored on your computer, not the computer in the room where you'll be giving your presentation. What do you do? You have several options.

If your presentation file is less than 1.4 megabytes, copy it to a floppy disk. You can probably run it from the floppy; but if you'd like your slide transition to run faster, copy it onto the hard disk of the computer you'll use to present.

What if your presentation won't fit on a floppy disk? You can use a compression program, such as windup, to temporarily shrink your file so it will fit on a floppy. When you arrive for the presentation, you can restore your file to its original size on the presentation computer.

You can also make clever use of a notebook computer, if you have one. Create your presentation on your notebook computer and carry it to the presentation. Just check ahead of time to make sure you can connect your notebook to the projection system in the room where you'll give your presentation.

You might be able to use a network connection. Suppose you create your presentation in your office at work, where your computer is connected to the corporate computer network. You'll be giving your presentation in the board room, which also has a computer connected to the network. If you store your presentation on the network server's shared disk drive, you should be able to access it from the board room.

DO I NEED TO INSTALL MY PRESENTATION SOFTWARE ON THE COMPUTER I'M USING FOR MY PRESENTATION?

Suppose you create a presentation using PowerPoint presentation software. You're going to give the presentation at a conference in, say, Ireland. Do you need to take all your software with you?

If you're taking your notebook computer to the conference, it would be a good idea to make sure your presentation software, PowerPoint in this case, is loaded on the notebook along with your presentation slides. When you arrive at the conference, you can connect your computer to the projection device and everything should go smoothly.

But what if you're not taking a computer? Your PowerPoint presentation is just a data file that requires software to run the slide show. If the full version of

PowerPoint is not available, you can use the **PowerPoint viewer**—a stripped-down version of PowerPoint that's designed to display slide shows, but not to create or revise slides. Such viewers take up only a small amount of disk space and are easy to install.

WHAT IF I DON'T HAVE A PROJECTION DEVICE?

Computer projection equipment is expensive, so not all conference facilities have it. You might have to consider alternatives. If a 35mm slide projector is available, you can send your presentation file to a commercial media house to have slides made. Several media houses offer 24-hour turn-around.

Many presentation facilities have an overhead projector like the one in Figure 10. You can print out the slides from your presentation on transparencies, then use these transparencies on the overhead projector. With this method, your output will often be back and white—but you can add some color with felt pens.

Figure 10 *An overhead projector substitutes for a computer projector, but you must first print your slides on transparencies.*

Another alternative is to give a paper presentation. Print out your slides on paper. Most presentation software will print three or four slides per page. Make a nice booklet or folder of the slides for each participant. As you speak, you can direct the audience to look at the appropriate slide.

CAN I AVOID TECHNICAL DIFFICULTIES DURING MY PRESENTATION?

Professional presenters know something is bound to go wrong, so they plan for unpleasant surprises—the projector's been stolen, there's a power failure, the window curtains have gone to the dry cleaner.

You can't be absolutely certain that your presentation will go without a hitch, but you can take steps to minimize problems by checking the room and equipment ahead of time. It's also a good idea to have a low-tech Plan B, such as handouts containing critical information or your most important slides.

CheckPoint _____

1 The computer images you create with presentation software are usually referred to as _____.

2 When you plan a presentation, you should find out as much as you can about your audience. List at least six factors you might consider when characterizing an audience.

3 As you plan your presentation, what features of the presentation hall environment should you consider?

4 A presentation script might be in the form of an outline, _____, or _____.

5 True or False? One way to create a presentation in which all slides follow a visual theme is to use a pre-designed template, included with your presentation software.

6 What are the four keys to presentation color?

7 A(n) _____ is a symbol that precedes an item in a list.

8 Suppose you want to add a graphic to one of your slides. You found the perfect image on the Internet. You copy the image to your computer, but when you try to add it to a slide, it looks too small. You try to enlarge the image, but it becomes distorted; smooth curves now appear jagged and blocky. Is this image a vector graphic or a bit-mapped graphic?

9 Explain how copyright laws affect or restrict your use of graphics.

10 _____ elements such as graphics, sounds, and video emphasize important points and help keep your audience alert.

11 List three ways you can transport your slides to the presentation hall.

12 A presentation software _____ is essentially a stripped-down version of the software that allows you to show a presentation, but not create or edit one.

Microsoft PowerPoint

Tutorial 1: PowerPoint Basics

Tutorial 1

PowerPoint Basics

Giving Power-Packed Oral Presentations

In your career you'll frequently find yourself nervously standing in front of a group of managers, trying to persuade them to adopt your ideas. Learn how to use a PowerPoint slide show to help get your point across more professionally and effectively.

Doing the e-Thing

You'll find out how to get started with the e-Course instructional software. This is an easy way to learn how to use Microsoft PowerPoint.

Projects

Tutorial 1 Projects are designed to help you review and develop the skills you learned in Tutorial 1. Complete each Project using Microsoft PowerPoint. You should not need to use the e-Course software to complete the Projects, except to create a Project Disk containing practice files. If you have not yet made the Project Disk for Tutorial 1, start the e-Course software, click Project Disk on the e-Course Welcome screen menu bar, and follow the instructions on the screen.

   If you've forgotten some of the skills you need to complete these Projects, refer to the Task Reference.

Disks

If you would like to keep track of your progress, you should have a blank formatted disk ready when you begin the online Steps for Tutorial 1. As you log in, the e-Course software will create a **Tracking Disk** for you. The Tracking Disk will keep a record of the length of time you spend on each e-Course session and your scores on the CheckPoint questions you answer online. If your instructor will collect your Tracking Disk for grading, make sure you have a backup copy! You should have a second formatted disk to use as a **Project Disk**. You'll find out how to make and use your Project Disk when you get to the Projects section of the WorkText.

scenario

Time Out!

As our society has evolved from the agricultural era through the industrial era, and now into the information age, we find ourselves with more time on our hands. No longer do we have to spend time growing our own food, building our own homes, making and even washing our own clothes. All of the necessities are relatively easy to come by. Computers and automated machines do more and more of our work.

Our standard of living is far beyond what even the wealthiest of kings would ever have dreamed possible. This increased standard of living has brought much more leisure time—and in response to this increase we have more games, toys, recreational activities, sports, entertainment media, and other similar activities than anyone can handle. Can you imagine a time when there was radio, but no TV, board games but no video games, movies but no videos? This describes how it was less than 20 years ago!

Consider the many types of recreational activities available—cycling, kayaking, skiing, snow boarding, roller blading, skydiving, fishing, surfing, rappelling, and playing countless "ball" sports—basketball, football, soccer, and golf...to name just a few. Think of how much attention is paid to golf alone! This sport originated in Scotland in the fifteenth century. Early golf clubs looked more like hockey sticks than today's clubs did, and early golf balls were made of wood. King James II of Scotland banned golf because he thought his citizens were spending too much time on golf and not enough time at archery and wouldn't be able to defend themselves against an English invasion.

Since that time, golf has become an international sport and is still growing in popularity. Golf courses by the thousands can be found in the United States, Canada, and around the world. And numerous PGA and LPGA tournaments compete for prime sports coverage on television.

Commercial leisure activities have become big business. And people in the leisure business use many communications media to get their message across. TV, radio, newspapers, magazines, brochures, and the Internet are used to entice prospective customers. And the computer now provides another powerful communications tool—the slide show. Software packages such as PowerPoint are readily available and easy to learn. Even novice computer users can quickly create colorful, dynamic slide shows to help market their products and services. Slide shows are used for customer presentations and for behind-the-scenes work where people in the leisure business inform and persuade their colleagues.

Let's take a specific example related to the game of golf. What if you worked for a city recreation department and wanted to persuade the city council to approve plans to develop a municipal golf course? Where would you start? You might decide to first gather information on the location, the finances, and the demand. You might think that all of this information justifies the decision to proceed with the golf course. But when you informally poll the council members, you discover that not everyone is convinced. You decide that a professional and persuasive oral presentation with a hard-hitting slide-show would be just the thing to persuade the reluctant council members. Further, you decide to distribute a handout at the conclusion of your presentation so all the members can study the facts later on their own. Preparing such a slide show used to take weeks to complete, but with PowerPoint you can do it in less than an hour. Will the council approve the golf course proposal?

In Tutorial 1, you'll learn how to create slide shows to help you communicate persuasively. You'll learn how to start and exit PowerPoint, create slides using different backgrounds and layouts, enter text as headings and bulleted lists, and sort and edit slides to create a polished presentation.

GET STARTED ONLINE WITH e-COURSE

The e-Course software is designed to teach you how to use the Microsoft PowerPoint software. The first time you use the e-Course software, you'll probably want to set up a Tracking Disk, which keeps track of your progress and your CheckPoint scores. Now it's time to use your computer:

To start the e-Course software and set up a Tracking Disk:

1: Label a formatted disk **Tracking Disk** and place it in the disk drive. (This step is optional, but if you do not insert a disk, you will not have an electronic record of your progress.)

2: Start your computer, then click the **Start** button.

3: Point to **Programs**.

4: Point to **e-Course**.

5: Click **e-Course PowerPoint**.

6: If you see the message "The tracking file was not found on drive A," click the button labeled **Copy the tracking database to a disk in drive A**. This will copy some files onto your disk, and then display the Login window.

scenario

➔ If you're in a computer lab and e-Course is not on the Programs menu, ask your technical support person how to start the e-Course software. If you're using your own computer, you must install the e-Course software before you use it. Refer to the TechTalk section of this WorkText.

The first time you log in, e-Course asks you to enter your name and other information that automatically appears on your CheckPoint Reports. This information is stored on your Tracking Disk, so you won't have to enter it the next time you log in.

To log in the first time:

1: On the Login screen, fill in the blanks with your **first name**, **last name**, **course section**, and **student number**. If you don't know your course section or student number, just type anything—you can change it later.

2: Click the **OK** button. In a few seconds, you should see the e-Course Welcome screen.

At the e-Course Welcome screen, you can print out your Task Reference. The Task Reference will help refresh your memory about how to do the tasks you learn in the tutorials.

To print out the Task Reference:

1: Click **Task Reference** on the Welcome screen menu bar.

2: Click **View/Print Task Reference**.

3: After the Task Reference appears, click **File** on the menu bar, then click **Print**.

4: When the printout is complete, click **File**, and then click **Exit**.

e-Course is easy to use. After the short e-Course Introductory Tour, you'll be ready to use all the e-Course features.

To start the e-Course Introductory Tour:

1: Click the **Introductory Tour** button on the Welcome screen.

2: Follow the instructions on the screen to navigate through the tour.

When you've finished the Introductory Tour, it's time to get started on Tutorial 1!

To start Tutorial 1:

1: Click **Tutorials** on the menu bar at the top of the Welcome screen.

2: Point to **Tutorial 1**.

Click a Topic—you should begin with Topic 1.

Review Questions

FILL-IN-THE-BLANKS

Fill in the blank with the correct word or phrase.

1 You can use PowerPoint to create slide show _____.

2 The filename extension automatically added to PowerPoint files is _____.

3 If you hold the mouse pointer over a PowerPoint screen button for a second or two, a(n) _____ appears, telling you the function of the button.

4 In PowerPoint a slide's background is called a _____.

5 The arrangement of text and graphics on a slide is referred to as the slide _____.

6 The dotted-line border on a PowerPoint screen where you can enter text is called the text _____.

7 A(n)_____ is a box, triangle, circle, or other symbol used to accent the beginning of a line of text.

8 If you're working on a slide and then decide to delete it, you would click _____ on the menu bar, and then click Delete Slide.

9 You can spell check a slide presentation in _____ View.

10 You can reorder PowerPoint slides best when in _____ View.

11 In _____ View, you can play a slide presentation for an audience.

12 _____ Effects change the way a new slide is first displayed.

13 _____ Effects make several bulleted items on a slide appear one at a time, instead of all at once.

review questions

14 Clicking the _____ button on the menu bar bypasses all the print options and makes the printer print immediately.

15 A bulleted slide usually consists of a(n)_____, plus several bulleted items.

MULTIPLE CHOICE

*Select the letter of the **one** best answer.*

16 **The extension of a PowerPoint file is:**

    a .prp   **c** .pwr

    b .ppt   **d** .pnt

17 **To run the PowerPoint spell checker, PowerPoint must be in _____ View.**

    a Slide   **c** Outline

    b Slide Sorter   **d** Slide Show

18 **A template dictates**

    a the slide background design.

    b whether a title or bulleted list slide shows on the screen.

    c where the text placeholder(s) will be on the screen.

    d what font will be used for the slide text.

19 **If you click the print button, PowerPoint will**

    a automatically print miniature-slide handouts.

    b display the Print dialog box.

    c display the Printer-selection dialog box.

    d skip all dialog boxes and send the job directly to the printer.

20 **How many total slides can you have in a PowerPoint presentation?**

    a 20   **c** 40

    b 30   **d** As many as your computer memory can accommodate

21 **Which of the following views does not permit you to add new slides?**

    a Slide View   **c** Slide Sorter View

    b Outline View   **d** Slide Show View

22 **To get PowerPoint to show bullets on a slide one at a time, you click:**

  a special effects   **c** text preset animation

  b animation settings   **d** slide transition

23 **Which of the following is the name of a slide layout?**

  a Bulleted list   **c** Bedrock

  b Comet   **d** Blueweave

24 **In Outline View, the button "collapse all" will display**

  a all the text of all the slides.

  b only the main titles of the slides.

  c the text and the placeholders of all the slides.

  d the text and the background of all the slides.

25 **Which of the following options will result in this action: The PowerPoint program disappears from the screen and is no longer available for you to use.**

  a Exit   **c** Save

  b Close   **d** Save As

26 **Which of the following options will result in this action: PowerPoint remains as an active program on the screen, but the presentation you were working on disappears from the screen.**

  a Exit   **c** Save

  b Close   **d** Save As

27 **Which of the following options will result in this action: PowerPoint overwrites the name previously given to a presentation and saves the presentation.**

  a Exit   **c** Save

  b Close   **d** Save As

28 **If you see "Slide 2 of 4" in the lower-left corner of your PowerPoint screen, it means**

  a you are using the Bulleted List layout.

  b you are using the Contemporary template.

  c you have eight slides in your presentation.

  d you are working on the second of four slides.

29 **In which of the following views can you click the scroll bar down arrow to advance PowerPoint to the next slide?**

   a Slide View

   b Outline View

   c Slide Sorter View

   d Slide Show

MATCHING

Select the letter from the right column that correctly matches each item in the left column.

30	**layout**	**a**	a small symbol at the beginning of a line of text
31	**template**	**b**	a printed version of the PowerPoint presentation used to give to audience members
32	**Slide Show View**	**c**	the colored graphic background that appears behind the slide text
33	**Slide Sorter View**	**d**	the PowerPoint feature that presents bulleted lines one at a time instead of all at once
34	**bullet**	**e**	the PowerPoint feature that determines where the slide placeholders will be positioned
35	**build/animation effects**	**f**	the PowerPoint mode you use for showing a slide show presentation to an audience
36	**handouts**	**g**	the view in which you reorder the sequence of slides

SHORT ANSWER

Use a separate sheet of paper to write out your answers to the following questions.

37 Explain the difference between a Title layout and a Bulleted List layout.

38 If a friend were to ask you what PowerPoint is, what would you tell him or her?

39 Although you could reorder slides in the Outline View, why should you use the Slide Sorter View for reordering your slides?

40 If you had 15 slides in a presentation, would you use a different transition for each slide? Why or why not?

Projects

These Projects are designed to help you review and develop the skills you learned in Tutorial 1.

Complete each Project using Microsoft PowerPoint. You should not need to use the e-Course software to complete Projects, except to create a Project Disk containing practice files. If you have not yet made the Project Disk for Tutorial 1, start the e-Course software, click Project Disk on the e-Course Welcome screen menu bar, and follow the instructions on the screen. If you've forgotten some of the skills you need to complete these Projects, refer to the Task Reference.

REVIEW SKILLS

1   Who Are You, Anyway?   File: Golf.ppt

When you give a presentation to a group of people who don't know you, it's often a good idea to put your name and job title on the first slide, even if someone else has formally introduced you. Seeing your name and title, as well as hearing them, will help the audience remember better and will help them feel more at ease asking questions and making comments.

1: Open the Golf.ppt presentation from your Project Disk.

2: Change the subtitle "The Time is Right" to your name.

3: Press the **Enter** key and then type your title as **Recreation Specialist**

4: Print the slide in black and white, and then close the presentation without saving it.

2   Too Much of a Good Thing?   File: Golf3.ppt

Text is often the most important element you can include on your slides, but how you present text can make or break its impact. Slides that appear to be poorly prepared reflect poorly on the presenter and reduce the chances that the presentation will achieve its goals. Here's where special transition effects can help…they can make a slide show appear more professional and well thought out. But don't overdo a good thing. Avoid using too many special transition effects, because instead of contributing to the effectiveness of the slides, too many transitions will detract and cause the audience to focus on the transitions instead of the message.

projects

Using the Golf3.ppt file, apply the Box Out transition to slides 1 and 3. Apply the Box In transition to slides 2 and 4. Remember to apply this effect while in Slide Sorter View. After applying the transition effect, create a build/animation for each slide with bulleted text (slides 3 and 4). In Text Preset Animation, select Fly from Bottom for these bulleted slides. Save your file on your disk as "Golftran.ppt". View your presentation. Write a paragraph telling whether you agree with the statement that "too many different transitions detract."

3   Seeing Is Believing   File: Cycling.ppt

For every presentation you create, consider the visual capabilities of the audience. For younger audiences, you can use smaller print because younger people can usually see very well. For older audiences, however, you should use larger type. Load the Cycling.ppt file you used in Tutorial 1 and print black and white handouts for an older audience. Instead of printing six miniature slides on a page, select the three-slides-per-page option.

4   Basketball Bullets

You can use PowerPoint to create more than presentations with numerous slides. You can also use PowerPoint to create a single slide from which you can then produce a chart or film transparency. Assume that you need to create a chart announcing the times and places of basketball tryouts for men's and women's teams. Start a new presentation with a Contemporary template. Use a Bulleted List layout, and type the following elements on the slide, and then print the slide:

Title: **Basketball Tryouts**

Bullet: **Men--Monday at 4 p.m., South Gym**

Bullet: **Women--Tuesday at 4 p.m., North Gym**

Create a second presentation like the first one, except using a template of your choice. Print it, and then write a paragraph telling:

   a   which template looks best on the screen, and

   b   which template looks best on paper. Explain why.

5   Nothing But Text   File: Golf4.ppt

Often it is helpful to see the text of all the slides at once, instead of having to move from slide to slide. This is where the Outline View comes in handy, because it shows no layout or template. Only the slide text appears. Another advantage of Outline View is that while you're in this view you can run the spell checker to help ensure that your words are spelled correctly.

Load the Golf4.ppt file, switch to Outline View, and run the spell checker.

Although you can print the outline in PowerPoint, if you export it to Microsoft Word, you have many more options for formatting. To do this from the File menu, point to Send To, then click Microsoft Word, Outline Only, then click the OK button. Microsoft Word will open and a new document will be created. On the Edit menu, click Select All, and change the font to Times New Roman, 12-point. With the text still selected, select Columns in the Format menu, and change the number of columns to 2. If necessary, click on the Line between option. On the Format menu, select Paragraph and change the Alignment to Center and the Line Spacing to Double.

Print this Word version of your outline.

Write a paragraph explaining whether you prefer the PowerPoint or Word version as a handout and why.

APPLY SKILLS

6   Playing It Safe

You've been asked to give a presentation to an elementary school class on playground safety. Create a new presentation with a template of your choice and with the layout you think will work best. Use the following text on the slide:

Slide 1 (title):   **Playground Safety**

Slide 2 (bulleted list):   **Swings**

Bullet 1:   **Don't swing too high**

Bullet 2:   **Don't jump from swings**

Bullet 3:   **Stay away when someone else is swinging**

Slide 3 (bulleted list):   **Slides**

Bullet 1:   **Hold onto the handrails when climbing the steps**

Bullet 2:   **Don't climb up the slide**

Bullet 3:   **Don't slide down the slide backwards or lying down**

projects

Slide 4 (bulleted list):   **General Rules**

Bullet 1:   **Play fair**

Bullet 2:   **Don't take chances**

Bullet 3:   **Don't fight**

Bullet 4:   **Report to a teacher any problems you see on the playground**

Save the presentation as "Playrule.ppt", and print the slide show in black and white as a handout.

7   A Special Flyer

Your friend is helping organize a Special Olympics in your town. She is worried that she cannot create a professional-looking flyer, because she claims she has no artistic talent whatsoever. "And if the flyer doesn't look professional," she says, "people won't take it seriously." With your ability to use PowerPoint, you volunteer your services for this worthwhile event. Your friend gladly accepts your offer and asks you to make a flyer that can be used as a handout or be enlarged and used as a poster to place on billboards. Create the document using a template and layout of your choice. The text of the slide is as follows:

Title: **Special Olympics**

Bullet: **Come cheer your favorite athlete to victory!**

Secondary bullet: **Where: Southside High School Track**

Secondary bullet: **When: July 18 from 10 a.m. to 4 p.m.**

Secondary bullet: **How much: $2.00 per adult (children under 10 free)**

Save the presentation on your drive A as "Specialo.ppt", and print the slide.

8   Reordering Slides

You're a teaching assistant for one of the physical education instructors at your college. During the past week, you've been busy receiving applications from women students who have organized teams and want to participate in the women's volleyball intramural program during the current semester. Next Friday you'll meet with all the women students who have applied and give them their first week's playing schedules. You decide to create a short slide show for the meeting. The following information gives the team names and the dates, times, and locations of their weekly games. Type this information on slides, using whatever template you choose. Create a title for the first slide, and then use bulleted list slides for the other slides you need.

Slide 1:

Title: **Women's Volleyball**

Subtitle: **Team Schedules**

Slide 2:

Title: **Slammers**

Bullet: **Schedule:**

Secondary Bullet: **January 24 at 4 p.m.**

Secondary Bullet: **Hanover Hall, Room 128**

Slide 3:

Title: **Hawks**

Bullet: **Schedule:**

Secondary Bullet: **January 24 at 5 p.m.**

Secondary Bullet: **Hanover Hall, Room 126**

Slide 4:

Title: **Flyers**

Bullet: **Schedule:**

Secondary Bullet: **January 24 at 4 p.m.**

Sccondary Bullet: **Simpson Hall, Room 128**

Slide 5:

Title: **Cruisers**

Bullet: **Schedule:**

Secondary Bullet: **January 24 at 5 p.m.**

Secondary Bullet: **Simpson Hall, Room 126**

Slide 6:

Bullet: **If you have any questions:**

Secondary Bullet: **Ask Kevin Walker**

Secondary Bullet: **Room 188, P.E. Building**

Secondary Bullet: **414-2298 (email: kwalker@oldu.xxx)**

Secondary Bullet: **Hours: 8 a.m. to 6 p.m.**

projects

Use the transition effect of your choice for each of the slides. After creating the slide show, switch to Slide Sorter View. To reorder the slides, click on the Cruisers slide to select it, and drag your mouse pointer between slides 1 and 2. When you release the mouse button, the Cruisers slide becomes slide 2. Continue reordering the slides until they are in alphabetical order by team name. Save the presentation as "Volleyball.ppt" on your drive A.

9 Using Bullets

You've been hired as a lifeguard for a youth summer camp. The camp has a small lake, and your job will be not only to watch the campers as they engage in water activities, but also to organize activities and teach the campers appropriate water-related skills. You decide to prepare a one-page document that lists the different water activities available; your plan is to then enlarge it into a poster to display in the dining hall and attract the campers' interest. Select a template appropriate for a summer camp, and use a Bulleted List layout. Type the following information on the chart, using Outline View.

Title: **WATER ACTIVITIES**

Bullet: **Canoeing**

Bullet: **Swimming**

Bullet: **Tubing**

Bullet: **Snorkeling**

Save the presentation as "WaterActivities.ppt" on your drive A and print the final presentation, using a colored sheet of paper, if possible, so it will be more noticeable. In a paragraph write about what more you could do to enhance the effectiveness of the poster.

10 Support Your Local Fish?

You work as an assistant to a manager in your state's fish and game office. Your manager will give a presentation to a girl scout group on the different game fish in the local lakes. You tell your manager about PowerPoint and how it can help her make an entertaining presentation. She asks you to prepare a demonstration slide show. Prepare the following demo presentation, using a template appropriate for the situation.

Slide 1: Title slide with **Blinds Horizontal** transition

Title: **Game Fish in our Area**

Slide 2: Bulleted-list slide with **Blinds Vertical** transition and build/animation
with **Fly From Left**

Title: **Freshwater Fish**

Bullet 1: **Yellow Perch**

Bullet 2: **Catfish**

Bullet 3: **Trout**

Bullet 4: **Largemouth Bass**

Save the presentation as "Fish.ppt" on your drive A and show it to a friend, explaining the template, layout, transition, and build/animation features. Write a short report answering the following questions: What did your friend like most about the presentation? What did s(he) like least? Had your friend seen a PowerPoint presentation before? Has s(he) ever created one? What changes would your friend suggest to make your presentation better?

BUILD SKILLS

11 Changing A Template   File: Sports.ppt

As you know, PowerPoint provides templates as a background for slides. Although you cannot use a different template for each slide in a presentation, you can change the template if you change your mind after creating a presentation. Suppose you want to change the template for the Sports.ppt presentation.

To change a template:

1: Open the **Sports.ppt** file.

2: Make sure you have slide 1 displayed in Slide View.

3: Select on the toolbar.

4: Select a different template and then click **Apply**.

5: Print your presentation with six slides per page so you can see how the template looks on the screen as well as on paper.

6: Close the file without saving it.

12 2-Column Text Layout

In Tutorial 1 you used the Bulleted-list layout for several applications. This layout gives you two text placeholders—a title and a place for several lines of bulleted text. A slightly different layout is also available for text. This is the 2-Column Text layout; it appears as the third slide in the New Slide dialog box. This layout works well when you have a larger number of short text items you want to include on one slide. Create a new presentation, using a template of your choice. Select the 2-Column Text layout, and type "Sport Options at RiverWoods" as the title. Next, click the left placeholder, and type the following items:

Bullet: **Summer**

Secondary bullet: **Hiking**

Secondary bullet: **Fishing**

Secondary bullet: **Canoeing**

Secondary bullet: **Bird watching**

Now click the right placeholder, and type the following items:

Bullet: **Winter**

Secondary bullet: **Sledding**

Secondary bullet: **Cross-country skiing**

Secondary bullet: **Snowmobiling**

Secondary bullet: **Snow shoeing**

Save the slide as "Summer-winter sports.ppt" on your drive A, and print the slide.

13 Primary and Secondary Bullets

Create a new presentation, to be called Menu.ppt. Choose whatever template you think is appropriate, and then select the Bulleted List layout. In Tutorial 1 you pressed the Tab key to create secondary bullets. In the Menu presentation, you'll return from the secondary-bullet level to the primary-bullet level. Type the following information:

Title: **Tuesday's Menu**

Bullet: **Breakfast**

Secondary bullet: **Eggs, sausage, hash browns, juice, toast**

After typing the word "toast", press the Enter key. Then hold down the Shift key and press the Tab key to return to the next primary bullet. Then type the following:

Bullet: **Lunch**

Secondary bullet: **Sandwiches, chips, fruit wedges, punch, cookies**

Bullet: **Dinner**

Secondary bullet: **Salad, roll, drink, steak, vegetable, dessert**

Select all the text in the bulleted list. If the ruler isn't displayed, click Ruler on the View menu. Notice the two sets of indent markers, one for each bullet level. Slide the right pair of indent markers to the 1" mark to increase the distance to the secondary-bullet level. Save the presentation on your drive A. Print this presentation in black and white.

14 Moving Through a Slide Presentation   File: Sale.ppt

In Tutorial 1 you learned to press on the scroll bar to move from one slide to another when in Slide View. But there are additional ways to move through a slide presentation. Open the Sale.ppt presentation and try the following options in Slide View:

Next slide:	Press the **Page Down** key on the keyboard.
	Click on the scroll bar.
	Click just below the box on the scroll bar.
Previous slide:	Press the **Page Up** key on the numeric keypad.
	Click on the scroll bar.
	Click just above the box on the scroll bar.
First slide:	Press **Ctrl+Home**.
Last slide:	Press **Ctrl+End**.

Using your word processing program, create a mini-manual on different ways to move through a presentation.

projects

15 Transitions and Effects with Multiple Slides
File: Cycling.ppt

In Tutorial 1 you learned how to add transitions and build/animation effects to individual slides. You'll now learn how to add these transitions and effects to multiple slides.

To use transitions and effect with multiple slides:

1: Open the **Cycling.ppt** presentation and click the **Slide Sorter View** button.

2: Click **Edit** on the menu bar, and then click **Select All** to select all the slides.

3: Select **Box In** for the slide transition.

4: Select **Fly From Left** for the build/animation effect.

5: Click outside the slide area to deselect all the slides. Then click the first slide, play the show, and view the transitions and animations on all the slides.

Save this presentation on your disk as "CycleTransition.ppt", and then submit it to your instructor.

EXPLORE

16 Creating a Continuous Presentation, Hiding Slides, and Using Pack and Go

South Hills Fitness Center is a state-of-the-art physical fitness business that will soon open in your town. During the three months remaining before the center opens, South Hills President Dan Walker wants to set up a temporary storefront in the largest mall in town. Here people can learn about the Fitness Center facilities and membership packages.

Dan has hired you to develop a presentation that he will use when people come in to the store. You'll create this presentation in Outline View, using a pre-defined presentation format, as explained in the following Steps.

To use Outline View and a pre-defined presentation format:

1: If necessary, start PowerPoint and create a new slide show. Click the **Present** or **Presentations** tab in the New Presentation dialog box. The resulting screen gives you numerous pre-packaged presentation strategies, which you can follow exactly or modify to meet your needs.

2: Scroll down and select the **Company Meeting (Standard)** template.

projects

3: After the first slide appears on your screen, save this presentation on your disk as **Meeting.ppt**

4: Click the **Outline View** button. The entire text of this predesigned meeting agenda appears.

5: With the first line of text of slide 1 highlighted, type **South Hills Fitness Center** (Don't press the Enter key after you type.)

6: Highlight the subtitle **Presenter** and type **Dan Walker**. Nothing else should be included on slide 1.

7: Click the **slide 2** icon, highlighting the text. Press the **Delete** key and click the **OK** button, if necessary, to accept the deletion message. Modify the new slide 2 (Review of key objectives…) to read:

Title:	**Our Objectives**
Bullet:	**State-of-the-art Fitness Facilities**
Bullet:	**Affordable Pricing**
Bullet:	**Good Location** (Don't press the Enter key.)

8: Delete **slide 3**, **How Did We Do?**.

9: Change the new slide 3 to read as follows:

Title:	**What We Offer**
Bullet:	**Weight Room**
Bullet:	**Aerobics**
Bullet:	**Basketball**
Bullet:	**Racquetball**
Bullet:	**Child Care**
Bullet:	**Restaurant**

10: Change the next slide to read as follows:

Title:	**Pricing**
Bullet:	**Family and Group Rates**
Bullet:	**Day and Season Passes**

11: Change the next slide to read as follows:

Title:	**Location**
Bullet:	**Easy Access**
Bullet:	**Close to Major Neighborhoods**

You're not sure if you will need any of the other sample slides so instead of deleting them, you decide to hide them until Dan approves your presentation.

To hide slides in a presentation:

1: Hold down the **Shift** key and select slides 6 through 10. On the Slide Show menu, click **Hide Slide**. To verify that they are hidden, click on **slide 5** and run the Slide Show. It should skip from slide 5 to slide 11, the Summary.

2: Go back to Outline View, and modify the last slide to read as follows:

Title:	**Summary**
Bullet:	**Great Facilities**
Bullet:	**Great Rates**
Bullet:	**Great Location**

3: Run the spell checker and correct any spelling errors you find.

4: Click the slide 5 icon, highlighting the text. Drag it up between slides 3 and 4. Modify the last slide to reflect this change. The last two bulleted items should now be:

Bullet:	**Great Location**
Bullet:	**Great Rates**

Save the presentation once again, and then print it in black and white, with six slides per page.

When you show your presentation to Dan, he approves it and asks you to prepare it to run on a PC at the mall. He wants the presentation to run by itself, continuously, repeating every few minutes.

To create a continuously running presentation:

1: Click **Slide Show**, then click **Slide Transition**.

2: In the Advance section, deselect "On mouse click" and select **Automatically after**; enter 15 seconds as the time interval. Click the **Apply to All** button to apply this timed transition to every slide in the presentation.

3: Click **View** on the menu bar, click **Slide Show** and then click **Set Up Show**. In the dialog box, click two options: **Using Timings, if Present** and **Loop Continuously Until Esc**. Click the **OK** button.

4: Run the slide show to be sure it's not too slow and that it runs continuously.

Although you can simply save the presentation to a disk and open it on another computer, you can't always be sure that the other computer will have PowerPoint installed. The Pack and Go Wizard will help you to package the presentation so that it can run on any PC.

To use the Pack and Go Wizard:

1: Click **File**, then click **Pack and Go**. As you progress through the Pack and Go Wizard, make the following selections, then click **Next** to continue or **Finish** at the end.

    Select: **Active Presentation**

    Select: **A:\ drive**

    Select: **Include linked files**

    Select: **Embed TrueType fonts**

    Select: **Viewer for Windows 95 or NT**

To run the presentation, Dan will have to install it on the PC at the mall by running the Pack and Go Setup file that is included on the disk. If any changes are made to the presentation, the Pack and Go Wizard will have to be repeated to include the changes.

17 More on Transitions and Animations File: Racquet.ppt

You're working as a teaching assistant for one of the physical education instructors at your school. She is preparing for her first day of class in an introductory racquetball class and has given you a short slide show to work on. She has already entered the text, but she wants you to add some creativity to it so it doesn't look so boring.

To add transitions and animations to an existing presentation:

1: Open the presentation **Racquet.ppt**, and then click the **Slide Sorter View** button.

2: Add a different transition to each slide.

3: While holding down the **Shift** key, click **slides 2**, **3**, **4**, and **5**. Give these slides the build/animation effect of **Fly from Top Right**.

4: Click **slide 6** and then click **Slide View** to make the slide appear as a large slide. Click the placeholder in which the words "Practice, practice, practice" appear. On the toolbar near the top of the screen, click [icon]. An Animation Effects palette appears on the screen. Click [icon] on the Animation Effects palette. Click [icon] again to remove the Animation Effects palette.

projects

5: Save the presentation on your disk as **Racquet1.ppt**. To check the effects on slide 6, run the Slide Show for just that slide. Press the **Escape** key to return to Slide View. You should also play the entire presentation to see how you like the way the transitions work together.

Write a paragraph answering the following question: Do you think it's a good idea to have a different transition for each slide in this presentation?

18 Changing Text Effects and Printing in Color
File: Sportcol.ppt

All text comes from the basic alphabet, but there are dozens of different effects you can give to make text more eye catching. For example, you can change the typeface itself, from Times New Roman to Arial. Or you can change the size, the color, the shadow effect, the slant, or some other element of style. Let's experiment with the title slide of Sportcol.ppt.

To change the text style, font, and color:

1: Open the presentation **Sportcol.ppt**, and then click ⬜ to display the full-sized slide.

2: Click the title **South Hills Fitness Center**, and then highlight the title.

3: Enlarge the highlighted title by clicking 🅰 twice on the toolbar above the slide.

4: Click 𝐼 on the Formatting toolbar to italicize the title.

5: Click 𝐒 on the Formatting toolbar to place a shadow behind the title.

6: Click **Format** on the menu bar and then click **Font**. Click ▼ beside the *Color* box and click the text **More Colors**. Then click one of the colors from the color palette, and click the **OK** button to return to the font dialog box.

7: In the *font* box, change the typeface from Times Roman to something else, such as Arial. Click the **OK** button to close the dialog box.

8: Click outside the text placeholder to release the text highlight.

9: Click **File**, then click **Print**. If you have a color printer, deselect the "Black & white" option at the bottom of the dialog box, and print the slide in color. Then print again, in black and white. If you don't have a color printer, you could compare printing as "Black & white" and as "Pure black & white." Write a paragraph giving your opinion about which printout took longer to print and which is easier to read.

19 Enhancing Continuous Presentations   File: Sale.ppt

You're working as an administrative assistant to the manager of a sporting goods store in the local mall. The owner has asked you to create a continuously running slide presentation that can be seen by people as they walk down the main hallway. Your manager hopes the movement of the slide show will capture people's attention and entice them to come in and shop.

To enhance a presentation with color and sound:

1: Open the presentation **Sale.ppt** and then click 🖩.

2: Click **Edit** on the menu bar, and then click **Select All**.

3: Add a **Fly From Left** build/animation effect to all slides.

4: Click **Slide Show** on the menu bar, and then click **Slide Transition**.

5: Click the **Automatically after** option button.

6: In the *Automatically after _____ seconds* box, type **2**. Click the list arrow next to [No Sound] and select **Whoosh**. If your PC has sound capability, the sound will attract passersby to look at the screen.

7: Click the **Apply to All** button.

8: Click **View** on the menu bar, click **Slide Show,** and then click **Set Up Show**. In the dialog box, click two options: **Using Timings, if Present** and **Loop Continuously Until Esc**. Click the **OK** button.

9: View the slide show to make sure all slides are advancing properly. After viewing all slides, press the **Escape** key to stop the presentation.

10: Click **slide 2**.

11: Click **Format** and then click **Custom Background** or **Background**.

12: Click 🔽 beside the colored bar, and select one of the color options. Click the **Apply** button to change the background of slide 2.

Save the presentation on your disk as "Sale2.ppt".

The owner notices that the store experienced record-breaking sales while your slide show was running by the store entrance. He decides to use the technique again for his Memorial Day Sale.

projects

To create an alternate form of the presentation:

1: Go to slide 1 in Slide View, and click **Edit**, then click **Replace**. In the *Find What:* box, type **springtime**. In the *Replace With:* box, type **Memorial Day**. Click **Find Next**, then click **Replace**. You notice that on that slide, it says the sale ends on Saturday. Memorial Day is always celebrated on a Monday, so you should also replace Saturday with Monday.

2: Save the presentation again as **Sale3.ppt**, so both versions can be used again.

20 A Complete Presentation

You are enrolled in a speech class and have been assigned to give an informative presentation on your three favorite movies of all time. You are required to briefly describe the plot of each movie and then tell why you liked it. You want to use PowerPoint to help make it a more impressive presentation.

To create a new presentation using the PowerPoint wizard:

1: Click **File** on the menu bar and then click **New**. Click the **Present** or **Presentations** tab, and then click **AutoContent Wizard**. Click the **OK** button.

2: In the AutoContent Wizard dialog box, click the **Next** button, and then answer the questions concerning presentation type, output options, presentation style, and presentation options. Type your own name when it is requested, and type **My Three Favorite Movies** when you are asked for the subject matter.

3: Click the **Next** button after entering the appropriate information, and click the **Final** button after all the questions are answered.

4: Click ▣ to enter Outline View, and then modify the text of the slides as needed to create your presentation.

5: After the text is finalized, switch to **Slide Sorter View** and change the template by clicking ▣ on the Standard toolbar. Pick the template of your choice. Also, on all slides, apply a transition effect and a build/animation effect of your choice. Use the same transition effect and build/animation effect on all slides.

Save the presentation on your disk as "Movies.ppt", and then print handouts in black and white, with six slides per page.

INVESTIGATE

21 How Useful a Tool Is PowerPoint?

For one week, keep track of the instances where you think a slide show would have been useful to better communicate the message of the speaker. Consider yourself and anyone else you listen to in compiling this list. At the end of the week write a one-page summary of the value of slide shows in improving communication. Discuss the impact of having both visual and oral information in communication settings, rather than just oral.

22 Asking for a Handout

Many times you'll see teachers, trainers, or other speakers use overhead transparencies in their presentations. But far fewer use handouts along with their presentations. If you were listening to a speaker, would you want handouts? Why? What are the advantages and disadvantages of using slide handouts versus just using projected visuals? If you were to use handouts, would you give them before or after your presentation? Why? Write your answers and submit them to your instructor.

23 Come Through with Flying Colors

Analyze the impact of text and background colors. For example, what difference would the color of the text and background make in the following situations: Yellow text on blue background, red text on black background, orange text on red background, yellow text on green background, and white text on black background. What text/background color combination do you think is appropriate for almost any audience? Cruise the Internet and investigate the best and worst text/background combinations you see. Write a one-page report about your findings and conclusions.

24 Just My Type

Type height is measured in points, and 72 points equal one inch. In other words, 72-point type is about 1 inch tall. Most of the text you read is from 10 to 12 points tall. Experiment with different type sizes in a presentation, using the Font Size feature on the Formatting toolbar to change highlighted text in a presentation. How small is too small to be seen by an average audience? How small is too small to be read easily on a handout? Write a brief report of your findings and conclusions.

projects

25 The History of Type and Print

Read about typography in an encyclopedia, and learn about the history of printing. Create a concise slide show to summarize the major points you learn from your reading. Print handouts of the presentation, with six slides per page. Submit the handout to your instructor.

Microsoft PowerPoint

Tutorial 2: PowerPoint Graphics, Charts, and Tables

Tutorial 2

PowerPoint Graphics, Charts, and Tables

WHAT'S INSIDE

Adding Color to Your Business Graphics

During your career, you'll probably need to communicate lots of statistics. And nothing beats a colorful bar chart or pie chart for summarizing data and grabbing an audience's attention.

Enhancing Presentations with Clip Art

PowerPoint comes equipped with dozens of pieces of clip art just waiting to add extra visual interest to your presentations. You'll even learn how to animate these figures so they appear to be running on to the screen.

Building Impressive-Looking Tables

Tables are indispensable when it comes to presenting numbers in easy-to-read rows and columns. And with PowerPoint's Table AutoFormat feature, you can enhance the tables you create in many ways.

WHAT'S ONLINE

1 Work with Clip Art & Graphics
- Add Clip Art
- Work with Graphics
- Move a Graphic
- Scale a Graphic
- Delete a Graphic

2 Add a Shape
- Add an AutoShape
- Change the Fill Color of a Shape
- Type Text inside a Shape

3 Create a Graph
- Add a Bar Graph
- Change Data in a Bar Graph
- Edit a Graph
- Insert Titles
- Change the Graph Type

4 Work with Tables
- Create a Table
- Modify a Table

5 Add an Organization Chart
- Create an Organization Chart
- Delete a Chart Box
- Add a Chart Box

scenario

Health and Fitness

Health and fitness—you can't pick up a newspaper or turn on the TV without hearing advice about good nutrition or seeing hard bodies. If you're under 30, fit and active, you might not have given much thought to what will happen to you as you get older. But be forewarned. As you age, the advantages of youth will disappear. The years of cheeseburgers, fries, and sweet rolls will take their toll. One day even you will face the challenge of fitting exercise into a busy schedule of work, family, and other activities.

So what do you do? Can the computer help? The computer is a tremendous laborsaving device, but it doesn't help when it comes to exercise. The only exercise some people get is typing at a keyboard. On a daily basis, people of all ages are lured away from running, hiking, and playing soccer to instead surf the net or run through dungeons tracking demons in a computer game.

The fact is, there's no way to become and stay healthy and fit without hard work, some sacrifice, some sweat, and maybe even some pain. But don't despair. Many tools and services can help you. All these providers use a variety of communications media to publicize their message. TV, newspapers, magazines, brochures, and the Internet are all visual media used to communicate with the public. Slide shows are also frequently used to educate the general public about the importance of health and fitness.

Suppose, for example, that you are a high school teacher and that you are quite fit. You try to eat well and you follow a regular exercise program. One day the principal asks if you would consider creating a presentation on health and fitness that you could give to a group of students. You agree and then you panic. You know you won't have much success reaching your audience if you stand up and lecture for 45 minutes. You decide to spice up your presentation—a plastic model of the human body, photos of blackened lungs caused by years of smoking, samples of high-fat foods, and brochures. And you decide that the core of your presentation will be a colorful, informative slide show.

In this tutorial, you'll learn how to add graphics to your slide shows, including clip art, geometric shapes, and bar graphs. You'll also learn how to create tables and organization charts. All these elements can help complement the text, which was the focus of Tutorial 1.

Review Questions

Fill in the blank with the correct word or phrase.

1 Pre-drawn graphic images that can be purchased for use in your presentations are known as _____.

2 To remove the handles of a selected graphic, just click _____ the handles.

3 2-D bar graphs have a(n) _____ and _____ axis.

4 To delete a graphic, you select it and then press the _____ key on the computer keyboard.

5 To duplicate a clip-art item, hold down the _____ key, click the item with the left mouse button, and drag.

6 A pre-drawn geometric PowerPoint shape is known as a(n)_____.

7 A "marble" appearance inside an AutoShape is an example of a(n) _____ fill.

8 A data sheet is a matrix of vertical _____ and horizontal _____.

9 Each little box in a data sheet is called a(n) _____.

10 The title of the _____ axis goes at the bottom of a vertical-bar graph.

11 The title of the _____ axis goes at the left side of a vertical-bar graph.

12 A number placed at the top of each bar in a vertical-bar graph is called a(n) _____.

13 If Alison and Derek report to the same manager at their work, Alison will appear as a(n) _____ to Derek on an organization chart.

MULTIPLE CHOICE

*Select the letter of the **one** best answer.*

---

14 Six people's names, ages, and salary levels would be best shown on a(n)

    a bar graph.   **c** pie graph.

    b table.   **d** line graph.

---

15 Which of the following is an example of clip art?

    a a cartoon picture of a horse   **c** a rectangle

    b a bar graph   **d** an organization chart

---

16 To make a graphic both taller and wider, click the _____ handle and drag.

    a top   **c** right

    b left   **d** corner

---

17 Which of the following is not one of the options available in the organization chart boxes?

    a co-worker   **c** assistant

    b supervisor   **d** manager

---

18 To scale a graphic means to

    a crop off unwanted portions of the graphic.

    b evaluate the visual weight of the graphic.

    c make the graphic larger or smaller.

    d change the height but not the width, or vice versa.

---

19 If you want to compare two test scores of five students, which type of graph would be least appropriate?

    a vertical-bar graph   **c** pie graph

    b horizontal-bar graph   **d** line graph

---

20 Pie and bar graphs are examples of

    a tables.

    b organization charts.

    c business graphs.

    d clip art.

21 What does the Undo function do?

   a It returns the slide show to what it was before the last step you took.

   b It puts the software in edit mode.

   c It enables you to fix the system in case of an error message.

   d It gives you the option of changing the slide layout.

22 You are creating a vertical-bar graph that compares the calories consumed by two people over a five-day period. The y axis will have the

   a number of calories.

   b names of the two people.

   c day 1, day 2, day 3, and so on.

   d main title of the graph.

23 The information you type down the left-most column in the datasheet is placed

   a on the y-axis.

   b on the x-axis.

   c on the z-axis.

   d in the legend.

24 When typing information in a table, if you add more text than the width of a cell, PowerPoint

   a automatically widens the cell to accommodate the text.

   b wraps to the next line.

   c stops and does not accept any more text until you widen the cell.

   d decreases the size of the font so the text will all fit.

25 For best readability, you would most likely use _____ for the color of text on a dark blue background.

   a red

   b purple

   c yellow

   d black

MATCHING

Select the letter from the column on the right that correctly matches each item in the column on the left.

26 **handles**

27 **scale**

28 [button icon]

29 **AutoShape**

30 **fill**

31 **row**

32 **x axis**

33 **column**

34 **y axis**

35 [shape icon]

a to make a graphic larger or smaller

b a series of datasheet cells arranged horizontally

c a series of datasheet cells arranged vertically

d the horizontal axis in a vertical-bar graph

e the vertical axis in a vertical-bar graph

f a co-worker box in an organization chart

g the color and texture inside an AutoShape

h a pre-drawn geometric figure

i eight small rectangles around an object that has been selected

j the Undo button, which reverses the last PowerPoint action you did

SHORT ANSWER

Use a separate sheet of paper to write out your answers to these questions.

36 Explain how to scale a graphic and move it from one spot to another.

37 List three different AutoShape attributes (e.g., color), and explain how to change them.

38 You can orient bar graphs either vertically or horizontally. When would you use a vertical orientation, and when would you use a horizontal orientation? Why?

39 If you have data that could be placed in either a table or a bar graph, what factors would you consider in deciding which option to choose?

40 Do you think it is a good idea to use data labels on a bar graph? Why or why not?

Projects

T he following Projects are designed to help you review and develop the skills you learned in Tutorial 2. Complete each Project using Microsoft PowerPoint. You should not need to use the e-Course software to complete the Projects, except to create a Project Disk containing practice files. If you have not yet made the Project Disk for Tutorial 2, start the e-Course software, then click the Copy Files menu.

If you've forgotten some of the skills you need to complete the Projects, refer to the Task Reference.

REVIEW SKILLS

1   Getting into Shape and AutoShape

To add interest to a basic slide, you can use more than just text. AutoShapes, clip art, bar graphs, tables, and organization charts all help add variety to the visual impact of a slide. In this Project you're going to create a title slide and add a simple AutoShape with text inside it.

Suppose you were creating a title slide for a presentation in a class you were taking on physical fitness. Create a new slide show using the Contemporary template, and choose the Title Only layout (not the Title Slide you used in the online steps). Type the title "Fitness and You". Below the title, create an AutoShape in the shape of a basic rectangle. Change the fill color to yellow and the text to black. Inside the rectangle type "A few tips . . .". Save the presentation as "Fitness1.ppt" and print it. Your slide should look very similar to the following slide.

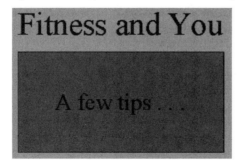

2   The Big Three in Conditioning

The Information Age in which we live provides many advantages, but one of its disadvantages is that computer work doesn't provide any physical activity. As a result, people have to schedule exercise around the hours they work. Some people wake up early for a before-work exercise session, while others schedule time for exercise in the evenings. Still others have access to fitness facilities where they work and take a half-hour or so for exercise during their lunch hour.

Where or when you exercise is less important than how you exercise and how frequently. Exercise physiologists recommend that you exercise at least three times a week and that you include three critical conditioning elements in your exercise routine: strength, endurance, and flexibility.

Using a template of your choice, create a Clip Art & Text slide showing the three critical conditioning elements. Select an appropriate clip-art image. Change the size of the clip art so it is about four inches tall, and move it so it looks centered on the left side of the slide. Your slide should look like the following slide, except that you'll have different clip art. Save your presentation as "Fitness2.ppt" and print it.

3   Bob and Sam

Bob has a good exercise program. Sam, well, Sam tries—sometimes. Anyway, Bob and Sam provide good examples of good and not-so-good exercise programs. Create a slide with a bar graph comparing the time Bob and Sam exercise each week. Use the following data:

Name	Week 1	Week 2	Week 3	Week 4
Sam	35	45	30	21
Bob	105	100	110	115

Choose a template and include the title "Which one are you?" Save the presentation as "Fitness3.ppt" and print the slide you just created. Your slide should look similar to this one:

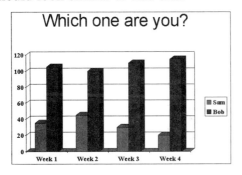

4 How Much Should You Eat?

The number of calories a person should consume each day varies according to several factors, including amount of physical activity and body weight. Create a new presentation with your choice of templates, and choose the Table layout for your first slide. Type "How Many Calories?" as the title. The table should have five columns and four rows as follows:

Lifestyle	100 lbs.	125 lbs.	150 lbs.	175 lbs.
Inactive	1300	1624	1950	2275
Moderately active	1500	1875	2250	2625
Very active	1700	2125	2550	2975

For the heading row, use Arial 24-point type. For the next three rows, use Arial 18-point type. Change the color of the text to white. Save the slide show as "Fitness4.ppt" and print it. After you print the slide, delete the 100 lbs. column. Then save the presentation again, and print the revised slide.

5 Let's Get Organized

If you were making a presentation on health and fitness, you might want to show cause-and-effect relationships. For example, weight lifting *causes* new muscle tissue to grow. Or, in reverse, new muscle tissue is *caused by* working the muscles. Cause-and-effect relationships are better shown as a graphic than as a word description. Organization charts are particularly effective for showing these relationships.

You're afraid that words alone will soon be forgotten, so you decide to create a slide that presents the three critical elements with some graphic impact. You think

an organization chart will be an effective graphic. Using a template of your choice, create an organization chart, and type "A Balanced Exercise Program" as the slide title. Type "Exercise Components" as the manager (the cause), and beneath it type "Strength", "Endurance", and "Flexibility" as three subordinates. Type the following effects under each subordinate:

Strength: **Weight Lifting**

Endurance: **Cycling**

Flexibility: **Racquetball**

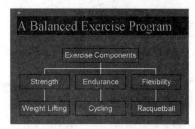

Save the slide as "Fitness5.ppt" and print it.

APPLY SKILLS

6   Clip Art, Scanning, and AutoShape   File: Baskball.tif

Run & Fun, a sporting goods store, is holding a sale on its team sports equipment. The sales manager wants an attention-grabbing flyer to post throughout the store. She wants the flyer to indicate what is on sale, and have appropriate graphics. Create a slide in Clip Art & Text layout, using whatever template you'd like, and include the following text.

- **Basketball**

- **Soccer**

- **T-ball**

- **Baseball**

- **Football**

You've already learned how to add a clip-art image. Another option for graphics images is to scan them from print sources, such as photographs, drawings, and the like.

If you have a scanner available, click Picture on the Insert menu, and then click From Scanner. Scan a picture of your choice to see how it looks. The Microsoft Photo Editor, a program you can use to edit the picture, will open. When you close the Photo Editor, your picture will appear on your slide. Scale and move it as necessary for a good fit.

If you don't have a scanner available, click Picture on the Insert menu, and then click From File. Select Baskball.tif, a graphic that was created by scanning a photograph. Click Insert, then scale and move it as necessary for a good fit.

To really grab the customers' attention, create an AutoShape with text inside it saying "SALE 25 % OFF". Select the AutoShape, then click Format on the menu bar, and click AutoShape. On the Size tab, type "–30%" and click the OK button. Your slide might look something like this:

Save the presentation as "Sale6.ppt". Then print the slide, in color if possible.

7   More with AutoShape

Create a slide (you choose the template) with a Blank layout. Click the Rounded Rectangle Tool AutoShape and insert it in the middle of the slide. Scale the rectangle so it is very large. Change the color of the AutoShape to white. Inside the AutoShape, type the four items listed in the following text column, modifying the text as shown in the next three columns:

Text	Font	Size	Color
CITY LEAGUE	Arial	40 point	Dark Blue
Jr. League	Times Roman	32 point	Green
Little League	Times Roman	32 point	Red
Youth League	Times Roman	32 point	Purple

In the top-right corner of the slide, add another AutoShape of your choice. Inside the shape, type "Join Now!" Modify the shape and text attributes as you'd like. Save the slide as "League7.ppt" and print it.

8 Using Table AutoFormat

In the online Steps, you learned how to create a basic table. In this Project, you find out how to improve the appearance of your table using Table AutoFormat. Suppose you're going to make a presentation to the prestigious Chaine de Rotisserie on "heart smart" gourmet cooking. Create a slide using the template of your choice.

Select the table layout, and title the slide "Dinner Options". Then type the following information in the table:

Menu Options	Calories	Fat Grams
Roast Chicken	284	6.14
Fried Chicken	557	29.8

After typing the text in the cells, click outside the table to return to Slide View. Then double-click the table to enter table edit mode. On the menu bar, click Table, and then click Table AutoFormat. In the Formats box, click Colorful 1. Make sure the box is checked (✓) for all of the following: Borders, Shading, Font, Color, and AutoFit. Click the OK button, then click outside the table to return to Slide View.

Save the file as "Chicken8.ppt" and print a copy of the slide. Your slide should look similar to this:

Dinner Options		
Menu Options	Calories	Fat Grams
Roast Chicken	284	6.14
Fried Chicken	557	29.8

9 Creating a Vertical Bar Graph

As you learned in the online Steps, PowerPoint enables you to create vertical-bar graphs or horizontal-bar graphs. The graph you use depends on your preferences and on the type of data you're displaying. Most bar graphs are arranged vertically, but if you have too many bars to fit across an 8½ x 11-inch sheet of paper, you can use horizontal bars, giving more room for all the bars.

projects

For this Project, create a new presentation, using the template of your choice. Select the Chart layout, and create a vertical-bar graph. Type the title as "Caloric Needs (150-lb. Person)". The data for this graph shows the differences in caloric needs, depending on a person's lifestyle. Enter the following data:

	A	B	C
	Nonactive	Mod. Activ	Very Active
	1950	2250	2550

Save the vertical-bar graph as "Calories.ppt" and print a copy. Then change to a horizontal-bar graph and label the X-axis as "Activity Level". Save the graph again and print a new copy.

10 Creating a Diagram

An effective way to explain step-by-step procedures is to display the steps inside boxes connected with lines. This visual approach is used often by systems analysts whose work consists largely of automating procedures. For this project develop a simple chart to show the step-by-step procedure for how to determine your target heart rate.

1—Subtract your age from 220.
   Result: Maximum Heart Rate.

2—Multiply Maximum Heart Rate by 0.85.
   Result: Maximum Target Heart Rate.

3—Multiply Maximum Target Heart Rate by 0.50.
   Result: Minimum Target Heart Rate.

Using the template of your choice, create an Organization Chart slide. Enter the slide title as "Finding your target heart rates". Enter the three steps in three boxes arranged as shown here. Save your file as "Heartrate.ppt" and print a copy.

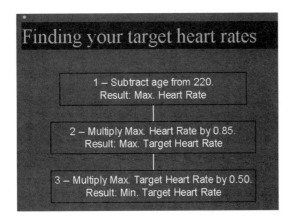

projects

BUILD SKILLS

11 Creating a Pie Graph

Many companies encourage fitness programs for their employees—whether by fully or partially paying for memberships in nearby health and fitness centers or by building a fitness facility right inside the building, encouraging employees to use the facility before work, during lunch break, or after work.

Assume that your firm has hired a fitness expert, Dr. Joseph Harmon, to help establish an on-site fitness center and program. You have been working with Dr. Harmon, who has conducted research on the exercise habits of people in your company. He obtained the following percentages regarding the number of times women employees exercise each week:

0 per week	1 per week	2–3 per week	4+ per week
28	14	34	24

In this Project you'll create a presentation that contains a pie graph showing the results of this research. Using a template of your choice, create a slide with the Chart layout. Type the title as "Women's Exercise Frequency". Click ▤ on the Formatting toolbar to center the title. Double-click the graph/chart placeholder, and enter the data in the datasheet. Click outside the datasheet when you're finished. Next, you'll change the bar graph to a 3-D pie chart.

To change a bar graph to a 3-D pie chart:

1: With the bar graph selected, click **Chart** on the menu bar, and then click **Chart Type**.

2: On the **Standard Types** tab, click **Pie** and then click the middle chart sub-type on the top row (Pie with a 3-D visual effect). Click the **OK** button.

3: Click **Chart**, and then click **Chart Options**. Click the **Data Labels** tab, and click **Show Label & Percent**. Click the **OK** button.

4: If there is a legend on the right side of the graph, click it and then press the **Delete** key.

Save the graph as "Pie.ppt" and print a copy. Your final product should look like the following slide:

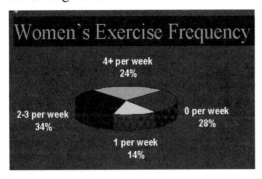

12 2-D Horizontal Bar Graph with Labels

Do men and women exercise with different frequency? At your company, a researcher conducted a survey and came up with some interesting results. Create a two-dimensional (2-D) horizontal-bar graph with data labels. Include the following data:

Group	0 per week	1 per week	2-3 per week	4+ per week
Women	28	14	34	24
Men	29	19	28	24

Use the template of your choice and create a chart using the Chart layout. Type the title as "Employees' Exercise Frequency". Double-click the graph placeholder and enter the data. Click outside the datasheet when you're finished. Next, you can change the graph to 2-D and add data labels and axis titles.

To change the graph to 2-D and add labels:

1: With the graph selected, click **Chart** on the menu bar, and then click **Chart Type**. Change the graph to a 2-D bar chart with horizontal bars. Click the **OK** button.

2: Click **Chart**, click **Chart Options**, and click the **Data Labels** tab.

3: Click **Show Value**, and then click the **OK** button.

4: Click **Chart**, click **Chart Options**, click **Titles**, and then type **Percent** in the **Value (Y) axis** box. Click the **OK** button.

Save the file as "2DBar12.ppt" and print a copy. Your slide should look similar to the one shown here:

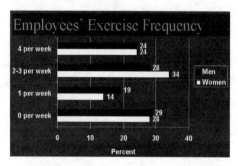

13 Spreading One Cell Across Columns and Importing an Excel Chart   File: Prefchart.xls

Sometimes you'll want to place a title over two or three columns in a table. To do this, you need one cell that spreads across the columns, as shown in the following table. PowerPoint can help you do this with its merge-cells feature. PowerPoint can also center text inside the cells.

Age	Preferred Activity (Ranked)		
	Aerobics	Cycling	Jogging
20-29	2	3	1
30-39	1	3	2
40-49	1	2	3
50+	2	1	3

Start by creating a Table slide, using the template of your choice. Title the slide "Preferred Fitness Activities". Now you're ready to merge the cells and center the ranking data.

To merge cells:

1: Highlight the second, third, and fourth cells in the first row. On the menu bar, click **Table**, and then click **Merge Cells**.

2: Type **Preferred Activity (Ranked)** in the new cell that spans columns 2, 3, and 4. Highlight this text and click the [U] **Underline** button.

3: Type the remaining data in the appropriate cells, then highlight the bottom four rows in columns 1 through 4 and change the type size to **26**.

4: Highlight the bottom four rows in columns 2, 3, and 4, and click the [≡] **Center Alignment** button on the Formatting toolbar.

Return to normal slide mode and save the file as "Prefer13.ppt". If necessary, to make the text more readable, re-enter Table Edit mode and change the text color. Print a copy, in color if possible. Your slide should look similar to the one shown here:

Preferred Fitness Activities

Age	Preferred Activity (Ranked)		
	Aerobics	Cycling	Jogging
20-29	2	3	1
30-39	1	3	2
40-49	1	2	3
50+	2	1	3

This data would have more impact if it were presented as a graph. Rather than enter this data again in a datasheet, you can import a pre-existing chart from Excel.

To import a chart from Excel:

1: Insert a new slide with the Chart layout. Leave the title blank. Click the graph placeholder to select it.

2: With the graph selected, click **Insert** on the menu bar, and then click **Chart**. A sample chart will appear in the placeholder. Click **Edit** on the menu bar, and then **Import File**. Select the file **Prefchart.xls** from your data disk.

3: In the Import Data Options dialog box, select **Sheet 1** and then select **Import: Entire Sheet**. Click the **OK** button.

projects

Your second slide should look similar to this:

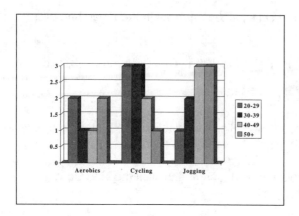

Save the file again and print it as handouts (two slides per page).

Write a paragraph explaining if you agree that the chart increases the data's impact. Also show your presentation to a friend to get another opinion and write up your friend's opinion.

14 Copying and Pasting an Image   File: Swimming.ppt

To give a presentation continuity, you can use similar elements and colors on all the slides, as well as on other documents used in connection with the presentation (memos, flyers, and so on). For example, you might want a certain graphic or your company logo to appear on every slide. For this Project you'll place an image in the bottom-right corner of all your slides. Open Swimming.ppt and add a second and third slide (Blank layout). Return to slide 1.

To copy and paste an image:

1: Click the clip-art image, and then copy and paste the figure so you have a second clip-art image on the slide.

2: Scale the image down so it's much smaller than the original, and move it to the bottom-right corner of the slide.

3: With the image still selected, click **Edit**, and then click **Copy**.

4: Scroll to slide 2 and click **Paste**. Repeat the procedure for slide 3.

5: Save the presentation as **Swim17.ppt**.

Print the presentation, with three slides per page.

15 Using the Slide Master   File: Armchair.ppt

It's handy to use the Slide Master to maintain consistency throughout a presentation. Suppose you're creating a humorous slide about office fitness. Open the Armchair.ppt file and add three new slides (Title Only layout). Type the following text in the title placeholder of each slide:

--Exercise your options.

--Jump to conclusions.

--Throw your weight around.

Now you're ready to use the Slide Master.

To use the Slide Master:

1: Go to slide 1 and select the clip art. Click **Edit** and then click **Copy**.

2: In the **View** menu, select **Master**, and then **Slide Master**. Click **Edit**, and then **Paste**. The graphic will be pasted on your Slide Master. The only objects you want on your slides are the graphic and a title. Click each of the other objects (Master text placeholder, Date placeholder, and so on) and delete each one.

3: Scale and move the clip art to the bottom-left corner of the Slide Master. Move the title placeholder (and scale it, if necessary) to fill the right half of the Slide Master.

4: Select the text **Click to edit Master title style** and change its font to Comic Sans, or any font of your choice. Change the text's alignment to **Right Alignment** using the Formatting toolbar. You have changed the Master title style, so all your slides will use this format.

5: Go to **Slide Sorter View**. Notice that slide 1 has two copies of the graphic, and its title would look better centered. Go to **slide 1** in the Slide View. In the **Format** menu, click on **Background**. Put a check mark in the **Omit background graphics from master** box, and click the **Apply** button. Click inside the title **Armchair Exercises** and change its alignment back to **Center**.

Save the presentation as "Armchair2.ppt" and print handouts with two slides per page.

projects

16 Adding a Moving Figure and Speaker Notes

File: Jogging.ppt

For your presentation on fitness, you think a moving figure would add a nice touch of energy. Open the Jogging.ppt file, and go to slide 2.

To add a moving figure:

1: Select the figure on the right, click **Slide Show** and then click **Custom Animation**.

2: Click the **Effects** tab, click the ▼ in the *Entry animation and sound* box, and then click **Fly From Left**. Repeat Steps 1 through 3 for the figure on the left.

This is an example of a presentation in which the slides enhance what you are saying, rather than repeat it for the viewers. To help you remember what you will say, you can include Speaker Notes and print them for yourself.

To include Speaker Notes:

1: Go back to slide 1 in the Slide View. On the View menu, click **Speaker Notes**. In the *Notes* box, type a list of jogging tips:

> **Schedule a regular time of day.**
>
> **Start slowly: "walk jog walk jog."**
>
> **Select a short route in advance.**
>
> **Work up to a longer distance gradually.**
>
> **If you get tired, turn around and go home!**

2: Close the *Notes* box, and go to slide 2. Create Speaker Notes for this slide, such as:

> **The best tip is to jog with a friend!**

Play the slide show, clicking the left mouse button to advance the slides and to launch the figures. Notice that your Speaker Notes are not visible. Save the file as "Jogging2.ppt". Print it, selecting Notes Pages. These notes pages will help you remember your planned comments.

17 Copying and Recoloring an Image

File: Tennis.ppt

Your company is sponsoring a tennis tournament for all employees who want to participate. Your task is to encourage people to enter. A slide show that is informative, as well as warm and friendly, just might do the job. On the title slide, you decide to add three brightly colored cartoon figures to get the presentation off to a lively start. Open the Tennis.ppt file, and then complete the following Steps to duplicate the image and change its color.

To duplicate an image and change its color:

1: Hold down the **Ctrl** key, click the left mouse button on the figure and drag it to the right. When you release the mouse button, you'll see that you've created a second image. Duplicate the image again so you have three figures on the screen. Position them evenly across the slide.

2: Select the first image and click **Format**, click **Picture**, and click **Recolor** on the Picture tab. Click the **New** ⏷ by the green bar, then click **More Colors**. Click one of the red cells, and click the **OK** button until you return to the main slide.

Change the color of the other two images to a color of your choice, and then save the file as "Title14.ppt" and print it.

18 Cropping a Graphic and Using the Genigraphics and Internet Assistant Wizards   File: Halfoff.ppt

(Note: To complete this entire project, the GeniGraphics Wizard and/or the Internet Assistant Wizard must be installed.)

Sometimes you'll want to use only a portion of a graphic. PowerPoint includes a cropping feature that enables you to cut off part of a graphic on the top, bottom, left, or right sides. When you crop a graphic, the cropped portion will not appear on the screen and will not print; but it is still stored in the computer, and you can go back at any time and restore the graphic to its original form.

projects

Open the Halfoff.ppt file. Then go to Help and learn how to crop a portion of the clip-art image. Crop the image so only the top half of the figure is remaining. Your slide should look like the one shown here. Save the file as "Halfoff18.ppt".

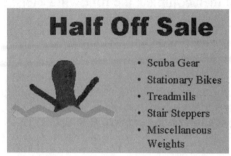

Once you have created a slide show, there are many interesting ways your slides can be presented. They don't always have to be used during a presentation with a fancy overhead projection system. You've already seen how one slide can become a poster, just by printing it as Slides. A simple variation is to print a single slide on transparency film (if your printer will accept it) or copy the poster to transparency film. Then, your slide can be shown whether or not your presentation is scheduled in a state-of-the-art meeting facility. The only equipment you will need is an overhead projector.

PowerPoint offers the options to format your slide show for 35mm slides, digital color overheads, large display prints, and posters, by using the Genigraphics Wizard.

To use the Genigraphics Wizard:

1: On the **File** menu, point to **Send To**, and then click **Genigraphics**.

2: Follow the instructions to send your file via modem, and they will return your printed materials overnight. If you didn't install the Genigraphics Wizard when you installed PowerPoint, the Genigraphics command won't be available.

You can also publish your slides directly to the Internet, if you have access to an account on the World Wide Web by using the Internet Assistant Wizard.

To use the Internet Assistant:

1: On the **File** menu, click **Save as HTML** to open the Internet Assistant. In this case accept all the default settings by clicking the **Next>** buttons, until the Wizard asks where you want to create the HTML folder. Type **A:** or select the appropriate location, then click the **Finish>** button. If the Wizard asks you to type a name for the HTML conversion settings, click **Don't Save**.

2: If you have access to a Web browser, open the file **HALFOFF18\sld001.htm** that was created. This file contains only one slide, but if there were more slides, the Navigation buttons would allow the viewer to control the transitions to the end of the slide show.

projects

19 Sharing Data with Other Office Programs
Files: Analysis.doc Analysis.xls

One of PowerPoint's most powerful capabilities is the ease with which it shares data files with other Office programs. During the first two months that your company's new fitness center is in operation, your manager has tracked how often the new center is being used and specifically what equipment is being used most.

The manager's data is stored in a Word document, which can be quickly converted into a PowerPoint slide show, and in an Excel workbook, which you'll use to make a chart.

To share data from Word:

1: In Microsoft Word, open the file **Analysis.doc**. In the **File** menu, click **Send To**, and then click **Microsoft PowerPoint**.

2: On the **Format** menu, click **Apply Design**. Select the **Ribbons** design, and click the **Apply** button. To lighten the background color, click **Slide Color Scheme** on the **Format** menu. Click a sample with a light background the select it, and then click **Apply to all**.

3: In Slide View, remove the bullet from slide 1. Center the line that reads "Two Months' Analysis."

4: On slides 2 and 3, remove the bullets. To improve the appearance of these slides, resize the bottom text placeholders so the left edge is nearer the center of the slide. On the View menu, be sure the **Ruler** is selected. Select all the text except the slide title, then set a tab by clicking on the ruler at the 3" mark. Slides 2 and 3 should look like this:

Your manager wants you to include a chart that she can use in a presentation to executive management. You'd like to use a pie chart, but you know that you can use pie charts for only one series of data. However, PowerPoint can adapt a pie chart, making it into a doughnut chart. **Doughnut charts** are round like pie charts, but they can have more than one ring so they can show additional data.

projects

To share data from Excel:

1: Add a fourth slide, using the Chart layout. Select the chart placeholder, then on the **Insert** menu, click **Chart** on the **Edit** menu, click **Import File**, and open the file named **Analysis.xls**. In the **Import Data Options** dialog box, select **Sheet 1** and **Entire Sheet**. Click the **OK** button.

2: On the **Chart** menu, click **Chart Type**, and select **Doughnut**.

3: On the **Chart** menu, click **Chart Options**. On the **Data Labels** tab, select **Show percent**. Resize the objects on the slide, and add a title and text until the slide looks similar to this:

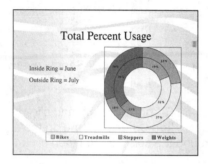

Finally, your manager decides that she would like to be able to flip from the chart slide to the data slide for each month, if the management executives have any questions. This requires you to create hyperlinks between the slides.

To create hyperlinks

1: On slide 4, select one of the months. On the **Slide Show** menu, click **Action settings**.

2: On the **Mouse Click** tab, select **Hyperlink to:**, then click the ▼ to select **Slide**. Select the slide for that month, then click the **OK** button.

Run the slide show from the fourth slide to see if your hyperlinks to slides 2 and 3 work. Save the file as "Analysis.ppt". If you have access to the Internet, this would be a good slide show to save as HTML. Your hyperlinks will work even better when viewed with a Web browser program.

20 Using the Presentation Conference Wizard

One of the latest trends in business is the use of online meetings. Rather than spend time and money on travel expenses, companies are conferencing via their own networks or via the Internet. PowerPoint's Presentation Conference Wizard can assist you in creating and managing a meeting wherever the participants may be. Unfortunately, you lose some of the features of your presentation when you go online. Multimedia objects (sound or video) and some objects that were created in other programs may not transmit well.

When setting up a presentation conference, one person has to be in charge. That person, called the Presenter, uses the Stage Manager tools to supervise all activities. To set up a Presentation Conference, each participant must select Presentation Conference on the Tools menu. The Presenter must be the last person to click Finish in the Presentation Conference Wizard.

To begin using the Presentation Conference Wizard:

1: Start a new presentation by selecting the **Company Meeting (standard)** design. Since this Project is just a simulation, don't change any of the text to personalize this presentation. Save this file as **Conference.ppt** — this is important since the name of the file will print in the minutes of the meeting later.

2: On the **Tools** menu, click **Presentation Conference**. The wizard reminds you to get everyone on the phone. In this Project, you don't have to include other participants. You will participate as the Presenter, but the other participants would select Audience. Click **Next>** three times to proceed through the wizard. In Connection details, all participants would add their own names and select their own connection options. Remember, as Presenter you must be the last person to click Finish.

When the Presentation Conference is set up, the Presenter controls the slide navigation just like you would during a traditional presentation. You would use the telephone to transmit your verbal comments. In addition, there are several Stage Manager tools that you could use to manage and record the conference.

To use some of the Stage Manager Tools:

1: On the **Tools** menu, click **Meeting Minder**. On the **Meeting Minutes** tab, type these sample comments that could occur during a typical meeting:

> **Tom said we need to increase sales in the Southeast.**
>
> **Sue agreed, but is also concerned about the Midwest.**
>
> **John asked to meet again on Tuesday.**

2: On the **Action Items** tab, assign some tasks based on these comments by entering:

Description: **Southeast sales analysis**
Assigned to: **Tom**
Due Date: **type in the date for next Tuesday**

3: Click the **Add** button to continue.

    Description: **Midwest sales analysis**

    Assigned to: **Sue**

    Due Date: **use the same date**

4: Click the **Add** button to continue.

5: Click the **Meeting Minutes** tab, and then click **Export**. Select the option to **Send meeting minutes and action items to Microsoft Word**. Click the **Export Now** button. Word will automatically open and a new document will be created, containing the notes you entered above.

6: Close the Meeting Minder, and run the Slide Show. Right-click on any slide to open a shortcut menu. You can also select the Meeting Minder this way, to take notes while the slide show is progressing. Click **End Show** to end this demonstration.

Notice that the Action Items have been added to the end of the slide show—on a new slide that was automatically generated when you selected End Show. This is immediate feedback for all the participants to see. In addition, you can transmit the Microsoft Word version of the meeting notes by attaching them to e-mail messages, or via fax, among other ways.

Save the presentation file. Print the meeting notes from Microsoft Word. Notice that the presentation file name (Meeting) appears as part of the title of this document. To use this effectively, you should name your presentation files descriptively, such as "Executive Meeting 9/1/98".

projects

21 Find a Client

Find a businessperson who has a definite need for a slide show. Have him/her describe in detail what content the show should contain. Create the show, including text, graphics, and anything else that is needed. Have him/her evaluate your results. Implement the suggestions, and then print the presentation as a handout with six slides per page. Save the slide as "Project21.ppt". Write a paragraph describing what it was like doing a project like this for another person. Would you do anything differently the next time you create a presentation for another person?

22 Survey the Business Community

With a fellow class member, create a questionnaire that collects data on how business people use slide show presentations. Interview 8 to 10 people, using the questionnaire. Prepare a slide show presentation to show your results.

23 Annual Report Graphics

Go to the library and survey the annual reports of ten companies. Make a record of what types of graphics they contain. Classify the graphics as bar charts, line charts, pie charts, organization charts, and miscellaneous. Determine the average number of graphs used in the reports. Develop a presentation to report your results.

24 Internet Graphics

Search the Internet and visit 10 sites related to a particular subject of interest to you (for example, mountain biking). Examine how graphics are used in companies' Web sites. Write a one-page paper describing what graphics you liked and disliked at these sites and why. Discuss specifically how these graphics were useful or not useful in communicating the message.

projects

25 Market Analysis

Research the software industry and see if you can find information on the history and current status of presentation software. Learn who are the industry leaders, how the software is evaluated, which packages have the greatest market share, the price differences, and so forth. Then write a one- to two-page summary discussing which package you would buy and why.

Answers to Odd-Numbered Review Questions

Tutorial 1

1   presentation

3   ToolTip

5   layout or AutoLayout

7   bullet

9   Outline

11   Slide Show

13   Build

15   title

answers

MULTIPLE CHOICE

17 c

19 d

21 d

23 a

25 a

27 d

29 a

MATCHING

31 c

33 g

35 d

answers

SHORT ANSWER

37 A Title layout has a placeholder for only a title. A Bulleted List layout has placeholders for a title and for bulleted text.

39 PowerPoint is a software program used for creating and showing slideshow presentations to an audience. PowerPoint can also print hard copies of the slides to use as audience handouts.

answers

Tutorial 2

1   clip art

3   x and y

5   control

7   texture

9   cell

11   Y

13   co-worker

MULTIPLE CHOICE

15 a

17 b

19 c

21 a

23 d

25 c

MATCHING

27 a

29 h

31 b

33 c

35 f

answers

37 AutoShape attributes include color, shade, texture, and pattern. To change them, select AutoShape, click Format, click Colors and Lines, and then make the attribute changes.

39 Consider mainly which format would be easier to read. But also consider whether you want to give a quick visual message or give details for analysis, which would take more time to produce, and whether the reader prefers a table or a graph.